Dennis P. Farmer

American Longarms

Other Titles in the Warner Collector's Guides Series

Available Now

The Warner Collector's Guide to American Toys
The Warner Collector's Guide to American Clocks
The Warner Collector's Guide to American Longarms

Forthcoming

The Warner Collector's Guide to American Pottery and Porcelain
The Warner Collector's Guide to American Sterling and Silver-Plated Hollowware
The Warner Collector's Guide to Dolls
The Warner Collector's Guide to American Glass

The Warner Collector's Guide to American Longarms

H. Michael Madaus

A Main Street Press Book

A Warner Communications Company

Warner Books, Inc.
75 Rockefeller Plaza
New York, N.Y. 10019

A Warner Communications Company

Printed in the United States of America

First printing: March 1981

10 9 8 7 6 5 4 3 2 1

Library of Congress Cataloging in Publication Data

Madaus, Howard Michael
The Warner collector's guide to American longarms.

(The Warner collector's guides)
Bibliography: p. 9
1. Firearms—America—Collectors and collecting.
I. Title.
TS532.4.M32 683.4'0097 80-25449
ISBN 0-446-97628-8 (USA)
ISBN 0-446-97971-6 (Canada)

Contents

How to Use This Book

The Warner Collector's Guide to American Longarms is divided into fifty chapters, each of which treats a different basic type of arm. More generally, however, for ease in indentification, these chapters are grouped into two major parts. Chapters 1 through 21 cover shoulder arms loaded from the muzzle, while chapters 22 through 50 treat breechloading arms. Each of these major categories, in turn, is subdivided into single-shot (chapters 1 through 19 and 22 through 24) and repeating or multiple-fire arms (chapters 20 and 21 and 25 through 50). Within each of these subdivisions, distinctive characteristics of the arms types covered—such as the number of barrels (single or multiple), the character of the bore (smooth or rifled), the type of ignition system (flintlock, percussion, or cartridge), the functional use (civilian or martial), the method of generating repetition, if applicable (revolving action, bolt action, or lever action), and the type of magazine (cylinder, tubular, or box)—are the bases for categorizing the arms into the fifty chapters. These characteristics, rather than markings found upon the arms which are too often nebulous or partially effaced, are the distinctions that should guide the collector in using this book. While most of these distinctions are well understood by the advanced collector, the beginner or novice would do well to familiarize himself with the common terms employed.

Use of this collector's guide is designed with ease, speed, and portability in mind. Suppose you spot what a dealer explains is a slide-action, tubular magazine rifle. But there are many such models. Exactly what kind of arm is it? What kind of markings, if any, should it carry? What should be its overall length, its barrel or bore length? What period does it date from? Is it real or a reproduction?

By turning to the Color Key to American Longarms (pp. 17-48), you will find among the fifty color illustrations a photograph of an arm that bears a close "family resemblance" to the one you're interested in. Under the color illustration will be found the name of the classification—"Slide Action, Tubular Magazine Repeating Rifles and Carbines." By turning to the black and white pages covering this classification, chapter 24, you will be able to find the identical arm you are examining or one similar to it.

All of the approximately 500 arms discussed in this guide are treated in a separate numbered entry, containing basic information. The majority of the entries are arranged in the manner illustrated on p. 8. In the remaining cases when one arm shares many of the same specifications as another, these particulars are not given each time but are summed up in an introductory paragraph before the group of similar entries.

It would be impossible to include in a portable guide all the types and variations of longarms that were produced during the 125 years of production that are covered herein. For this reason, emphasis has been given to the more common types—that is, those which the collector are more likely to encounter today. Although there are rare types described in almost every chapter and especially in those

A Typical Entry

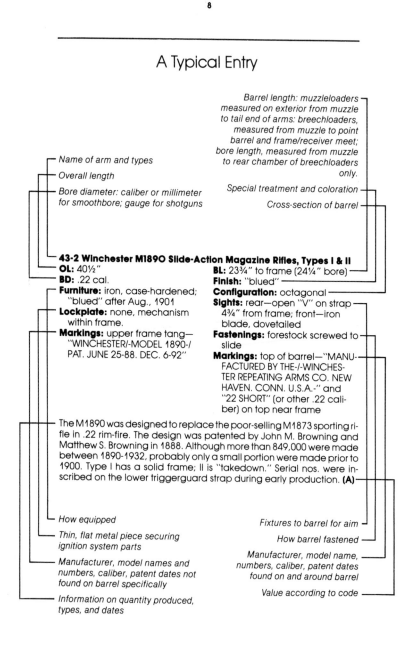

Barrel length: muzzleloaders measured on exterior from muzzle to tail end of arms: breechloaders, measured from muzzle to point barrel and frame/receiver meet; bore length, measured from muzzle to rear chamber of breechloaders only.

Name of arm and types

Overall length

Bore diameter: caliber or millimeter for smoothbore; gauge for shotguns

Special treatment and coloration

Cross-section of barrel

43-2 Winchester M1890 Slide-Action Magazine Rifles, Types I & II

OL: 40½"
BD: .22 cal.
Furniture: iron, case-hardened; "blued" after Aug., 1901
Lockplate: none, mechanism within frame.
Markings: upper frame tang—"WINCHESTER/-MODEL 1890-/PAT. JUNE 25-88. DEC. 6-92"

BL: 23¾" to frame (24¼" bore)
Finish: "blued"
Configuration: octagonal
Sights: rear—open "V" on strap 4¾" from frame; front—iron blade, dovetailed
Fastenings: forestock screwed to slide
Markings: top of barrel—"MANUFACTURED BY THE-/-WINCHESTER REPEATING ARMS CO. NEW HAVEN. CONN. U.S.A.-" and "22 SHORT" (or other .22 caliber) on top near frame

The M1890 was designed to replace the poor-selling M1873 sporting rifle in .22 rim-fire. The design was patented by John M. Browning and Matthew S. Browning in 1888. Although more than 849,000 were made between 1890-1932, probably only a small portion were made prior to 1900. Type I has a solid frame; II is "takedown." Serial nos. were inscribed on the lower triggerguard strap during early production. **(A)**

How equipped

Thin, flat metal piece securing ignition system parts

Manufacturer, model names and numbers, caliber, patent dates not found on barrel specifically

Information on quantity produced, types, and dates

Fixtures to barrel for aim

How barrel fastened

Manufacturer, model name, numbers, caliber, patent dates found on and around barrel

Value according to code

dealing with early production, these are exceptions. A code letter from A through F, reflecting rarity, follows each entry. Rarity is based on the approximate number of estimated surviving examples, as follows:

A	"Common"	Probably more than 5,000 survive
B	"Uncommon"	Probably between 1,000-5,000 survive
C	"Rare"	Probably between 500 to 1,000 survive
D	"Very Rare"	Probably between 50 to 500 survive
E	"Extremely Rare"	Fewer than 50 are known to survive
F	"Exceedingly Rare"	Fewer than 10 are known to survive

Selected Bibliography

Albaugh, William A. and Edward N. Simmons. *Confederate Arms.* New York, 1957.

Anthony, William E. and Richard Taylor Hill. *Confederate Longarms and Pistols: A Pictorial Survey.* Charlotte, N.C., 1978.

Bailey, D. W. *British Military Longarms, 1715-1815.* Harrisburg, Pa., 1971.

Blackmore, Howard L. *British Military Firearms, 1650-1850.* New York, 1961.

______. *Guns and Rifles of the World.* New York, 1965.

Brown, Stuart E., Jr. *The Guns of Harpers Ferry.* Berryville, Va., 1968.

Cromwell, Giles. *The Virginia Manufactory of Arms.* Charlottesville, Va., 1975.

Edwards, William B. *Civil War Guns.* Harrisburg, Pa., 1962.

Flayderman. Norm. *Flayderman's Guide to Antique American Firearms and Their Values.* Chicago, 1977.

Fuller, Claud E. *The Rifled Musket.* New York, 1957.

______. *Springfield Muzzleloading Shoulder Arms.* New York, 1930.

______ and Richard D. Steuart. *Firearms of the Confederacy.* Huntington, W. Va., 1944.

Gluckman, Arcadi. *United States Muskets, Rifles, and Carbines.* Buffalo, N.Y., 1948.

Grant, James J. *More Single Shot Rifles.* New York, 1959.

______. *Single Shot Rifles.* New York, 1947.

Hanson, Charles E. *The Northwest Gun.* Lincoln, Nebr., 1955.

______. *The Plains Rifle.* Harrisburg, Pa., 1960.

Hicks, James E. *French Military Weapons, 1717-1938.* Reprint ed. New Milford, Conn., 1964.

______ and Andrew Jandot. *U.S. Military Firearms, 1776-1956.* Reprint ed. La Canada, Calif., 1962.

Huntingdon, R.T. *Hall's Breechloaders. . . .* York, Pa., 1972.

Kaufman, Henry J. *The Pennsylvania-Kentucky Rifle.* Harrisburg, Pa., 1959.

Kindig, Joe, Jr., et al. *Thoughts on the Kentucky Rifle in Its Golden Age.* York, Pa., 1960.

Lewis, Berkeley R. *Small Arms and Ammunition in the United States Service.* Washington, D.C., 1956.

Lindsay, Merrill. *The Kentucky Rifle.* York, Pa., 1972.

______. *One Hundred Great Guns: An Illustrated History of Firearms.* New York, 1967.

______. *The New England Gun: The First Two Hundred Years.* New Haven, Conn., 1975.

Logan, Herschel C. *Cartridges: A Pictorial Digest of Small Arms Ammunition.* New York, 1959.

______. *Underhammer Guns.* Harrisburg, Pa., 1960.

Lustyik, Andrew F. *Civil War Carbines: From Service to Sentiment.* Aledo, Ill., 1962.

Moore, Warren. *Weapons of the American Revolution . . . And Accoutrements.* New York, 1967.

Mouillesseaux, Harold R. *Ethan Allen, Gunmaker: His Partners, Patents & Firearms.* Ottawa, Canada, 1973.

Neumann, George C. *The History of Weapons of the American Revolution.* New York, 1967.

Peterson, Harold L. *The Treasury of the Gun.* New York, 1962.

Reilly, Robert M. *United States Military Small Arms, 1816-1865.* Baton Rouge, La., 1970.

Roads, C.H. *The British Soldiers Firearm, 1850-1864.* London, 1964.

Roberts, Ned H. *The Muzzle-Loading Cap Lock Rifle.* Harrisburg, Pa., 1947.

Seller, Frank M. *Sharps Firearms.* North Hollywood, Calif., 1978.

Sharpe, Philip B. *The Rifle in America.* New York, 1947.

Shumway, George. *Pennsylvania Longrifles of Note.* York, Pa., 1977.

______. *Rifles in Colonial America.* York, Pa., 1979.

Sutherland, R.Q. and R.L. Wilson. *The Book of Colt Firearms.* Kansas City, Kans., 1971.

Thomas, H.H. *The Story of Allen and Wheelock Firearms.* Cincinnati, Ohio, 1965.

Watrous, George R. *The History of Winchester Firearms, 1866-1966.* New Haven, Conn., 1966.

Wolff, Eldon G. *Ballard Rifles in the Henry J. Nunnemacher Collection.* Milwaukee, Wis., 1945.

Illustration Credits

Nearly all the illustrations for this guide have been drawn from the Nunnemacher Collection, Milwaukee Public Museum, one of the major North American collections of firearms. Other sources include The Museum of the Fur Trade (19-1), the West Point Museum (26-11, 26-29), George Moller (6-2), and George Shumway, photographer (5-1a, 5-1b, 5-1c, 5-1d, 5-2, 5-3). The author wishes to extend special thanks to Andrew Mowbray of Man at Arms magazine for the use of color plate 5.

Introduction

Why do people collect antique firearms and, more specifically, antique shoulder arms? The answer to this question is not easily supplied, but the usefulness of such weapons is rarely a consideration. In large part they are antique because they are obsolete. Antique arms are often excellent investments, but financial gain is usually secondary in importance to aesthetic or historical reasons. In Europe, where many firearms were made for royalty and gentry and exhibit rich ornamentation and exquisite craftsmanship, the collector often makes his choice on artistic grounds. In America, firearms were produced for a much different class of people with more practical and democratic tastes. While some arms, especially the "Golden Age" or so-called "Kentucky" rifles made by German-American gunsmiths, may be lavishly ornamented, the vast majority are more interesting as historical objects than as decorative pieces. The American collector often seeks an historical "document," a tangible link to the past. Shoulder arms, primarily a product of the modern age, are especially relevant to the development of the American nation, and its place in world history.

The story of shoulder arms made or used in the United States is primarily a technological one. The method by which combustion is achieved in a particular arm is an important key to understanding its place in the overall development of modern weaponry, civilian and military. Ever since at least the late 13th century, the main source of propulsion of a projectile was not gunpowder as it is known today (smokeless) but rather a mixture now called "black powder." Composed of a mix of three finely ground substances (carbon, sulfur, and potassium nitrate), this relatively slow burning composition took its name from two of its characteristics—its black color prior to ignition, and the grimy residue that coated all surfaces after firing. Although "black powder" was at first restricted to large and cumbersome cannons, by the 14th century improved means to harness the power were developed. The result was the hand cannon, requiring the services of only two men—one to hold the tube and the other to ignite the charge at a touchhole drilled into its rear end. A refinement of this crude device took place during the first half of the 15th century whereby a mechanism was incorporated that permitted the person holding the stocked tube to ignite the charge by himself. The resulting arm, the arquebus, was slow to load and required a separate, detachable barrel support, but it could be deployed in practical, maneuverable military units. The era of "modern warfare" was born with this change, and firearms would play a dominant role in the expansion of European influence to the far corners of the globe.

Not knowing what to anticipate from the natives and rightfully fearing their European rivals, the first colonists who came to the Americas arrived fully prepared for combat in the European fashion. Their preparations proved fully justified. Still reeling from a century of bitter religious strife and intensely jealous of their newly found domains, the competing European powers spared no effort to bring rival settlements under control. The initially friendly American natives, in opposition to the encroachment of their tribal territories, entered into open warfare with the European settlers. Consequently, military garrisons became a necessity, and in the English settlements. the ancient Anglo-Saxon militia tradition was revitalized to supplement the small regular garrisons. This English militia system basically required that each citizen arm himself at his own expense with a suitable military weapon. As firearms development became more technologically refined, the edged weapons (spear or pike, sword, and bow and arrow) gave way to the musket, and the militia was expected to possess a longarm capable of delivering a man-killing ball. The pragmatic English colonists soon adapted a shoulder arm that had been popular for hunting wild fowl in the mother country to a shortened version that could double at militia musters. This colonial "fowler," often locally stocked with a variety of imported or obsolete military parts, became America's first native longarm. As the colonists trekked westward from their seaboard enclaves, the dual needs of security and sustenance were met through the use of increasingly sophisticated longarms.

The German-speaking settlers of Pennsylvania and neighboring areas brought with them a tradition that would influence American firearms development—hunting with rifled arms. Rifling, a series of spiraling grooves cut into the bore of the barrel, imparted a spin upon the round leaden projectiles that universally served for bullets until the 19th century. The gyroscopic effect of this spin gave the projectile a much greater accuracy than those that simply rebounded off the sides of the tube of a smoothbore longarm. Rifled shoulder arms were therefore much more reliable for hunting forest game. When combined with refinements of the wheel-lock mechanism devised in the German states during the 16th and 17th centuries, a fast igniting, flintlock longarm resulted.

To rectify problems in muzzle loading and in accuracy, as well as to economize on the use of lead, the Pennsylvania gunsmiths decreased the size of the bore of the traditional "jäger" rifle, often .50 cal. or greater. To give the projectile increased momentum to kill at distance, they were thereby forced to revert to a larger charge (relative to ball size) of powder. This in turn necessitated lengthening the barrel to give the rifling a "slow twist." The loading problem was overcome by not only reducing the size of the bullet but also by wrapping the lead projectile in a linen or leather patch that would serve as a catalyst to impart the spin on the bullet and yet easily grip the rifling while loading. As the originators of this hybrid arm migrated first south into the Shenandoah Valley of Virginia and then westward beyond the Appalachians, this "American rifle" (as the British respectfully termed it) acquired a new pseudonym—the Kentucky rifle. Modified in the Ohio and Mississippi/Missouri valleys by slightly shortening the overall length and replacing the delicate full-length wooden forestock with a shorter wooden piece supplemented by an iron rib, this rifle was used extensively in the Rocky Mountains and acquired yet another name—the "plains" rifle.

The Pennsylvania rifle won laurels for American marksmen in the Revolutionary War, but its importance in that conflict has been dramatically overemphasized. Independence was secured on the battlefield courtesy of the smoothbore flintlock musket—both American-made "committee-of-safety" copies of British patterns and European imports that Benjamin Franklin's tactful diplomacy secured for the infant nation. In addition to British-captured weapons, these "adopted" American muskets included Dutch castoffs and the obsolete products of the French arsenals.

The smoothbore flintlock muzzleloading musket would also dominate the battlefield, both in Europe and North America, for the next half century. Its tactical legacy—linear tactics (lines of soldiers, two ranks deep, standing shoulder to shoulder to permit effective volley fire)—would carry over into the early years of the American Civil War with tragic results. By 1861 this standard arm had been supplanted by those making use of two revolutionary technological innovations—the percussion ignition system and the easily loaded rifle projectile. Suddenly the effective killing power of opposing musketmen was increased from a mere 75 yards to 300 yards or better. The opposing lines of battle could now fire 5 to 6 times instead of 1 or 2 before closing with the bayonet. The rate of fire was increased by an improvement in the projectile used.

The new projectile that emerged during the 1850s was the end result of a long series of inventions undertaken during the 19th century by members of the French military in an effort to insure that muzzleloading rifled military shoulder arms might load with ease under combat conditions. The first attempt had involved minor alterations to the interior of the breech end of the rifle bore. A separate breech-piece with a chamber smaller than the rifle bore was screwed permanently to the rear of the barrel, leaving a lip above the chamber for the powder. A ball of the diameter of the lands of the bore was loaded from the muzzle with ease (since it did not engage the grooves) and then hammered against this lip with the ramrod to expand it into the rifling. This same principle was used in a later method devised by Thouvenin. In this case, however, a cylindrical pillar (a **tige**) emanating from the breechplug was substituted for the lipped chamber. This pillar served as the platform against which the bullet (now cylindro-conical in shape) was hammered into the rifling grooves. Both systems, though widely adopted throughout Europe in the 1840s and early '50s, had the disadvantage of deforming the projectile while hammering it into the rifling. The resulting deformed bullet occasionally deviated from its proper course.

In an effort to eliminate this defect, a French officer named Minie produced a design which called for placing a surrogate pillar directly within the Thouvenin projectile. The projectile was modified by casting it with a hollow base. Into this base Minie inserted an iron cup that would force the sides of the cylindrical base of the bullet to expand when rammed against the powder charge. The pillar was thereby totally eliminated. The English experimented favorably with Minie's system, substituting a wooden or clay plug for the metal cup. And in America after experiments at Harpers Ferry in 1852-53, it was discovered that gas pressure alone was sufficient to expand the lead side walls of the projectile into the rifling; no plug was necessary at all. These last projectiles were the primary bullets used by both sides during the Civil War. The longarms that used them were called rifle-muskets because they were in effect a crossbreed between the old-style smoothbore musket and the deeply grooved rifles using the round ball.

The Civil War rifle-muskets were all of the percussion ignition system that had been perfected in the same period as the "Minie ball." This system eliminated a major disadvantage of the flintlock mechanism—failure to ignite in rain or damp inclement weather. Essentially, the percussion ignition system was very similar in appearance and operation to the old flintlock mechanism. The "cock" whose jaws had previously held the flint was simply modified to form a solid iron striker or hammer. Since the flint was eliminated, the flat-faced iron "frizzen" that produced the spark when struck by the flint was no longer required, nor was the spring needed that held it in place until struck. Instead, an iron cone, often called a "nipple," was screwed into a metal bolster that had been forged or otherwise affixed to the side of the barrel where the vent had communicated the priming flash from the pan to the main charge. Since the cone was channeled directly to the main charge the pan was eliminated totally. Upon this cone a separate copper truncated cone, hollowed and filled with a small amount of mercury fulminate, was placed after the muzzle had been loaded and the hammer drawn back to "cocked" position. When the trigger released the hammer, it arched forward and struck the copper "cap" against the cone with sufficient force to detonate the fulminate. The resulting detonation was channeled to the main charge in an instant, firing the bullet.

The percussion ignition system was initially applied to firearms in 1807 by Scotch inventor Alexander Forsyth, but it was not generally adopted until nearly 40 years later. With the expiration of Forsyth's patents in 1821, however, improvements in the system made by Joshua Shaw and Joseph Manton circulated freely throughout the arms trade. The new system was first applied to sporting arms; its near instantaneous ignition proved highly advantageous, especially in hunting wild fowl. The removal of several cumbersome parts from the lock mechanism also endeared it to the makers of pocket pistols. The concept was quickly taken up in America and was so well-liked that many flintlock arms were altered by local gunsmiths. The public authorities in both the United States and Europe, however, were far more skeptical of the innovation, and were among the last to apply it in a widespread manner; U.S. specialty services, nevertheless, began receiving military percussion arms on a systematic basis in the 1830s.

With the final adoption of the percussion system to newly manufactured production, methods were also sought to alter existing stocks of flintlock arms. In the United States some of these alterations incorporated mechanical priming systems that eliminated the need to separately affix the small copper cap to the cone with each loading sequence. The most notable American mechanical priming system, that invented by a Washington, D.C., dentist, Edward Maynard, closely resembles a modern toy cap pistol with its roll of paper caps. In 1855 this system was adopted for all military longarms manufactured for the U.S. government, and even several thousand flintlock muskets were altered to it. The production demands of the Civil War, however, forced the government to revert to the standard copper cap in lieu of the roll of mechanically-fed primers.

The implementation of the copper percussion cap did much to indirectly stimulate the adoption of practical, efficient breechloading longarms. The problem had long been to find an effective method to seal the breechloading mechanism from the corrosive and fouling gases caused by the burning of the main powder charge. In 1812 a Swiss gunsmith working in Paris had invented a cardboard cartridge with a separately primed brass head that would expand with the head of the explosion of the main charge and thereby seal the breechloading mechanism from fouling. In 1848 Christian Sharps, an American arms maker, patented a variation of this concept, incorporating a brass "obdurator" as part of the lever-activated dropping breechblock that also integrated a percussion cone and a version of Dr. Maynard's priming mechanism.

The bullet and powder were contained in a combustible linen cartridge that was cut open when the breechblock sealed the breech. In the same year another American, Walter Hunt, patented a different style of cartridge that required no extraction of debris from the previous shot. Like the later-invented Minie ball, the base of the cylindro-conical projectile was hollow so as to hold a charge of powder which was sealed in place with a cork wad pierced in its center to permit ignition from the detonation of a separately affixed cap or priming device. An improved version of Hunt's "rocket ball" was patented in 1856 by his successors in the arms trade, Smith and Wesson. Their improvement, designed for the Volcanic repeating arms, included a fulminate primer integrated directly into the composite cork and brass base plug of the bullet. The cavity of these cartridges, however, was relatively small, and because black powder was a low-power explosive, not enough powder could be accommodated by the cavity to propel the bullet with any great force over a large distance.

Other attempts were made to create a self-contained cartridge incorporating the lead bullet, the powder charge, and the fulminate detonator during the late 1850s by the use of copper cylinders variously shaped at the rear. The state of the art of copper extrusion only permitted the manufacture of small caliber (up to .44), relatively short cartridges that did not provide the room for the powder charge desired in longarms. Until 1862 when the extrusion process was perfected for larger caliber rim-fire cartridges, inventors turned to other media for cartridges or abandoned the self-contained concept for more easily constructed separately primed percussion copper cartridges. Numerous patented breechloading carbines were adapted to such ammunition and were purchased during the Civil War, much to the consternation of supply officials in the field. Even after machinery had been developed for the manufacture of large carliber rim-fire cartridges, the unevenness of the copper sheeting used for the crucial rims housing the fulminate caused serious problems. This deficiency led to experiments with center-fire cartridges, and these came into general use during the 1870s for most longarms. The development of this type of cartridge guaranteed the success not only of the single-shot breechloading shoulder arm, but also that of the repeater, first with tubular magazines and later with box magazines.

The rim-fire arms (most notably the Spencer, the Henry, and the '66 Winchester) and then center-fire, single-shot rifles and repeating rifles (including the retrogressive U.S. M1873 rifle and carbine, the stately Sharps "buffalo rifles", and the '73 Winchester) were the prime arms responsible for the "civilizing" of America's Great Plains. With the closing of this last frontier, Americans turned their eyes and thoughts abroad. Almost coincidentally with the universal adoption of the smokeless powder cartridge, the country shed its cloak of isolationism and sought to become a world power. The old black powder cartridge arms were still very much in evidence during the Spanish-American War, but most of the Western World had adopted the more potent smokeless product. Confronted with that superiority, the American arms industry, both private and governmental, followed suit.

This guide to selected American antique shoulder arms attempts to categorize for the collector the major types used or made in the United States prior to the 20th century. This restriction to arms produced before 1900 should not be as judged to imply that arms made after that date are somehow not collectible as "antiques." Indeed, many of the longarms produced in the early years of this century are highly prized and are occasionally highly-priced collector's items. For this survey, however, it has been necessary to exclude smokeless powder arms, the vast majority of which have yet to attain the degree of obsolesence to qualify them as true "antiques." Although there are honest differences of what is and isn't antique, few can dispute the fact that the most significant developments in arms-making took place in the United States during the 125 years encompassed by this guide.

H. Michael Madaus
Milwaukee, Wisconsin
March, 1981

Color Key to American Longarms

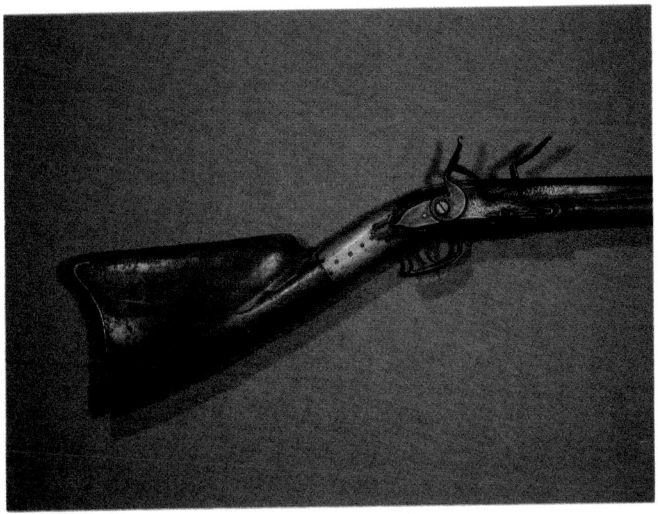

1. American Stocked Fowlers

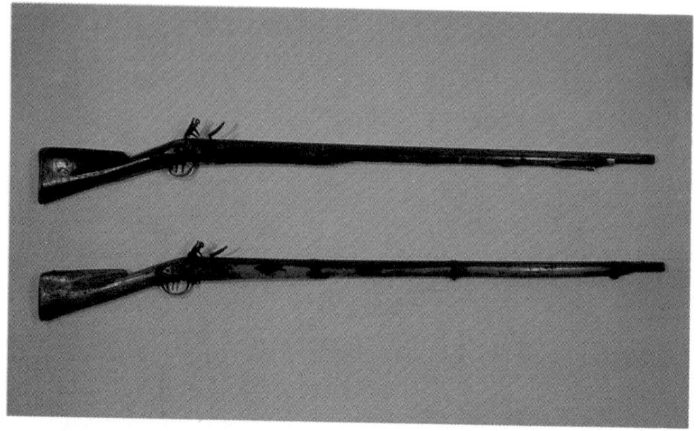

2. American-Used Foreign Flintlock Muskets

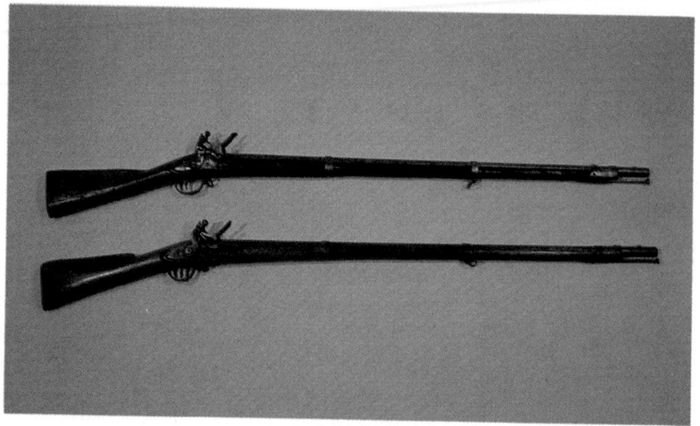

3. American-Made Flintlock Muskets

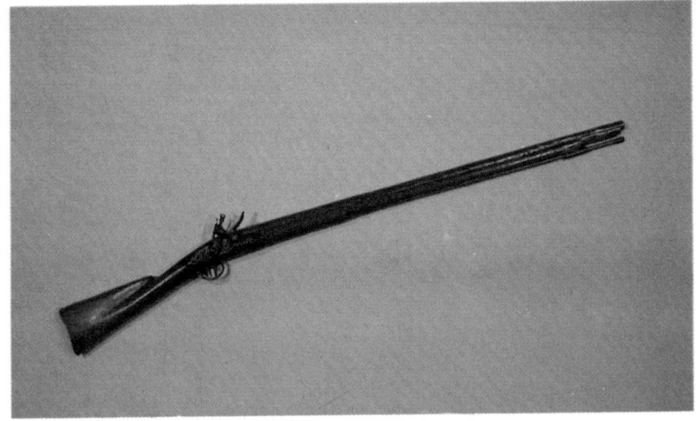

4. Indian Fusils, Carbines, and Musketoons

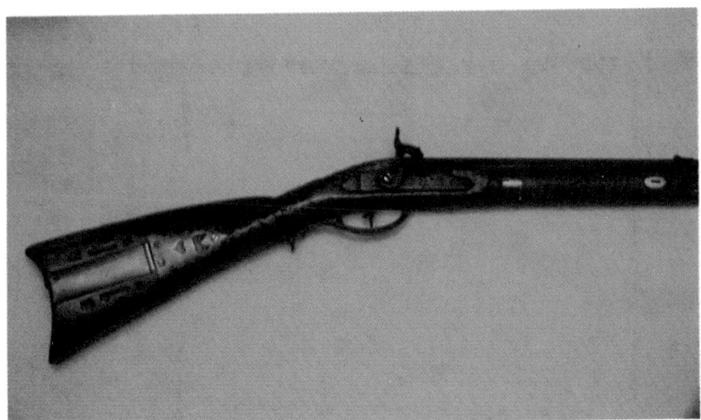

5. American Flintlock Rifles

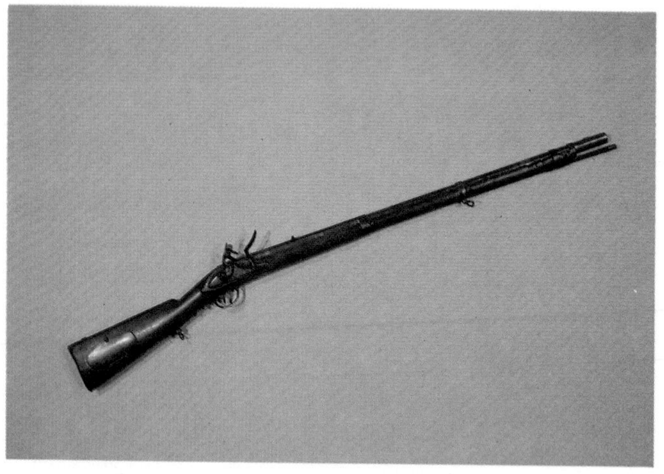

6. Military and Contract Flintlock Rifles

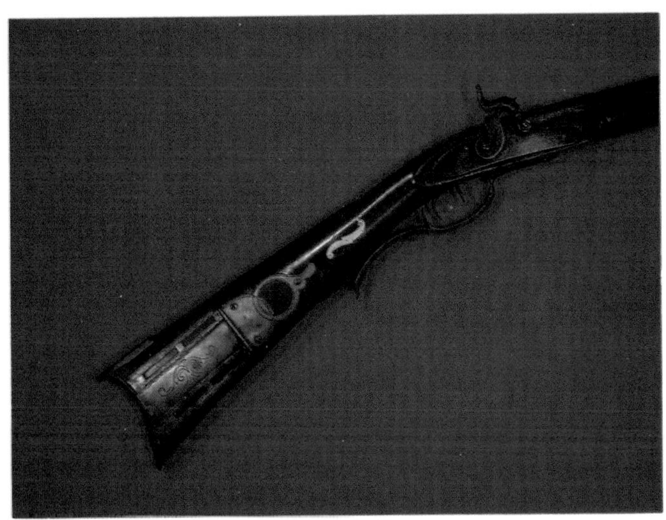

7. Civilian Alterations from Flintlock to Percussion

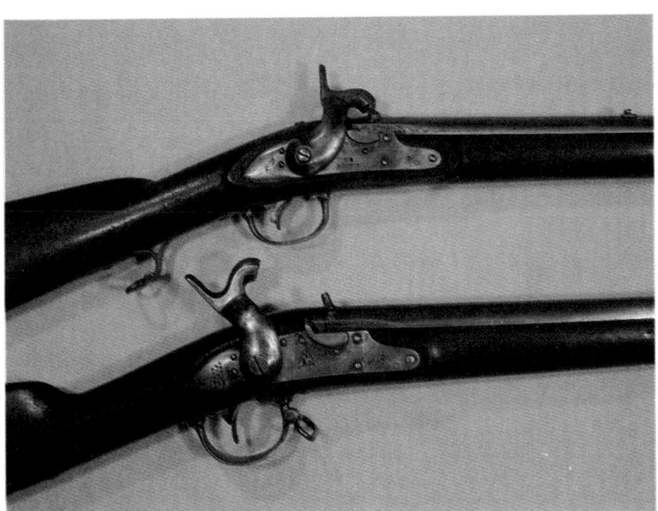

8. Arsenal Alterations from Flintlock to Percussion

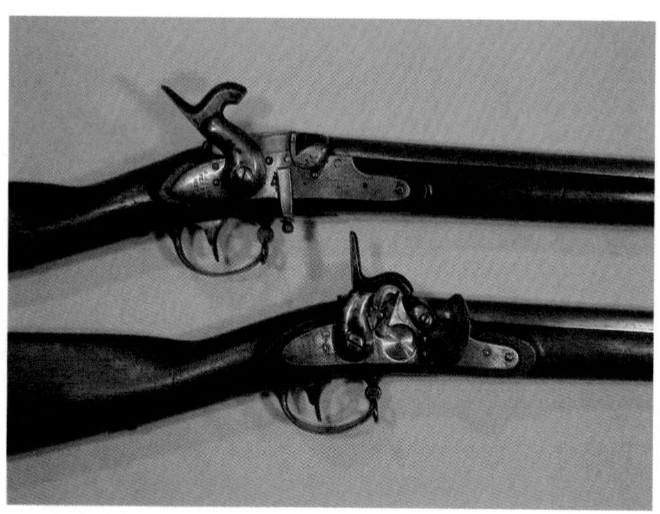

9. Alterations of Flintlocks to Mechanical Priming Systems

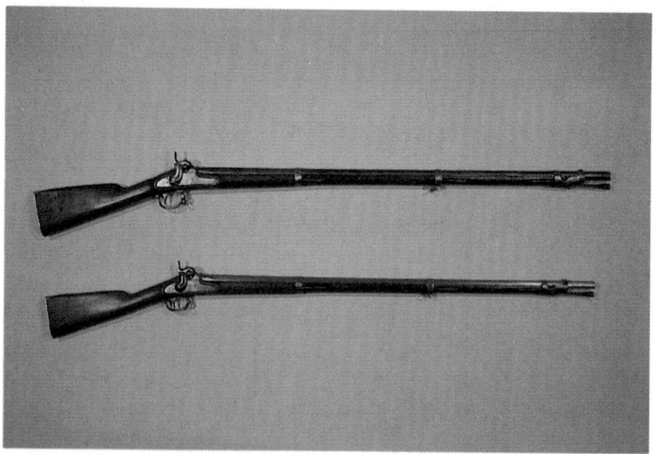

10. U.S. Smoothbore Percussion Muskets

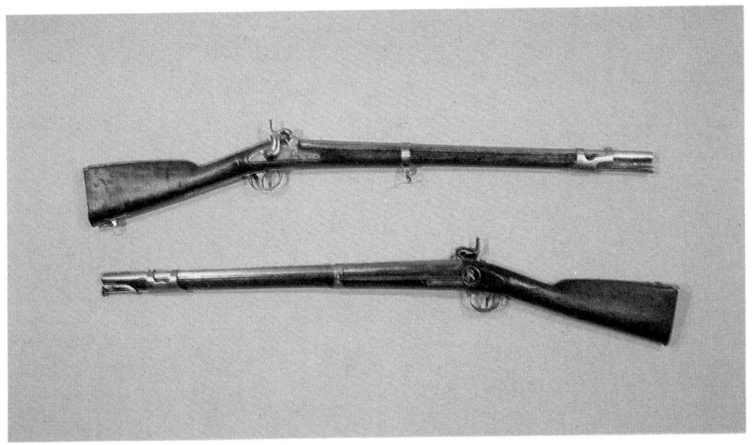

11. U.S. Smoothbore Percussion Musketoons

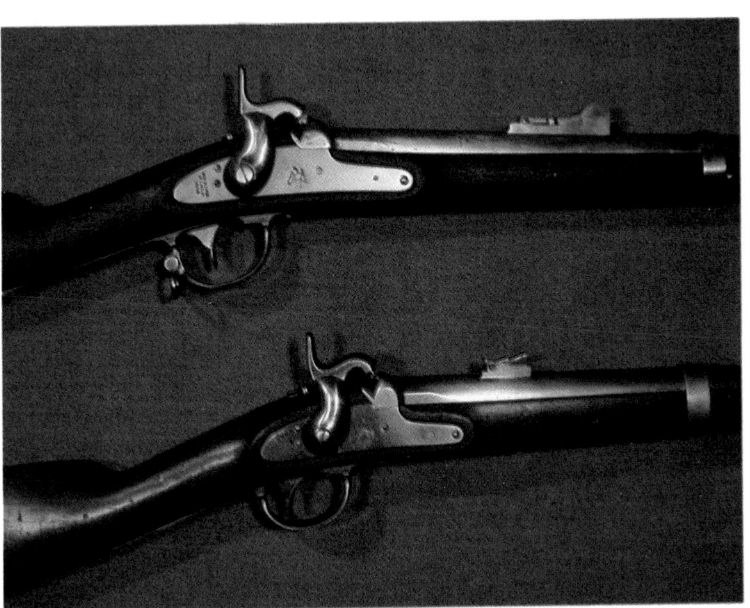

12. Rifled Smoothbore Percussion Alterations

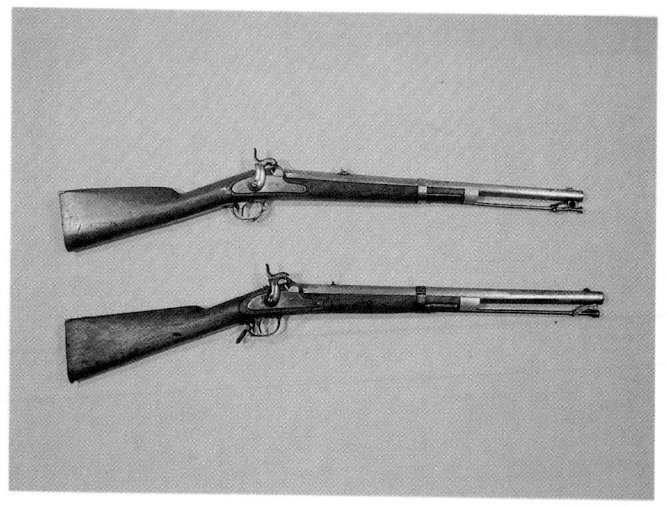

13. Rifled Percussion Carbines

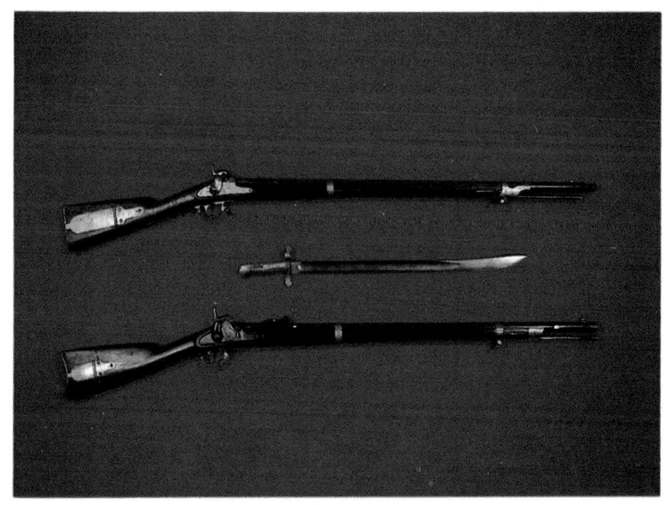

14. Arsenal-Made Percussion Military Rifles

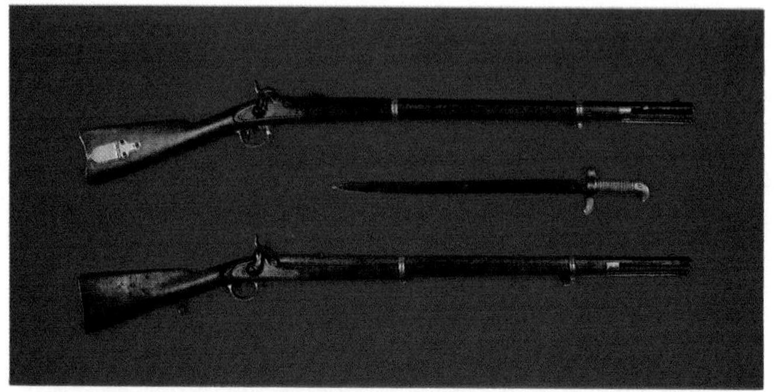

15. Contract Percussion Military Rifles

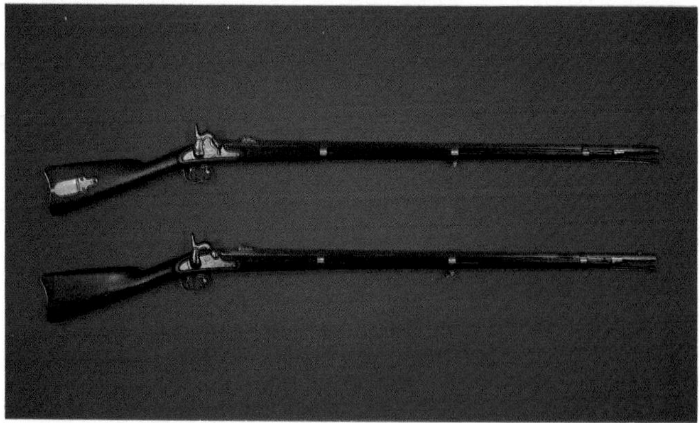

16. U.S. Military Rifle-Muskets

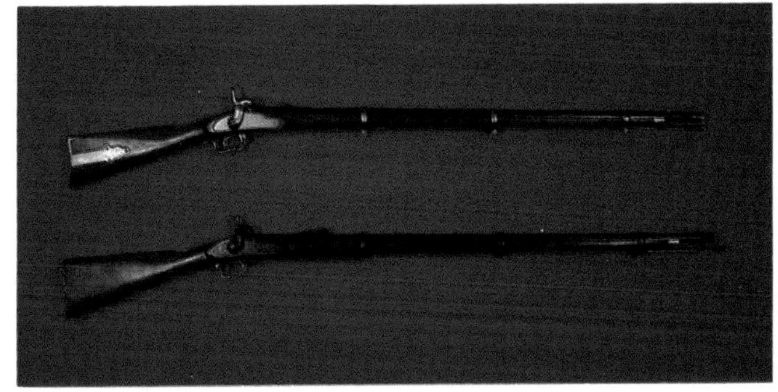

17. Special Contract Military Rifle-Muskets

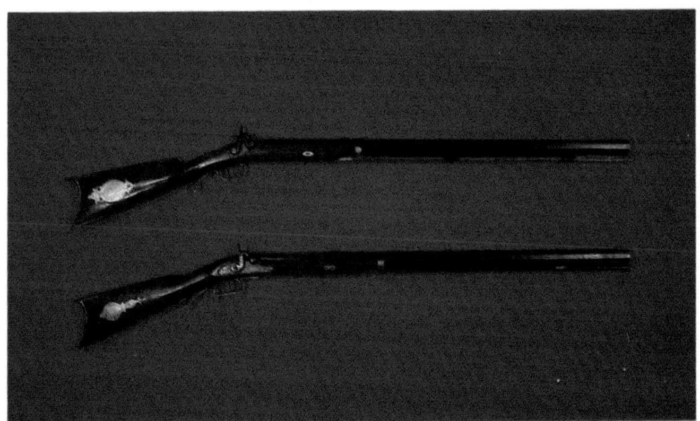

18. Percussion Sporting Rifles

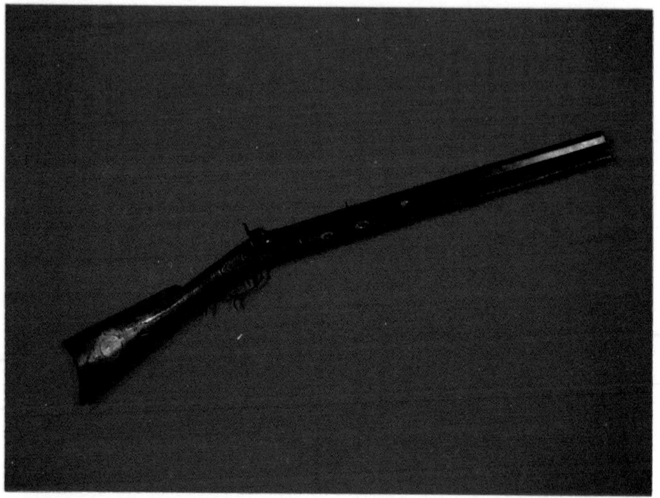

19. The "Plains" Rifle

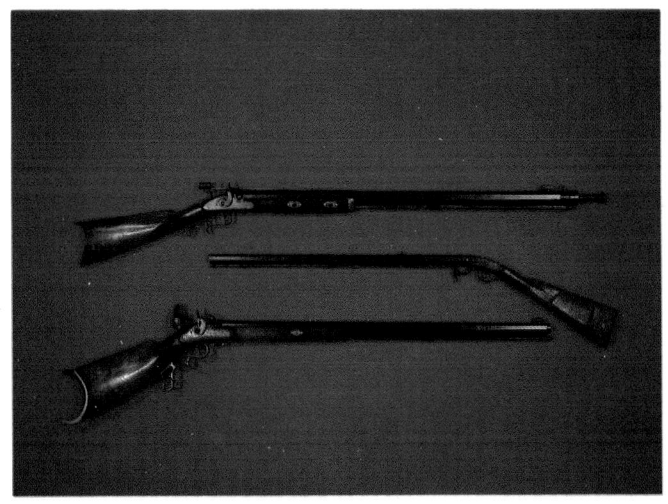

20. American Percussion Target Rifles

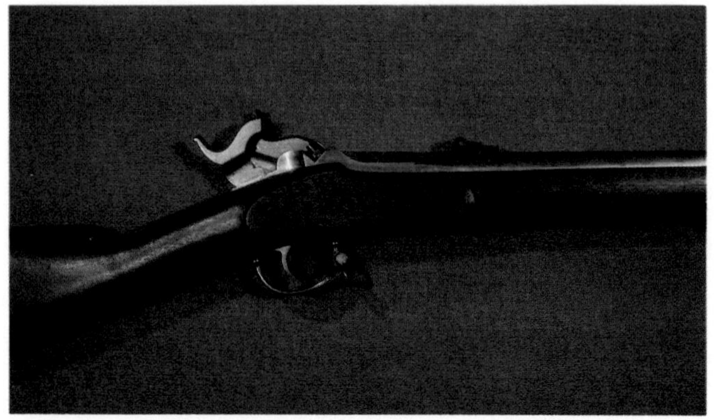

21. Multi-Shot, Single-Barrel Muzzleloading Rifles

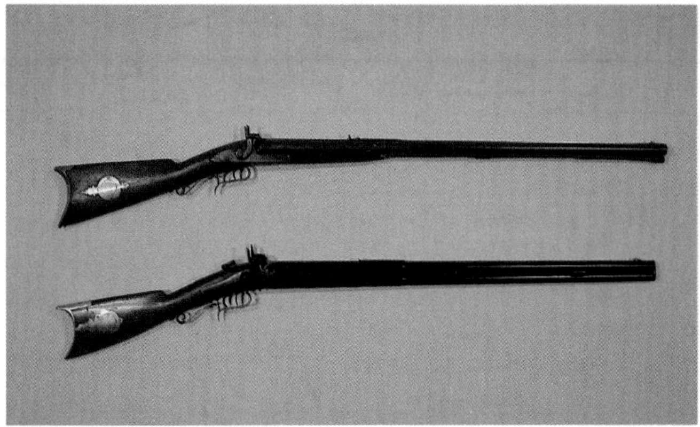

22. Multi-Barreled Muzzleloading Rifles and Shotguns

23. Breechloading Flintlock Rifles

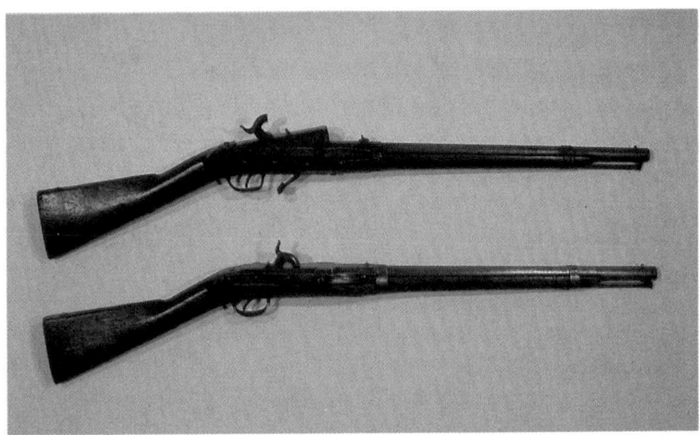

24. Breechloading Percussion Smoothbores

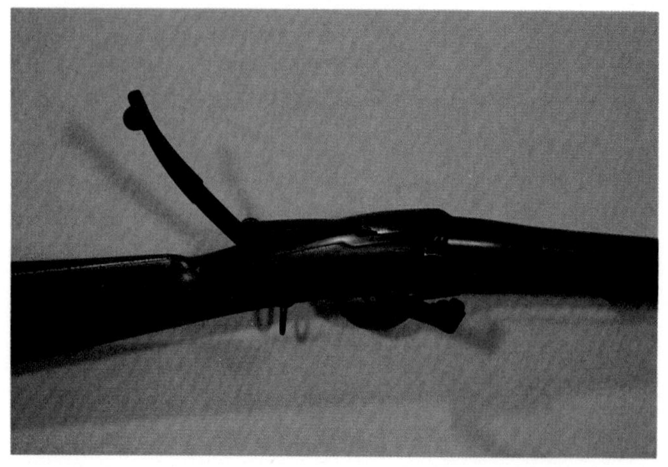

25. Breechloading Smoothbore and Rifled Alterations

26. Percussion Breechloading Rifles and Carbines

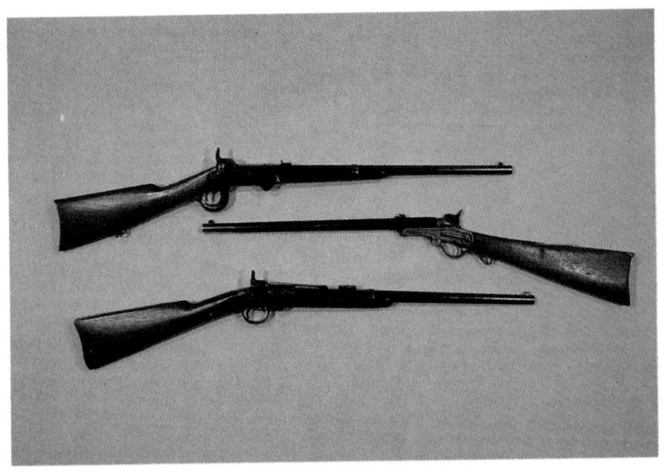

27. Patented Breechloading Percussion/Cartridge Rifles and Carbines

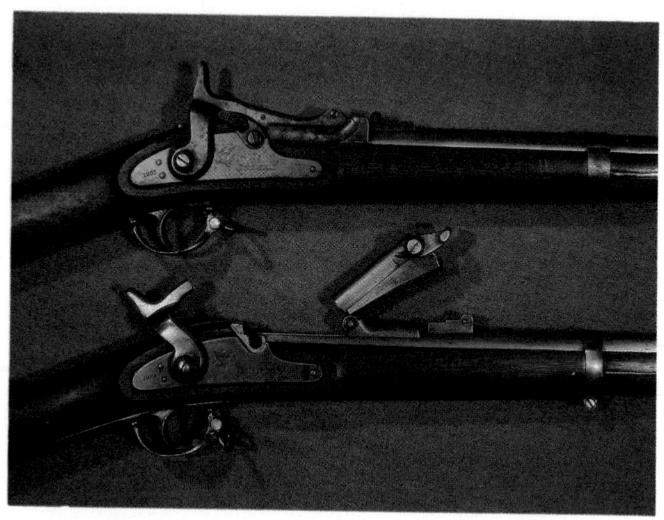

28. Percussion Muzzleloaders Altered to Cartridge Breechloaders

29. Single-Shot, Martial Breechloading Rifles

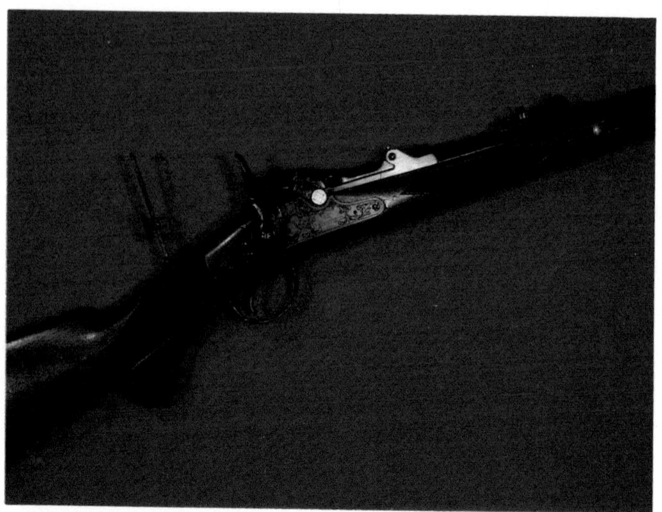

30. Special Arsenal Production of Martial Breechloaders

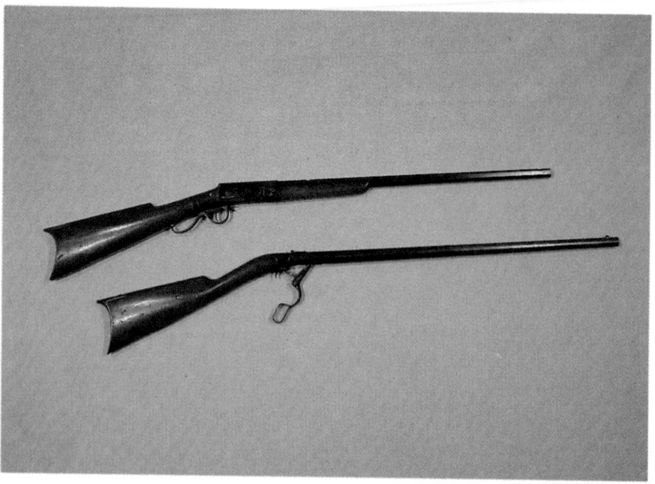

31. Patented Breechloading, Single-Shot Cartridge Rifles

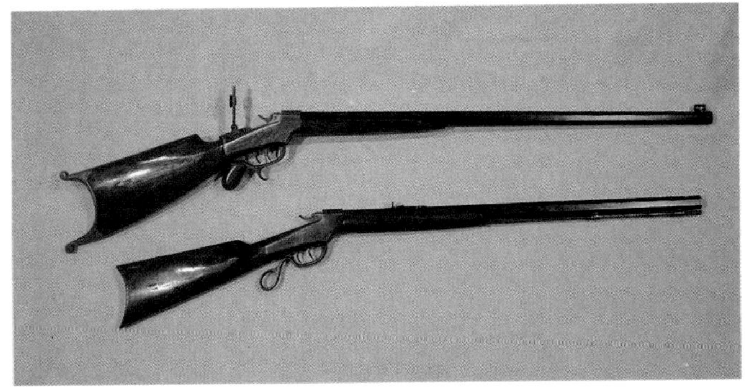

32. Ballard-Action Breechloading, Single-Shot Cartridge Rifles

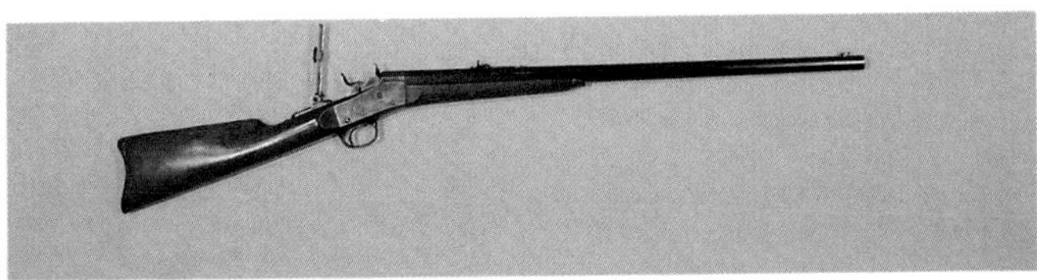

33. Remington/Rider-Action Breechloading, Single-Shot Cartridge Rifles

34. Sharps Single-Shot Cartridge Rifles

35. Patented, Single-Shot Breechloading Martial Cartridge Rifles

36. Flintlock, Repeating Magazine Longarms

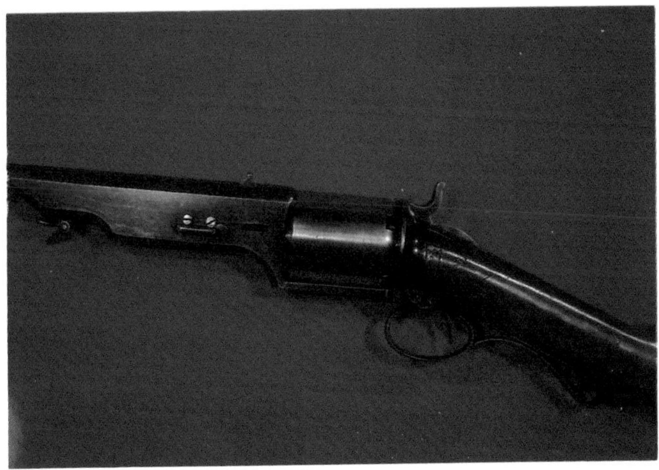

37. Percussion, Revolving Cylinder Repeating Longarms

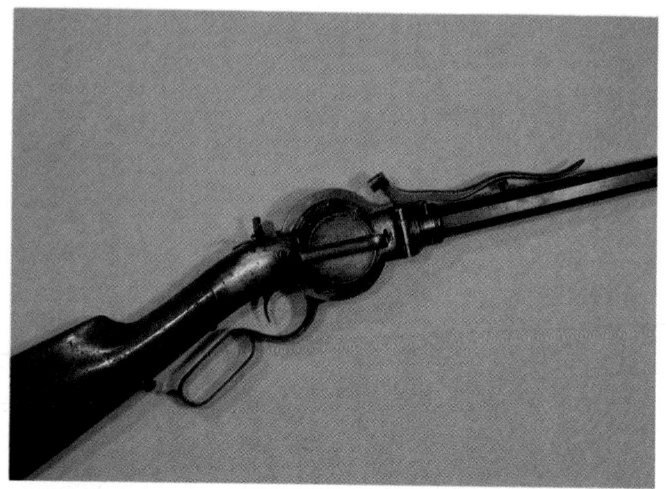

38. Percussion, Revolving Turret Magazine Repeating Longarms

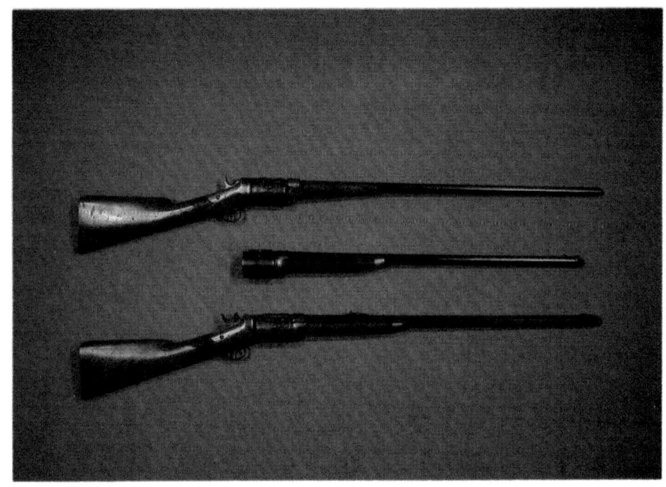

39. Metallic Cartridge, Revolving Magazine Repeating Longarms

40. Lever-Action, Tubular Magazine Repeating Rifles and Carbines

41. The Predecessors of the Winchester Longarms

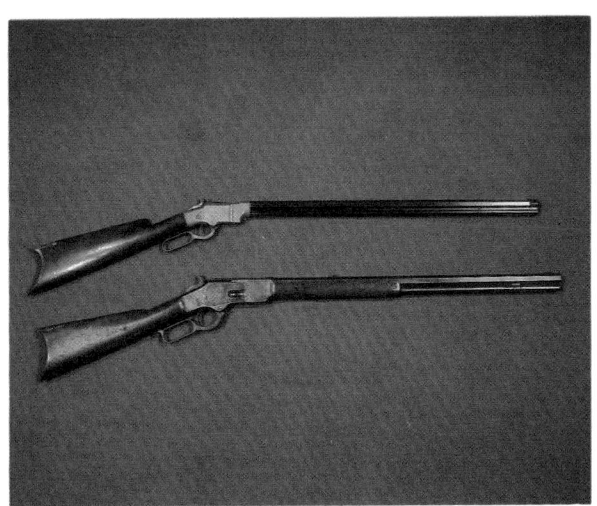

42. Winchester Lever-Action, Tubular Magazine Repeating Rifles

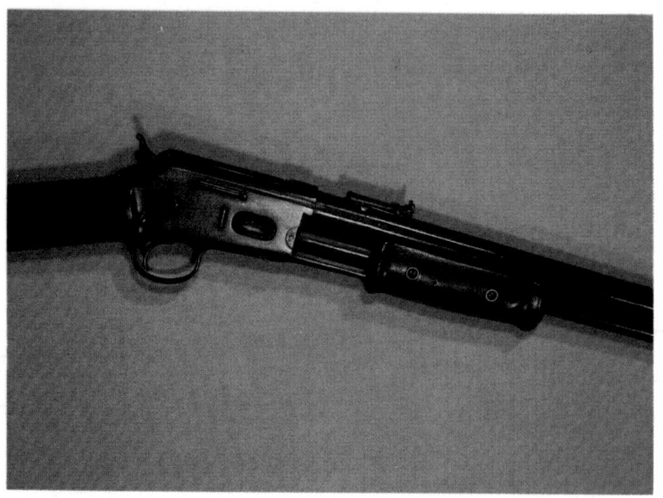

43. Slide-Action, Tubular Magazine Repeating Rifles and Carbines

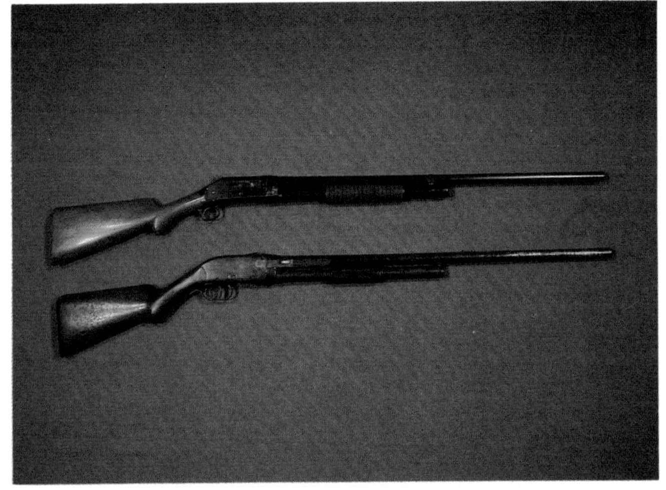

44. Slide-Action, Tubular Magazine Repeating Shotguns

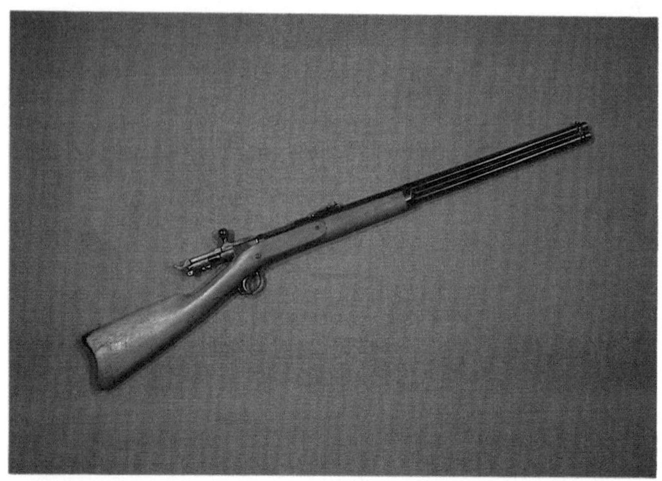

45. Bolt-Action, Tubular Magazine Repeating Sporting Rifles

46. Bolt-Action, Tubular Magazine Repeating Martial Rifles

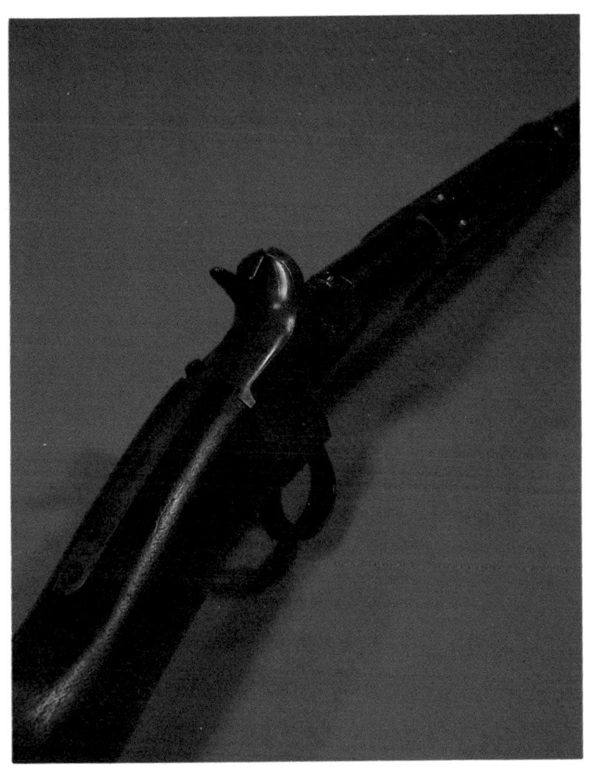

47. Other Tubular Magazine Repeating Rifles and Carbines

48. Bolt-Action, Box Magazine Repeating Rifles and Carbines

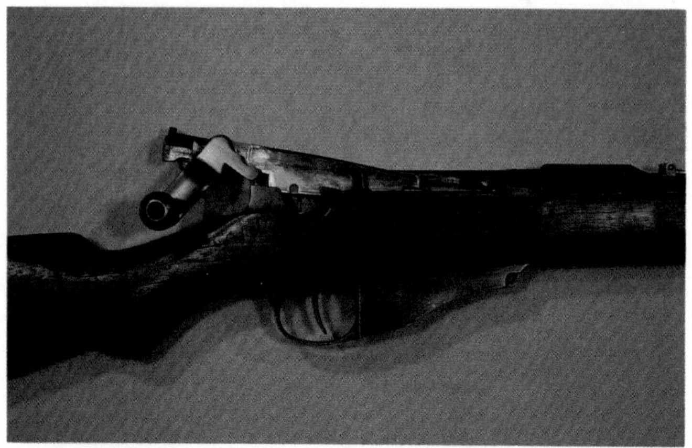

49. Quasi-Bolt-Action, Box Magazine Repeating Rifles

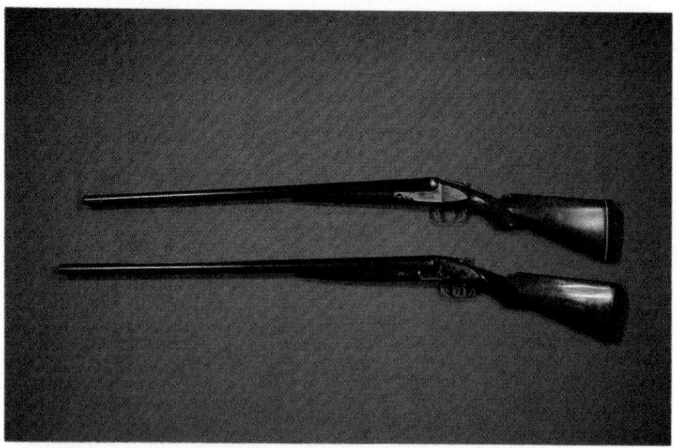

50. American Double-Barrel, Breechloading Shotguns

1 American Stocked Fowlers

Early black powders were uneven in consistency and therefore erratic in combustion. To insure that an entire charge of powder had ignited before a bullet left the barrel, early pistols and shoulder arms were made with relatively long barrels. The French are credited with making the earliest "long fowlers"—flintlock shoulder arms specifically designed for hunting wild fowl and having barrels of very large bore exceeding four feet in length. Some of these long fowlers were brought to the French colonies of North America. The same style arm was also copied in England, and as a result of both foreign influences, the long fowler came to New England and the Hudson Valley area. Because they proved very effective in the virtually shrubless virgin forests of North America, demand grew, and many were assembled in the colonies. Because the colonies lacked a domestic source for iron until after 1734, barrels and usually the flintlocks and furniture were either imported from Europe or stripped from broken or obsolete military weapons. The fowlers were stocked in the colonies, usually in American walnut or cherry or occasionally maple.

These American stocks were produced in two regional styles. The mode in the Hudson Valley followed the general configuration of a right triangle for the buttstock, the hypotenuse following a generally straight line and not angling sharply from the forestock. Furniture, especially the elaborately-wrought pierced keyplates, followed old Dutch patterns. In New England, however, the butts were made heavier with a "fish belly" convex lower edge that gave the stock the name "club butt." Keyplates, usually of brass, were large, but simple in design. Later, a "Roman Nose," a deeply dropping but thinner buttstock, came into vogue as well.

As powder quality improved during the 18th century, the barrels of fowlers were gradually reduced, approaching those of the military muskets. In many instances the barrels of the old long fowlers were shortened, the forestocks being reduced proportionately so that the fowler could double as a militia shoulder arm, though few were equipped with bayonet lugs.

1-0 Hudson Valley Long Fowlers (color plate)

OL: 58½''
BD: .66 cal.
Furniture: brass
Lockplate: flat with integral, iron-faced pan
Markings: none

BL: 42½''
Configuration: round with top rib and two long (17¾'') side flats
Fastenings: pins
Markings: on top "SAN/TOS" in gold cartouche and Spanish proofs on upper left.

A typical Hudson Valley long fowler with Spanish barrel (so highly respected during the 17th and 18th centuries), shortened to 42¼'' for militia usage. Forestock has been crudely cut back, wrist has been repaired with brass sheeting and tacks, and frizzen has been refaced, evidencing hard service. Missing upper jaw and jaw screw from cock. **(D)**

1-1 American Long Fowlers

OL: 81¼''

BL: 65¼''

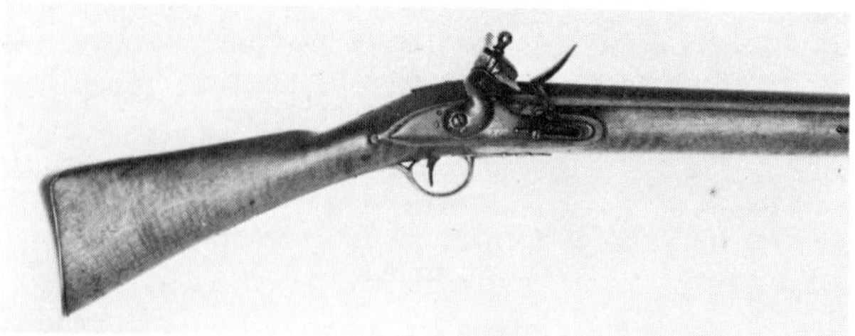

BD: .77 cal.
Furniture: brass
Lockplate: convex with integral, iron round pan
Markings: "Ketland/& Co." (script) forward of cock

Configuration: round
Fastenings: wedges
Markings: on top "London" (script); upper left, "TK" and English proofs

A typical late-type American fowler stocked in American walnut. Note there is no nosecap, and the forestock is accordingly damaged. **(D)**

---

2 American-Used Foreign Flintlock Muskets

Prior to the Revolution, America's sole source of military arms were those sent by the mother country. Most were of English manufacture, although during the French and Indian War Dutch muskets had been purchased to meet the pressing needs of the British service. For the most part, however, the muskets found in the colonies during the 1700s were one of two types: the English Long Land Pattern (introduced 1720-30) with a 46-inch long barrel, and a later version (introduced c. 1755, formally adopted 1768) with a 42-inch long barrel first known as the Militia or Sea Service Pattern and later as the Short Land Pattern musket. Quantities of these muskets were confiscated and captured during the early years of the Revolution. They also were widely copied by the suppliers of the various Committees-of-Safety.

The main source of Revolutionary Army arms, however, was France. In 1776 and 1777 American commissioners procured over 100,000 obsolete muskets. Some were old Dutch and German weapons, but most bore the names of the three major French armories inscribed upon their locks: St. Étienne, Maubeuge, or Charleville, with the last predominating in such numbers that the entire assemblage carries the misnomer "Charlevilles." As France was in the process of adopting a new musket model, to be known as the M1777, the government was quite willing to dispose of the stored relics dating back to the first standardized type, the M1717. Most, fortunately, were of the more recent M1763 types and its offshoots.

Because the separate colonies also made purchases of muskets, orders were issued on January 30, 1777 to insure that those secured by Congress would be readily recognizable. These were to be surcharged, usually with the initials "US" stamped into the top of the barrel and/or the tail of the lockplate, frequently in conjunction with

the brand "U. STATES" in the buttstock. The colonies also utilized various abbreviations upon the metal of their respective arms. "US" surcharge markings are among the easiest of all to fake, and the collector should regard them with great care. It should also be noted that legitimately surcharged lockplates, and less frequently barrels, have been transposed to arms that were not Revolutionary War imports. Some of this was done after the disposal of surplus and damaged arms after the conclusion of hostilities in 1783.

2-0 British Long Land Pattern "Brown Bess" Muskets (color plate, above)

OL: 61¾''
BD: .75 (.78) cal.
Furniture: brass (buttplate with long pin-held tang); iron sling swivels set on triggerguard and forestock
Lockplate: convex (banana-shaped on earlier production) with integral, iron round pan; rounded gooseneck cock
Markings: "GR" surmounted by crown forward of cock, contractor's name and date of contract (e.g., "GALTON/1759") on tail until 1764, simple "TOWER" after 1764
BL: 46'' (45½'')
Configuration: round; bayonet lug on top near muzzle
Fastenings: pins
Markings: English proofs and occasionally regimental markings (see comments); captured muskets usually have "US" surcharge at the breech

Regimental markings usually consist of the numerical rank of the regiment of foot, such as "IX," in Roman numerals followed by the abbreviation "REG^T." near the breech of the barrel. Rack numbers, consisting of a letter and number combination were inscribed in the brass wrist escutcheon. **(C)**

French M1754 Muskets (color plate, below)

OL: 62¼'' (59⅞'')
BD: .69 (.70-.73) cal.
Furniture: iron (sling swivels located on forward strap of triggerguard and middle band)
Lockplate: flat with detachable, iron-faceted pan; gooseneck cock
Markings: armory code marks forward of cock; if surcharged, "US" on tail
BL: 44½''-45⅝''
Configuration: part of octagonal (10'') and round; bayonet lug on top near muzzle
Fastenings: 3 bands
Markings: contractor's/inspector's letters on upper left flat; if surcharged, "US" on top flat

If surcharged in wood, usually "U STATES" branded into buttstock below lower tang of triggerguard. Armory code letter (e. g., "D" for Charleville Armory) stamped into buttstock as well. Note, 1746 furniture occasionally legitimately used in the early production of this arm. **(C)**

2-1 British Short Land Pattern Muskets

OL: 58'' (−½'')
BD: .75 (.78) cal.
Furniture: brass (buttplate with short, pin-secured tang), iron sling swivels set on the triggerguard and forestock
Lockplate: convex with integral, iron round pan; rounded gooseneck cock
BL: 42''
Configuration: round; bayonet lug on top near muzzle
Fastenings: pins
Markings: English proofs and occasionally regimental markings, but most frequently with regimental number in Arabic numerals; captured muskets usually surcharged "US" at the breech

Markings: "GR" surmounted by crown forward of cock; "TOWER" or "DUBLIN/CASTLE" on tail; "US" if surcharged

In the 1790s, with the outbreak of war with Revolutionary France, England modified this pattern by first eliminating the wrist escutcheon and then by adopting the convex, tailless keyplate similar to the new "India Pattern" musket. On Nov. 26, 1800, 3000 British "Tower" muskets were imported for the United States by James & Ebenezer Watson, and these may have been of this modified Short Land pattern or of the India pattern. **(B)**

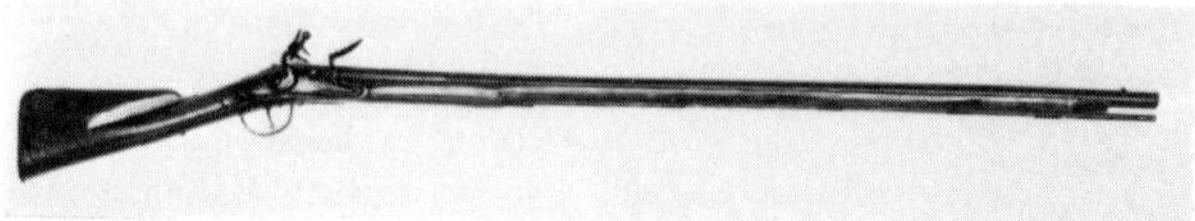

2-2 American Purchased Continental Muskets, Dutch Variant

OL: 61¼"
BD: .80 cal.
Furniture: iron
Lockplate: convex (banana-shape) with detachable, iron rounded pan; gooseneck cock
Markings: none

BL: 45⅞"
Configuration: part octagonal/part round; narrow bayonet lug on top near muzzle
Fastenings: pins
Markings: various numbers and letters near breech, proofs, bayonet mating
Markings: in script near muzzle

Illustrated is only one example of many styles of Dutch and German muskets imported to America during the French and Indian War and the War of Independence. **(D)**

2-3 French M1746 Muskets

OL: 63"-62¼"
BD: .69 (.72) cal.
Furniture: iron (sling swivel rings on left side of middle band and in left side of stock behind keyplate)
Lockplate: flat with integral iron-faceted pan; gooseneck cock
Markings: occasionally surcharged "US" on tail in addition to French armory and contractor's markings (letters)

BL: 46½" (−½")
Configuration: part octagonal (7"), part round; bayonet lug on top near muzzle
Fastenings: 2 iron bands and short, double strapped upper band
Markings: occasionally surcharged "US" on top flat

This arm was originally equipped with an iron ramrod. **(D)**

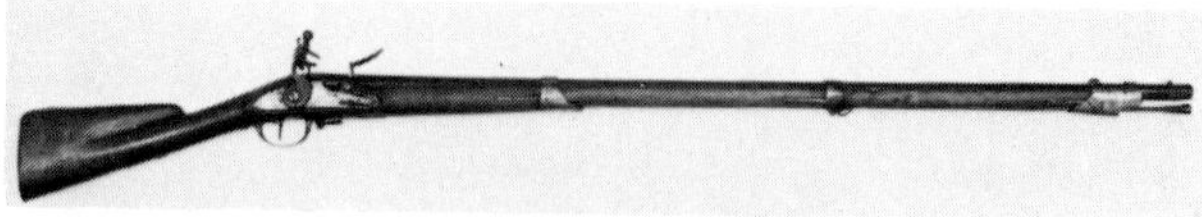

2-4 French M1768 Derivative of M1763 Muskets

OL: 60" (59¾")
BD: .69 (.70) cal.
Furniture: iron

BL: 44¾" (44½")
Configuration: round; bayonet lug under barrel near muzzle

Lockplate: flat with detachable iron pan; reinforced cock

Markings: armory name (in script) such as "Charleville," "St. Etienne," or "Manuf/Maubeuge" and armory code letter forward of cock

Fastenings: 3 bands, the upper double strapped

Markings: "M1763" on breechplug tang; if surcharged, "US" on top of barrel near breech

This arm, the original M1763, and its other derivatives—the M1766, the M1772, and the M1774—were the most commonly exported arms for the American cause of Independence. The distinctions for the derivatives, including the M1768, are: **M1766:** Both stock and lock made slightly smaller in weight and bulk; front, double strapped band modified slightly in shape. **M1768:** Alterations of the M1766 continued; furthermore, spring band inletted behind rear band to secure it in uniformity with the other bands; bayonet lug returned to top of barrel near muzzle; ramrod retaining spring screwed into the lower band. **M1772:** Lockplate surface made convex at the tail and bottom of the pan is rounded; "M1772" inscribed on breechplug tang. **M1774:** Locking spring to secure bayonet is riveted to the barrel so as to protrude slightly forward of upper, double strap band; "M1774" inscribed on breechplug tang.

All derivations of the M1763 have been noted with "U.S." surcharges on locks and barrel and with "U STATES" branded into the buttstocks. In addition to these muskets, fusils and dragoon musketoons were exported to America for the use of the Continental Army. These arms are quite rare. **(B)**

---

3 | American-Made Flintlock Muskets

The earliest flintlock muskets actually made in quantity—lock, stock, and barrel—in America were those ordered by the Committees-of-Safety. These arms followed the general characteristics of the British Land Pattern muskets. With the influx of French arms during the war, American makers were presented a new basis for home manufacture. In the late 1790s the most common of the French arms, the M1763 and its derivatives, particularly the M1768, became the model upon which production was based at the two national armories established at Springfield, Massachusetts, and Harpers Ferry, Virginia. Although supposedly following the same pattern, the early production of these armories evidenced a significant dichotomy. These differences became even more marked as each armory (without coordinating with the other) sought to improve manufacturing techniques.

When war was threatened with France in 1797-98 and after federal legislation was passed in 1808 requiring the supplying of the militia with arms, the government was forced to rely on private contractors to meet pressing needs for military muskets; only a small portion could be produced by the new armories. These contractors generally copied divergent samples provided either by the Springfield or Harpers Ferry armories. Eli Whitney, however, based his contract muskets on the French M1777 and claimed (erroneously) that his arms were interchangeable. To add further to the diversity, several

states independently contracted for arms of differing patterns, and in one instance (Virginia) established a state armory that made a completely different product. As late as the 1820s Massachusetts was still contracting for muskets that were very similar to the new English musket patterns.

The problem was near resolution in 1812 when a board was convened to determine a common pattern, but the War of 1812 intervened. Although a new model finally went into production at Springfield, improvements were almost immediately incorporated, necessitating the adoption of another new model in 1816. Contracts were let for its manufacture, and production also began at the armories as old parts were cleared. After a minor change was incorporated in 1822, a rigid standard of uniformity and, gradually, interchangeability was established that would guide public and private production until the improvements of the French M1822 musket were incorporated into the American M1835. With minor alterations this became the U.S. M1840 musket, and although the flintlock mechanism was by then on the wane, production would continue at the public armories until 1844 and at private contractors until 1848.

3-0 U.S. M1822 Muskets (Armory Type), Types I (color plate, above), **& II**

OL: 57¾''
BD: .69 cal.
Furniture: iron
Lockplate: beveled edge, flat; detachable, brass round pan; round reinforced cock
Markings: eagle over "US" forward of cock; "HARPERS/FERRY/(date)" or "SPRING/FIELD/(date)" on tail

BL: 42''
Configuration: round; bayonet lug on top near muzzle
Fastenings: 3 iron bands, the upper double strapped
Markings: "P," eaglehead, "V" near breech; date on top of breech-plug tang

The U.S. M1822 musket differed from the M1816 in only two major characteristics, one of these applicable to type I only. The most evident change is the relocation of the rear swing swivel. Formerly located on a separate lug piercing the forward strap of the triggerguard plate, this swivel was instead riveted directly to the front of the triggerguard bow. From 1822-30 (I), the M1822 musket's furniture (lockplate and screw heads excepted) was finished "brown"; after 1831-44 (II) all metal furniture and barrels were finished "bright." Although fully interchangeable at both armories, the Harpers Ferry muskets continued to have an assembly number (figures in Arabic numerals) struck into all metal furniture; Springfield production did not. Harpers Ferry inspection marks in the wood opposite the lockplate consisted of a pair of initials surmounted with a "V", neither in cartouches. The inspection mark placed in the same place at Springfield consisted of script initials within an oval cartouche (also used on contract arms). Almost all U.S. armory-made M1822 muskets were altered to percussion during the 1850s. **(C)**

Virginia Manufactory Muskets, Type IV (color plate, below), **& I-III**

OL: 59'' (I), 57'' (II-IV)
BD: .69 cal.
Furniture: iron
Lockplate: beveled edge, flat (smaller size during 1810-15); integral, iron round pan (I-III) and detachable brass round pan after 1818 (IV); flat-faced, gooseneck cock (I) until 1809; rounded, rein-

BL: 44'' (I), 42'' (II-IV)
Configuration: round; bayonet lug on top near muzzle
Fastenings: 3 iron bands, the upper double strap secured by band strings from behind (I-II) until 1815; the rear and middle from front (III-IV) after 1815
Markings: "P" (proof) on top near

forced cock (II) during 1810-11; and flat faced reinforced cock (III-IV) from 1812-21.
Markings: "Virginia/(script)Manufactory" forward of cock; "RICHMOND (arced)/(date) on tail breech; Virginia county markings on top below rear band on early production, often effaced.

The principal distinctions between types will be found in the lockplate which reflected changes effected at the Springfield Armory. Furniture also was changed in 1816, the former teardrop ends to the triggerguard being changed to the smooth, rounded ends during that year and the band springs being located forward for the rear and middle bands. 58,428 produced. **(B)**

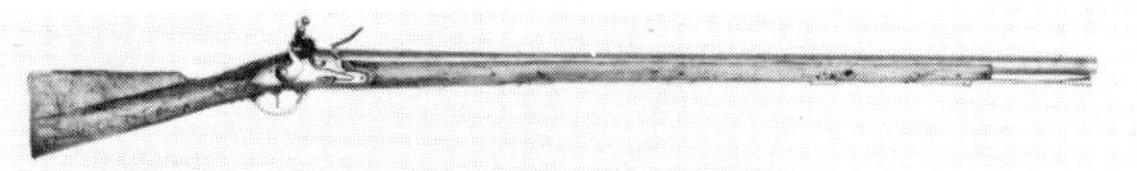

3-1 Maryland Committee-of-Safety Muskets
OL: 57''-58'' (57¾'')
BD: .75 (.78) cal.
Furniture: brass buttplate, iron sling swivels (set on triggerguard and forestock)
Lockplate: convex, integral iron rounded pan; gooseneck cock
Markings: none
BL: 42'' (42¼'')
Configuration: round; bayonet lug on top near muzzle
Fastenings: pins
Markings: view mark "V" on left and "M" on top near breech

This arm is typical of those supplied by Massachusetts, Pennsylvania, Maryland, and Virginia in 1775. Furniture varied from state to state and contractor to contractor; many eliminated the brass wrist escutcheon. With the exception of the arms made at the Fredericksburg Manufactory and John Hunter's Iron Works near Falmouth, Va. (respectively marked on their tails "FRED^{G}/(date)" and "RAP^{A}/FOREGE". Committee-of-Safety arms are unmarked to their manufacture. **(E-Maryland), (D-others)**

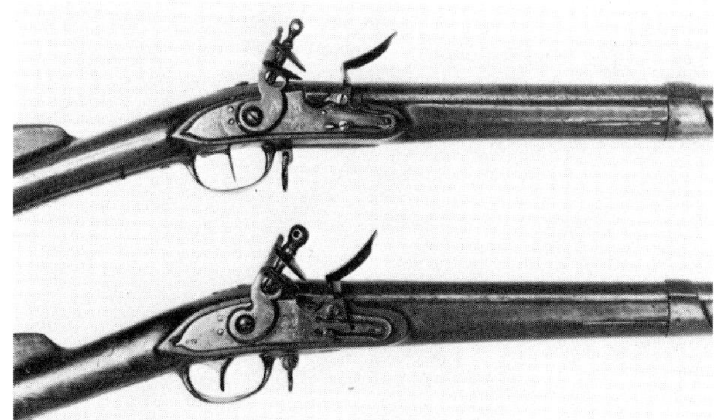

I

II

3-2 Springfield Armory M1795 Muskets, Types I-III
OL: 60'' (−½'')
BD: ?
BL: 44½''-44¾'' (−½'')
Configuration: round, bayonet lug

Furniture: iron
Lockplate: beveled edge, flat; I—detachable, iron-faceted pan (1799-1806); II—detachable, iron rounded pan (1806-12); III—integral, iron rounded pan (1813-14)
Markings: 1799-1802—script over eagle forward of cock and arced "SPRINGFIELD" (vertical on tail of lock); 1802-1804—same as earlier model, but with "SPRINGFIELD" horizontal; 1804—eagle over script "US" forward of cock, date and arced "SPRINGFIELD" (horizontal) on tail of lock; 1805—eagle over script "US", date, and arced "SPRINGFIELD"; 1806-14—eagle over script "US" over arced "SPRINGFIELD" (horizontal), and date

on top near muzzle
Fastenings: 3 iron bands, the upper double strapped
Markings: "P," eagle head, "V" near breech

This musket was produced as early as 1795, but no distinguishing marks were applied until 1799. In addition, distinctions of the pan configuration identify the three subvarieties of this model. The other major change occured in the configuration of the triggerguard strap, which originally (1799-1805) terminated in teardrop finials. First the rear (1806-1809) and finally both ends (1809-14) were finished in a round fashion. 101,000 produced. **(C)**

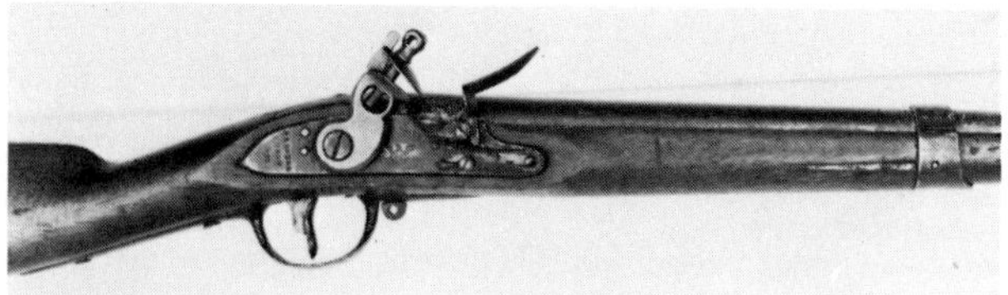

III

3-3 Harpers Ferry Armory M1795 Muskets, Types I-IV

OL: 60''-61'' (I-III)
57''-58'' (IV)
BD: .69 cal.
Furniture: iron
Lockplate: beveled edge, flat; integral, iron round pan; reinforced cock
Markings: spread eagle surmounting script "US" forward of cock; "HARPERS/FERRY/(date)" on tail.

BL: 44''-45'' (I-III)
42'' (IV)
Configuration: round; bayonet lug on top near muzzle (I); on bottom near muzzle (II-IV)
Fastenings: 3 iron bands, the upper double strapped
Markings: eagle head, "V," "P," "US" and serial number (until 1811); serial no. deleted afterward

Harpers Ferry did not change the configuration of the triggerguard strap to the simpler rounded end type until 1812. This is the distinctive characteristic between types II and III. The shortened barrel that distinguishes type IV was more likely a war-induced economy measure than an attempt to adopt the characteristics of the M1812 produced only at the Springfield Armory. 72,300 produced. **(C)**

3-4 Virginia State Contract Muskets

OL: 60'' (−½'')

BL: 44¾''

BD: .69 cal.
Furniture: iron
Lockplate: beveled edge, flat surface with detachable, iron round pan, reinforceable
Markings: according to contractor
Configuration: round; bayonet lug on top near muzzle
Fastenings: 3 iron bands, the upper double strapped
Markings: impressed "P" proof mark and Virginia regimental abbreviation and county name.

Marks are as follows: 1) "V" and M^C^CORMICK" forward of cock, "GLOBE/MILL" on tail; 2) "MILES" on tail; 3) "VIRGINIA" forward of cock, "WHEELER MANUFACTORY" on barrel; 4) "HASLETT" on tail. **(E)**

3-5 Pennsylvania State Contract Muskets

In 1797 the Pennsylvania legislature ordered 20,000 muskets following the pattern of the French M1768 musket (see 2-5). The distinguishing features are the proof marks on the barrel-an impressed "P" surmounted by a liberty cap (changed to an eagle's head after 1799) and the stamped ownership letters "CP" (for Commonwealth of Pennsylvania) on the barrel. "CP" was also struck into the lockplate together with the contractor's name. Known marks are: 1) "EVANS" forward of cock, "CP," "EVANS/CP" on tail; 2) "W HENRY" forward of cock, "CP" and "W HENRY NAZ'H" on tail; 3) "CP" forward of cock, "HENRY" on tail; 4) "LETHER/& CO/CP" on tail; 5) "MILES/CP" ontail; 6) "D. SWEITZER" or "SWEITZER & CO" forward of cock, "CP" on tail; 7) "M. BAKER/CP" on tail. **(D)**

3-6 1798 and 1808 Federal Government Contract Muskets (except Eli Whitney's)

The anticipation of war with France in 1797-98 and the requirement that the states be apportioned an allotment of muskets annually for their militia under the Militia Act of 1808 necessitated the issuance of private contracts. Each contractor received a sample musket from either the Harpers Ferry or the Springfield armory to guide production. Depending on the date of the contract, the 1798 and 1808 contract muskets may incorporate the progressive improvements made in the M1795 muskets (see 3-2 and 3-3) at these two public armories. The main distinguishing characteristic of the contract muskets is their lock parking. **(B-F, depending on mark).**

Barstow 1808

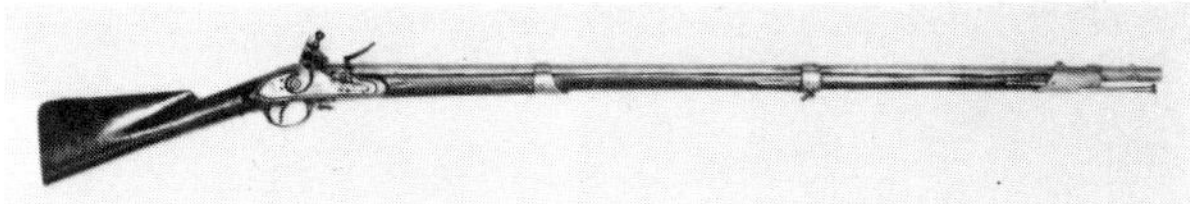

Known marks, 1798 contracts: 1) "US/(date)/E.BROWN" forward of cock or "E.BROWN/(date)/US" on tail; 2) "DANBURY" forward of cock; 3) "NORWICH" on tail; 4) "US/E.D. & Co." forward of cock; 5) "KENT" forward of cock or on tail; 6) "EVANS/US" arced on tail; 7) "US" and script "FALLEY" forward of cock, "MONTGOMERY (date)" on tail; 8) "US/D GILBERT" forward of cock, date on tail; 9) "US" forward of cock, "HENRY" on tail; 10) "US" forward of cock, "SJ" or "HH" on tail; 11) "(eaglehead)/US" forward of cock, "McCORMICK/(date)" on tail; 12) "E. STILLMAN/CT" on tail; 13) "WELTON" forward of cock and on keyplate.

Known marks, 1808 contracts: 1) "US/(eagle)/EXETER" forward of cock, "J.& C.B." on tail or "(eagle)/U.S." forward of cock, "J.& C.B./EXETER" on tail; 2) "(eagle)/US/BARTLETT" forward of cock, date on tail; 3) "(eagle)/O.BIDWELL"

or "(eagle)/O. BIDWELL/MIDDLETOWN" or "(eagle)/MIDDLETOWN" or "(eagle)/US" forward of cock, "US (date)", or "US" on tail; 4) "(eagle)/US" forward of cock, "EVANS" on tail; 5) "(eagle)/US (T)FRENCH" or "T. FRENCH/(eagle)/US" forward of cock, "CANTON/(date)" on tail; 6) "(eagle)/US" forward of cock, "G&W/PHILADA" or "WESTPHAL/PHILADA" on tail; 7) "(eagle)/US", or "US" or "(eagle)/US" and "PHILA" forward of cock, "J. HENRY/PHILA", "W. HENRY/NAZRTH", or "W. HENRY/JR." on tail; 8) "(eagle)/US" forward of cock, "JENKS'S/RI/(date)" or without date on tail; 9) "(eagle)/US/R&C LEONARD" forward of cock, "CANTON" on tail; 10) "(eagle)/US" forward of cock, "MILES" on tail; 11) "(eagle)/US/BRIDGEWATER" (arced) forward of cock, date on tail; 12) "(eagle)/US" forward of cock, "W & H S/PHILA" on tail; 13) "(eagle)/US/STILLMAN" (arced) forward of cock, date on tail; 14) "(eagle)/US/SUTTON" or "(eagle)/US/MILLBURY" forward of cock, date on tail; 15) "(eagle)/US" forward of cock, "W.N.&S/PHILAD" on tail or "(eagle)/US" forward of cock and "NIPPES/& CO." on tail.

Other important markings—on M1795 type muskets include: "S. ALLEN", "E. BUELL", "CASWELL & DODGE", "I. BROAD", "L.B.&CO./ASHFORD", "H. OSBORNE", "PICKELL", "A. PRATT", "SCITUATE/(date)", "UPTON", "L. WOOD".

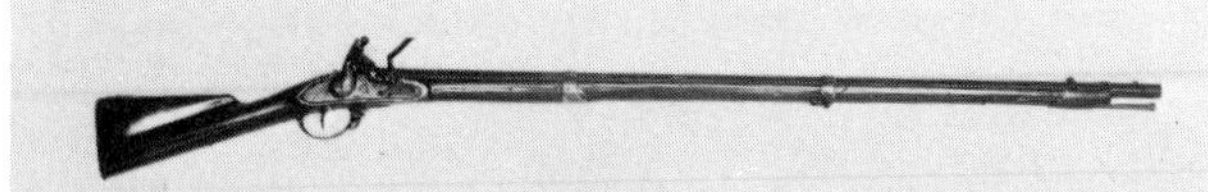

II

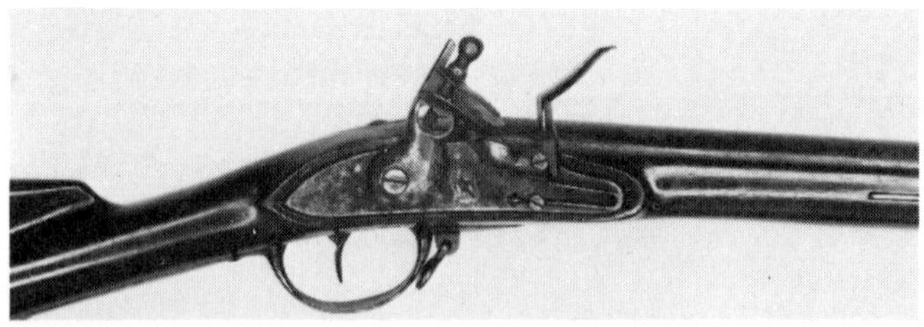

3-7 Eli Whitney 1798 Contract Muskets, Types I-II

OD: 57½''-58¾''

BD: .69 cal.

Furniture: iron

Lockplate: beveled edge, flat (I) integral, iron-faceted pan and flat-surfaced reinforced cock; (II) detachable, brass round pan and rounded surface reinforced cock

Markings: eagle surmounting "NEW HAVEN" forward of cock; "U STATES" in arc on tail.

BL: 42''-43¾''

Configuration: round, bayonet lug on top at muzzle

Fastenings: 3 iron bands, the upper double strapped

Markings: U.S. proof marks and inspector's initials near breech.

Eli Whitney's first 1,000 muskets copied the Evans contract pattern musket the governemnt had furnished as his guide and included the faceted iron pan and flat-surfaced, reinforced cock that had been copied from the French M1763 musket. In 1802, in order to gain extensions on his delivery schedule, Whitney changed to the brass pan and the rounded cock of the French M1777 musket. Because the French had experimented with interchangeability with this model, Whitney claimed that his change would permit his arms to accomplish the same end. The actual products, however, were neither interchanged nor well made. **(D)**

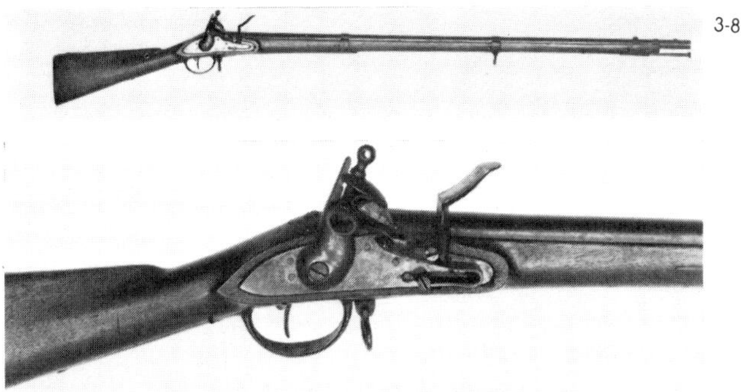

3-8

3-8 Eli Whitney 1808-12 Contract Muskets, Connecticut Variant

OL: 56½''-57¼''

BD: .69 cal.

Furniture: iron

Lockplate: beveled edge, flat; detachable, brass round pan; round cock

Markings: early, 1808-10—eagle surmounting "NEW HAVEN" forward of cock; later, 1812-16—"N. HAVEN" in scroll forward of cock.

BL: 41½''-42''

Configuration: round; bayonet lug at top near muzzle

Fastenings: 3 iron bands, the upper double strapped

Markings: "P" struck in oval, and contract variations

With only minor differences in lock part configuration and barrel length, the principal distinctions of the contracts between 1808-15 are in the markings. Known marks, N.Y. contracts, 1808 and 1812: "S.N.Y." or "SNY" across barrel and N.Y. inspection in clover on left in wood; Conn. contracts, 1809-12: "P" in oval on barrel and Conn. state seal in shield-like border on left in wood opposite lock; Mass. contract, 1815: "M.S." and "P" near breech, five-digit serial no. on barrel between upper band straps; U.S. contract, 1812, including 1,000 sold to N.Y.: "P" and U.S. inspector's initials on barrel (first 1,000 sold to N.Y., "SNY" on barrel) and U.S. inspector's initials and "V" on left in wood opposite lockplate. **(D)**

3-9 Eli Whitney State Contract Musket Derivatives

New York, Connecticut, and Massachusetts contracted for additional muskets (of unknown quantities) using Whitney's contract musket as the pattern, except that the reinforced cock is flat-faced instead of round. Whitney's detachable, brass round pan is the salient feature in these arms. Known marks are: 1) "SNY/ALBANY/S. COGSWELL (arced)" or "SNY/ALBANY" on lock and "SNY" forward of cock, "SNY" across, and "NA", "P", "SNY" on

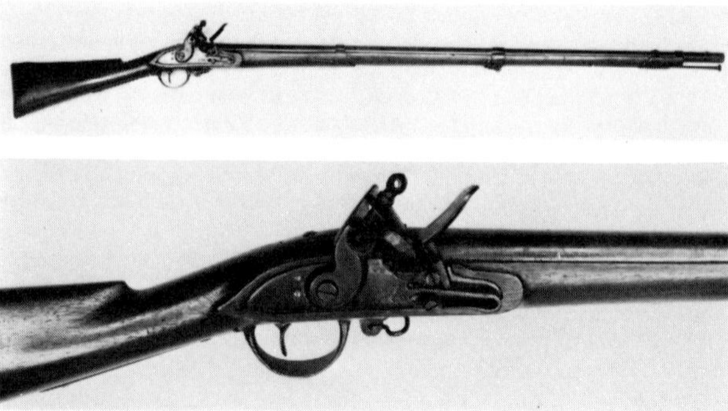

barrel axis; 2) "S.CT." forward of cock; 3) "MASS" forward of cock. Arms of the same style as 2) and 3) are known marked simply "POMEROY" forward of the cock. He is believed to be the maker of this type. **(D)**

3-10

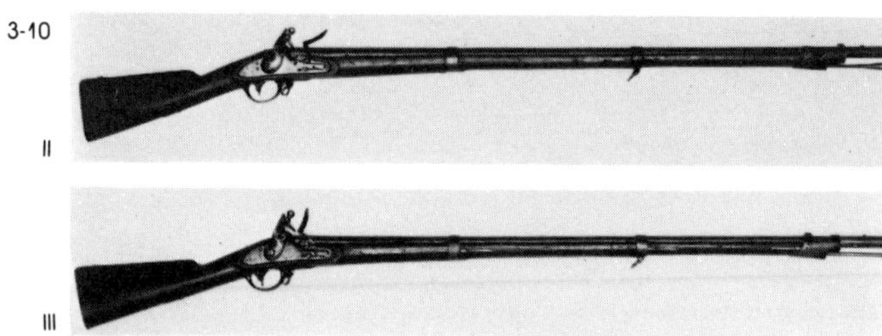

II

III

3-10 Springfield Armory M1812 Muskets, Types I-III

OL: 57"
BD: .69 cal.
Furniture: iron
Lockplate: beveled edge, flat; integral, iron round pan and reinforced round cock
Markings: "US" (script) over eagle, all surmounting arced "SPRINGFIELD" forward of cock; date (1815 or 1816) on tail

BL: 42" (−½")
Configuration: round; bayonet lug on top near muzzle
Fastenings: 3 iron bands, the upper double strap secured by band springs from behind (I); by "Wickham" stud springs in front (II); and by band springs in front (rear and middle bands) and behind upper (III)
Markings: "P", eagle head, "V"

The left side of the buttstock was dished out on this model (as well as a few late produced M1795 Springfields), and the early production utilized some earlier pattern parts (such as flat surface cocks). This arm was designed by master armorer, Marine T. Wickham. The rounded cock distinguishes the model; the location and type of band retainers distinguish the three types. About 14,500 produced. **(C)**

3-11 U.S. M1816 Muskets, Armory Types

OL: 57¾"
BD: .69 cal.
Furniture: iron

BL: 42"
Configuration: round; bayonet lug on top near muzzle

Lockplate: beveled edge; flat; detachable, round brass pan; round reinforced cock

Markings: (for U.S. armory production) eagle over "US" forward of cock; "HARPERS/FERRY/(date)" or "SPRING/FIELD/(date)" on tail

Fastenings: 3 iron bands, the upper double strapped

Markings: (for U.S. armories)—"P", eagle head, "V" near breech; date on top of breechplug tang

The two key features of this model are the brass pans of the French M1777/Eli Whitney pattern and the combless configuration of the buttstock, whose top edge neatly flows into the wrist. It should be noted, however, that Springfield continued to use up its old supply of M1812 locks well into 1817 (and reportedly, 1818), thereby producing a transitional model during those years. Springfield production, 73,215; Harpers Ferry production, 45,605. **(D)**

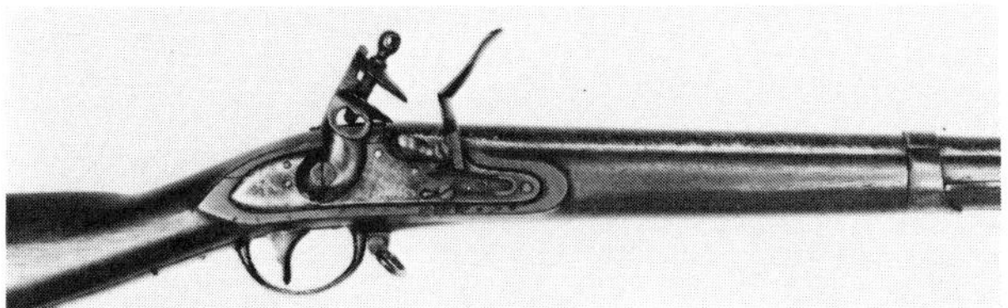

3-12

3-12 U.S M1816 Muskets, Contract Type

In dimensions and configuration, these muskets conform to the armory-manufactured U.S. M1816 muskets; only the markings differ. Barrels are marked near the breech with the letters "US" and the U.S. inspector's initials surmounted by either "V" (viewed) or "P" (proofed). Locks are marked according to contractor. Known marks are: 1) "(eagle)/A. CARRUTH" forward of cock, "(date)/US" on tail; 2) "(eagle-large)/L. POMEROY" forward of cock, "(date)/US" on tail; 3) "(eagle-small)/L. POMEROY" forward of cock, "(date)/US" on tail; 4) "B. EVANS (arced)/(eagle)/VALLEY FORGE (arced)" forward of cock, (date) on tail; 5) "US (script)/MILLBURY" forward of cock, (date) on tail; 6) "(eagle)/US (script)" forward of cock, "A. WATERS/(date)" on tail; 7) M.T.WICKHAM (arced)/PHILA" forward of cock. **(C)**

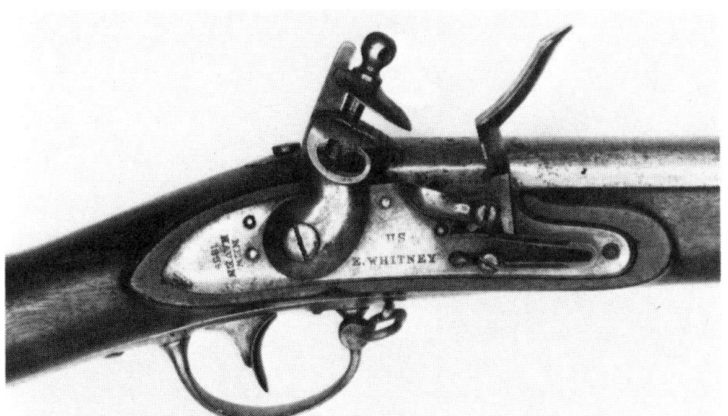

3-13
II

3-13 U.S. M1822 Contract Muskets, Types I and II

In dimensions and configuration, these arms were identical to the U.S. 1822 muskets produced at the U.S. armories. Barrel markings, however, are like those of the U.S. M1816, and stock inspection marks are like those appearing on the Springfield M1822 musket, but usually with two oval cartouches with script inspector's initials. The lock markings vary according to contractor. Known marks are: 1) "US/J.BAKER" forward of cock, "PHILA/(date)" on tail; 2) "W.L.EVANS/(eagle)/V. FORGE" forward of cock, (date) or "US" on tail; 3) "US/(eagle)/JOHNSON" forward of cock, "(date)/MIDD^{N} CONN. (arced)" on tail; 4) "US/D.NIPPES/PHILA" forward of cock, (date) on tail; 5) "(eagle)/L. POMEROY" forward of cock, "(date)/US" on tail; 6) "US/(sunburst)/N. STARR (arced)" forward of cock, "MIDD^{TN}/CONN/(date)" on tail; 7) "US/A. WATERS" forward of cock, "MILLBURY/(date)" on tail; 8) US/M.T.WICKHAM (arced)" forward of cock, "PHILA/(date)" on tail; 9) "US/(small star)/P.&E.W.BLAKE" forward on cock, "NEW HAVEN (arced)/(date)" on tail; 10) "US/(crossed arrow and olive branch)/E. WHITNEY" forward of cock, "NEW HAVEN/(date)" on tail; 11) "US/E.WHITNEY" forward of cock, "NEW HAVEN/(date)" on tail. **(B)**

E. Buell M1816

3-14 U.S. M1816 and M1822 State Contract Muskets

Two state contracts are known to have been issued for U.S. M1822 contract muskets that are identical to the U.S. contract types except for markings. These two contracts were issued by South Carolina (c. 1835) and Texas (1840). Due to attrition during the Civil War, both types are extremely rare. In addition to these two known state contracts, muskets following the general characteristics of the U.S. M1816 and M1822 survive, differing only in using furniture from previous models (principally the middle band, which is wider and secured by a band spring from behind instead of forward). The most frequently found makers of these arms are E. Buell of Marlborough, Mass., and H. Osborne of Springfield, Mass. The former's muskets were marked only upon the lockplate, either with "(eagle)/MARLBOROUGH" forward of the cock and "E.BUELL" on the tail or with only "(eagle)/E.BUELL" forward of the cock. Osborne's muskets are marked upon the barrels with a large "P" and a large eaglehead. Four variations of the lockmarking have been found, all forward of the cock: "H.OSBORNE", "H.OSBORNE/SPRINGFIELD", "(eagle head)/SPRINGFIELD" (in conjunction with an eagle head on the tail), and "(eagle head)/H. OSBORNE/SPRINGFIELD". Known marks are: 1) "SC/E.WHITNEY" forward of cock, "NEW HAVEN/(date)" on tail, and "S^{O} CAROLINA" on keyplate; 2) "(large star)/TEXAS" forward of cock, "TRYON/PHILAD^{A}" on tail. **(C)**

3-15 Massachusetts Militia Muskets

OL: 54''-57''
BD: .69 cal.
Furniture: brass
Lockplate: small, flat (usually beveled edge; integral, iron round pan; flat-faced gooseneck

BL: 39''-42''
Configuration: round; bayonet lug on top (infrequently also on bottom) near muzzle
Fastenings: pins
Markings: all Massachusetts-made

cock; frizzen spring with roller cylinder attached (invariably English locks)

Markings: vary with contractor, all marked forward of cock; most frequently encountered markings —"D.DANA", "A. WATERS", "LANE & READ/BOSTON", "ADAMS", "J. COOPER", and "LONDON/Warranted"

arms have a "P" impressed within an oval and "M" near breech; Dana arms bear impressed "PC" cartouche and 1815 date on barrel; Lane & Reed arms the letters "LH" and dates in 1820s and '30s; others "TE" in cartouche and dates as late as 1841

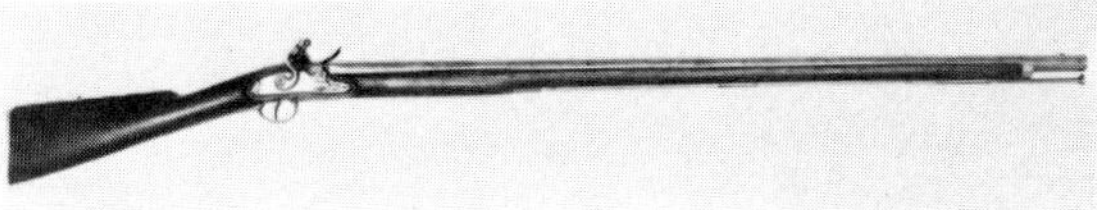

Prior to 1842, Massachusetts privately purchased a total of 1,391 muskets for the use of her militia. This figure is exclusive of the 1,455 arms contracted for in 1815. In addition to those bearing the Massachusetts proof marks, militia muskets of this same basic pattern are known with English proof marks (Birmingham crossed scepters, the first of the pair with "V" in crux, the other with "B," "C," and "P"). **(B)**

3-16 U.S. M1840 Muskets, Springfield Armory Type

OL: 57¾''

BD: .69 cal.

Furniture: iron

Lockplate: beveled edge (convex at tail), flat; detachable, brass round pan; round, reinforced cock

Markings: "SPRING/FIELD/(date)" on tail; "(eagle)/US" forward of cock

BL: 42''

Configuration: round, bayonet lug below barrel, near muzzle

Fastenings: 3 iron bands, the upper double strapped

Markings: "V", "P", and eagle head near breech; date on top of breechplug tang

Unlike its predecessor, the M1822 musket, this arm has a pronounced comb on the buttstock, and the bayonet lug is located below the barrel. This arm took a socket bayonet with a locking ring. The flint version is exceedingly rare, most having been subsequently altered to percussion. 30,421 produced. **(D)**

Nippes

3-18 U.S. M1840 Muskets, Contract Type

Due to the strict gauging requirements instituted with the new series of U.S. arms adopted in 1840-41, only two of the old suppliers under the Militia Act of 1808 opted to tool up for the new model. In all characteristics except the lock markings, the products of these contractors agreed with those made at Springfield. The two suppliers were Daniel Nippes and Lemuel Pomeroy. Known marks are: 1) "D. NIPPES/US" forward of cock, "MILL/CREEK/PA." on tail, later production with date added; 2) "(eagle)/L. POMEROY" forward of cock, "(date)/US" on tail. **(C)**

Indian Fusils, Carbines, and Musketoons

"Fusil" (corrupted in English as "fuzee" or "fuke" in some early texts) was originally a French term for a military musket. By the middle of the 18th century, however, the term had taken on a new connotation —a flintlock longarm of approximately musket caliber but lighter in weight. It had become a specialty weapon, one carried by officers. Due to its lighter weight, it also became a popular firearm among the French colonists and voyageurs in North America. Through them it became the favored firearm of American natives during the 18th and first quarter of the 19th century. After the French and Indian War, the main suppliers of these "Northwest" guns were the two major English trading companies, the Hudson Bay Co. and the Northwest Co. (merged into the former in 1821). The prime English manufacturers were William Wilson & Co.; William Grice; Ketland & Co.; Edward Bond; Parker, Field & Co.; and Thomas Barnett & Sons.

The new United States government initially created an Indian Department to manage a series of government-owned "factories" to carry out trade with the natives on an equitable basis. Firearms were not at first an important item of trade, although a number of chief's presentation arms were made. During the War of 1812, however, the government contracted for a quantity of fusils to be delivered to her Indian allies. After 1822, trade was to be conducted through the private fur companies, and "Northwest" guns, usually of British make or a Belgian copy and occasionally from an American maker, once again became the prime bartering tool on the frontier. Even the U.S. government purchased American-made fusils to meet its treaty commitments.

During the early 1800s, the government also found itself in need of another specialty flintlock of a light nature. These shorter and less weighty muskets (eventually called "musketoons" and later "carbines") were required primarily for artillery soldiers manning heavy guns. The mounted forces of the Army (called the dragoons at that time) also required a shorter weapon. In addition, the Navy needed a shorter longarm that could be loaded readily without interfering with the ship's rigging. And, lastly, military cadets required a short and light version of the current musket. Although attempts were eventually made to create specialty arms to meet these needs, most of the requirements were met by supplying shortened versions of the musket, usually made from barrels that had failed full proofing.

4-0 Springfield U.S. M1807 Indian Fusils (or Carbines) (color plate)
OL: 47½" **BL:** 33¾"
BD: .54 (.56) cal. **Configuration:** round; bayonet lug

Furniture: brass
Lockplate: flat surface with integral, iron round pan; flat-faced reinforced cock
Markings: "US (script)/(eagle)/SPRINGFIELD" arced horizontally forward of cock; date (1808, 1809, 1810) on tail
added to top near muzzle on cadet version
Fastenings: pins
Markings: "P", eagle head, "V" near breech; also dated on tang of buttplate the year of assembly

A total of 1,202 were made at Springfield between 1808-10. They were intended as chief's presents in the treaty ceremonies. Few were actually presented, however, as 950 were still in store in 1830 when it was recommended that some be altered as cadet musketoons for the U.S. Military Academy. Apparently 260 were so altered by cutting back the forestock and adding a bayonet lug, as only 690 remained in store in 1848. **(E)**

4-1 "Bridgewater" (Perkins' Contract) Indian Fusils, Types I & II

OL: 54"-57"
BD: .69 cal.
Furniture: brass
Lockplates: (I) small (5½" long) flat; integral, iron round pan; flat-faced gooseneck cock; probably a surcharged English import lock. (II) large musket size, flat; integral, iron round pan; flat-faced reinforced cock; probably locks remaining from Perkins' 1808 musket contract.
Markings: "(eagle)/US" forward of cock; "BRIDGEWATER (arced)/(date)" on tail.
BL: 39"-42"
Configuration: round
Fastenings: pins
Markings: either unmarked or "V", "P" (both in oval cartouches), and "UNITED STATES" near breech.

The earliest record of the purchase of Perkins' Indian guns by the Superintendent of Indian Trade was in 1808, when 20 were ordered in 48" and 42" barrels of .60 caliber. All surviving specimens, however, are dated 1815, 1818, and 1819. **(E)**

4-2

4-2 American-Made "Northwest" Fusils

OL: 46", 49", 52", 55", 58", 64" (according to barrel size)
BD: .58 cal. (24 ga.)
Furniture: brass buttplates (nailed early, screwed later), cast, ornate serpentine keyplate, ramrod tubes (2 or 3), and nosestrap; iron triggerguard with large bow
Lockplate: slightly convex; integral, iron round pan; rounded gooseneck cock
Markings: among makers are
BL: 30", 33", 36", 39", 42", 48" (+¼")
Configuration: round, part octagonal, 6½"-8½"+ from breech
Fastenings: pins
Markings: usually specious Birmingham proofs and maker's name

Joseph J. Henry, Henry Deringer, Henry E. Leman, and E. K. Tryon & Co.

In addition to American-made fusils, private fur companies placed orders for significantly larger quantities of English arms (primarily through Chance, Son & Co. of Birmingham) and Belgian copies of the same. "Northwest guns" with markings such as "W. CHANCE & SON/LONDON" or "BURNETT" (specious representation of "BARNETT"), or "SARGENT BROTHERS/(date)" should be considered importations of American fur trading firms. **(D)**

4-3 U.S. M1795 Shortened Muskets

Prior to 1800 the Secretary of War had ordered that bayonets be soldered to the arms then in store to prevent their loss. Some 15,000 muskets were so altered. In 1812-13, between six and eight thousand were shortened by cutting back the barrel by 12" and the stock accordingly so that only two bands were required, the former lower band and the upper double strap band. **(D)**

4-4 Virginia Manufactory Artillery Muskets

To utilize barrels that had blown near the muzzle during proofing, Virginia Manufactory mounted about 300 muskets per year with either 36" or 39" barrels for issue to Virginia's artillery or mounted forces.
Except for barrel length, these "artillery" muskets follow the characteristics of the four Virginia Manufactory musket types. **(C)**

4-5

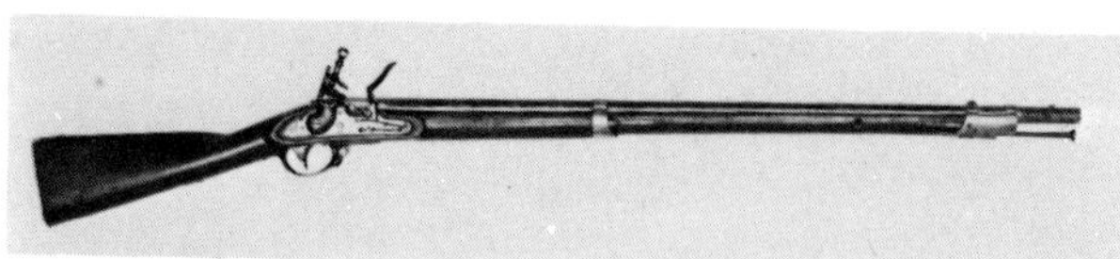

4-5 U.S. M1817 Artillery Muskets

OL: 51½"
BD: ..69 cal.
Furniture: iron
Lockplate: beveled edge (convex on the tail), flat; detachable brass round pan; rounded, reinforced cock
Markings: "(eagle)/U.S." forward of cock; "SPRING/FIELD/(date)" on tail

BL: 36"
Configuration: round; bayonet lug on top near muzzle
Fastenings: 2 iron bands, the upper double strapped
Markings: "P", eagle head, "V" on upper surface near breech; occasionally marked "S.M. Co." on left side flat for the Springfield Manufacturing Co., a barrel subcontractor; date on breechplug tang

To provide muskets for the U.S. Military Academy Cadets, 200 were ordered made in 1817, primarily to conserve barrels that had burst in proof. A total of 1,540 were eventually manufactured until production ceased in 1821. **(D)**

American Flintlock Rifles

The American flintlock rifle (in all its derivatives) is a direct descendant of the German jäger (hunting) rifle of the 18th century. During the early 1700s, Pennsylvania-German settlers modified the jäger rifle by giving it a longer barrel, but they retained the original design elements. The patchbox (a recess in the buttstock for the greased patches that envelop the ball when loading) was covered by a wooden lid that dovetailed into the rear of the stock and locked with a springcatch. On the opposite side of the stock a trapezoidal cheekpiece protruded from the stock, frequently with carved "C" scrollwork surrounding it. The brass triggerguard incorporated a raised hand grip terminating in a spur. The brass keyplates were generally composed of sharply angled projections rather than of a curvilinear configuration. Finally, the tail of the flat lockplate was cut in European fashion with one or two vertical slashes behind the cock.

Just prior to and during the American Revolution, the wooden patchbox lid was replaced with a metal (usually brass), hinged cover. Initially of two pieces (the lid and the hinge support), the patchbox became increasingly more ornate, first by adding metal side panels adjoining the lid, and later by fashioning both these side panels and the hinge support into intricate, often pierced, designs. Additional ornamentation in the forms of brass, silver, or German silver inlays to the cheekpiece, the upper wrist, and eventually the forestock produced what has been termed the "Golden Age" of the "Kentucky" rifle (1790-1815). Mistakenly termed "Kentucky"—from a song popularized after Jackson's victory at New Orleans in 1815—the rifle was made almost exclusively in Pennsylvania and the immediately adjoining counties.

5-0 Pennsylvania ("Kentucky") Rifles (color plate)

Lebanon School, Nicholas Beyer. **(D)**

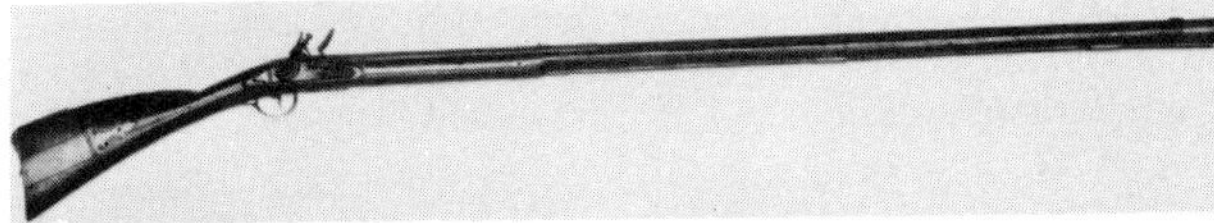

5-1 Pennsylvania ("Kentucky") Flintlock Rifles

OL: generally 57''-63''

BD: .46-.53 cal., rifled, but occasionally smooth or bored out smooth

Furniture: usually brass, consisting of buttplate, heelplate, keyplate, triggerguard, patchbox, ramrod

BL: generally 41''-46''

Configuration: octagonal, infrequently part octagonal/part round

Sights: open "V" for rear; dovetailed blade for front

tubes (3 or 4), and nosecap; brass, silver, or German silver ornaments

Patchbox: usually 4-piece, hinged forward; hinge support and sideplates fashioned in accordance with maker or school

Ornaments: if present, invariably a wrist escutcheon and horizontally elongated, six-pointed star, crescent moon, or eagle upon cheekpiece; carved "C" scrolls on buttstock; occasionally wedge ferrules and other forestock ornaments

Lockplate: flat-faced with integral or detachable, iron-faceted pan; flat-faced gooseneck cock and usually roller on frizzen

Markings: usually unmarked; German imports and locally made with vertical slashes on pointed tail; English locks often with maker's name over "WARRANTED" forward of cock

Fastenings: pins or wedges

Markings: either unmarked or inscribed with maker's name or initials in script

Because civilian-purchased Pennsylvania rifles were all handmade to order, no two are exactly alike and the measurements given are only the most frequently encountered parameters. Decoration varied as well, but generally followed the style common to the county school whence the rifle originated. The major schools and their distinguishing characteristics are as follows. **(D)**

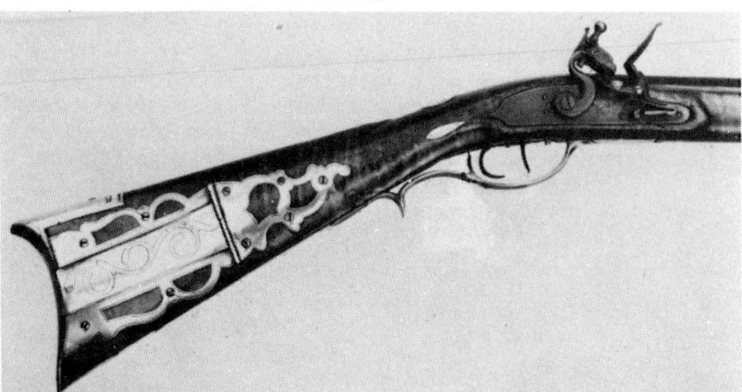

5-1a Bedford Joseph Mills

Very pronounced drop to the low-combed buttstock; side pieces and hinge support of patchbox pierced with half moons; eagle inscribed on elliptical cheekrest ornament; teardrop ornaments inlaid behind lockplate and keyplate; long, narrow lockplates, usually with truncated tails.

5-1b Bethlehem

Very pronounced drop to low-combed, Roman nose buttstock; either 2-piece patchbox with convex lid and fleur-de-lis-shaped finial to hinge support or 4-piece with elaborate piercing and engraving; Indian head

Jacob Kunz

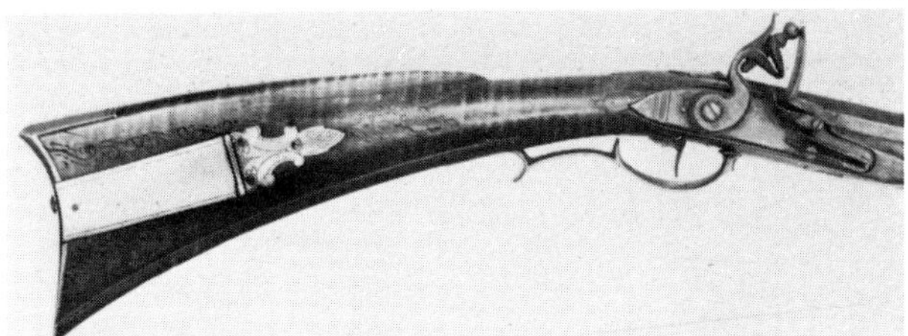

ornament frequently inlaid forward of triggerguard. A subschool associated with the Bethlehem makers utilized one- or two-piece patchboxes hinged below.

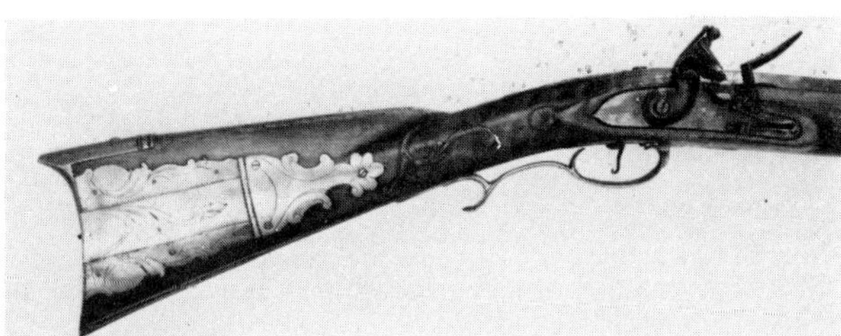

5-1c Attrib. to John Noll

5-1c Chambersburg

Moderate drop to low-combed buttstock, sidepieces of 4-piece patchbox occasionally separated from lid by a section of the stock (also a design employed by Melchior Fordney of Lancaster); pierced sidepieces and pierced oval hinge support usually terminating with a rococo floral flourish finial; often with eagle inscribed upon elliptical silver cheekrest ornament; frequently with heart-shaped ornaments inlaid behind lockplate and keyplate.

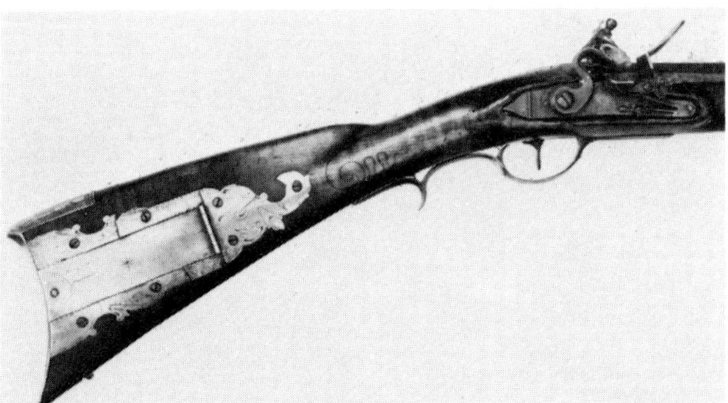

5-1d John Brooks

5-1d Dauphin

Moderate drop to pronounced combed buttstock; 4-piece patchbox with occasionally pirced sidepieces and either pierced rococo hinge support terminating in a pointed trefoil or a symmetrical floral hinge support, pierced and terminating in a pointed quadfoil.

5-1e Emmitsburg (Maryland)

Moderate to pronounced drop to buttstock; 4-piece patchbox usually with pierced sidepieces; hinge support invariably pierced and formed into rococo scrolls terminating either in a pointed quadfoil or a floral flourish.

5-1f Lancaster

Moderate drop to pronounced combed buttstock; 4-piece patchbox with rococo hinge support frequently terminating in a "daisy"-shaped floral finial. Several makers of this school preferred to shape the hinge support as a horse head, but that design was utilized by other schools as well.

5-1g Lebanon

Both moderate drop and pronounced drop to pronounced and occasionally convex-combed buttstock; 4-piece patchbox with rococo "chicken head," "resting swan," or floral hinge support terminating occasionally with quadfoil or "daisy."

5-1h Littlestown

Pronounced drop to low-combed buttstock; 4-piece patchbox in a variety of hinge support designs, including human half torsos, eagles, horse heads, and other animal or floral designs.

5-1i Reading

Moderate drop to pronounced, convex-combed, Roman nose buttstock; 4-piece patchbox, seldom pierced; symmetrical or rococo "chicken head" patchbox used by some makers only.

5-1j York

Moderate or pronounced drop to pronounced combed buttstock; 4-piece patchbox frequently extensively pierced with rococo scroll hinge support varying in configuration according to maker; occasional engraved bird finial on hinge support.

5-2 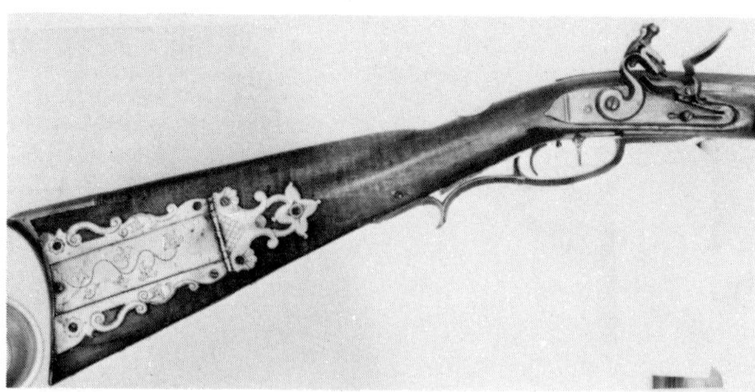

5-2 Virginia/North Carolina Flintlock Rifles

The migration of many Pennsylvania-German families to the Shenandoah

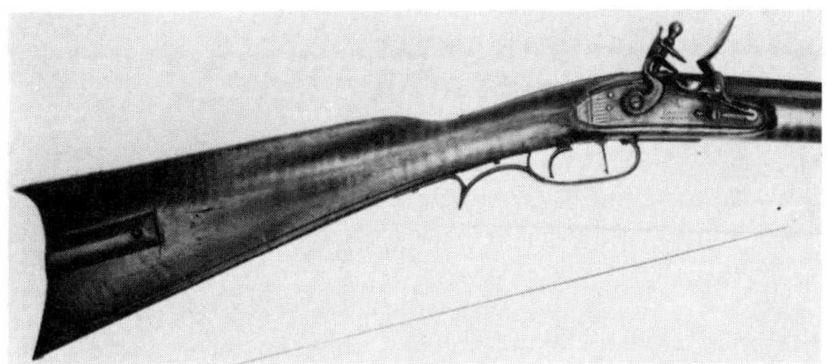

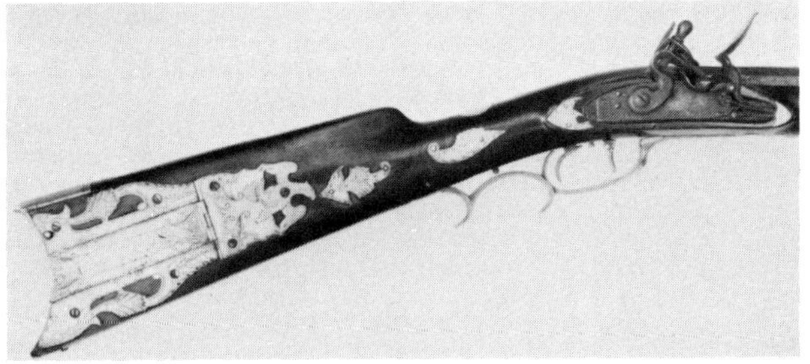

Henry Ledford

Valley of Virginia and to a lesser extent further south into piedmont North Carolina, brought with it the manufacture of Pennsylvania rifles. Generally conforming to the overall dimensions and design of their predecessors, these Southern "Kentuckies" are distinguished by their symmetrical, elaborately pierced, 4-piece patchboxes, often ornamented with additional silver insets. Other brass and silver inlays are often found decorating other sections of the stock. **(D)**

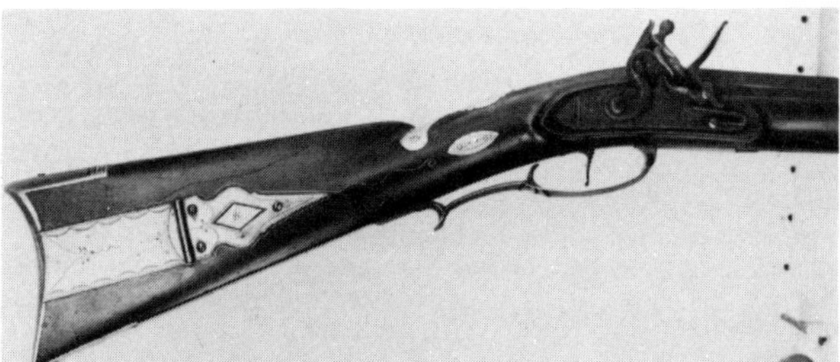

5-3 Mason & Baldwin

5-3 New England Flintlock Rifles

A variant of the Pennsylvania rifle was also made in New England. Although the 4-piece patchbox having a horse-head hinge support was copied by some New England rifle makers (Silas Allen and W. Mathewson), most New England rifles have 2-piece patchboxes with a symmetrical hinge support formed as a disc with an elongated finial at its top. These rifles frequently employed inlaid brass or silver wire designs in the stock and usually have a triggerguard forward strap terminating in a squared projection. Half-stocked variants with these characteristics also survive. **(D)**

6 Military and Contract Flintlock Rifles

Privately purchased Pennsylvania rifles had seen limited but effective use during the Revolutionary War. Rifle units were therefore incorporated into the post-War regular army as well as the state militias. At first arms with simpler furniture were secured from established Pennsylvania rifle makers. Gradually, however, the requirements for a stronger, more uniform product brought forth military rifles with different characteristics. Three major changes were gradually made. The first alterations to the federal-government-purchased arms made them lighter and more manageable under combat conditions. Barrels were shortened and lightened by making them part round and part octagonal at the breech instead of fully octagonal. The patchbox and its ornamentation was greatly simplified as a second step. By the end of the War of 1812, the two- and four-piece brass boxes had been reduced to a single piece of iron. Lastly, and reluctantly, the pin or wedge fastenings yielded to the more substantial iron barrel bands.

Traditional Pennsylvania rifles, however, continued to be made. Those purchased by the states often followed the old style. At the same time that the War Department had been purchasing and modifying the Pennsylvania rifle for military usage, the Office of Indian Trade was also purchasing the arm for treaty presents and for trade goods to be stocked at the government-operated "factories". Established Pennsylvania riflemakers, whose work varied little from their predecessors, supplied the Office and, after 1822, independent trading companies. Later, with the decline of the great fur companies, the government again assumed the responsibility of furnishing rifles to the Indian tribes under the agreements that were called for in treaties. Contracts were again let to major Pennsylvania riflemakers. The government subsequently had many of these same armsmakers produce similar rifles in percussion and altered those in the possession of the tribes, usually by the drum bolster percussioning method.

6-0 U.S. M1814 Flintlock Military Contract Rifles (color plate)

OL: 48½'' (+½'')
BD: .54 cal. (7 grooves)
Furniture: iron; triggerguard with finger ridges on rear strap
Patchbox: 1-piece, elliptical iron lid, hinged below
Lockplate: beveled edge, flat (convex on tail); detachable, brass round pan; reinforced rounded cock
Markings: either "US/H. DERINGER/PHILADA" or "US/R. JOHNSON/MIDDLETOWN" forward of cock.

BL: 32¾'' (+½'')
Configuration: part octagonal/part round
Sights: rear—open "V", 5'' from breech
Fastenings: 3 iron bands, the upper double strapped, all secured by stud springs forward of bands
Markings: "H DERINGER/PHILADA" on top only, viz: "GF", "P/US"

Robert Johnson of Middletown, Conn., and Henry Deringer of Philadelphia received contracts in 1814 for 2,000 each of these rifles. Deringer was exceedingly slow in his deliveries, delivering only 50 of the 980 required in 1814 while making Pennsylvania contract rifles at higher prices. **(E)**

6-1 U.S. 1792-1794 Contract Rifles

To arm the four rifle battalions that formed a part of the "Legion of the United States" between 1792 and 1796, the War Department entered into agreements with York, Lancaster, and Philadelphia-area gunmakers for nearly 2,000 plain Pennsylvania rifles. Although no example has survived in complete condition, the 42" long octagonal barrels were to be bored for a .49 cal. (40 ga.) bullet, and the rifle was to be marked "UNITED STATES" or at least "US," preferably the former. Deliveries under these agreements were made at least through 1794. There are 19 known makers. Because no authenticated rifles of this contract have yet been positively identified, the potential for forgery is extremely high. Known barrel signatures are: 1) "A. Angstadt" and "A.A."; 2) "H. Albright"; 3) "P. Brong"; 4) "J. Demuth"; 5) "J. Dickert"; 6) "P. Gonter"; 7) "J. Graeff"; 8) "C. Gumpf"; 9) "J. Messersmith"; 10) "A. Schweitzer"; 11) "J. Welshans" and "J.W." **(X)**

6-2

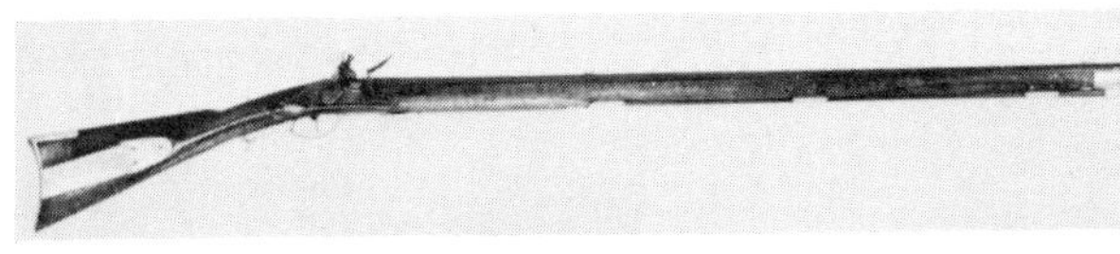

6-2 U.S. 1807/1808 Contract Rifles

OL: about 54"
BD: .53 (.56) cal. (32 ga.)
Furniture: brass
Patchbox: 2-piece, hinged forward, very plain hinge support
Lockplate: flat, integral iron faceted pan; flat-faced gooseneck cock
Markings: unmarked; vertical slash on tail
BL: 38" (+¾")
Configuration: part octagonal/part round
Sights: rear—open "V" on octagonal
Fastenings: pins
Markings: "US" and "(eagle head)/P" cartouche or "P" in cartouche near breech; maker's name (in script) on facet.

The same threat of war that prompted the production of the U. S. 1808 musket caused the War Department to issue contracts to Pennsylvania gunmakers for military rifles. Known makers are: John Joseph Henry; Jacob Dickert, George Miller, John Bender, and Charles Gumpf; Abraham Henry, John Guest, and Peter Brong; and Henry Pickel. **(F)**

6-3 U.S. M1803 Rifles Types I & II

OL: 47"-48" (I)
BD: .54 cal.
Furniture: brass; triggerguard with Pennsylvania rifle-style handgrip
Patchbox: 2-piece, hinged forward; hinge support bell-shaped; release on buttplate tang
BL: 33" (I—31¾"-33½"), 36" (II)
Finish: "browned"
Configuration: part octagonal (11"-13")/part round, with iron rib beneath round part
Sights: rear—open "V" 8" from breech; front—brass blade

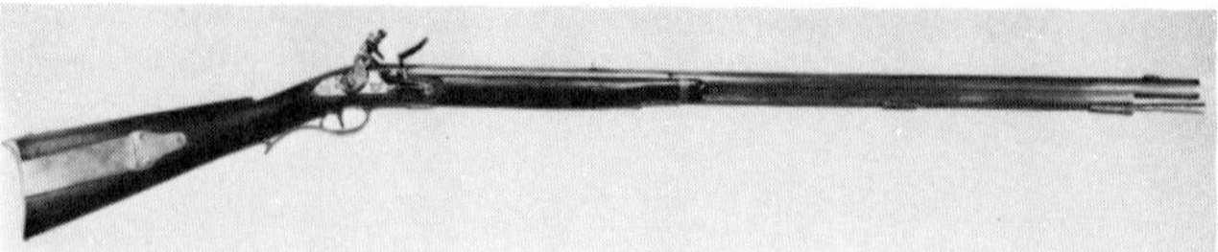

Lockplate: beveled edge, flat; integral iron round pan; flat-faceted reinforced cock

Markings: "(eagle)/US" (I); eagle with "US" on shield (II) forward of cock; "HARPERS/FERRY/(date)" on tail

Fastenings: single wedge

Markings: "US" in cartouche, "(eagle head)/P" in cartouche, and serial number near breech

Although a number of component parts for 3,000 rifles were made at Springfield between 1814 and 1817, this rifle was manufactured solely at Harpers Ferry. Between 1803 and 1807 a total of 4,023 of the shorter-barreled version (I) were manufactured. Most of these arms remained in storage until the War of 1812. With the addition of three new rifle regiments to the service in 1814, 3,000 additional rifles were ordered. The first 1,600 of this later production followed the dimensions of type I but bore the markings common to type II. 15,703 type II produced. **(D)**

6-4 U.S. M1817 Contract Rifles

OL: 51½" (+¼")

BD: .54 cal. (7 grooves)

Furniture: iron; triggerguard with handgrip terminating in projection; all "browned"

Patchbox: iron elliptical 1-piece lid, hinged below, catch above

Lockplate: beveled edge, flat (convex on tail); detachable brass round pan; reinforced round cock

Markings: according to contractor

BL: 36"

Finish: "browned"

Configuration: round

Sights: rear—open "V" 7½" from breech; front—iron lug/blade

Fastenings: 3 iron bands, the upper double strapped

Markings: "US/P (inspector's initials)" near breech; date of manufacture on breechplug tang; "U.S." on buttplate tang

This rifle was manufactured by four prime contractors—Henry Deringer, Robert and John D. Johnson, Simeon North, and Nathan Starr—over a span of 30 years. It was alluded to in contemporary correspondence as the "common rifle." **(C)**

---

7 Civilian Alterations from Flintlock to Percussion

Recognition of the superior reliability of the percussion ignition system developed quickly in America. With the termination of Forsyth's patent rights in 1821, Joshua Shaw's copper percussion cap was freed from the legal constraints that had hampered its commercialization since its invention in 1816. Since Shaw had emigrated from his native England to Philadelphia in 1817, it was only natural that the gunsmiths of that city would be among the first to wholeheartedly embrace the percussion principle. By the 1830s the system had been introduced into York and Lancaster counties. Coming at the

same decade that saw the expanded use of surcharged Birmingham mass-produced locks and other commercially mass-produced gun furniture, the percussion system effectively closed the "Golden Age" of the Pennsylvania/"Kentucky" rifle.

As the system became increasingly more popular, country gunsmiths sought an inexpensive method to extend the lifespan of their regions' flintlock longarms. The method devised by some unidentified gunsmith was quite simple. The old flintlock battery (cock, pan, frizzen, and frizzen spring) was removed from the lockplate face. The vent was enlarged and threaded. An iron cylinder or "drum" was made and tapped on its periphery for a percussion cone and then this drum bolster was screwed into the former vent. A flat-faced percussion hammer was easily filed or hand forged and attached in place of the former cock. The "American" type alteration (often erroneously dubbed "French") was thus born.

Pennsylvania/"Kentucky" rifles and their derivatives were not the only longarms to receive this treatment. Old muskets were quickly purchased from the Federal and state governments by speculators who recognized the potential of these muskets if altered to percussion. Considerable numbers of these were altered by the "American" drum bolster method, both with simply-fashioned filed or crudely-forged percussion hammers. After European wars and revolutions spawned a market for inexpensive percussion muskets, several of the country's larger private armories (such as Colt and Whitney) turned to this cheap method of fashioning percussion arms. The final use of this method of alteration took place in the South during the Civil War. Southern gunsmiths, particularly in the Mississippi Valley and trans-Mississippi theaters of the War, turned to this method to alter nearly every available flintlock sporting rifle or old musket to a weapon that could serve the cause of the vastly underarmed Confederacy.

7-0 Drum Bolster Alterations of Flintlock Rifles (color plate)

The drum alteration was most frequently applied to Pennsylvania/"Kentucky" rifles and their derivatives. Usually the new percussion hammers were hand-forged in the configuration known as the "dog's head." A number of military rifles, most notably the U.S. M1803 (see 6-3), the Virginia Manufactory rifles, and Pennsylvania contract rifles were altered in this manner. Fewer of the U.S. M1817 contract rifles were so modified but examples exist, including Southern Civil War alterations. **(B)**

7-1

7-1 Drum Bolster Alterations of Pre-1819 U.S. Muskets

Consequent to the classification of arms that took place between 1842-45 for the purpose of determining which muskets in store might prove suitable for percussioning, the U.S. government disposed of all made prior to 1812

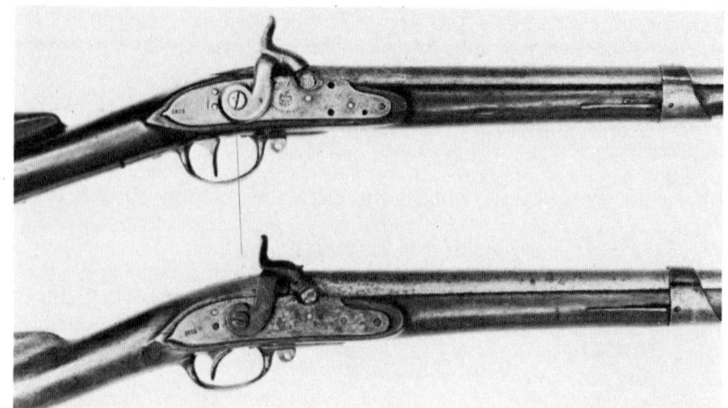

and those made after 1812 that were deemed too poor to repair. These arms were quickly purchased by speculators in the arms trade and altered to percussion by the drum bolster method. This is the type of musket most frequently "reconverted" to flintlock today. Beware of "bushed" vent holes. **(B)**

Springfield M1822 Musket

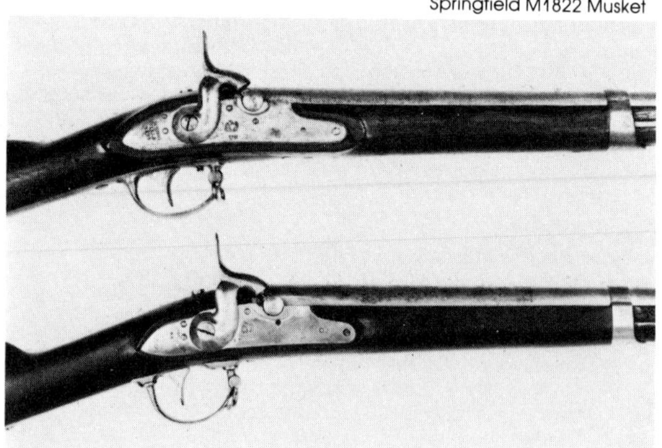

U.S. M1840 Pomeroy Contract Musket

7-2 Drum Bolster Alterations of Post-1819 U.S. Muskets

During the 1850's several states disposed of quantities of flint muskets that had been issued under the Militia Act of 1808, either by direct sale or by exchange for percussioning of a portion of the number or for newly-made percussion arms. Many of these arms were secured by the larger private gunmakers and altered to percussion using a finer quality drum bolster and a forged iron or steel hammer. Assembly numbers or marks frequently were struck into the barrels, lockplates, drums, hammers, and upper bands. **(B)**

7-3 Colt "Patent" Drum Bolster Musket Alterations

The Crimean War prompted pistol maker Samuel Colt to alter condemned U.S. military muskets (primarily M1816s and M1822s) to percussion for entre-preneur George Law. Colt altered these arms, utilizing a drum bolster with a

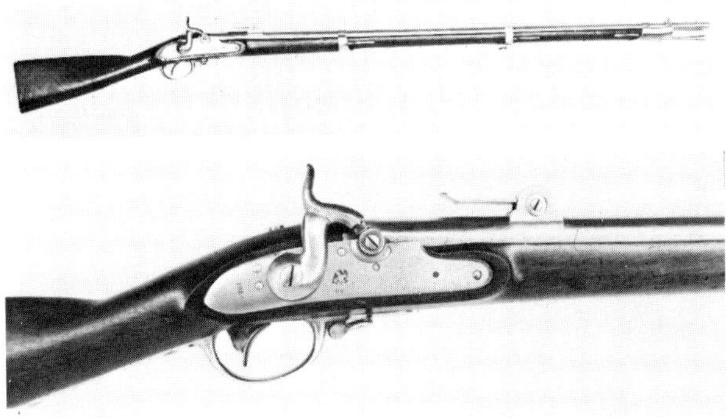

clean-out screw through its head, marked around the screw in an arc: "COLT'S" and "PATENT" (a reference to his English patent issued in 1855). A forged steel "S"-shaped hammer with rounded surface replaced the flint cock. Barrels were rifled with 4 narrow grooves, and accordingly sighted. The rear sight followed the Russian rifle pattern (which Colt patented in England in 1856) while the front consisted of a large rounded iron blade affixed to the forward strap of the upper band. Colt polished the old dates and substituted the date of alteration on the tail of the lockplate and the breechplug tang. Disassembly numbers were struck into the tang of the buttplate, the breechplug, the back of the barrel, the interior of the lockplate, and the interior of the hammer, and finally, the interior of the upper bands.**(F)**

---

8 Arsenal Alterations from Flintlock to Percussion

With the general adoption of the percussion ignition system for the arms of the U.S. infantry service in 1841-42, the War Department determined to alter as many as possible of the more than half-million flint muskets then in store. Between 1842-45 the government inventoried its stock, classifying it according to alteration potential. All muskets made after 1831 were automatically deemed acceptable for alteration and of first-class standing. Likewise, all arms made prior to 1812 were considered totally unworthy and were sold at auction in New York City. Those made between 1812-20 and all arms that had seen actual service were judged third class, and while not suitable for alteration were held for emergencies. All third-class arms received a number "3" inspection mark. Those which had been manufactured between 1821-30 were judged second-class arms but potentially suitable for alteration. After inspection the acceptable were stamped with a number "2" over the inspector's initial(s) in a cartouche on the left side of the stock opposite the lockplate.

The actual alteration of arms began in 1848. The method selected was the Belgian variation of the French altering system, known familiarly as the "cone-in-barrel" method, and continued at several arsenals through 1857. The adoption of the "Minie ball" projectile in

1855, however, ended the era of the smoothbore musket and effectively negated the cone-in-barrel alterations which could not withstand the combination of barrel weakening caused by the rifling and the increased pressure caused by the "Minie ball." After "dumping" as many as possible upon the states under the 1808 Militia Act, the government began in 1859-60 to sell many of these arms at auction or to interested Southern states girding for the impending conflict. With the outbreak of the war, many of the alterations were still in store and were reluctantly issued. Beginning in 1862, however, the U.S. government adopted a new method of altering stored flintlocks and, in many cases, of realtering the alterations. This method utilized an added steel breechpiece with integral bolster, variations of which had been used on earlier mechanical primer alterations.

In the exigencies of 1861, the Confederacy and some of its states (most notably Virginia) endeavored to alter muskets and rifles. The alterations most frequently employed copied the brazed side bolster adopted by South Carolina in 1852 to alter her flint muskets. In addition to Virginia and the Confederate eastern ordnance depots, at least one North Carolina contractor used variations of this method.

8-0 Cone-in-Barrel ("Belgian Style") Martial Alterations (color plate)

The cone-in-barrel alteration adopted by the United States to alter its muskets and rifles from flintlock to percussion was a Belgian adaptation of the French system of 1842. This method was applied to 370,938 muskets, rifles, and pistols at ten armories or arsenals between 1848-59. Although about 3,000 U.S. M1817 contract rifles were altered in this manner, most of the arms were U.S. M1822 muskets or U.S. M1840 muskets. Unless part of the 6,027 Navy weapons altered in 1853, all muskets made prior to 1831 should bear the reinspection "2" classification. **(A)**

top/U.S. M1822 Musket

8-1

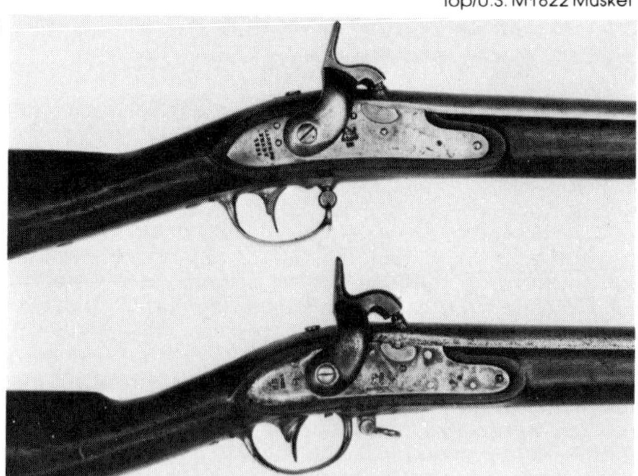

8-1 New York State Hitchcock Contract Alterations

In 1853 New York entered into an agreement with the U.S. government to have 10,000 muskets altered from flintlock to percussion. Because the machinery for this alteration was subsequently forwarded to the wrong U.S.

arsenal, the state contracted separately with A. Hitchcock & Co. of New York City for the alterations, and, when the machinery was properly installed at Watervliet Arsenal, had 5,000 altered at that place as well. Those altered at Watervliet conformed to the federal cone-in-barrel alterations, but were done on state muskets that had never gone through the classification of 1842-45. Those altered by Hitchcock & Co. were likewise on state muskets. The hammer utilized by Hitchcock & Co. was slightly heavier than the arsenal alteration hammer and had a smooth, concave surface between the shank and the head rather than the clean line found on an arsenal alteration hammer. **(C)**

8-2

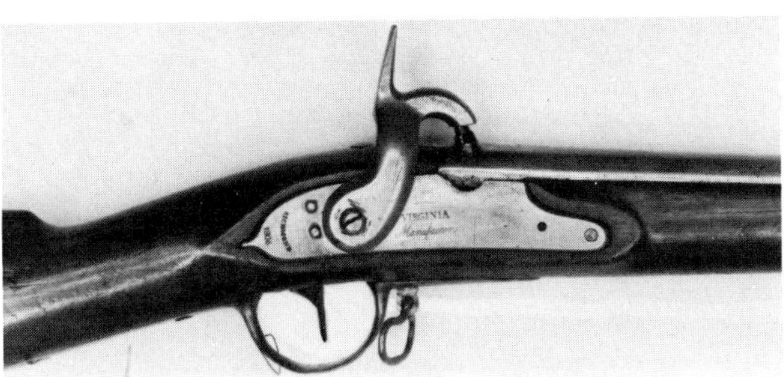

8-2 Virginia Contract Cone-In-Barrel Alterations

To alter nearly 50,000 flintlock muskets in 1861, Virginia contracted with several Richmond firms. Most apparently followed the brazed bolster alteration method (see 8-7), but one may have been altered by means of the cone-in-barrel method as a few rare examples of such Virginia Manufactory arms survive. These may instead represent some of the arms secured by Cooper & Pond of New York City from the Tredgar Iron Works. **(F)**

I

8-3 New Jersey Patent Breech Alterations, Types I and II

In 1861 New Jersey contracted with two firms (Hewes & Phillips of Newark and Field & Horton of Trenton) to alter muskets. A total of 7,481 were altered and another 400 were altered at the state arsenal in 1862-63. All of these arms were altered by cutting away the breech section and applying a patent breech with integral bolster with clean-out screw piercing its right side. The muskets were primarily U.S. M1822 flintlocks or cone-in-barrel alterations thereof. In altering the former a 1'' breechpiece with bulbous bolster was used (I). In realtering the cone-in-barrel alterations, a 1⅛'' breechpiece was used with a flat-faced bolster (II). Barrels were rifled at the state arsenal with 3 grooves. Muskets were sighted by placing the 2-leaved

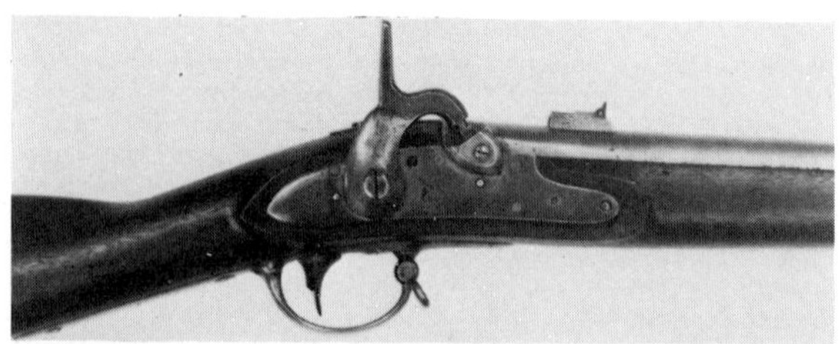

II

pattern 1858 rifle-musket sight backwards upon the barrel 2⅛'' from the breech and affixing an iron blade to the forward strap of the upper band. Hewes & Phillips struck their logo "H&P" across the junction of the barrel and patent breech and dated the tang of the breechpiece "1861". All parts removed from the arm were struck with a common assembly number. Both contract and arsenal alterations utilized a percussion hammer of the 1855 style but of the size employed on the Frankfort Arsenal (Remington) primer alterations (see 9-0), and without knurling upon the hammer spur. Except for those muskets that went directly to the volunteers from New Jersey (4,291), "N.J." was marked upon the left side of the barrels and the left side of the stock opposite the lockplate. Because some cone-in-barrel alterations were used, classification marks will also occasionally be found in wood. **(C)**

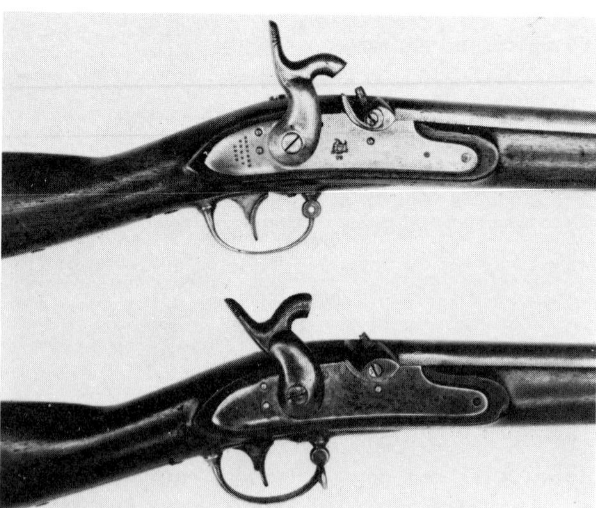

8-4

8-4 Leman Pennsylvania Contract and U.S. Patent Breech Alterations

Beginning in 1861 Henry E. Leman of Lancaster, Pa., altered 16,123 of Pennsylvania's flintlock arms, rifling those which would withstand the resulting weakening of the barrel and sighting the same. Leman applied a patent breech 1¼" long (+1/16") having an integral M1842 musket-like bolster but pierced through the flat right face with a clean-out screw, frequently entering at a slight angle. The hammer applied was also of the U.S. M1842 musket type. Under an agreement with the U.S. War Department, he also altered 7,993 muskets in late 1862 and early 1863, chiefly U.S. flintlock muskets dating from 1812-20, but also including Austrian M1842 tubelock muskets. In addition to these, Leman altered 978 rifles from flint. **(C)**

8-5

I

II

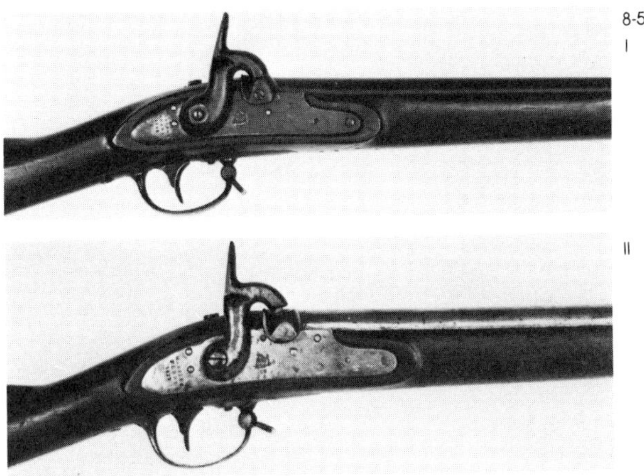

8-5 Butterfield Pennsylvania Contract Patent Breech Alterations, Types I and II

In 1861 Pennsylvania agreed to an amendment to Jesse Butterfield's contract to provide the state with 1,000 of his patent primer alterations to flintlock muskets, permitting Butterfield to deliver instead 4,000 muskets without the primer but altered to percussion. Butterfield simply utilized the already-made patent breechpieces he had prepared for the primer musket contract haphazardly so that they may be found with clean-out screws on the right side piercing the bolster (I) or through the left side of the breechpiece (II). The old hammers from the primer contract were also used simply by deleting the plunger in the cup of the hammer head (see 9-0). The barrel was marked "BUTTERFIELD'S/PHILADA" forward of the new patent breech section. All metal parts (and the wood immediately forward of the trigger-guard) were stamped with a serial number consisting of a Roman letter and an arabic figure between 1 and 100. 1,010 muskets, 10 rifles produced. **(D)**

8-6 U.S. Contract Patent Breech Alterations

In 1862 the Chief of Ordnance authorized the Frankford Arsenal Commander to contract for the alteration of several thousand flintlock muskets recently received from the St. Louis Arsenal, including some Austrian tubelocks. These were distributed to 24 gunmakers and machinists in the general area of Philadelphia who altered a total of 33,508 muskets to percussion (of which approximately 15,295 were realterations). Except for the 7,993 altered by Henry E. Leman (see 8-4) all of these arms were altered in the same style. All used a steel patent 1⅛" long (1$^{3}/_{16}$" long for realterations) with integral, flat-faced bolster like that of the M1842 musket. All took similar-style U.S. M1842 musket pattern hammers. Some took the rear sight adopted for the rifle musket in 1858, and an iron blade was added to the forward strap of the upper

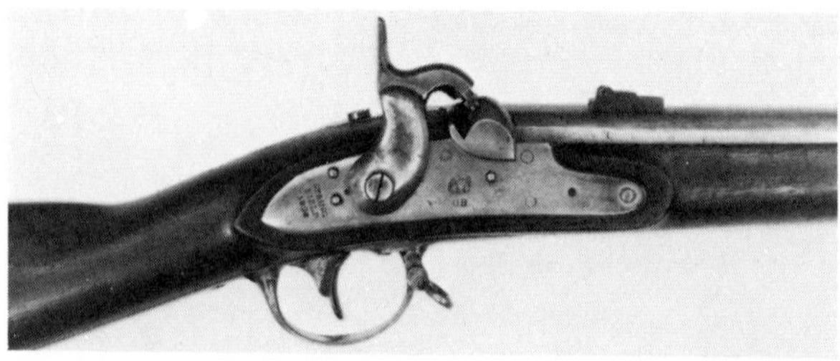

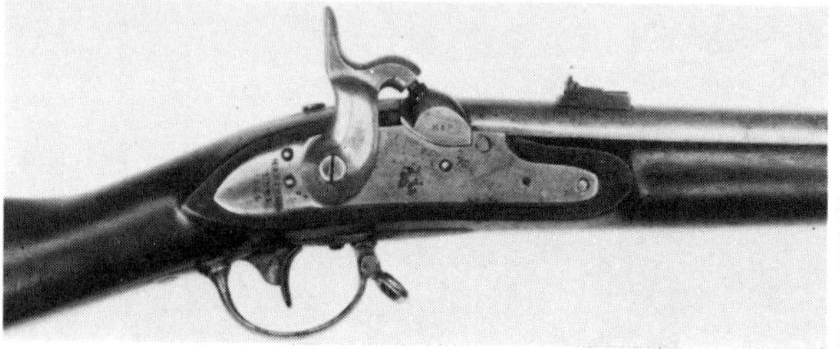

Hewes & Phillips

hand. Only a few, however, were actually rifled, these being generally realtered U.S. M1840 muskets, in which case the old brass front blade remained unchanged. Only Hewes & Phillips of Newark, N.J. marked its alterations, stamping its "H&P" logo upon the face of the bolster and the date of alteration upon the top of the breechpiece. Each contractor stamped a differing set of reassembly numbers or letter/number combinations on all altered parts. **(B)**

8-7 Harpers Ferry M1795 III

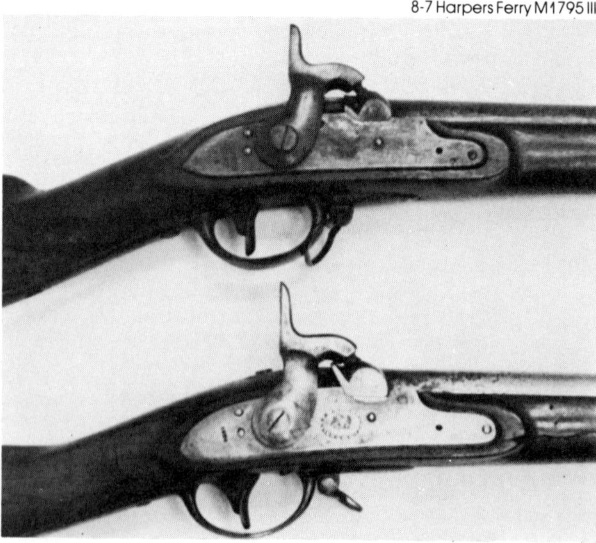

U.S. M1816 Evans Contract Musket

8-7 Virginia Contract Brazed Bolster Alterations

In 1861 Virginia took measures to alter nearly 50,000 flintlock Virginia Manufactory muskets and rifles. Contracts were let with six Richmond gunsmiths or firms (S.B. Cocke, Thomas Addams, Jr., Francis Perpignon, Samuel C. Robinson, Samuel Sutherland, and the Union Manufacturing Co.). All utilized the brazed bolster method similar to that employed by South Carolina in 1852. The configuration, however, more closely followed the M1842 musket bolster and had a straight, flat bottom that rested on the top of the lockplate. A new hammer, also of the M1842 musket style, completed the alteration. All parts altered and the new hammer were marked with mating disassembly numbers either in arabic or Roman numerals, occasionally preceded by a letter. Those numbers preceded by the letter "U" may have been the alterations of the Union Manufacturing Co., but the makers' codes have yet to be fully deciphered. In addition to Virginia Manufactory muskets (see 3-0) and late-type rifles, arms received under quotas of the 1808 Militia Act, principally Harpers Ferry M1795 muskets (see 3-3) and Evans M1816 U.S. contract muskets (see 3-12), were altered in the same manner. **(C)**

8-8

I

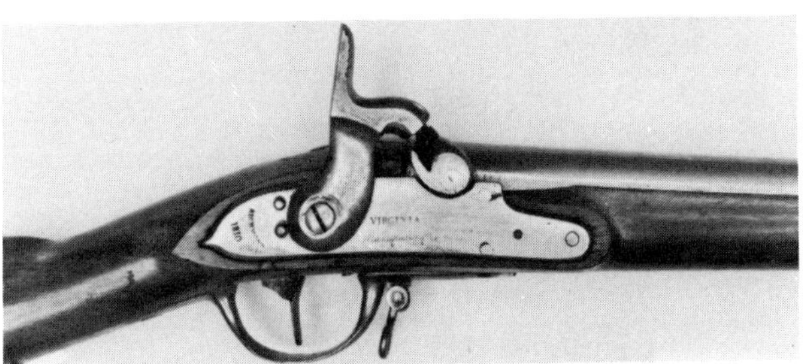

II

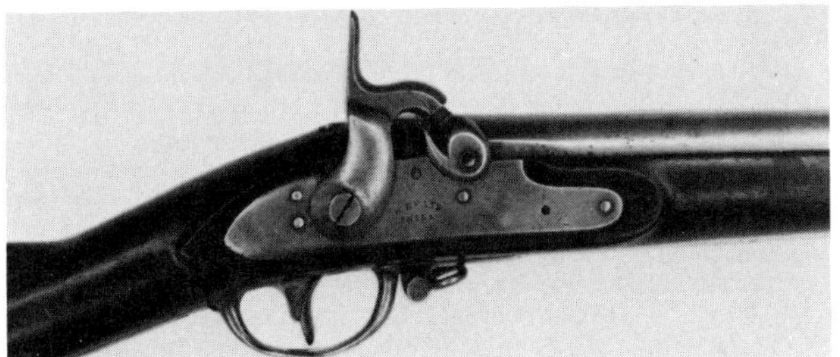

8-8 Confederate Contract Brazed Bolster Alterations, Types I and II

Many of Virginia's flintlock muskets were issued to volunteers in service during the arms crisis of 1861, and the Confederacy attempted to alter these by brazing a percussion bolster over the flintlock vent which had a rounded bottom. Most of these bolsters had an iron plug through the face to block the hole drilled to communicate the cone hole to the old vent hole (I), but a few utilized a screw in place of the plug (II). Most of the flintlocks having come from Virginia stores, this alteration is most frequently encountered on Virginia Manufactory muskets (see 3-0) but will also be found on Evans M1816 U.S. contract muskets (see 3-12), usually with the clean-out screw. Disassembly codes were like those struck into Virginia Contract alterations, frequently with the "U" prefix to the number in arabic figures. **(C)**

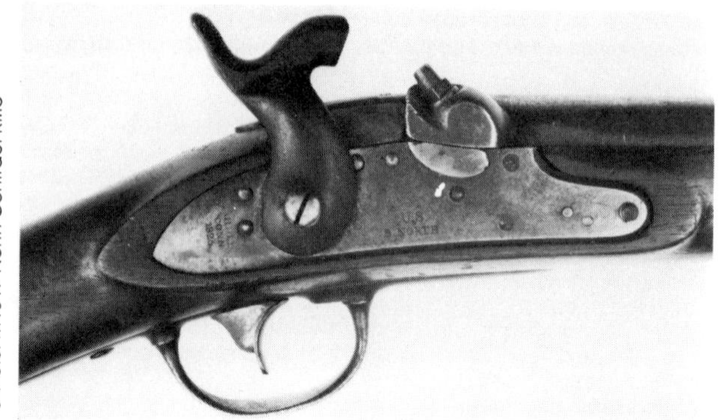

8-9 U.S. M1817 North Contract Rifle

8-9 M. A. Baker North Carolina Contract Brazed Bolster Alterations

M. A. Baker of Fayetteville received contracts from North Carolina in 1861 to alter arms. Although he is known to have delivered altered muskets as well, to date only U.S. M1817 contract rifles (see 6-4) and U.S. M1836 contract pistols are known with his peculiar alteration. Baker cut away a quarter section of the breech of the weapon and brazed into it an M1842-style bolster that rested directly upon the cutaway brass pan. An 1842-style hammer completed the alteration once the rest of the flint battery had been removed. Baker alterations bear the "N. CAROLINA" surcharge upon the barrel top. **(D)**

9 Alterations of Flintlocks to Mechanical Priming Systems

In September, 1845 Edward Maynard of Washington, D.C., was issued a patent for a percussion "priming cock" invention. In place of separate percussion caps, he formulated a means to affix the fulminate percussion compound to strips of paper formed into rolls. This roll of primers was housed in a compartment built into or into the lockplate. By cocking the hammer, the roll was mechanically unwound so that one primer was advanced over the cone with each cocking motion of the hammer. After studying and testing the Maynard system, the government decided to alter 5,000 arms. Accordingly, the Navy ordered 1,000 Jenks patent breechloading carbines made with the mechanism attached, and the Army contracted with Daniel Nippes for the alteration of two lots of 1,000 muskets. After further trials the government purchased the unrestricted right to use the Maynard system. After first considering altering muskets at Springfield armory, the government contracted with E. Remington & Sons to provide the necessary parts (breechpieces and new locks) to modify 20,000 flintlock muskets to the new primer. The alteration work took place at the Frankford Arsenal and included rifling. 2,000 New Jersey militia muskets were altered there as part of the 20,000.

In spite of the U.S. government's acceptance of Maynard's system, others endeavored to improve upon it. In 1856 James N. Ward de-

vised a method by which the primer rolls could be housed in the hammer instead of the lockplate. After altering a small number of muskets, the U.S. Ordnance Department rejected Ward's device. It was adopted, however, for New York and New Hampshire militia muskets, and considerable numbers of these had been set aside for alteration when Ward's untimely death terminated the projects. Likewise, in 1859 the government became sufficiently interested in both W. H. Bell's and J. S. Butterfield's patented disc priming devices to contract for the right to apply these to several thousand arms. The Civil War, however, intervened to prevent completion of the experiment. Pennsylvania did contract with Butterfield to apply his primer to 1,000 of its militia muskets in 1861 and 200 were delivered before the contract was renegotiated to eliminate the primer.

9-O Pennsylvania Contract Butterfield Primer Alterations (color plate, above)

In 1861 Jesse Butterfield of Philadelphia and the commonwealth of Pennsylvania entered into a contract by which he would alter to his patented disc priming system 1,000 militia muskets. Only 200 were delivered, however, before the contract was modified to permit Butterfield to alter the muskets without the primer attachment (see 8-5). Two alteration methods were used. In the earliest (I) a castement was added to the lock's exterior after the removal of the flintlock battery, housing the primer tube and mechanism. This alteration required an elongated bolster that was integral to the $1\frac{1}{16}$" long patent breech section. A clean-out screw pierced the right side of this bolster. In the later (II) alterations, the lock was instead modified so that the primer tube sat flush with the lockplate, all of the mechanism being recessed into a cavity built behind the hammer. The bolster was similar to I, but the clean-out screw entered the patent breech from its **left** side and was considerably larger. Both types received the marking "BUTTERFIELD'S/PATENT DEC. 11 1855/PHILADA" forward of the hammer, and both were rifled with three broad grooves equal in width to the lands. The hammers placed on these alterations have peculiar plungers inset into the cavity of the hammer-head face. Although a few 1808 contract muskets were altered by this method, most were U.S. M1822 Harpers Ferry Armory-produced muskets dating between 1836-39 (see 3-0). A number of these muskets were later altered to breechloaders experimentally. **(E)**

Frankford Arsenal (Remington) Maynard Primer Alterations, Types I and II (color plate, below)

In 1854 a federal contract was let with E. Remington & Sons of Ilion, N.Y. for 20,000 breechpieces and 20,000 new percussion locks incorporating the Maynard tape primer. The lockplates bear the marking on their rounded tail, "REMINGTON'S/ILION, N.Y./(date)/U.S." and the mechanism and primer compartment is recessed into the lockplate. The hammer used resembles those employed on the U.S. M1855 series rifles and rifle-muskets but is larger in proportions. The breechpieces are 1" long (exclusive of the tang) and marked on the top of the tang with the date. All the alterations done at Frankford Arsenal were rifled with 3 broad grooves, equal in width to the lands. Sights (distinguishing type I from type II—unsighted) were affixed to 14,989 of these, of the style identical to those used on the rifled M1822 muskets (see 12-1). In the process of sighting, the altered front band and the tang of the breechpiece were struck with a letter/no. code. 17,996 muskets produced. **(B)**

9-1 

9-1 Nippes Contract Maynard Primer Alterations

In 1848 Daniel Nippes received two contracts to alter 1,000 U.S. muskets to the Maynard tape primer. The muskets were altered by removing the old flintlock battery. Into the enlarged and threaded vent, he screwed a drum bolster with a clean-out screw. Using the old frizzen screw hole and a new one, a castemate for the primers and its advancing mechanism was attached to the exterior of the lockplate, bearing on its face the marking, "EDWARD MAYNARD/PATENTEE/1845". A new, flat-faced hammer completed the alteration, made only on U.S. M1840 contract muskets (see 3-17) that had been produced by Nippes. **(D)**

9-2 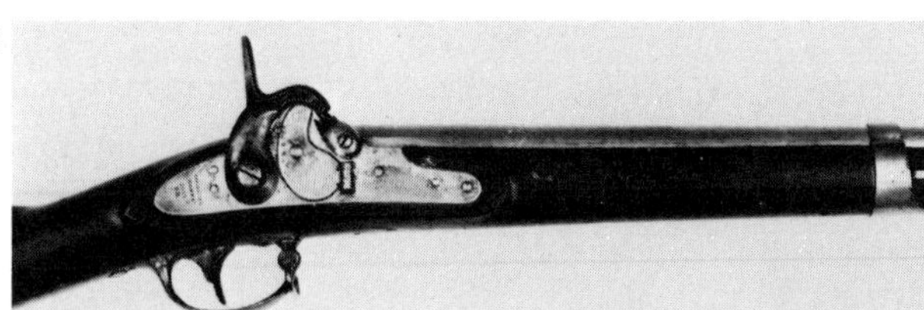

9-2 New Jersey Frankford Arsenal Maynard Alterations

By an agreement between New Jersey and the Chief of Ordnance, the state sent 2,000 "browned" M1822 contract muskets (see 3-13, type I) to Frankford in 1858 for alteration with Remington contract breechpieces and lockplates. A majority were type II, i.e. unsighted, but 200 followed the characteristics of the type I Frankford Arsenal (Remington) Maynard Primer Alterations (9-0). The only distinguishing markings (other than the absence of classification marks upon the stock) is the state ownership surcharge "N.J." stamped into the left side of the barrel near the breech. 1,978 produced. **(D)**

9-3

9-3 New York Arsenal Ward Primer Alterations

In fiscal year 1857-58 100 smoothbore "rifle muskets" were fitted with J.N. Ward's patented primer hammer. It is possible that the identification of this particular sighting to the New York Arsenal is incorrect, in which case this type should be considered a variant of the New York state contract alterations (see 9-4). The arms are all U.S. M1822 contract muskets (see 3-14). The locks were modified by removing the flintlock battery and substituting the new hammer which was marked on its left side "J.N. WARD USA/PATENTED JULY 1 1858" and serially numbered in four places. Minor lock modifications were made to activate this hammer mechanism. The barrel was modified by brazing a percussion bolster of unique configuration having a flat base that rests deeply in a recess cut into the lockplate. A long range, single-leaf ladder rear sight was dovetailed into the barrel 3¼" from the breech, and a new conical brass front sight was soldered to the upper band's rear strap. Lock, lock cavity, left side of barrel, and upper band were all marked with a common reassembly code consisting of a letter followed by a number between 1 and 9. **(F)**

9-4

9-4 New York State Contract Ward Primer Alterations

After evaluating the Frankford Arsenal (Remington) Maynard Primer Alteration against the Ward Primer Hammer Alteration, New York determined to have 1,200 of its old flintlock muskets altered to the Ward hammers. The alterations were identical to those described before (9-3) except that the rear sight was a simple curved "squirrel tail" leaf set into a block. Most of the alterations were made on Whitney 1808-12 contract muskets (see 3-8) or Blake contract U.S. M1822 muskets (see 3-13). **(E)**

10 U.S. Smoothbore Percussion Muskets

Although the percussion ignition system had been in practical existence since the mid-1820s, there was great reluctance to adopt the concept for military use. When it was finally partially adopted during the 1830s, conservative ordnance officers reserved percussion arms for highly trained specialty services. When the United States adopted the system for the Hall breechloading mechanism in 1833, the weapons were intended solely for the two mounted dragoon regiments. Similarly, the rifle and cadet muskets adopted in 1841 were specialty arms not intended for the great mass of uneducated soldiers.

When the percussion system for all services was accepted by the major European powers between 1837-42, the United States realized that it must conform. As a result the recently adopted 1840 flintlock musket was slightly modified for percussion, becoming the U.S. M1842. Production commenced at the two national armories in 1844. Too few had been produced and the percussion cap supply was too unreliable, however, for the arm to be introduced for infantry use in the Mexican War. Production of this smoothbore, percussion musket continued at the armories until the adoption of the "Minie ball" rifling in 1855.

No private contracts were let for production of the U.S. M1842. The cost of the tooling to meet the government's standards of interchangeability was high, and two of the major private musket makers already were under contract to produce the U.S. M1840 flintlock. Asa Waters, one of the most famous musket contractors, apparently was given assurances of a contract, for his firm did tool up for its manufacture. His death in 1844, however, together with the press of Mexican War orders, delayed potential contracts. Nevertheless, the successor to his firm, A. H. Waters & Co., did eventually produce a brass-mounted version of the M1842, including a few with the distinctive "Sea Fencible" knobbed buttplate. These muskets were probably made under contract with Massachusetts, although 100 may have been sold to South Carolina in 1849. Waters' former foreman and successor in musket production, Benjamin Flagg, secured the Waters' machinery and produced direct copies of the U.S. M1842 which he sold to South Carolina under his marking in 1850. Flagg eventually transferred the machinery to Columbia, S.C. There, in conjunction with William Glaze, 6,000 brass and iron-mounted versions of the U.S. M1842 musket were manufactured for South Carolina in 1852-53.

10-0 U.S. M1842 Muskets, U.S. Armory Production (color plate, above)

OL: 57¾"
BD: .69 cal.
Furniture: iron
Lockplate: flat, beveled edge
BL: 42"
Finish: "bright"
Configuration: round; bayonet lug below near muzzle

Markings: "(eagle)/US" forward of hammer; either "SPRING/FIELD/(date)" or "HARPERS/FERRY/(date)" on rounded tail

Sights: rear—none; front—brass blade on upper strap

Fastenings: 3 iron bands, the upper double strapped

Markings: "V", "P", and eagle head near breech; date on top of breechplug tang

Between the fiscal year 1844-55, 106,629 of these muskets were manufactured at Harpers Ferry and 165,936 were made at Springfield. Springfield records indicate that 6,020 more were made during the calendar years 1856-58; however, these were undoubtedly immediately altered to the rifled musket version before leaving the production lines (see 12-0). **(A)**

U.S. M1851 Cadet Muskets (color plate, below)

OL: 55¼"

BD: .57 cal.

Furniture: iron

Lockplate: flat, beveled edge

Markings: "(eagle)/US" forward of hammer; "SPRING/FIELD/(date)" on rounded tail

BL: 40"

Finish: "bright"

Sights: rear—none; front—brass blade on upper band

Fastenings: 3 iron bands, the upper double strapped

Markings: "V", "P", and eagle head near breech; date on top of breechplug tang

A total of 4,000 cadet muskets were manufactured at Springfield in 1852-53. **(C)**

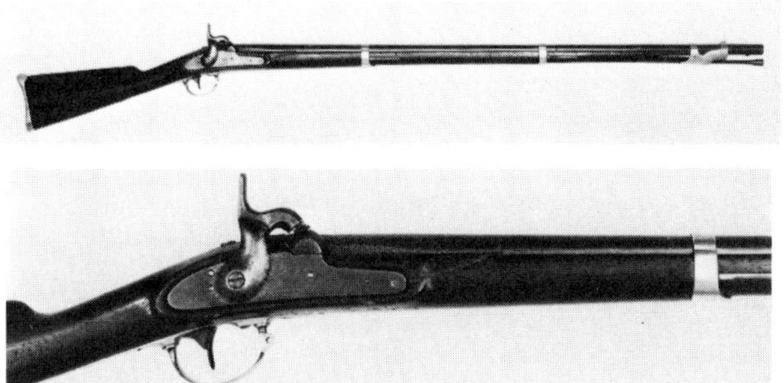

10-1
II

10-1 A. H. Waters & Co. M1842 Muskets Types I & II

OL: 57¾"

BD: .69 cal.

Furniture: brass, (I) with standard buttplate; (II) with "Sea Fencible" heavy knobbed buttplate

Lockplate: flat, beveled edge

Markings: "(eagle)/A.H. WATERS & CO./MILBURY, MASS." forward of hammer

BL: 42"

Finish: "browned"

Sights: rear—none; front—brass blade on upper band

Fastenings: 3 brass bands, the upper double strapped

Markings: "V", "P", and eagle head near breech

For whomever intended, this arm was produced in exceedingly small numbers in both types I and II lockplate configurations. It is suspected that 100 may have been purchased through Glaze and Radcliffe for South Carolina in 1849. **(E)**

10-2

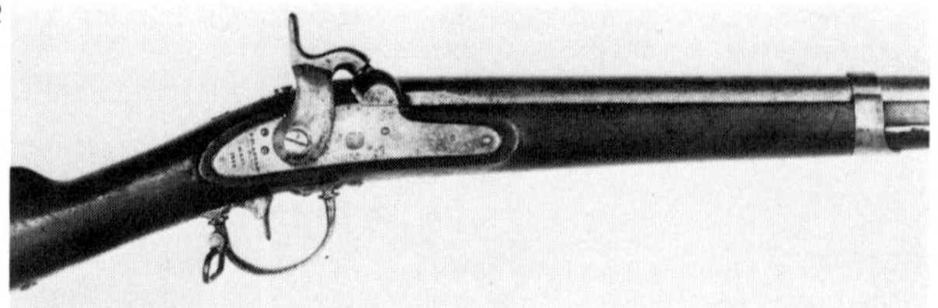

10-2 B. Flagg & Co. M1842 Muskets

OL: 57¾''
BD: .69 cal.
Furniture: iron; triggerguard bow incorrectly reversed in illustration
Lockplate: flat, beveled edge
Markings: "(eagle)/US" forward of hammer; "B. FLAGG & CO./MILL-BURY/MASS./1849" on rounded tail

BL: 42''
Finish: "bright"
Configuration: round; bayonet lug on bottom near muzzle
Sights: rear—none; front—brass blade on upper strap
Fastenings: 3 iron bands, the upper double strapped
Markings: "V", "P", and eagle head near breech; "1849" on breech-plug tang

In conjunction with William Glaze, Benjamin Flagg sold 640 of these muskets to South Carolina in 1850. "US (slanted)" appears upon the buttplate tang, and a serial number is stamped on the buttplate tang, the top of the barrel near the breech, and on the top of each of the bands. This is a direct copy of the U.S. M1842 percussion musket. **(E)**

10-3

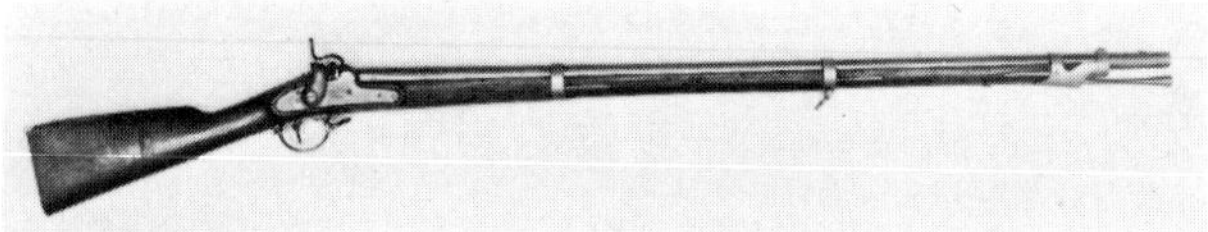

10-3 "Palmetto Armory" South Carolina Contract Muskets

OL: 57¾''
BD: .69 cal.
Furniture: brass (I); iron (II)
Lockplate: flat, beveled edge
Markings: "PALMETTO ARMORY" and "S*C" around a palmetto tree, forward of hammer; "COLUMBIA/S.C. (date)" on tail

BL: 42''
Finish: "bright"
Configuration: same as 10-2
Sights: rear—none; front—brass blade on upper band
Fastenings: 3 brass (I) or 3 iron (II), the upper double strapped
Markings: "P", "V", and palmetto tree (upper left surface); "WM. GLAZE & CO." or "W.G.&Co." on left side; date on breechplug tang

A total of 6,020 muskets of this type were delivered in 1852-53 in accordance with a contract between William Glaze & Co. (B. Flagg) issued in 1851. **(D)**

10-4 Morse South Carolina State Armory Muskets

OL: 57¾''
BD: .69 cal.
Furniture: iron
Lockplate: flat, elliptical plate
Markings: none

BL: 42''
Finish: "bright"
Configuration: round; bayonet lug on top near muzzle
Sights: rear—none; front—brass

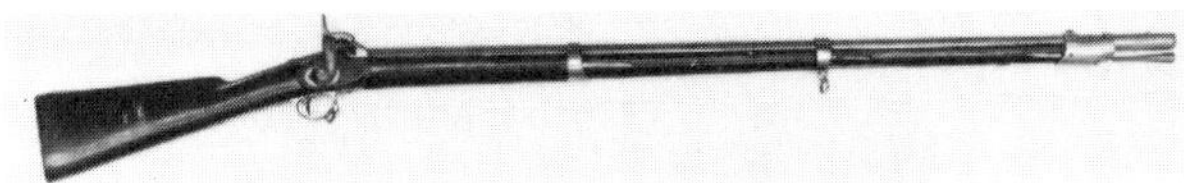

blade on upper strap
Fastenings: 3 iron bands, the upper double strapped
Markings: none

The only markings on this type musket will be found upon the brass triggerguard straps. The date of manufacture will be found on the forward strap, e. g. "1863"; the rear strap is marked "MORSE'S LOCK." and "STATE WORKS./GREENVILLE S.C." and the serial number. **(F)**

---

11 U.S. Smoothbore Percussion Musketoons

In 1844 a decision was made to arm the U.S. 2nd Regiment of Dragoons with muzzleloading arms rather than Hall breechloaders. Before the M1839 flintlock musketoon could be modified to percussion, the war with Mexico intervened. As a result, it was not until 1847 that this version was readied for production.

The actual production of the M1847 musketoon was divided into three versions for the specialty forces for which they were intended, including, by this time, the unmounted field artillery and the enlisted men of the Engineer Corps. The version adopted for the dragoons was furnished in brass and had a ring swivel bar attached to its left side. In lieu of a provision for a bayonet, the dragoon version had a special attachment to prevent loss of the ramrod while loading on horseback. That made for the artillery was furnished in iron, and the barrel was arranged to accept the socket bayonet used on the U.S. M1842 musket. The version adopted for the Corps (called "Sappers and Miners") was also furnished in iron but had a special attachment on the barrel and upper band to accept the long double-edged saber bayonet copied from the English P1837.

Although production of the artillery version was significant, the quantities produced failed to meet the needs of both the regular army and the militia. To remedy this, a large number of dragoon musketoons and a portion of the Engineer production was altered to the characteristics of the artillery to the greatest extent possible. In addition to these two alterations from the standard models, another version was produced, commonly referred to as the "Naval" musketoon. Rather than a true alteration, this arm is made up of parts similar to, but not officially assembled into any of the three standard models.

11-0 U.S. M1847 Artillery Musketoons (color plate, above)
OL: 41"
BD: .69 cal.
Furniture: iron
Lockplate: flate with beveled edge
Markings: "(eagle)/US" forward of hammer; "SPRING/FIELD/(date)" on rounded tail
BL: 26"
Finish: "bright"
Configuration: round; bayonet lug underneath near muzzle
Sights: rear—none; front—brass blade on upper strap

Fastenings: 2 iron bands, the upper double strapped
Markings: "V", "P", and eagle head date on breechplug tang

A total of 2,501 of these artillery musketoons were manufactured at Springfield between 1848-55. Prominent characteristics include the sling swivels upon the special mount on the buttstock and lower band, plus the bayonet lug under the barrel near the muzzle. **(C)**

U.S. M1847 Dragoon Musketoons (color plate, below)
OL: 41''
BD: .69 cal.
Furniture: brass, except for iron ring bar on left side between keyplate and lower band
Lockplate: flat with beveled edge
Markings: "(eagle)/US" forward of hammer; "SPRING/FIELD/(date)" on rounded tail
BL: 26''
Finish: "bright"
Configuration: round; ramrod swivel lug near muzzle
Sights: rear—none; front—brass blade on upper strap
Fastenings: 2 brass bands, the upper double strapped
Markings: "V", "P", and eagle head near breech; date on breechplug tang

Springfield produced 6,703 of these cavalry musketoons between 1847-54. However, in addition to the 630 later modified to artillery musketoons, 346 others were rifled and sighted in 1859. Note that the forestock protrudes beyond the upper band on the model, as no bayonet was intended. In 1851 a spring spoon was added to retain the ramrod. **(C)**

11-1 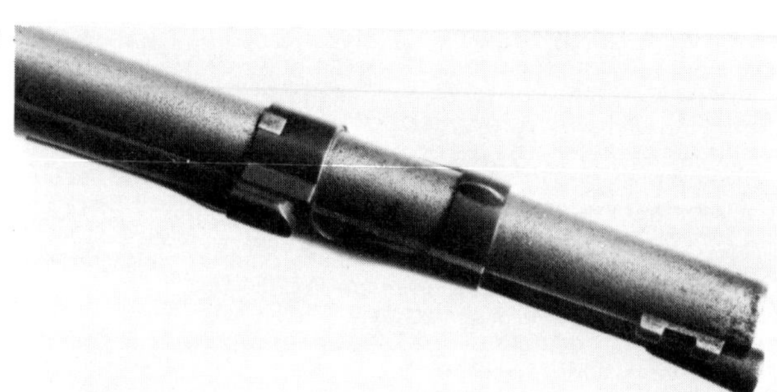

11-1 U.S. M1847 Sappers & Miners Musketoons
OL: 41''
BD: .69 cal.
Furniture: iron
Lockplate: flat with beveled edge
Markings: "(eagle)/US" forward of hammer; "SPRING/FIELD/(date)" on rounded tail
BL: 26''
Finish: "bright"
Configuration: round; band locking lug on top, and bayonet guide on right side of barrel near muzzle
Sights: rear—none; front—same as art
Fastenings: 2 iron bands, the upper double strapped with bayonet lug on right side
Markings: "V", "P", and eagle head near breech; date on top of breechplug tang

Only 830 of these musketoons for enlisted Engineers were manufactured at Springfield, 250 in 1848 and the balance in 1855-56. Of these, 228 were subsequently modified to artillery musketoons. The bayonet was copied from the British "Brunswick" rifle and locked into a guide on the right side of the barrel and a lug on the right side of the upper band, requiring the locking lug on top of the barrel. **(D)**

11-2 U.S. M1847 "Naval" Musketoons

In all dimensions and markings, this arm matches the U.S. M1847 artillery musketoon. However, it lacks both sling swivels and provision for a bayonet. Other elements of the all-iron furniture also distinguish this arm from the artillery musketoon. The upper double-strap band is shorter than the artillery and mounts the sight blade on the rear instead of the forward strap. The iron keyplate is of the dragoon configuration. **(E)**

12 Rifled Smoothbore Percussion Alterations

With the adoption of the "Minie ball" projectile by the U.S. Army in 1855, the military was confronted with the same dilemma that had been posed by the general adoption of the percussion system in 1841-42. What could be done with obsolete arms? This dilemma was deepened by another problem. In adopting the rifled bore for its new muzzleloading arms, the government had reduced the bore diameter from .69 caliber to .58. Rifling of the old models, even when possible, would pose an ammunition supply problem for the Ordnance Department in the event of a conflict. In spite of that possibility, the economy-conscious War Department opted to rifle its old smoothbore weaponry.

The rifling and sighting of both cone-in-barrel altered M1822 and M1840 muskets and M1842 smoothbore percussion muskets began in 1856. The rifling of the former alterations, however, was unsatisfactory as the barrels were weakened at the breech by the upsetting of the metal for the cone seat. After a few thousand alterations, rifling of this type was discontinued. Rifling of the U.S. M1842 muskets went ahead as did the rifling of the flintlock muskets that were being altered at Frankford Arsenal to the Maynard tape primer with the Remington contract lockplates and breechpieces (see 9-0).

Attempts to assign these rifled alterations to the militia met with only limited success. The more informed state militia officers demanded weaponry that would fire the newly adopted .58 caliber "Minie ball," but the Ordnance Department argued that it could not furnish the newly-produced arms according to the provisions of the 1808 Militia Act. A few states circumvented this restriction by requesting .58 caliber cadet muskets (which had only been made at federal armories and for which precedents existed for issuance to the states under the 1808 legislation). This resulted in the rifling and sighting of the M1851 cadet muskets in store during 1857. Some of the dragoon officers complained that they did not care for the breechloading arms furnished under the Army's experimental programs, and several hundred of the M1847 cavalry musketoons were rifled and sighted as well.

12-O U.S. M1842 Rifled Muskets, (Types I & II) (color plate, above)

Between 1855-59, 55,290 U.S. M1842 smoothbore percussion muskets (see 10-0) were rifled at government armories and arsenals. Like the cone-in-barrel alterations rifled in the same period (see 12-1), the M1842 musket bores were cut with three broad grooves equal in width to the lands. Rear sights of the same type were affixed in the same manner and location on most of these rifled muskets, distinguishing type I. In 1856, 500 of this type were also "browned" at Harpers Ferry. As many as 20,074 of the rifle muskets may never have received rear sights, distinguishing type II. **(B)**

U.S. M1847 Rifled Calvary Musketoons (color plate, below)

In 1859, after two samples had been prepared at Springfield, Frankford Arsenal altered 344 U.S. M1847 dragoon musketoons (see 11-0). As with other pre-Civil War federal alterations, the bores were cut with three broad grooves equal in width to the lands. A new 1$\frac{5}{16}$" long-stepped sight base was dovetailed and screwed to the barrel 3" from the breech face. The old ramrod swivel having proved impractical, a chain with slide replaced it. Finally, to reduce recoil, an 8 oz. slug of lead was melted into a cavity drilled into the buttstock base beneath the brass buttplate. **(D)**

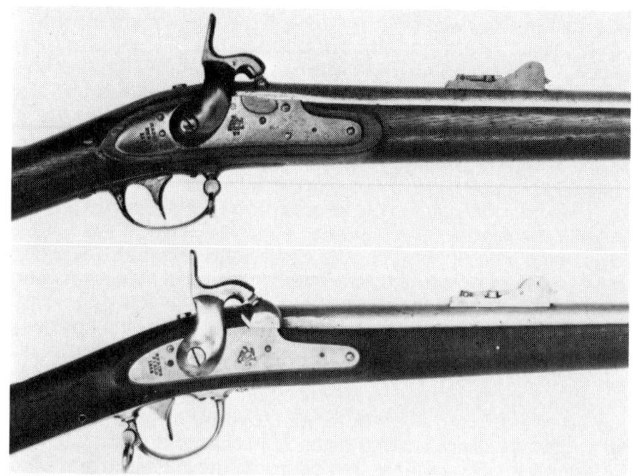

12-1 Cone-in-Barrel Realtered Rifled Muskets

Only 2,000 "browned" M1822 alterations were rifled and sighted at Harpers Ferry in 1856-57 before it was determined that the prior alterations of the muskets to percussion had too weakened the barrels to withstand the increased pressure generated by the tighter seal of the new rifle projectile. Rifling of the barrels of these muskets was with three broad grooves equal in width to the lands. The rear sight was a lengthened (2$\frac{11}{16}$" long base) version of the U.S. M1855 rifle-musket rear sight, dovetailed and screwed to the barrel 5½" from the breech face. The brass blade was removed from the upper band rear strap and a new iron blade was brazed upon the forward strap of the same brand. **(D)**

12-2

12-2 U.S. M1851 Rifled Cadet Muskets

In 1857-58 323 M1851 cadet muskets were rifled and sighted at Springfield. Three were rifled with three broad grooves equal in width to the lands. The rear sight, having a 2⁷⁄₁₆" long base graduated from 100 to 400 yards on the side walls and from 500 to 900 yards on the ladder, was dovetailed and screwed to the barrel 4" from the breech face. A new iron blade replaced the shorter brass blade upon the front strap of the upper band. **(D)**

12-3 Greenwood Ohio Contract Rifled Muskets, Types I & II

In 1861 Ohio received from the U.S. Ordnance Department several thousand U.S. M1842 smoothbore muskets and an equally large number of cone-in-barrel altered muskets. These muskets were to be issued to the Ohio volunteer regiments mustering into federal service. The volunteers begrudgingly accepted the arms only when assured that the "Minie rifle" could not be had. Miles Greenwood & Co. of Cincinnati rifled and sighted 16,918 cone-in-barrel alterations and 8,406 U.S. M1842 percussion muskets. Rifling consists of four narrow grooves. The rear sight soldered to the barrel follows the general characteristics of the English P1853 rifle-musket sight with a slightly different slide on the graduated ladder. The front sight is a simple, high brass blade mounted upon the upper band. **(D)**

12-4 Greenwood Austrian M1842 Musket Alterations

In 1861 Major-General John C. Fremont, in command of an ill-armed volunteer force in Missouri, purchased 25,000 obsolete Austrian M1842 smoothbore muskets. These were percussion, but in a variant system peculiar to the Austrian military, known as the Augustin tubelock, requiring a special primer. The facilities in St. Louis Arsenal being taxed to their limit, 10,000 of these muskets were sent to Cincinnati for alteration to the standard percussion cap system and rifling by Miles Greenwood & Co., who, in turn, subcontracted half the work to Hall, Carroll & Co., of the same city. The alteration effected is believed to have been a copy of the cone-in-barrel method, and the rifling and sighting is believed to have followed the style Greenwood used for his Ohio contract (see 12-3). Although similar in style to the U.S. M1842 musket, the Austrian version is readily identified by its longer (43") barrel, and the distinctive lock markings which consist of the date of manufacture (deleting the "1" first digit) forward of the cock and the Austrian imperial (double-headed) eagle on the tail. **(D)**

12-5 Palmetto Armory South Carolina Contract Alterations

In 1861 South Carolina contracted with W. Glaze & Co. for rifling and sighting the Palmetto Armory muskets made by the firm for the state in

1852-53 (see 10-3). A total of 3,720 were altered in the exact same manner as the U.S. M1842 rifled muskets (see 12-0), except that the original brass front sight blade was retained. **(C)**

---

13 Rifled Percussion Carbines

In 1855 the Ordnance Department ordered the Springfield Armory to manufacture 900 rifle-carbines for two new U.S. cavalry regiments, the 1st and 2nd. The weapons produced in that year—basically short rifles for mounted service utilizing some of the U.S. M1851 cadet musket components—were issued to three squadrons each, the other two squadrons of each regiment receiving experimental arms or the newly adopted pistol-carbine. Because production commenced prior to the official U.S. adoption of the Maynard tape primer, this arm utilized the standard percussion lock manufactured for the M1847 musketoons and the M1851 cadet musket.

Although the M1855 rifle-carbine was the only muzzleloading carbine specifically made for the U.S. service, rifle-carbines played an important role in arming the Confederate cavalry. One manufactured rifle-carbine was a close copy of the U.S. M1855. The others, however, tended to follow two distinct patterns. The English P1856 cavalry carbine (which had been extensively imported by the Confederacy) provided the basis for the carbines produced by Cook & Brother of New Orleans and Athens, Ga., and for the carbines produced late in the war at the Tallassee, Ala., Confederate Armory. The other Confederate rifle-carbines were little more than shortened versions of the rifles and rifle-muskets made at the various public and private Southern armories. These carbines were generally not part of planned production, but rather were deliberate attempts to salvage barrels that had burst near the muzzle during proofing. This was accomplished by shortening the remaining section to a standard length and fitting it into a stock furnished with the same parts as the rifle or rifle-musket. The Richmond Armory produced short versions of the rifle-musket in 1863-64, and such private makers as J. B. Barrett, Davis & Bozeman, Dickson, Nelson & Co., and the partnership of Greenwood & Gray adapted the rifle barrels that had failed proof into limited production carbines whose characteristics occasionally did not match the other arms of the same production.

13-0 U.S. M1855 Rifle-Carbine (color plate, above)

OL: 36¾''
BD: .54 cal.; 3-groove rifling
Furniture: iron, except brass nosecap
Lockplate: flat, beveled edge
Markings: "(eagle)/US" forward of hammer; "SPRING/FIELD/1855" on rounded tail

BL: 22''
Finish: "bright"
Configuration: round with ramrod swivel lug below near muzzle
Sights: rear—block with 2 leaves; 5'' from breech; front—iron block/blade
Fastenings: single iron band
Markings: "V", "P", and eagle head near breech; date on breechplug tang

The sling ring is attached to the rear section of the triggerguard bow. A total of 1,020 were made at Springfield in 1855. **(D)**

D. C. Hodgkins & Son Confederate Carbines (color plate, below)

OL: 37½''
BD: .58 cal.; 3-groove rifling
Furniture: iron, except brass nosecap; swivel ring on rear of triggerguard bow
Lockplate: flat with beveled edge; rounded tail
Markings: none
BL: 22''
Finish: "bright"
Configuration: round; ramrod swivel lug at muzzle
Sights: rear—open "V" c. 3'' from breech; front—iron block/blade
Fastenings: single iron band
Markings: "P/CS" near breech; "CSA" on top

This arm, made in small numbers by D. C. Hodgkins & Son of Macon, Ga., is a near copy of the U.S. M1855 rifle-carbine. Hodgkins had extensive arms contracts with the state from 1860 until taken over by the Confederate government in 1862. **(E)**

13-1 Cook & Brother Confederate Artillery Carbines, Types I & II

OL: 39¾''-40''
BD: .58 cal.; 3-groove rifling
Furniture: brass with iron swing swivels
Lockplate: flat
Markings: "COOK & BROTHER" and either "N.O. (date)" or "ATHENS, GA./(date)" and serial no. forward of hammer; Confederate flag on round tail
BL: 24''
Finish: "browned"
Configuration: round
Sights: rear—open "V", 3'' from breech; front—(see below)
Fastenings: 2 brass bands
Markings: "PROVED" near breech; "COOK & BROTHER" on top

Type I (New Orleans production) has a long iron block with brass inset blade for a front sight; type II (Athens production) uses a simple iron block/blade. This arm was copied from the British P1853 artillery carbine. **(E)**

13-2 Cook & Brother Confederate Cavalry Carbine, Types I & II

OL: 37''-37⅛''
BD: .58 cal.; 3-groove rifling
Furniture: (I) brass with enlarged ferrules; iron sling swivels; (II) brass with ring bar attached to ferrules
Lockplate: flat
Markings: "COOK & BROTHER" and "ATHENS, GA" and serial no. over date, forward of hammer; Confederate flag on rounded tail
BL: 21¼''-21½''
Finish: "browned"
Configuration: (I) round; (II) round with ramrod swivel lug at muzzle
Sights: rear—open "V", c. 4'' from breech; front—iron block/blade
Fastenings: 2 brass bands
Markings: "PROVED" near breech

The very rare Cook & Brother cavlry carbine was patterned after the English P1856 cavalry carbine. Most carbines are dated 1864. **(E)**

13-3 Dickson, Nelson & Co. Confederate Carbines

OL: 39¾''
BD: .58 cal.; 3-groove rifling
Furniture: brass
Lockplate: flat with swiveled edge
Markings: "DICKSON/NELSON & CO./CS" forward of hammer; "ALA/(date)" on rounded tail
BL: 24''
Finish: "bright"
Configuration: round with ramrod swivel lug at muzzle
Sights: rear—open "V" c. 3'' from breech; front—iron block/blade
Fastenings: single brass band
Markings: none

The few carbines of this type made are undoubtedly produced from rejected rifle barrels intended for Dickson, Nelson & Co.'s Alabama rifle contract. **(E)**

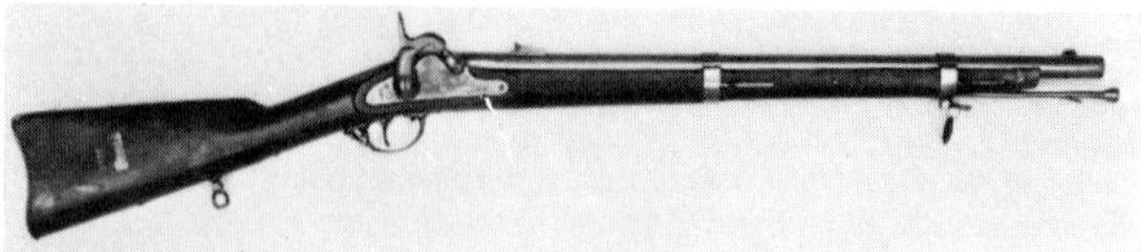

13-4 Richmond Armory Confederate Carbines

OL: 41⅛"-41½"
BD: .58 cal; 3-groove rifling
Furniture: iron, except brass nosecap and buttplate
Lockplate: "lowhump" flat surface with beveled edge
Markings: "C.S./RICHMOND, VA." forward of hammer; date on rounded tail
BL: 25⅛"-25½"
Finish: "bright"
Configuration: round
Sights: rear—U.S. M1858 two-leaf block 3" from breech; front—iron block/blade
Fastenings: 2 iron bands
Markings: "V", "P" and eagle head near breech

This arm was the result of a request by Robert E. Lee to produce a muzzle-loading cavalry weapon that could compete with the Union Cavalry's Sharps carbines. Of these arms, 19,764 were made from 1863 until the carbine factory was removed to Tallassee, Ala., in mid-1864. **(D)**

---

14 Arsenal-Made Percussion Military Rifles

In 1841 the U.S. government adopted a percussion rifle different in nearly all respects from the M1717 flintlock rifles still in production with two contractors. At first this rifle was produced only at Harpers Ferry. To meet militia demands, however, contracts were soon let with four private armories. Surprisingly, these contracts were given to musket maker Eli Whitney, Jr., and three firms that had little experience making military arms to high tolerances. During the war with Mexico, the M1841 won laurels and the nickname "Mississippi rifle" in the hands of Jefferson Davis's regiment of Mississippi riflemen at the battle of Buena Vista. The resulting popularity necessitated further contracts with three of the contractors, including Robbins & Lawrence, who exhibited the rifle at London's Crystal Palace Exhibition in 1851.

With the general adoption of the Maynard tape primer and the "Minie ball" by the U.S. armories in mid-1855, a new percussion rifle was devised—the long-range M1855 rifle with its long saber bayonet. Like its forerunner, it was manufactured at Harpers Ferry. It was cosmetically modified in 1858-59, but the 1855 title was retained. Production continued until the capture of the manufacturing machinery by Virginia forces in 1861. Virginia loaned this machinery to North Carolina, and it was re-established at the old Fayetteville federal arsenal where a primerless series of variations of the M1855 rifle was produced until the end of the war.

Many contractors refrained from seeking orders for the M1855 rifle because of their experience with the high tolerance requirements on the M1841. To meet the needs of the militia, therefore, the government made numerous alterations to the M1841 to give it the characteristics of the M1855. With the outbreak of war, these efforts were accelerated, but the loss of Harpers Ferry forced the government to turn elsewhere for alterations. A large number of rifles were delivered to Colt, and others were sold to northern states to be altered for their volunteers. A few M1841 rifles were also modified in the South in 1861, but their characteristics remain nebulous. The popularity of the rifle was so great, however, that many of the private armories set up after secession endeavored to produce arms that copied the classic, but none were able to copy it exactly.

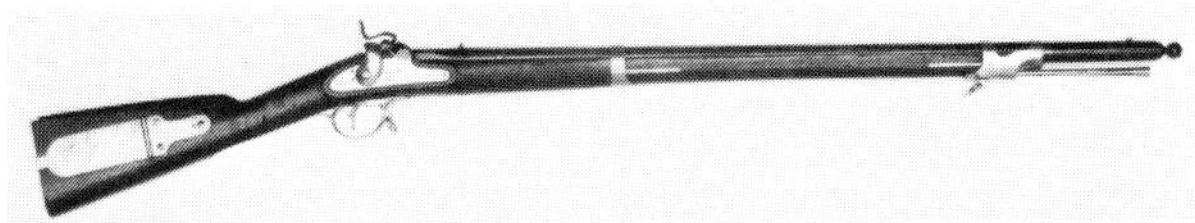

14-O Harpers Ferry U.S. M1841 Rifles (color plate, above)

OL: 52¾"
BD: .54 cal.; 7-groove rifling
Furniture: brass
Patchbox: brass, 2-piece hinged forward
Lockplate: flat, beveled edge
Markings: "(eagle)/US" forward of hammer; "HARPERS/FERRY/(date)" on tail

BL: 33"
Finish: "browned"
Configuration: round
Sights: rear—open "V" 2⅞" from breech; front—brass blade
Fastenings: 2 brass bands, the upper double strapped
Markings: "V", "P", and eagle head; "AW" or "WW" over "P", all near breechplug; date on breechplug tang; small "S" forward of bolster after 1851 denotes "steel" barrel

Three minor features distinguish Harpers Ferry-made stocks and furniture from those used by contractors. All buttplate tangs are devoid of the "US". The stocks are subtly different: three centering machine holes appear in the cavity of the patchboxes of Harpers Ferry rifles. And the rifles bear only the block letter inspector's initials "JHK" or "J.L.R." on the left side of the stock instead of the usual two script sets of initials found within cartouches. 25,296 produced. **(C)**

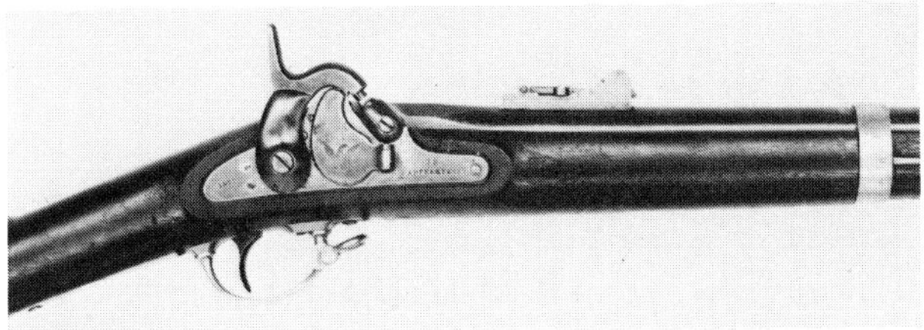

Harpers Ferry U.S. M1855 Rifles, Type I (color plate, below)

OL: 49⅜"
BD: .58 cal., 3-groove rifling

BL: 33"
Finish: "browned"

Furniture: brass; long brass nosecap
Patchbox: brass, 2-piece, hinged forward
Lockplate: flat, beveled edge
Markings: "U.S./HARPERS FERRY" forward of primer door; eagle on primer door; date on rounded tail

Configuration: round; saber bayonet lug on right side near muzzle
Sights: rear—2$\frac{7}{16}$" long block with side walls numbered "2", "3", "4", and "5", and folding leaf with slide dovetailed and screwed 2$\frac{7}{8}$" from breech; front—iron block/blade
Fastenings: 2 brass bands
Markings: "V", "P", and eagle head and date near breech

A total of 3,645 of these rifles were manufactured between 1857-58. The "patchboxes" are inletted for a special iron figure "8" cross-hair sight that could be attached to the muzzle with a set screw. Most of the rifles were believed destroyed when the armory arsenal was destroyed in 1861 to prevent the arms from falling into the hands of Virginia forces. **(D)**

14-1 U.S. M1841 Contract Rifles

Although the lockplate markings are the most distinctive difference between the armory-manufactured arms and those of contractors, other differences are also evident. In addition to the absence of machine holes in the patchbox cavity and the double cartouche inspection initials in the stock, contractor arms are marked on the buttplate tang with a "U.S." (of a slightly small size in the case of the Tryon production). "US" (in conjunction with the inspector's initials over "P" or "V" and "P") are also struck into the barrel. Due to parts mixing, these differences, though seemingly inconsequential, are important. **(B)**

14-2

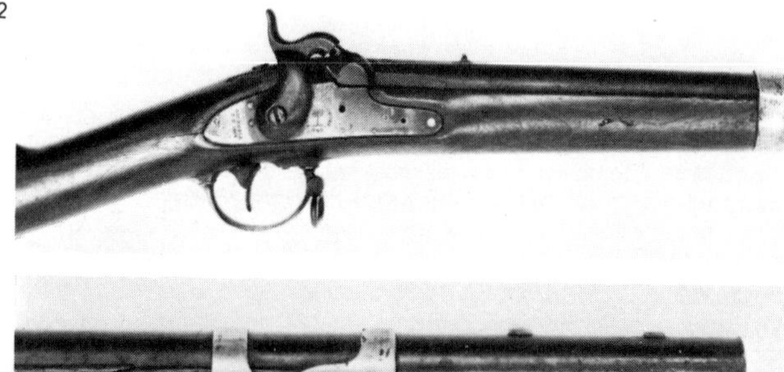

14-2 South Carolina Armory Contract Rifles

In 1851 South Carolina contracted with William Glaze & Co. for 1,000 U.S. M1841 rifles. The products differ from the U.S. contract rifle in two respects beside the markings. The South Carolina-made arms have a bayonet lug on the top of the barrel for a triangular socket bayonet, but lack the hole in the cavity of the patchbox for the extra cone. The barrels are marked with "V", "P", and a Palmetto tree on the upper left surface and with either "W.G.&Co." or "WM. GLAZE & CO." on the left side flat. The locks are marked with a Palmetto tree surrounded by "PALMETTO ARMORY" and 'S*C" forward of the hammer and "COLUMBIA/S.C. (date)" on the tail. **(D)**

14-3

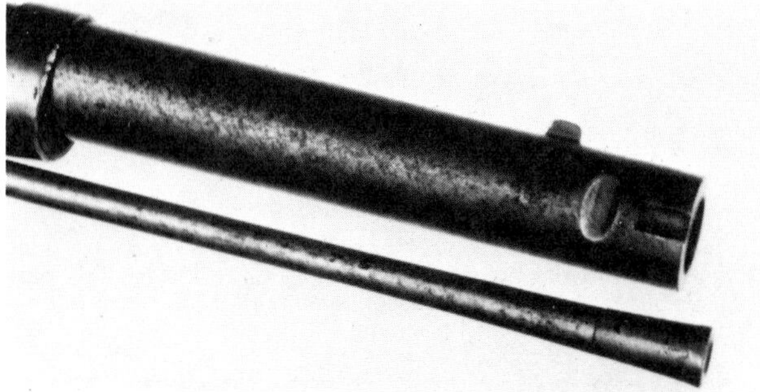

14-3 Harpers Ferry U.S. M1841 "Snell"/Screw Sight Alterations

In 1854-55 590 Harpers Ferry rifles and 1,041 rifles from the Washington arsenal were altered with a new, long-range rear sight consisting of a ½"-long base dovetailed $2^{15}/_{16}$" from the breech which has a single-standing ladder with screw adjustable range setting. These rifles were also altered to take the Snell-pattern saber bayonet, requiring that a horizontal slot be milled at the muzzle, and an elliptical cut be milled on the right side slightly down from the slot. The face of the barrel was stamped with a letter/number code mating it to the same code on the quillion on the bayonet. Although the bayonet attachment was partially successful, the rear sight was unsatisfactory, and they were replaced with simple open "V" block sights. The bore diameter (.54 cal.) remained unchanged as the .58 caliber was not adopted until mid-1855. **(E)**

14-4 U.S. M1841 Harpers Ferry and Whitney Alterations, 1854-56

Along with the Harpers Ferry "Snell" alterations, 449 rifles of the 1854-55 Harpers Ferry production and 1,200 rifles stored at the Washington

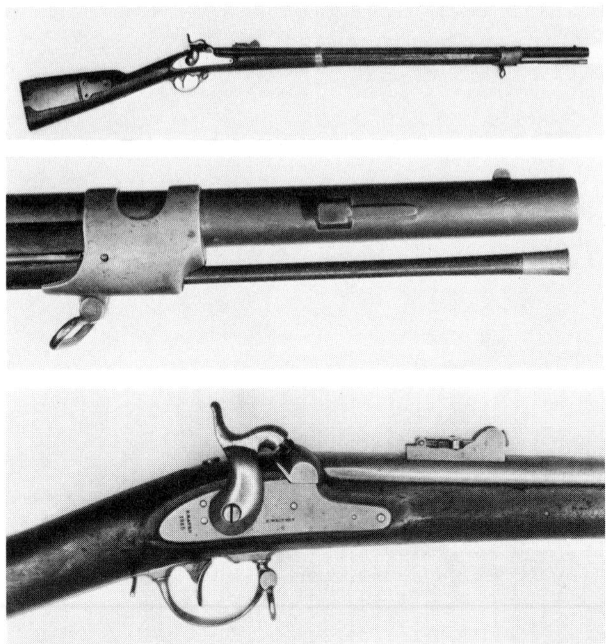

Arsenal (all prior Harpers Ferry products) were altered to accept a different pattern saber bayonet and long-range rear sight. The latter (copied from the English P1853 rifle-musket sight) consists of a 2³⁄₁₆"-long base soldered to the barrel 2⅞" from the breech. The base supports a graduated ladder with slide. At least two side wall variations were used. That used during 1854-55 is marked on the side walls with only "2", "3", and "4" 100-yard gradients while the adjustable folding ladder is marked from 500 to 1000 yards. That used on the 250 similarly altered rifles made in 1855-56 has the side wall gradiants marked "200", "3", and "4", and has intermediate 50-yard steps. Both rifles have a saber bayonet lug brazed to the right side of the barrel with a 1" guide. To permit dissassembly, a new short double-strap front band was substituted for the old longer version (which did continue in use with the Snell alteration.) In addition to the 1,899 rifles altered at Harpers Ferry in this manner, all 600 of the 1855 deliveries of Whitney's 1853 and 1855 contracts were altered to the earlier sight and the bayonet lug with guide before leaving his factory. A new altered (cupped) ramrod was affixed to these rifles as well as those that he had delivered in 1854 to accept the "Minie ball." **(D)**

14-5 U.S. M1841 Harpers Ferry Alterations, 1857-58, Types I & II

The 803 M1841 rifles altered in 1856-57 to .58 cal. (II) and the 1663 rifles altered in 1857-58 (presumably .54 cal.) as well as the 842 altered in 1858-59 in .58 cal. at Harpers Ferry were modified to take the saber bayonet and both sights of the M1855 rifle. The bayonet lug has no

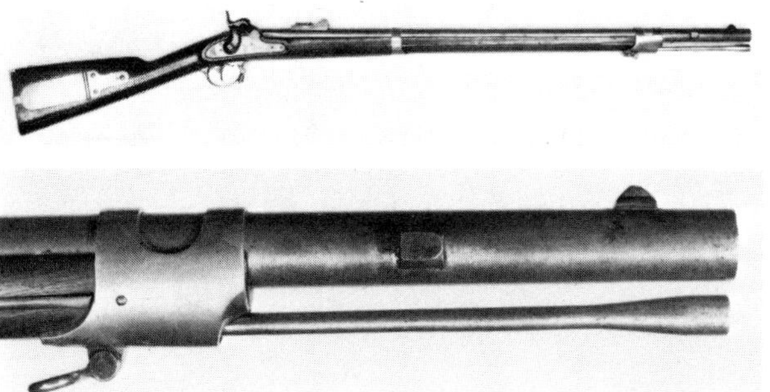

guide; the front sight is an iron block/blade; and the rear sight has a $2\frac{7}{16}$" base with side walls graduated for 100 yards, "2", "3", "4", and "5", dovetailed and screwed to the barrel $2\frac{7}{8}$" from the breech. These arms were reinspected after altering, the inspector striking his initials "W.C.K." upon the barrels forward of the bolster and into the wood opposite the lockplate. **(C)**

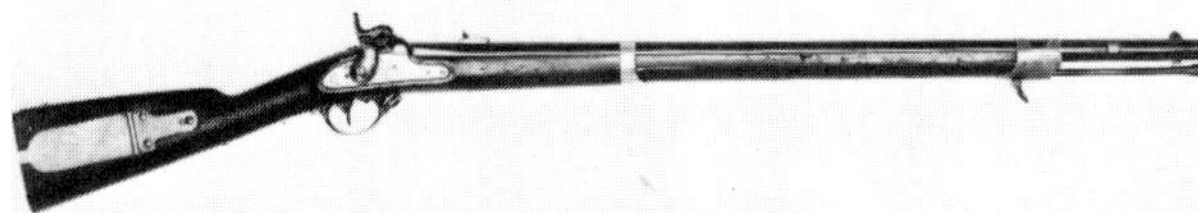

14-6

14-6 U.S. M1841 Harpers Ferry Alterations, 1858-60

With the adoption of the new M1855 rifle sight in 1858, alterations made at Harpers Ferry on M1841 rifles began to utilize this new pattern rear sight, a stepped block $1\frac{3}{16}$" long with two folding leaves for 300 and 500 yards (marked "3" and "5" respectively) dovetailed and screwed to the barrel $2\frac{15}{16}$" from the breech. The bayonet leg, front sight combination remained as the old M1855 rifle pattern, still necessitating the shorter front band. All 2,133 rifles so altered between 1858-60 were rebored to .58 cal. and rifled with three grooves equal in width to the lands. **(D)**

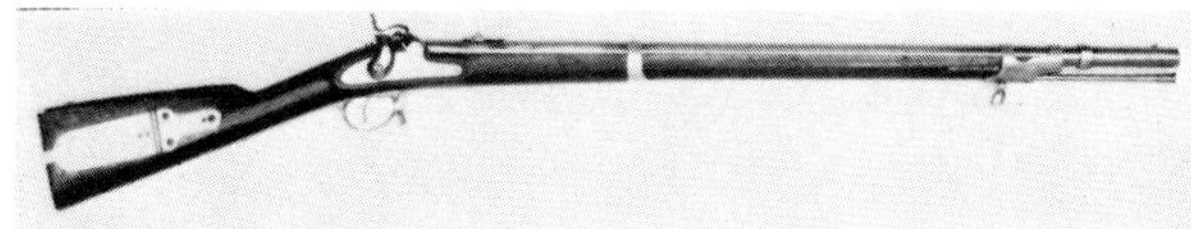

14-7

14-7 U.S. M1841 Rifles, Colt Contract Alterations

In 1861 Samuel Colt offered to purchase from the U.S. government all available .54 caliber M1841 rifles so that he might rebore them and make them available to the states for their volunteer services. He bought 11,500 rifles covering the full range of Harpers Ferry and contract production. Except for 468 which Colt sold directly to Connecticut in .54 cal., but with saber bayonets added, all of these arms were altered to .58 cal. (with 7-groove rifling), resighted, and altered to take the saber bayonet. The rear sight is of the pattern utilized on the Colt

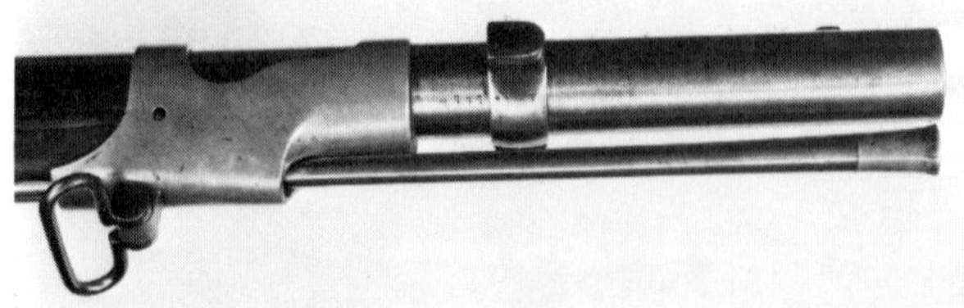

revolving carbine, with a $\frac{9}{16}$" base dovetailed $2\frac{15}{16}$" from the breech and having a 300- and 500-yard leaf, one of which drops forward and the other of which falls back on the barrel. The extremely long saber bayonet secured for these rifles is fastened to the barrel by means of a slip ring with integral stud that is screw clamped to the barrel. The clamp is serial numbered to the bayonet, and the barrel is struck with the same serial number on the lower right side near the muzzle. From February to May, 1862, Colt resold 10,200 of these altered rifles back to the U.S. government. Prior to acceptance, Colt's rifles were struck on the left side of the barrel with the reinspector's initials "CC" and upon either the side of the buttstock or comb with an oval cartouche with the initials "CGC" in script. **(C)**

14-8 U.S. M1841 Rifles, New York State (Remington) Alterations

In 1861 New York received 5,000 Remington M1841 contract rifles from the Watervliet Arsenal. The state contracted with E. Remington & Sons to attach saber bayonets to all. Soon this contract was altered to require that the bayonet lugs (which had no guide) be brazed to the barrels. Because Remington was unable to secure enough bayonets, the contract was reduced to 2,500, but later 768 more were produced. All remained in .54 cal. **(C)**

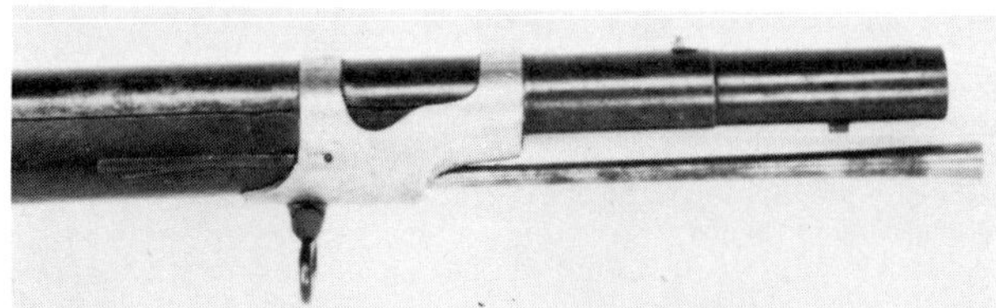

14-9

14-9 U.S. M1841 Rifles, New York State (Grosz) Alterations

Due to Remington's failure to deliver the full 5,000 alterations, 1,600 old M1842 musket bayonets were secured from Springfield Armory, and Frederick H. Grosz attached these to a portion of the rifles. Grosz turned down the barrel of the rifle at the muzzle for $2\frac{11}{16}$" to the inner diameter of the M1842 socket and simply moved the old brass blade further back on the barrel, behind the turning. All rifles remained in .54 cal. **(D)**

14-10 U.S. M1841 Rifles, Pennsylvania (H.E. Leman) Alterations

In 1861 Pennsylvania sent Henry E. Leman of Lancaster 2,352 M1841 rifles which he bored out to .58 cal. and rifled with three wide grooves (equal in width to the lands). U.S. M1842 musket triangular socket bayonets were affixed by turning the barrel for the distance of $2\frac{11}{16}$" from

the muzzle to the inner diameter of the socket and brazing a bayonet stud below the barrel on this turning. The front sight having been removed, a new triangular brass blade was placed on the barrel behind the turning. As the turning had a slight taper to it, Leman also altered the bore on at least some of the bayonets to fit the taper. These alterations are serially numbered on the left side of the barrel and on the butt-plate tang. Invariably the alteration was effected on Tryon M1841 contract rifles. **(C)**

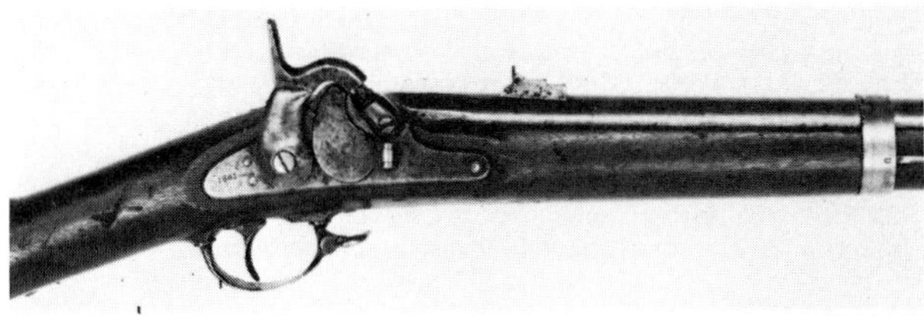

14-11 III

14-11 Harpers Ferry U.S. M1855 Rifles, Types II & III

Beginning in fiscal year 1858-59 significant cosmetic changes were made in the U.S. M1855 rifle. All furniture (except the shortened version of the brass nosecap, distinguishing type II from III with an iron nosecap of the same configuration) was made bright iron. The barrel was at first blued, but this was later brightened. The patchbox cavity is fully inletted and contains no special front sight. A new rear sight consisting of a 1$^3/_{16}$" long stepped base with two folding leaves for 300 and 500 yards is dovetailed and screwed into the barrel 2⅞" from the breech. 3,771 produced. **(C)**

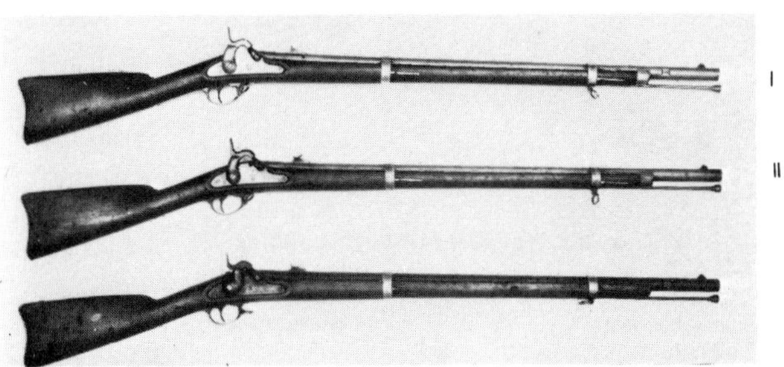

14-12

14-12 Fayetteville Confederate Rifles, Types I & II

With the capture of Harpers Ferry by Virginia in 1861, the machinery for the production of the U.S. M1855 rifle was transferred on loan to North

Carolina and set up at Fayetteville. Production began in 1862, at first utilizing captured unassembled parts. These included a few unmilled Maynard primer locks with the full "hump" (I). With the exhaustion of these lockplates, it was necessary to secure plates from Richmond where the lock making machinery had been sent for the manufacture of the Richmond rifle-musket. Type II rifles use the Richmond style "low-hump" lockplate. Both are marked forward of the hammer "(eagle)/CSA" and "FAYETTEVILLE", while the rounded tail bears the date "1862". Because it was easier to machine, brass was reverted to for the Fayetteville production, although the stock of iron nosecaps found at Harpers Ferry was used up first. The "patchbox" was also eliminated as a matter of economy, but otherwise the arm conforms to the basic characteristics of the M1855 rifle. "CSA" was stamped into the buttplate tang in lieu of "U.S." **(E)**

14-13 Fayetteville Confederate Rifles, Types III & IV

In late 1862 a new lock was devised for the Fayetteville rifle that distinguishes types III and IV from the earlier production. This lock resembles the U.S. M1861 special rifle-musket with a hammer that has the rounded surface of the type introduced by Colt. In 1864 production of the saber bayonet was discontinued throughout the Confederacy. Accordingly, the saber bayonet lug was eliminated from the right side of the barrel and the iron M1855 style block/blade was changed so that the block portion served as a lug for a triangular socket bayonet. The stocks are stamped on the left side opposite the lockplate with the inspector's initials "PB", first in block form, later in script within an oval cartouche like that utilized on the U.S. firearms. **(D)**

14-14

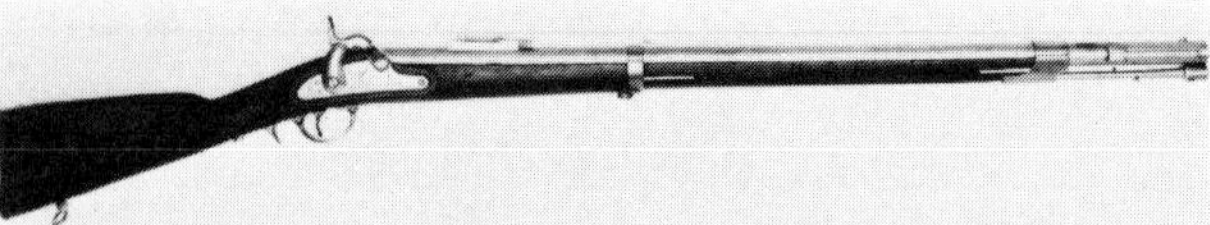

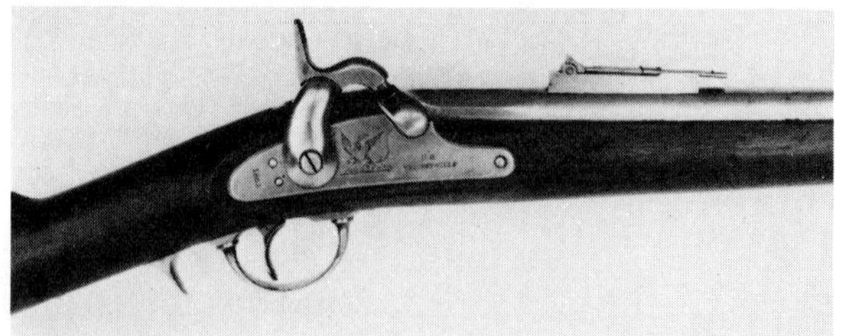

14-14 Whitney U.S. Navy M1861 Contract Rifles

OL: 50"
BD: .69 cal.; 3-groove rifling
Furniture: iron
Lockplate: flat, beveled edge
Markings: either large eagle with panoply of flags and "U.S./WHITNEY-VILLE", or (eagle)/U.S." and "WHITNEY-VILLE" forward

BL: 34"
Finish: "bright"
Configuration: round; saber bayonet lug with long guide on right side near muzzle
Sights: rear—2¾" long base with hinged leaf graduated to 1000 yards; front—iron block/blade

of hammer; date on rounded tail

Fastenings: 2 iron bands, the upper with extended lip

Markings: "V", "P", and eagle head; date, and inspector's initials near breech; serial no. on breechplug tang

Eli Whitney delivered an order for 10,000 of these rifles in 1863-64. They were made with a long "yatagan"-bladed saber bayonet made by Collins & Co., but a special "bowie knife" bayonet was devised by Captain Dahlgren for it as well. This triggerguard has a distinctive spur on the strap. Basically this arm was modeled after the French M1853 "carbine-a-tige." **(B)**

---

15 | Contract Percussion Military Rifles

With the completion of the M1841 U.S. contracts, the three major remaining contractors turned to other, more profitable pursuits. Only Whitney continued to manufacture military longarms, but not to the strict standards that had proved so unprofitable when working for the U.S. government. Instead he created a series of weapons especially appealing to the state militias, first using his M1841 machinery and rejected surpluses from his own and federal armories as well as a few of the machines from the defunct Robbins & Lawrence firm, with which he finally devised a rifle and rifle-musket strictly for the militia trade.

With the outbreak of hostilities in 1861, the federal government was hard pressed to arm the multitude of volunteers that flocked to the Union cause. In this crisis the government turned to many sources, including Whitney. Contracts were also let again with Remington to produce a modified cross between the U.S. M1841 and U.S. M1855 rifles. Philip Justice secured a federal rifle contract and produced a rifle similar to those that the other Philadelphia gunmakers had quickly produced in small quantities for the flank companies of departing volunteer militia companies. In spite of these various purchases of non-standard rifles, the rifle itself never found acceptance with the Union ordnance authorities, who favored in its stead the rifle-musket as the prime infantry arm (see chapters 16 and 17). As mentioned in the introduction to Chapter 14, several southern states entered into contracts with private armories for copies of the M1841 rifle, and a few private armories also began to produce it on their own initiative. Shortages of raw materials caused the elimination of the large brass patchbox on all of the rifles and resulted in the change to the brass nosecap in lieu of the double strapped front band in all but a few instances. Due to a considerable importation of English rifles and rifle-muskets, the Confederate ordnance officials eventually favored weapon designs that incorporated the major features of the widely distributed English P1856 rifle, especially its flat lockplate. As a result, several of the state contractors changed to this lock pattern in the middle of their production.

15-O Remington U.S. M1862 Special Contract Rifles (color plate, above)

OL: 49⅛"
BD: .58 cal.; 7-groove or 3-groove rifling
Furniture: brass
Patchbox: brass, 2-piece, hinged forward
Lockplate: flat
Markings: "(eagle)/U.S." and "REMINGTON'S/ILION, N.Y." forward of hammer; date on rounded tail

BL: 33"
Finish: "blue"
Configuration: round with saber bayonet stud with guide on right side
Sights: rear—U.S. M1858 rifle base, 3" from breech; front—iron block/blade
Markings: "V", "P", and eagle head near breech; "STEEL" on left side flat; inspector's initials and date near breech

Remington contracted in 1862 to deliver 10,000 rifles, and supplied 9,000. Before completing the work, he contracted for an additional 2,500, but delivered only 1,000. This rifle has been nicknamed "Zouave" because of its yatagan saber bayonet. **(B)**

II

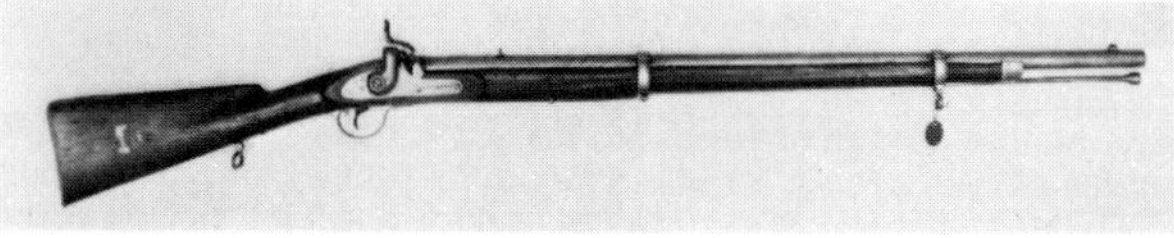

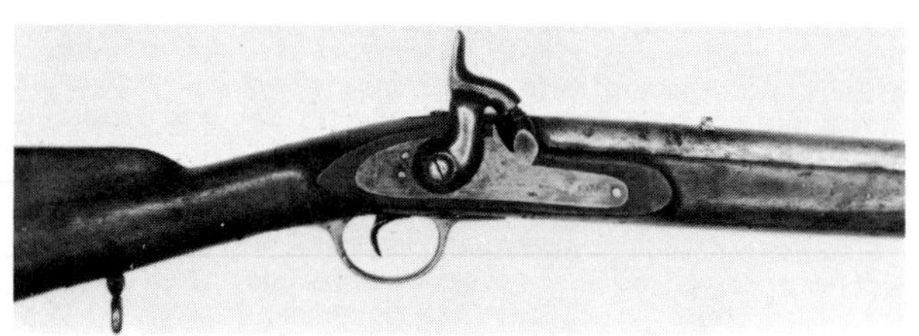

Cook & Brother Confederate Rifles, Type II (color plate, below), **& Type I**

OL: 48¾"
BD: .58 cal.; 3-groove rifling
Furniture: brass, including sling swivels
Lockplate: flat
Markings: "COOK & BROTHER" and (I) "N.O. (date)" or (II) "ATHENS, GA/(date)", and serial no. forward of hammer; Confederate flag on tail

BL: 33"
Finish: "browned"
Configuration: round; (I) saber bayonet lug with guide on right side
Sights: rear—open "V" 4³⁄₁₆" from breech; front—iron block/blade
Fastenings: 2 brass bands
Markings: "PROVED" near breech; "COOK & BROTHER N.O. 1861" on a few type I, on top of barrel

A few of both type rifles bear an Enfield rifle-musket long-range rear sight and a large iron block front sight base housing a dovetailed brass blade. The rifle was modeled after the English P1856 Sergeant's rifle. Approximately 1,000 were made in New Orleans before the capture of that city forced the removal of the machinery to Athens, Ga. Based on surviving serial numbers (struck on all metal parts) another 6,000 were made at Athens. **(D)**

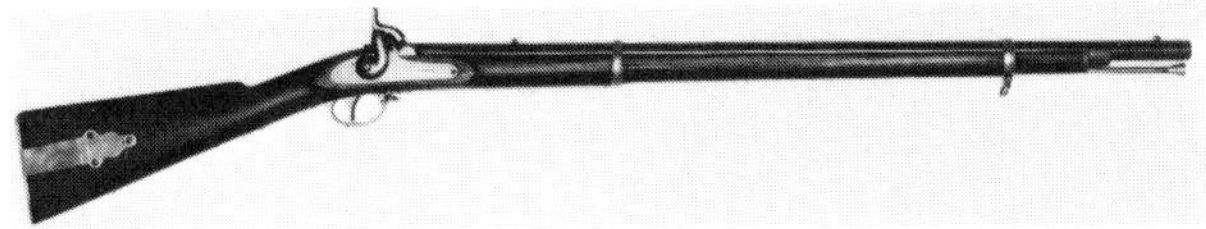

15-1

15-1 J. H. Krider Militia Rifles

OL: 49¼''
BD: .58 cal.; 7-groove rifling
Furniture: brass, except pewter Enfield-style nosecap
Patchbox: brass, 2-piece, hinged forward
Lockplate: flat
Markings: "KRIDER" forward of hammer

BL: 33''
Finish: "browned"
Configuration: round
Sights: rear—open "V" 5'' from breech
Fastenings: 2 brass bands
Markings: none or "PHILADA"

This type was only made in small quantities in 1861 for the flank companies of some of the Pennsylvania three-months' volunteer militia. **(E)**

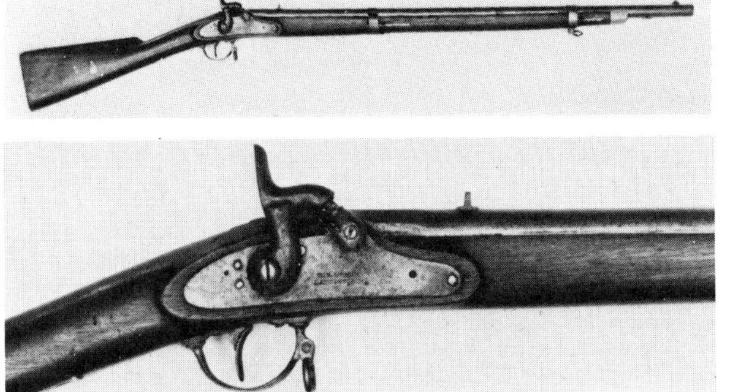

15-2

15-2 H.E. Leman Militia Rifles

OL: 49''
BD: .58 cal.; 3-groove rifling
Furniture: brass
Lockplate: flat
Markings: "H.E. LEMAN/LANCASTER, PA." forward of hammer

BL: 33''
Finish: "bright"
Configuration: round
Sights: rear—open "V" 3¼'' from breech; front—iron block/blade
Markings: "H.E. LEMAN/LANCASTER, PA." and serial no.

Probably no more than 200 of these rifles were manufactured in 1861 to arm the flank companies of a Pennsylvania 3-month's volunteer militia regiment. **(E)**

15-3 Whitney "Short Enfield" Militia Rifles, Types I-IV

OL: 49"
BD: .58 cal.; 7-groove rifling
Furniture: iron, except Enfield pattern, pewter nosecap and

BL: 33"
Finish: "browned"
Configuration: round with saber bayonet stud on right side

IV

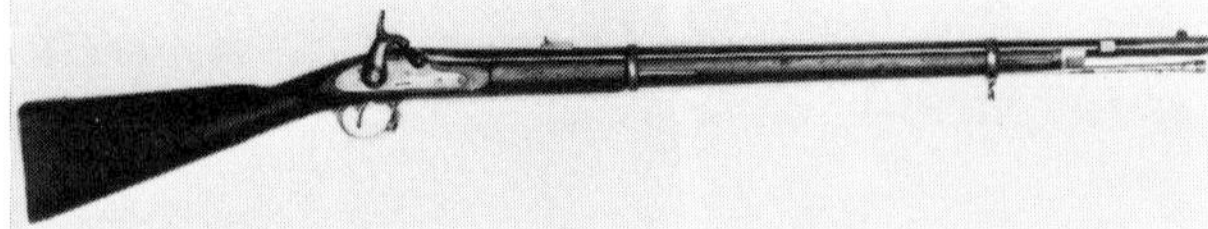

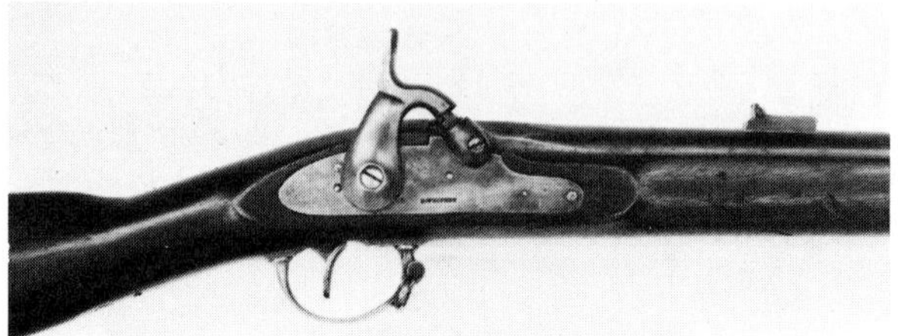

brass triggerguard, bow, ferrules, and buttplate
Lockplate: flat
Markings: "E. WHITNEY", forward of hammer.

Sights: rear—(see comments below); front—iron block/blade
Fastenings: 2 iron bands, the upper wider than the rear
Markings: serial code (letter/number) near muzzle in small figures, usually on top

Four variants, at least, were manufactured between 1859-61. Types I and II are distinguished by elliptical iron patchboxes (hinged below) in the buttstocks. The other types are distinguished by their sights. Type I has a simple open "V" dovetailed into the barrel. II & III (the latter without patchbox) utilized Whitney's 800-yard derivative of the US M1855 rifle musket rear sight ($2\frac{5}{16}$" base) dovetailed and screwed $5\frac{5}{8}$" from the breech. Type IV uses a short ($1\frac{1}{4}$" long) base supporting a single leaf from the breech. **(C)**

15-4 Whitney M1855 Derivative Militia Rifles

OL: 49"
BD: .58 cal.; 3-groove rifling
Furniture: iron, except brass bands, the upper being the shore M1841 type
Lockplate: "low hump" style
Markings: "E. WHITNEY" forward of hammer

BL: 33"
Finish: "browned"
Configuration: round; saber bayonet stud on right side
Sights: rear—Whitney M1855 type tangent sight 3" from breech; front—iron block/blade
Fastenings: 2 brass, the upper double strapped
Markings: "V", "P", and eagle head on upper left flat; date on top near breech (usually "1858")

Whitney offered this style rifle to the militia as early as 1859. The lockplates are unmilled U.S. M1855 Maynard primer rifle locks or locks with the "hump" ground off. The barrels are apparently Harpers Ferry U.S. M1855 rifle rejects, and the stocks were cut down rifle-musket stocks. Quantities produced must have been extremely limited as very few have survived. **(F)**

15-5

15-5 Asheville Armory Confederate Rifles

OL: 48¾″
BD: .58 cal.
Furniture: brass
Lockplate: flat, beveled edge
Markings: "ASHEVILLE/N.C." forward of hammer

BL: 33″
Finish: "browned"
Configuration: round; saber bayonet stud on right side
Sights: rear—open "V" 2¾″ from breech; front—brass blade
Fastenings: 2 brass bands
Markings: none

Most Asheville Armory lockplates are totally unmarked; at least one bears evidence of old "HARPERS/FERRY" markings from M1841 rifle production. The left side of the butt stock bears the rectangular cartouche with the script "Asheville, N.C." therein. Quantities were very small. **(E)**

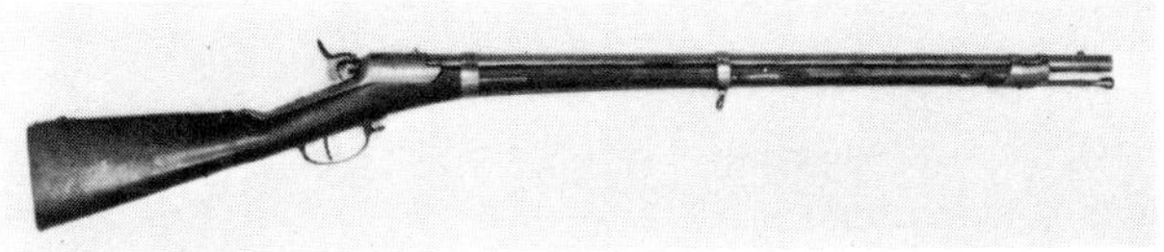

15-6 II

15-6 J. B. Barrett (N.T. Reed) Confederate Rifles, Types I & II

OL: 48-48½″
BD: .54 cal.; 16-groove rifling
Furniture: iron
Lockplate: none; mechanism set behind hammer
Markings: none

BL: 33-33⅛″
Finish: "browned"
Configuration: round with octagonal breech section
Sights: rear—open "V" on octagonal section; front—iron block/blade
Markings: "N T R" cypher on top of breech

The casting breech block of type I is sealed by means of a simple bronze casting housing the cone. The breech block of type II is a much more elaborate bronze casting that partially surrounds the octagonal breech section. Very few of these rifles were made by J. B. Barrett of Wytheville, Va. in 1861 from Hall breechloading rifle parts captured at Harpers Ferry. **(D)**

15-7 C. Chapman Confederate Rifles

OL: 48¾″

BL: 33″

BD: .58 cal.
Furniture: brass
Furniture: brass
Lockplate: flat, beveled edge
Markings: "C. CHAPMAN" forward of hammer
Finish: "bright"
Configuration: round
Configuration: round
Sights: rear-open "V" c. 3'' from breech; front—iron blade
Fastenings: 2 brass bands, the upper double strapped

The serial number is stamped upon all metal parts. Highest number recorded to date is only "4," suggesting extremely limited production. Chapman's location is not yet known; note, however, similarity to the Georgia Armory rifle (15-9)). **(F)**

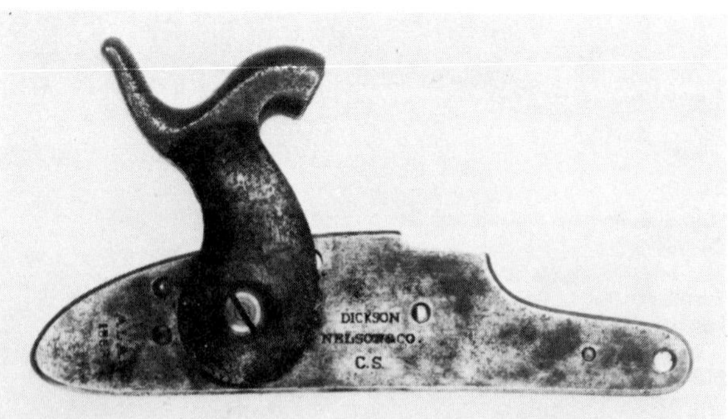

15-8 Dickson, Nelson & Co. Alabama Contract Rifles
OL: 48''
BD: .58 cal.
Furniture: brass
Lockplate: flat, beveled edge
Markings: "DICKSON/NELSON & CO./CS" forward of hammer; "ALA./(date)" on rounded tail
BL: 33''
Finish: "browned"
Sights: rear—open "V" c. 3'' from breech; front—iron blade, dovetailed
Fastenings: 2 brass bands
Markings: "ALA.(date)" on upper left surface near breech

The Shakanoosa Arms Co. (Dickson, Nelson & Co.) received a contract from Alabama for 5,000 rifles based on the U.S. M1841 rifle. Between 1863-64, 645 of these were delivered. **(E)**

15-9

15-9 Georgia Armory Rifles

OL: 48¾-49"
BD: .58 cal.; 5-groove rifling
Furniture: brass
Lockplate: flat, beveled edge
Markings: "GA. ARMORY/(date)" on rounded tail

BL: 33"
Finish: "bright"
Configuration: round
Sights: rear—open "V" 2$\frac{15}{16}$" from breech; front—brass blade
Fastenings: 2 brass bands, the upper double strapped
Markings: serial no. on barrel near breech

All metal parts are stamped with the rifle's serial no. The Georgia Armory was established at the state penitentiary at Milledgeville until the facility was destroyed by Sherman's Army in 1864. In spite of indications that production was 125 per month, very few survive. **(F)**

15-10 I

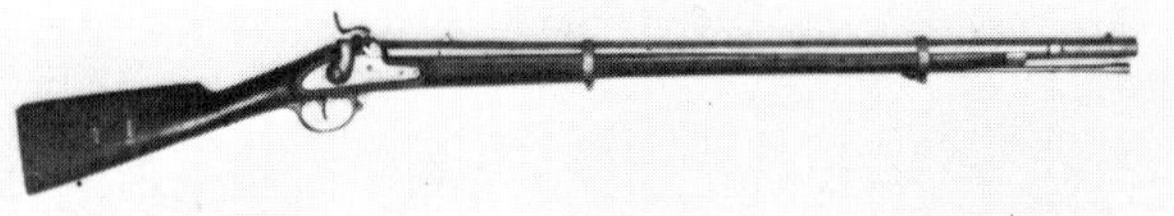

15-10 H. C. Lamb & Co. North Carolina Contract Rifles, Types I & II

OL: 49"
BD: (I) .58 cal.; (II) .50 cal.
Furniture: brass; (I) with M1841-style keyplate; (II) with round ferrules
Lockplate: (I) flat, beveled edge, U.S. M1841-style; (II) flat, English P1853-style
Markings: none

BL: 32½"-33½"
Finish: "bright"
Configuration: round, part octagonal (7") near breech; saber bayonet stud on right side
Sights: rear—open "V" on octagonal section; front—brass blade
Fastenings: 2 brass bands
Markings: "P" on top flat

This firm of Jamestown, N.C., received a contract for 10,000 rifles from the state in 1861. Production has been estimated at about 300 per month from 1862-65. Some parts were purchased from Clapp, Gates & Co. Some rifles have been noted with "N.C." struck into the wood opposite the lockplate and upon the buttplate face. **(D)**

15-11 I

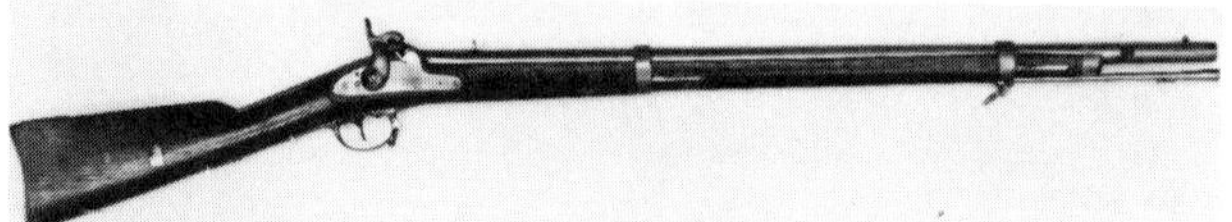

15-11 Mendenhall, Jones, and Gardner North Carolina Contract Rifles, Types I-III

OL: 48¼''-49½''
BD: .58 cal.
Furniture: brass, except for iron buttplate; (I) with U.S. M1841 keyplate; (II) with Enfield P1853 ferrules; (III) with round U.S. M1855 ferrules
Lockplate: flat beveled edge
Markings: either "M.J.& G./GUILFORD/N.C." (early) or "M.J.& G./N.C." (later) forward of hammer; either "C.S." or "C.S./(date)" on rounded tail

BL: 32¾''
Finish: "bright"
Configuration: round; saber bayonet stud on right side
Sights: rear—open "V" c. 3'' from breech; front—brass blade
Fastenings: 2 brass bands
Markings: "P/NC" (early), or none (later)

A rectangular cartouche enclosing the script initials "M J & G" will occasionally be found on the left side of the stock opposite the lockplate. The firm, first of Whitsett and later of Jamestown, N.C., received a state contract to produce 10,000 rifles in 1861. Production began in 1862 and continued until 1865. Late war production utilized a single-piece triggerguard casting instead of separate bow and plate. **(D)**

15-12

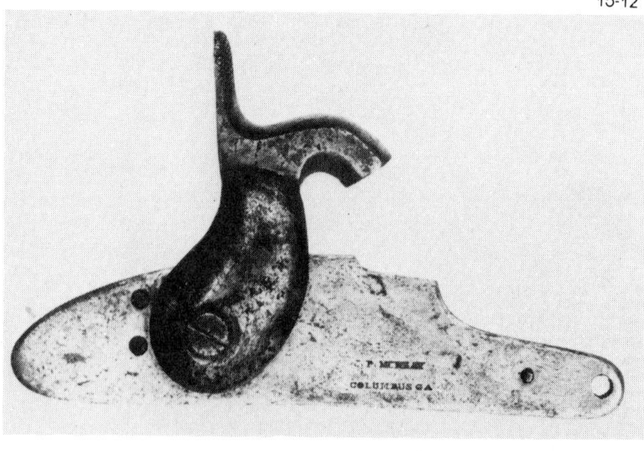

15-12 J. P. Murray (Greenwood & Gray) Alabama Contract Rifles

OL: 48½''
BL: 29⅞''

BD: .58 cal.
Furniture: brass
Lockplate: flat, beveled edge
Markings: "J.P. MURRAY/COLUMBUS, GA" forward of hammer

Finish: "browned"
Configuration: round
Sights: rear—open "V" c. 3" from breech; front—brass blade
Fastenings: 2 brass bands, the upper double strapped
Markings: "PRO./F.C.H." on upper left surface, near breech, or "ALA. (date)"

The firm of Eldridge S. Greenwood and William C. Gray of Columbus, Ga. (of which John P. Murray was master armorer) had contracts with both the Confederate government and the state of Alabama. In 1863-64 the firm delivered 262 rifles as part of its Alabama contract, but total quantities manufactured are unknown. **(D)**

---

16 U.S. Military Rifle-Muskets

The United States made extensive and highly favorable tests on the French "Minie ball" design at Harpers Ferry in 1852-53, and in 1854 adopted it for the .54 cal. U.S. M1841 rifle. The tests had shown that a bore closer to that adopted by the English in 1853 (.577 cal.) was nearer the ideal. Accordingly, when a new series of arms, consisting of a pistol-carbine for the mounted service, a short rifle for the engineers and rifle-corps, and a rifle-musket for the line infantry, was proposed, a new bore of .58 caliber was chosen. The government, having also secured unrestricted rights to the Maynard tape primer in 1854, incorporated this feature into the locks of all the new arms.

The prime infantry arm of this new series was manufactured solely at the two national armories at Harpers Ferry and Springfield. Due to the exacting tolerances adopted to achieve perfect interchangeability, no contractors were willing to undertake the new series. As a result, the militia was unable to obtain any of the new arms until political pressure forced the War Department to yield in the late 1850s. In the interim, a few minor cosmetic changes took place in the rifle and rifle-musket, primarily affecting the furniture and rear sights.

With the outbreak of the Civil War, Harpers Ferry armory was partially destroyed. Virginia moved the salvage rifle-musket machinery to Richmond where it was employed throughout the war to make an arm that followed the pattern of the modified M1855 rifle-musket, minus the complex Maynard primer. Springfield, to decrease production time, also eliminated this primer in 1861. In the same year, after consultations with Samuel Colt, a special model rifle-musket was devised that further decreased production time and costs. Although produced on contracts issued in 1861, these improvements were not incorporated into Springfield's production until a new model was approved in 1863. Although Springfield's production greatly increased, it was, nevertheless, also necessary to grant contracts to private firms for rifle-muskets. Over 1½ million of these arms were contracted for in the first year of the war alone. Although many makers defaulted, the net result was not only to provide the Union Army with its prime fighting weapon, but to reinforce the necessity

for tolerances and interchangeability among American manufacturers.

16-O U.S. M1855 Rifle-Muskets Type II (color plate, above)

OL: 56″
BD: .58 cal.; 3-groove rifling
Furniture: iron
Patchbox: iron, 2-piece, hinged forward
Lockplate: (incorporating Maynard primer), flat, beveled edge
Markings: eagle on primer door; "U.S./SPRINGFIELD" or "U.S./HARPERS FERRY" forward of hammer; date on rounded tail

BL: 40″
Finish: "bright"
Configuration: round, long-range, 1$\frac{5}{16}$″ stepped
Sights: rear—base with two leaves, dovetailed and screwed to barrel 2¾″ from breech; front—iron block/blade
Fastenings: 3 iron bands, marked "V"
Markings: "V", "P", and eagle head on upper left facet; date on top near breech

The major distinguishing characteristics are the change to the new 2-leaf rear sight adopted in 1858 and the addition of an iron grease box of the U.S. M1855 rifle configuration. A transitional variant will be found utilizing a brass nosecap. A total of 3,680 were made at Harpers Ferry and 22,394 were manufactured at Springfield. **(B)**

Springfield U.S. M1861 Rifle-Muskets, Types I (color plate, below) **& II**

OL: 56″
BD: .58 cal.; 3-groove rifling
Furniture: iron
Lockplate: flat, beveled edge
Markings: eagle and "U.S./SPRINGFIELD" forward of hammer on rounded tail

BL: 40″
Finish: "bright"
Configuration: round
Sights: rear—(I) U.S. M1858 rear sight; (II) U.S. M1861 rear sight, screwed and dovetailed 2¾″ from breech; front—iron block/blade
Fastenings: 3 iron bands, marked "U"
Markings: "V", "P", and eagle head on upper left facet, date on top near breech

The prime difference between the M1858 and the M1861 rear sight base is the addition of reinforcing metal to the section around the screw holes for the leaf screw. A total of 265,129 of these essentially simplified M1855, type II rifle-muskets were made between 1861-63. **(A)**

16-1 U.S. M1855 Rifle-Muskets, Type I

OL: 56″
BD: .58 cal.; 3-groove rifling
Furniture: iron, except brass nosecap
Lockplate: (incorporating Maynard primer), flat, beveled edge
Markings: eagle on primer door; "U.S./SPRINGFIELD" or "U.S./HARPERS FERRY" forward of hammer; date on rounded tail

BL: 40″
Finish: "bright"
Configuration: round
Sights: rear—long-range, 2$\frac{7}{16}$″ base with folding tangent ladder, dovetailed and screwed to barrel 5½″ from breech; front—iron block/blade
Fastenings: 3 iron bands, marked "V"
Markings: "V", "P", and eagle head on upper left facet; date on top near breech

Although three sample arms were made prior to July, 1856, production did not commence at Springfield until fiscal year 1856-57 or at Harpers Ferry until the following fiscal year. Including the sample arms, 24,721 type I rifle-muskets were produced at Springfield; another 15,071 were manufactured at Harpers Ferry. **(C)**

16-2

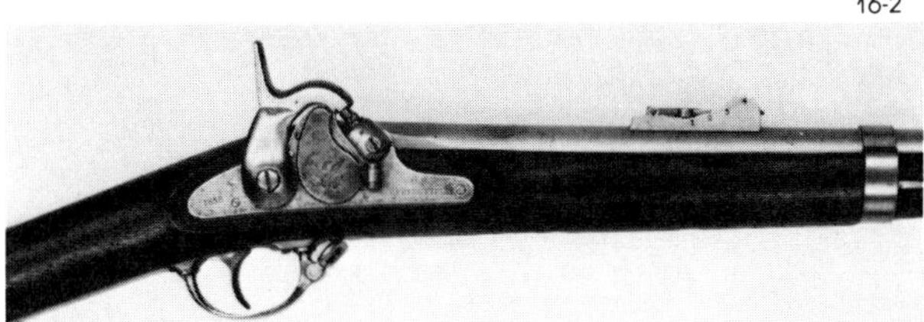

16-2 U.S. M1858 Cadet Rifle-Muskets, Type I

OL: 53″
BD: .58 cal.; 3-groove rifling
Furniture: iron, except brass nosecap
Lockplate: (incorporating Maynard primer), flat, beveled edge
Markings: eagle on primer door; "U.S./SPRINGFIELD" forward of hammer; "1858" on rounded tail
BL: 38″
Finish: "bright"
Configuration: round, long-range, $2\frac{7}{16}$″ base
Sights: rear—with folding tangent ladder, dovetailed and screwed to barrel $5\frac{1}{2}$″ from breech; front—iron block/blade
Markings: "V." "P", and eagle head on upper left facet; "1858" on top near breech

Cadet rifle muskets totaling 1,502 and agreeing to the characteristics of the type I rifle-musket except for the shortened barrel and stock were manufactured solely at Springfield in 1858. **(D)**

16-3

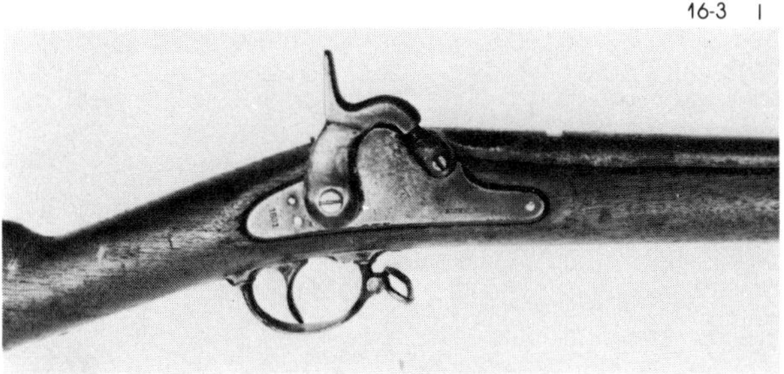

16-3 Richmond Confederate Rifle-Muskets, Types I-III

OL: 56″
BD: .58 cal.; 3-groove rifling
Furniture: iron, except copper alloy buttplate and nosecap on types II and III, the former marked "C.S.A." on tang
Lockplate: flat, beveled edge
Markings: (I) "RICHMOND, VA." forward of hammer, "1861" on
BL: 40″
Finish: "bright"
Configuration: round
Sights: rear—U.S. M1858-style screwed and dovetailed $2\frac{3}{4}$″ from breech; front—iron block/blade
Fastenings: 3 iron bands, marked "U"

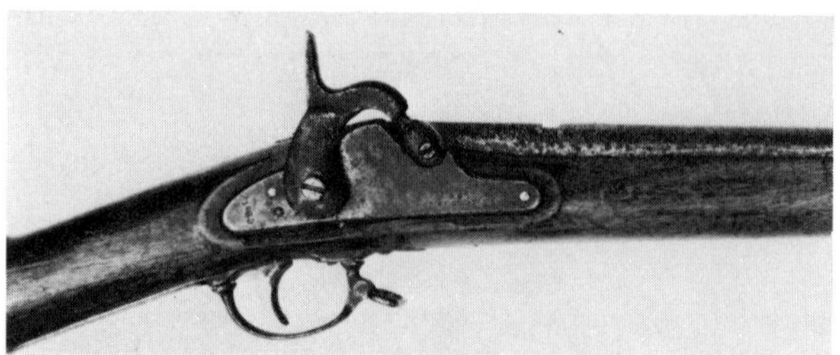

III

rounded tail; (II & III) "C.S./ RICHMOND, VA." forward of hammer, date on rounded tail

Markings: "V", "P", and eagle head on upper left facet; date on top near breech

Types I and II have the "high hump" lockplates unmilled for the Maynard tape primer, distinguished from one another by their different marking. Type III has a "low hump" lockplate. Due to the use of parts captured at Harpers Ferry and elsewhere, furniture variations are common. **(C)**

William Hahn/C.H. Funk 16-4

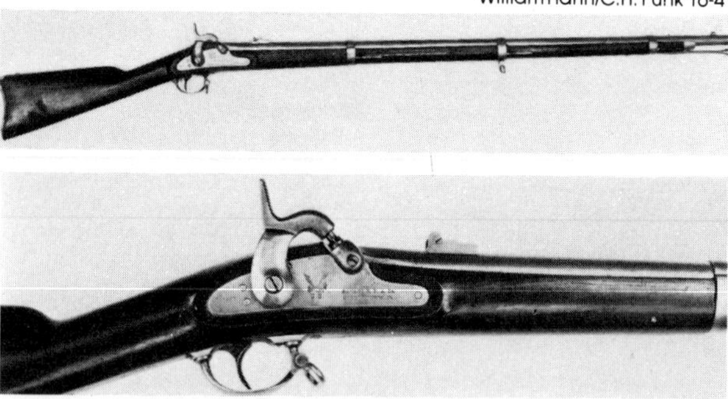

Savage

16-4 U.S. M1861 Contract Rifle-Muskets

Between 1861-65 private arms contractors in the North delivered no fewer than 643,439 rifle-muskets, primarily of the U.S. M1861 types I or II (depending on when a sample from Springfield had been furnished.) These arms differ from the Springfield M1861 rifle-musket only in the lock marking. Contractors' markings are as follows: 1. eagle and "U.S./ EAGLEVILLE"; 2. eagle and "U.S." and "C.H. FUNK/SUHL" under barrel; 3. eagle and "U.S./WATERTOWN"; 4. eagle and "U.S./BRIDESBURG/1861" or "U.S./BRIDESBURG" or "U.S./PHILADELPHIA" and date "1862"; 5. eagle and "U.S./JAS. D. MOWRY/NORWICH, CONN."; 6. "(eagle)/U.S." and "W[M] MUIR & CO./WINDSOR LOCKS, CT." or eagle and "U.S./WINDSOR LOCKS" and date "1863"; 7. "(eagle)/U.S." and "PARKERS' SNOW & CO./MERIDEN, CONN." and "1863"; 8. eagle and "U.S./NORWICH"; 9. "U.S./eagle" and "PARKERS' SNOW & CO./MERIDEN, CONN." and "1864"; 10. eagle and "U.S./PROVIDENCE", "1862", "U. (eagle) S./PROVIDENCE TOOL C[O]/PROVIDENCE R I"; 11. "(eagle) U.S." and "REMINGTON'S/ILION, N.Y."; 12. "(eagle)/U.S." and "U.A.CO. /NEW YORK:, "(eagle)/U.S." and "E. ROBINSON/NEW YORK", "1863", "(eagle)/U.S." and "(arched) E. ROBINSON/NEW YORK"; 13. eagle and "U.S./NEW YORK/1862"; 14. "(eagle)/U.S." and "SAVAGE.R.F.A. C^O/ MIDDLETOWN, CON."; 14. eagle and "U.S./C.D. SCHUBARTH/PROVIDENCE"; 15. eagle and "U.S./TRENTON"; 16. eagle (old style) and "U.S. /MILLBURY", "1864"; 17. eagle and "U.S./NORFOLK"; 18. "(eagle)/U.S." and "WHITNEYVILLE" or eagle with panoply of flags over "WHITNEYVILLE", "1863." **(A-E, depending on lock markings)**

16-5

16-5 U.S. M1861 New Jersey Contract Rifle-Muskets

In 1863-64 New Jersey contracted with three firms for 10,000 rifle-muskets. Of these, 2,200 delivered by Perkins & Livingston (Meridian Arms Co.) were Savage contract arms and marked identically to their federal contract; similarly, 5,300 delivered by the Trenton Arms Co. were identically marked to the federal contract arms. The 2,500 delivered by Schuyler, Hartley, & Graham of New York, however, were U.S. M1861 Special Model rifle-muskets manufactured by Colt and identical to those delivered under his federal contracts. All arms were surcharged with block letters "N.J." on the left side of the barrel and in the stock opposite the lockplate. The two oval cartouches with script inspectors' initials will not be found on the stock on the left side. **(B)**

16-6 U.S. M1861 New York Contract Rifle-Muskets

Consequent to the draft riots of July, 1863, New York purchased 8,000 M1861 rifle-muskets (probably 2nd class arms or federal contract rejects) from five New York City dealers. Of these, only William Muir was a manufacturer who undoubtedly delivered his own (1,000) products. In view of the New Jersey contracts, another of the dealers, Schuyler, Hartley & Graham, probably delivered Colt M1861 Special Model rifle-muskets. Precisely what the others delivered remains unknown since New York did not surcharge the arms. Like the New Jersey arms, these rifle-muskets should not have the inspectors' initials in cartouches on the left side of the stock opposite the lockplate. In 1864-65 another 2,000 each were purchased from William Muir in two lots, again both probably with his markings. **(A-D, depending on lock markings)**

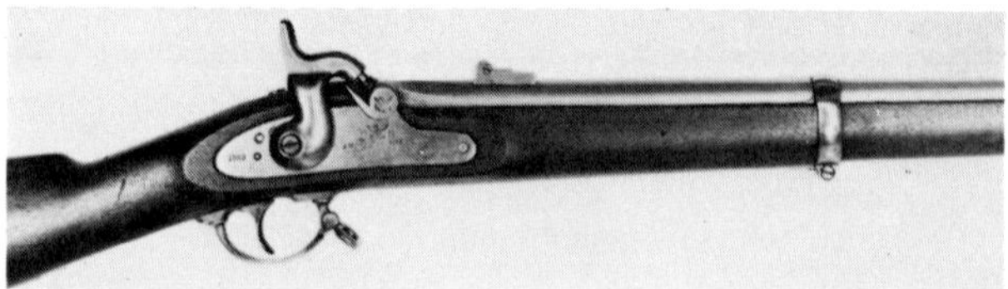

16-7 U.S. M1861 Special Model Rifle-Muskets

As a result of contacts between Colt and the master armorers of Springfield in 1861, it was determined that several changes might be made in the U.S. M1861 rifle-musket to speed and simplify its production. The resulting arm differs from the M1861 in three details, all other specifications being the same as the U.S. M1861. The lockplate was made of a slightly different configuration and utilized an "S"-shaped hammer instead of one that had been devised to curl around the Maynard primer. The bolster was shorter with a flat exterior surface and did not have a clean-out screw. Finally, the three iron bands were split, rounded screw-clamping instead of secured by band springs forward of the bands. This arm was produced only on contract with the following markings: 1. "U (eagle S./AMOSKEAG MFG. CO./MANCHESTER, N.H."; 2. eagle on bolster face and "U.S./COLT'S P^T F.A. M^FG C^O/HARTFORD C^T"; 3. eagle on bolster face and "U.S./L.G-&Y. WINDSOR-V^T", "(eagle)/U.S.", and L.G. & Y./WINDSOR-V^T"; "U.S./E.G. LAMSON & CO./ WINDSOR VT.", "1865". **(A-D, depending on lock markings)**

16-8 Springfield U.S. M1863 Rifle-Muskets, Type I

In 1863 the alterations suggested by Colt in 1861 were incorporated into the Springfield production with the exception of the lockplate which remained exactly the same configuration as the U.S. M1861. The new hammer, moreover, while "S"-shaped, was flat and faceted rather than rounded like the M1861 Special Model. Like the latter, the U.S. M1863 rifle-musket employed the flat-faced bolster (stamped with an eagle), rounded clamping bands, and a straight, spring-held ramrod. A total of 273,265 were produced in 1863-64. **(B)**

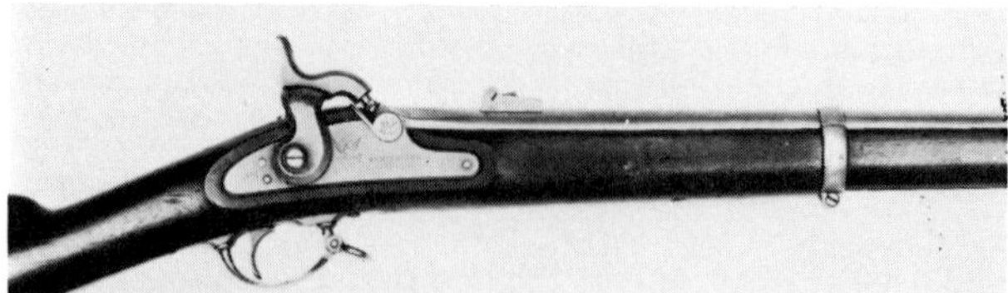

16-9 Remington

16-9 U.S. M1863 Contract Rifle-Muskets, Type I

Only two of the U.S. M1861 contract rifle-musket manufacturers altered their machinery to produce the new form, type I—Alfred Jenks & Son (eagle and "U.S./BRIDESBURG") and E. Remington & Sons ("[eagle]/ U.S." and "REMINGTON'S/ILION, N.Y.") **(D)**

16-10 U.S. M1863 Massachusetts Contract Rifle-Muskets, Type I

In 1863 Massachusetts bought 13,000 of these arms from Samuel Norris and W.T. Clement of Springfield. They were identical to the Springfield Armory and contract rifle-muskets of this type except for lock marking, which read: "(eagle)/U.S." and "S.N. &W.T.C./FOR/MASSACHUSETTS" forward of the hammer and the date on the tail. The inspector's initials "L.F.R." appeared on the left facet of the barrel instead of upon the stock. **(C)**

16-11 Springfield U.S. M1863 Rifle-Muskets, Type II

Because the screw-fastened clamping bands of the U.S. M1863 type I rifle-musket had a habit of loosening after repeated firing, it was decided in 1863 to revert to the solid, spring band-fastened barrel bands. The new solid bands, however, were rounded like the M1863 (I) and M1861 Special Model rifle-muskets. A total of 255,040 of these were produced only at Springfield during 1864-65. A new pierced single-leaf rear sight was adopted at the same time but was not installed on any of the arms until the close of the War. To distinguish this arm from the M1863, it has often been called the U.S. M1864. 25,000 of these were altered to breechloaders in 1866 and more during subsequent years. **(A)**

---

17 | Special Contract Military Rifle-Muskets

The outbreak of the Crimean War in 1854 significantly affected the American private arms industry. Some firms sought quick profits by upgrading obsolete muskets to sell. In the case of Robbins & Lawrence, however, it was a different matter. The firm had already impressed the English by their display of interchangeable firearms at the 1851 Crystal Palace Exposition. They received a contract (together with a false promise for a larger one) to produce the recently adopted English P1853 rifle-musket. The Crimean War ended, however, before the contract could be completed. And, because Robbins & Lawrence had delivered its initial shipments late, substantial penalties were invoked that bankrupted the firm. The English government ran the firm briefly, but, after producing a few thousand extra weapons, sold the plant and some of its machinery. Many of the firm's rifle-muskets returned to America in 1861 when Northern state purchasing agents and speculators scoured Europe for anything that would shoot.

Eli Whitney, Jr. was one of the parties to purchase some of Robbins & Lawrence's machinery. He had already suffered losses on his rigidly gauged U.S. M1841 rifle contracts, and the misfortune of the other firm (also caused in part by the gauging system) convinced him that he could not profit by making military longarms to the government's strict codes of uniformity. Instead, he turned to an inexpensive series of longarms whose cost and immediate availability appealed to the state militias, especially those of the South then girding for conflict. His first products were a cross between the U.S. M1855 and the English P1853 rifle-muskets, using also as much of his old M1841 rifle machinery as could be modified. His later products more closely approach the regulation U.S. M1861 rifle-musket, which he eventually did produce on the interchangeable basis.

The beginning of the Civil War caused a number of other gunmakers to produce their own rifle-muskets for the militias. Most who did so were located around Philadelphia and took advantage of surplus or rejected armory rifle or musket parts to quickly assemble small quantities. One of those who initially made arms in this manner was Philip S. Justice of Philadelphia, and he eventually secured a federal contract for 4,000 rifle-muskets.

17-O P.S. Justice Rifle-Muskets, Types III (color plate, above) **& II**

OL: 55″
BD: .69 cal., 3-groove rifling
Furniture: brass (triggerguard) with indented bow)
Patchbox: brass, 2-piece, hinged forward
Lockplate: flat
Markings: "P.S. JUSTICE/PHILADA" forward of hammer

BL: 39″
Finish: "browned"
Configuration: round, bayonet lug on bottom near muzzle
Sights: rear—(II) U.S. M1842 rifled musket, (III) U.S. M1858 rifle-musket; front—brass blade or iron block/blade
Fastenings: (II) 3 pins; (III) 3 brass bands
Markings: "P.S. JUSTICE/ PHILADA." on top

Except for a very few pin-fastened variants (II), the majority of the 2,174 rifle-muskets received in 1861 from Justice were the newly-made III variation. Most of Justice's arms were issued to the 58th, 88th, and 95th Pennsylvania Volunteers, who vociferiously complained of their poor quality of workmanship. **(C)**

P.S. Justice

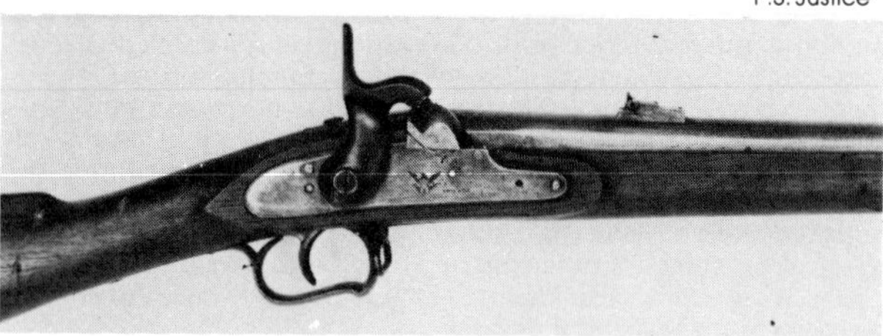

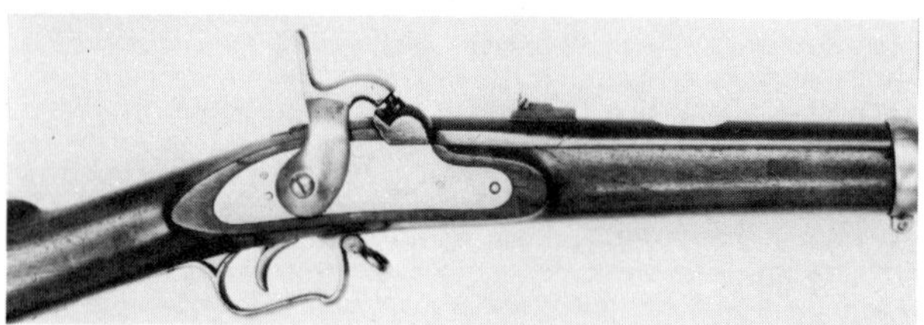

P.S. Justice

Orison Blunt "Enfield" Rifle-Muskets (color plate, below)

OL: 56″
BD: .58 cal., 3-groove rifling
Furniture: brass, except iron bands
Lockplate: flat
Markings: usually unmarked;

BL: 40″
Finish: "blued"
Configuration: round
Sights: rear—English-style long-range (2½″ long) base soldered and screwed 4⅜″ from

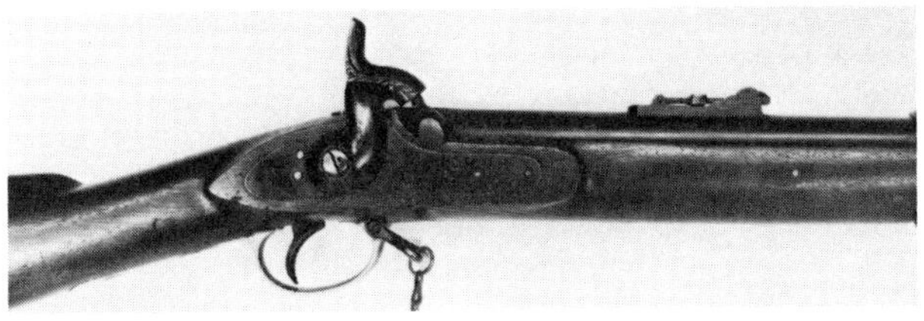

very few with "1862/UNION" forward of hammer and eagle on rounded tail

breech; front—iron block/blade
Fastenings: 3 iron bands
Markings: "DP/B" in oval near breech

Orison Blunt received a contract from the U.S. in 1861 for 20,000 American-made "Enfield-pattern" rifle-muskets. Only 500 were completed in May, 1862, when the government cancelled his contract because he had failed to have the arms properly proofed. **(E)**

17-1

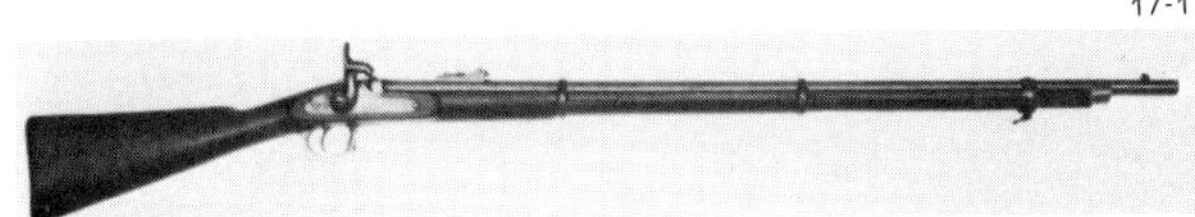

17-1 Robbins & Lawrence "Windsor" English P1853 Rifle-Muskets

OL: 55"
BD: .577 cal., 3-groove rifling
Furniture: brass, except iron bands
Lockplate: flat
Markings: "(date)/WINDSOR" and crowned arrow forward of hammer; crown on rounded tail

BL: 39"
Finish: "bright"
Configuration: round
Sights: rear—Enfield-pattern long-range base (2¼" long) soldered 3½" from breech; front—iron block/blade
Fastenings: 3 iron bands, the upper wider secured by spring bands
Markings: crowned "A/(numeral)" and crowned arrow near breech

In 1855 Robbins & Lawrence of Windsor, Vt. entered into a contract with Fox, Henderson & Co. (representing the British War Dept.) for 25,000 P1853 English rifle-muskets. Due to delays in obtaining gauges, production was delayed and the firm was forced to cease production in bankruptcy after delivering only 10,400. Agents of the British government ran the firm until mid-1858, making an additional 5,600. **(C)**

17-2 Whitney "Long Enfield" Militia Rifle-Muskets, Types I & II

OL: 56"
BD: .58 cal., 7-groove rifling
Furniture: brass, except pewter (Enfield-style)nosecap and iron bands and triggerguard strap (bow is brass)
Lockplate: flat

BL: 40"
Finish: "browned"
Configuration: round
Sights: rear—(see comments); front—iron block/blade
Fastenings: 3 iron bands, the upper wider

Markings: "E. WHITNEY" forward of hammer

Markings: serial code (letter over numbers) near muzzle

Most type I have the Whitney long-range tangent rear sight (2¼" long base) screwed and dovetailed to the barrel 5⅝ from breech. Later production (II) used the smaller (1¼" long) base supporting the single-leaf sight with 300-yard pierced window dovetailed and screwed to the barrel 2¾" from the breech. In addition to 2,000 sold to Maryland and 100 purchased by the federal government in 1861, small numbers are believed to have been sold to Georgia and Mississippi (about 75), respectively in 1860 and 1861. **(C)**

17-3

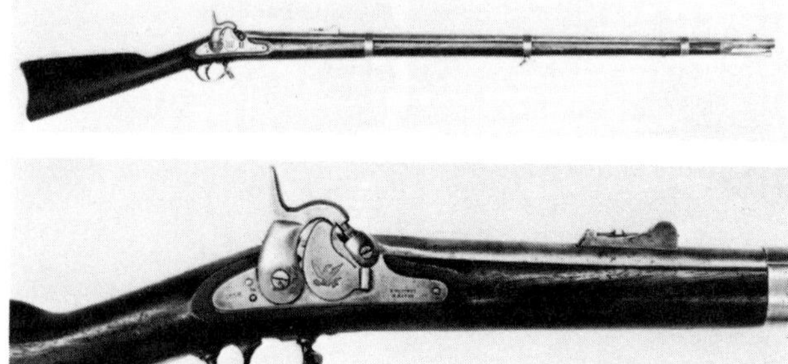

17-3 Whitney M1855 Derivative Rifle-Muskets

OL: 56"
BD: .58 cal., 7-groove rifling
Furniture: iron, except for pewter nosecap and brass ferrules, both Enfield-style
Lockplate: (incorporating Maynard primer), flat, beveled edge
Markings: eagle on primer door; "E. WHITNEY/N. HAVEN" forward of hammer; date (either "1858" or "1859") on rounded tail

BL: 40"
Finish: "bright"
Configuration: round
Sights: rear—Whitney long-range tangent sight dovetailed and screwed 5⅝" from breech; front—iron block/blade
Fastenings: 3 iron bands
Markings: serial code (letter over numbers) near muzzle

Using the same barrels that he produced for his "Enfield" militia rifles and rifle-muskets as well as his early Connecticut contract production, Whitney assembled a very few rifle-muskets incorporating the Maynard tape primer. The locks on these arms usually are flawed, suggesting that Whitney may have purchased U.S. Armory rejects and marked them with his name. Ramrods have brass heads. **(E)**

17-4 Whitney M1861 Derivative Connecticut Contract Rifle-Muskets

OL: 56"
BD: .58 cal., 7-groove rifling; later 3-groove
Furniture: iron, except pewter U.S. M1861-style nosecap
Lockplate: flat, beveled edge

BL: 40"
Finish: "bright"
Configuration: round
Sights: rear—(see comments); front—iron block/blade
Fastenings: 3 iron bands

Markings: (early) "E. WHITNEY/ N. HAVEN" forward of hammer; (later) large eagle with panoply of flags over "WHITNEY VILLE", date "1863" occasionally on rounded tail

Markings: "G.W.Q." on upper left facet; "V", "P", and eagle head on upper left surface; serial code near muzzle

Early production used the 1¼"-long Whitney M1858-type base, while later production used an unstepped 1$^{5}/_{16}$"-long Whitney variant of the M1861 base, both with a single leaf pierced with a 300-yard window, dovetailed and screwed 2¾" from the breech. A total of 14,077 of these were purchased by Connecticut in 1861-62. **(C)**

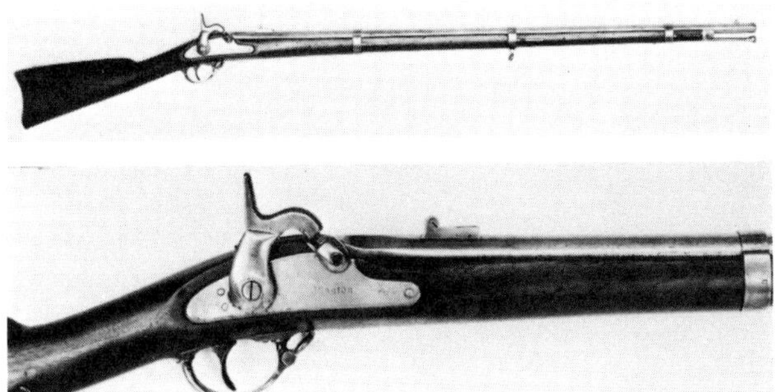

17-5 Whitney "Manton" M1861 Derivative Rifle-Muskets

OL: 56"
BD: .58 cal., 3-groove rifling
Furniture: iron, except pewter (M1861-style) nosecap
Lockplate: flat, beveled edge
Markings: "Manton" in old English letters forward of hammer; "1862" on rounded tail

BL: 40"
Finish: "bright"
Configuration: round
Sights: rear—M1861 Whitney base with single leaf with pierced window dovetailed and screwed 2¾" from breech; front—iron block/ blade
Fastenings: 3 iron bands
Markings: "G.W.Q. on upper left facet; "V" and "P" on top, near breech; serial code near muzzle

These were second-class arms made under Whitney's Connecticut contracts and marketed in New York to Fitch & Waldo under the spurious "Manton" trademark. A total of 1,385 were purchased by Fitch & Waldo, who probably moved them to other dealers. **(D)**

17-6 Whitney "High-hump" M1861 Derivative Rifle-Muskets

OL: 56"
BD: .58 cal., 3-groove rifling
Furniture: iron
Lockplate: flat, beveled edge
Markings: "E. WHITNEY/N.

BL: 40"
Finish: "bright"
Configuration: round
Sights: rear—U.S. M1861 rifle-musket; front—iron block/blade

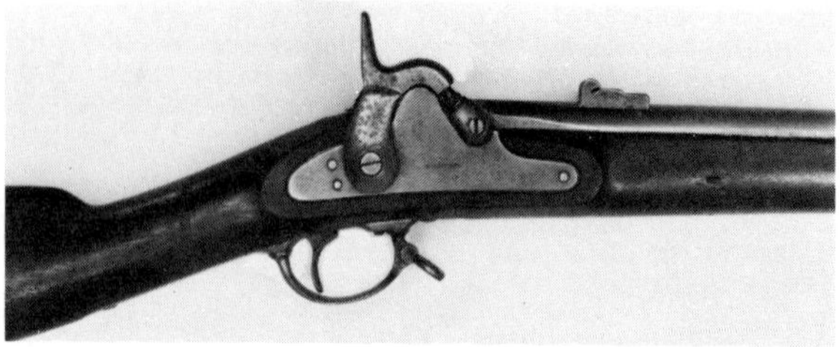

HAVEN" forward of hammer

Fastenings: 3 iron bands, marked "V"
Markings: "V", "P" and eagle head on upper left facet near breech

The extremely few surviving arms of this type are direct copies of the U.S. M1861 rifle-musket in all respects except the lockplate. This is a U.S. M1855 blank unmilled for the Maynard tape primer. **(F)**

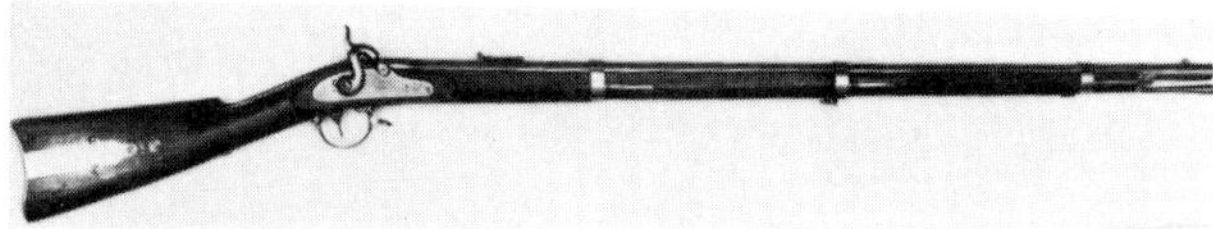

17-7

17-7 J. H. Krider Rifle-Muskets

OL: 56"
BD: .69 cal., 3-groove rifling
Furniture: iron, except brass patchbox and nosecap
Patchbox: brass, 2-piece hinged forward
Lockplate: flat
Markings: "KRIDER"

BL: 40"
Finish: "bright"
Configuration: round
Sights: rear—dovetailed block supporting folding ladder c. 5" from breech; front—iron block/blade
Fastenings: 3 iron bands
Markings: none

John H. Krider of Philadelphia probably made no more than 200 of these arms for departing Pennsylvania three-month's militia in 1861. The triggerguards may have been made for the U.S. M1842 musket. **(F)**

---

18 Percussion Sporting Rifles

Long before the military adopted the percussion ignition system for either smoothbore or rifled muzzleloaders, the civilian makers and their buyers fully accepted the new system. By the 1840s independent gunmakers were producing full stock rifles in original percussion. The more qualified gunsmiths built the new rifles with the "patent" breech that had originated on the Continent. This breechpiece with integral percussion bolster (often with a clean-out screw)

screwed very tightly into the open breech end of the barrel. "Country" gunsmiths made their new percussion arms in the same manner that they had used to alter flintlocks, i.e., simply by screwing a drum bolster into the side of the barrel in lieu of a vent.

With the great western expansion into the Ohio, Mississippi, and Missouri River valleys, a new demand for rifles emerged. Durability and economy guided the production of the "western" gunmakers; ornamentation was discarded and stocks became thicker and straighter. The resulting full stock rifle, otherwise generally following the lines of its Pennsylvania ("Kentucky") forebears, became known as the "plain rifle." In the border states, particularly Kentucky and Tennessee, the patchbox was even eliminated or occasionally supplanted with a simple "grease" hole in the buttstock side. Regional styles in rifle making developed in older parts of the "West" as well. In the northern Ohio Valley and the Great Lakes area, the full stock rifle gave way to the half-stocked ribbed version that had been popular in New England. These regional developments were influenced by the contributions of various ethnic groups in the 1840s. The Germans in particular brought with them their own preferences in design for both hunting and target shooting.

The great post-Civil War emphasis on breechloading cartridge arms, surprisingly, did not totally destroy the popularity of the muzzleloading rifle. In fact there was a great proliferation of such arms in the twenty years after the war, made all the more economical by the introduction of standardized, inexpensive locks, furniture, and fittings from such eastern establishments as E. K. Tryon & Co. of Philadelphia and J. H. Johnson's Great Western Gun Works and James Bown's Enterprise Gun Works, both of Pittsburgh. The availability of inexpensive quality parts permitted the local assemblers to spend more time refining their barrel making and decorating techniques, creating a "Silver Age" in American rifle making.

18-O Amory Half-Stock Percussion Hunting Rifles (color plate, above)

OL: 49¼″
BD: .45 cal., 5-groove rifling
Furniture: German silver
Patchbox: German silver, 2-piece, hinged to rear
Lockplate: Backaction, flat
Markings: only engraving
BL: 33″
Finish: "browned"
Configuration: octagonal (with patent breech)
Sights: rear—sliding open "V" 8″ from breech; front—brass bead
Fastenings: single wedge
Markings: "AMORY" and "FOND DU LAC WIS" and serial no. on top; serial no. and "AMORY" on muzzle face

This rifle is typical of the better quality handmade (and accordingly all different) hunting rifles popular in the upper Midwest during the 1870s and '80s. The furniture includes a decorative inlay of a deer on the cheekpiece, reminiscent of the designs of the Pennsylvania "Golden Age" rifles. Although the "bar lock" or "frontaction" lock was more common, the backaction lock came into its own during this period. **(B)**

W. H. Hyatt Half-Stock Percussion Hunting Rifles (color plate, below)

OL: 48½″
BD: .46 cal., 6-groove rifling
Furniture: brass, except pewter nosecap
BL: 32⅜″
Finish: "browned"
Configuration: octagonal
Sights: rear—open "buckhorn"

Patchbox: brass, 2-piece, hinged forward
Lockplate: flat
Markings: "MOORE", forward of hammer

7⅞" from breech; front—brass blade, dovetailed
Fastenings: single wedge
Markings: "1873" on top; "W.H. HYATT (arced)/WIS." and also WARRANTED" on upper right side

This relatively "plain" half-stock rifle with double-set triggers is very typical of the "Yankee"-style hunting rifle assembled in the Great Lakes and Ohio Valley. The lock (Moore was a New York importer) and barrel are English; the furniture may have been obtained from Eastern dealers by Hyatt, who worked in Minnesota. **(A)**

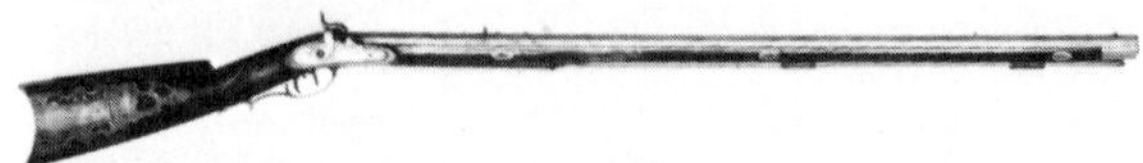

18-1 New York State Full-Stock Percussion Sporting Rifle

OL: 53¾"
BD: .44 cal., 9-groove rifling
Furniture: brass, except German silver wedge ferrules
Patchbox: brass, 2-piece, hinged forward; rococo, pierced support
Lockplate: flat
Markings: "A. BAKER" forward of hammer

BL: 38⅛"
Finish: "bright"
Configuration: octagonal
Sights: rear—open "buckhorn" 6¾" from breech; front—iron blade, dovetailed
Fastenings: 3 wedges
Markings: "BELKNAP" on top

The "Golden Age" of the Pennsylvania rifle ended about 1830 at the same time as the percussion ignition system to sporting arms was introduced. A few of the Eastern rifle makers, however, continued to decorate their original percussion long rifles in the classic manner. As with the Pennsylvania rifles, no two are exactly alike. **(C)**

18-2

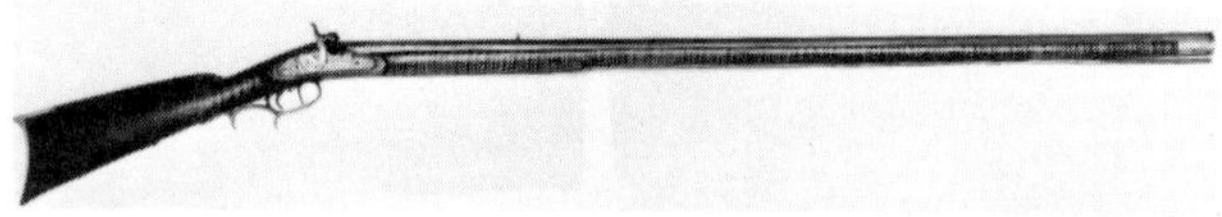

18-2 Kentucky Full-Stock Patent Breech "Plain" Percussion Rifles

OL: 57⅛"
BD: .37 cal., 7-groove rifling
Furniture: brass
Lockplate: flat
Markings: "J. GRIFFITH/LOUISVILLE" forward of hammer

BL: 41⅝"
Finish: "browned"
Configuration: octagonal
Sights: rear—open "buckhorn" 8¾" from breech; front—brass blade
Fastenings: pins
Markings: "N. VOYLES" in script on top

This rifle is typical of the style of "plain" rifle to evolve from the Pennsylvania rifle in Kentucky and Tennessee during the percussion era. No two were made exactly alike, since all were specially ordered by customers with specific requirements. **(B)**

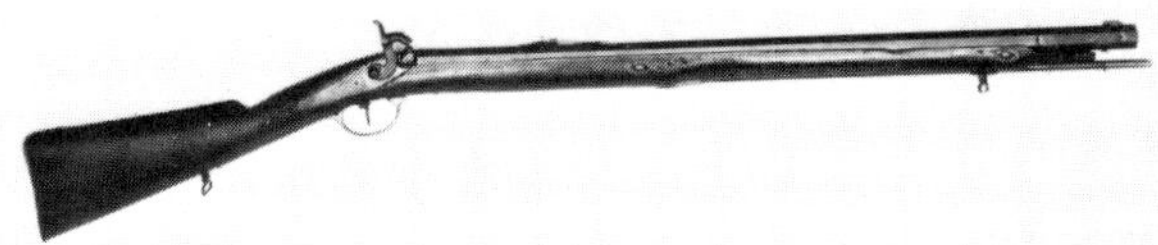

18-3

18-3 W. Kellermann Percussion "Turnverein" Rifles

OL: 45¼"
BD: .44 cal., 7-groove rifling
Furniture: brass
Lockplate: backaction, slightly convex
Markings: "W. KELLERMANN/ CHICAGO ILL." behind hammer
BL: 29½"
Finish: "brown"
Configuration: octagonal with sword ("hirschfanger") lug on right side
Sights: rear—sliding open "V" 5" from breech; front—iron blade, dovetailed
Fastenings: 2 wedges
Markings: none

This rifle typifies the kind made for the German-American "Turnverein" acrobatic/sporting societies during the late 1850s and '60s. The distinctive feature is the long notched bar on the right side of the barrel for the "hirschfanger" sword used in Germany for deer and boar hunting. Most have backaction locks. **(D)**

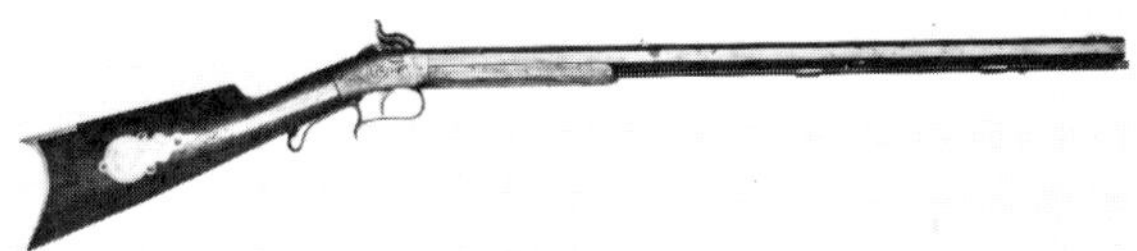

18-4

18-4 G. P. Foster New England Box-lock Percussion Rifles

OL: 43"
BD: .44 cal., 6-groove rifling
Furniture: iron, except nickled brass buttplate and patchbox
Patchbox: nickel-plated, 2-piece, hinged forward
Lockplate: box lock
Markings: none
BL: 27"
Finish: "browned"
Configuration: octagonal
Sights: rear—open "V" 8¼" from breech; front—German silver blade
Fastenings: single wedge, dovetailed
Markings: "Geo. P. Foster/Bristol, R.I." in script and "CAST STEEL" on top; serial no. on upper left side; "B" on left side

Foster made small percussion hunting rifles of this type probably shortly before the Civil War. Serial numbers through 143 have been observed making this one of the few production percussion muzzleloading rifles produced with any degree of uniformity. **(D)**

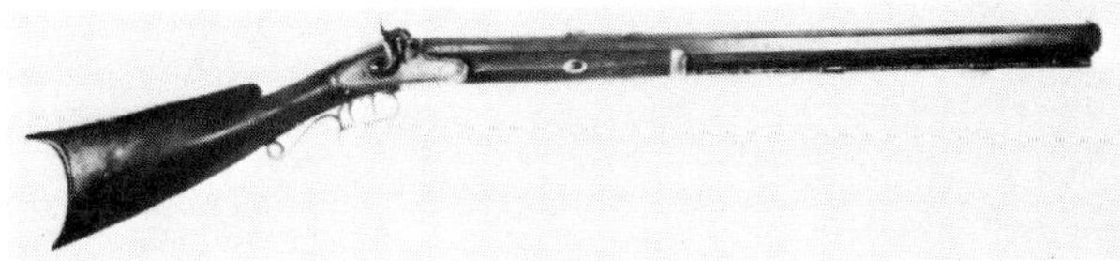

18-5

18-5 Norbert Wesle Half-Stock Percussion Hunting Rifles

OL: 43"
BD: .50 cal., 6-groove rifling
Furniture: iron, except pewter nosecap
Lockplate: flat
Markings: only engraving
BL: 27¾"
Finish: "browned"
Configuration: octagonal, with patent breech
Sights: rear—open "buckhorn" 6" from breech; front—brass blade, dovetailed
Fastenings: single wedge
Markings: "N. WESLE" and "MILWUAKEE" on top

This relatively large caliber rifle exemplifies the higher quality handmade percussion sporting rifle of the 1870s and early '80s. The iron furniture most likely was obtained from Philadelphia or Pittsburgh makers who were mass producing the separate parts for distrbution to the independent makers. Were it not for Wesle's name on the barrel and the single wedge, this rifle might easily be mistaken for a "Plains" rifle (see Section 19). **(B)**

18-6

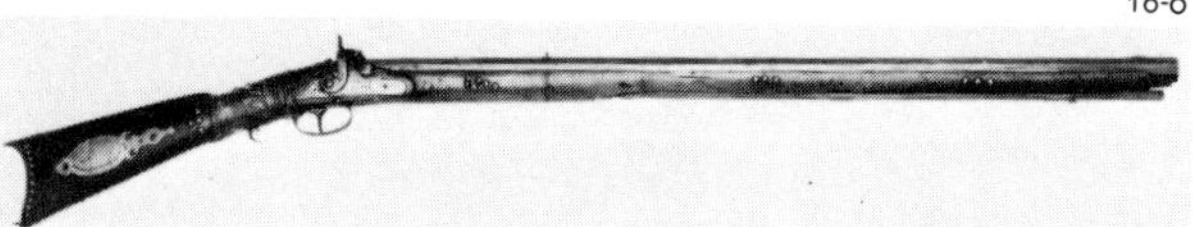

18-6 H. E. Leman Percussion Indian Trade/Treaty "Plain" Rifle

OL: 50½" (shorter versions made)
BD: .54 cal., 7-groove rifling; also made in .52, .54, .58 cal.
Furniture: brass
Patchbox: brass, 2-piece, hinged forward
Lockplate: flat
Markings: "H.E.LEMAN/LANCASTER, PA." forward of hammer
BL: 35⅛" (shorter versions made)
Finish: "bright"
Configuration: octagonal
Sights: rear—open "buckhorn" 8⅛" from breech; front—brass blade, dovetailed
Fastenings: pins
Markings: "H.E.LEMAN", "LANCASTER PA." and "WARRANTED" on top

Leman dominated the manufacture of the Indian Trade/Treaty rifle. The square-faced drum bolsters are original and not an attempt to alter from flintlocks. Leman had extensive U.S. contracts for these rifles, marked "US" in the stock behind the triggerguard strap. He also delivered percussion rifles to Pierre Choteau, Jr. & Co. from 1853 until the 1868 prohibitions on selling weapons to the Indians. Rawhide Indian repairs and brass tack decorations are quite common. **(D)**

---

19 The "Plains" Rifle

Originally known as the "mountain rifle", the "plains rifle" was quite distinct from the "plain", heavy barreled arm actually carried into the Rocky Mountains during the heyday of the fur trade (1828-42). It was, however, a direct descendant of it, modified in the St. Louis area by adopting some of the characteristics of the Ohio Valley/Upper Midwest half-stock rifle. Its prime period of manufacture was

1850-60.

The "plain"-style Pennsylvania rifle had been modified slightly by boring it to 32 gauge (.53 cal.) and, if rebarreled, remounting the old rifle with a new, shorter octagonal barrel having a minimum diameter of 1" across the parallel flats. Such a thick barrel was required to withstand the large powder charge and to absorb the recoil from the large lead ball; the resulting effect was guaranteed to bring down the most dangerous "game" the fur trapper might encounter in the wilds of the Rockies—four-legged or two-legged. The barrels were made shorter than the typical Pennsylvania rifle to permit easy loading and firing from the saddle. The earliest were flintlock, but most were percussion or flintlock altered to percussion with drum bolsters.

The "plains" rifle that evolved from the "mountain" type simply incorporated the heavy, large calibered barrel to a strengthened half-stock configuration. To reinforce the half-stock rifle the stocks were made somewhat thicker and secured to the barrel by means of two wedges through the forestock. Decorative furniture that only served to weaken the stock was kept to a minimum, but the double set triggers were retained. Patchboxes were only applied infrequently. The barrel remained short (34"-38"), at least 1" thick, and .48-.55 cal.

The name frequently associated with both the "mountain" and the "plains" rifles is Hawken. The Hawken brothers, Jacob and Samuel, migrated to St. Louis during the 1820s. Their heavy barreled modifications were renowned among the mountain men. With the end of the rendezvous system in 1842 and Jacob's death in 1849, Samuel turned to the local trade, providing rifles for western immigrants, particularly those headed for the California gold fields. In all likelihood, he developed and commercialized the "plains" rifle, cashing in on the reputation he and his brother had garnered. Other St. Louis makers produced rifles in the same style, though varying according to their taste in furniture and stocking. The Philadelphia gun trade sought to copy the basic features of the rifle and to market it to western-bound immigrants. The Civil War, however, not only shut off the great migration, but also forced the gunmakers of both St. Louis and Philadelphia to turn to other pursuits.

19-O John Krider Presentation "Plains" Rifles (color plate)

OL: 40¾"
BD: .75 cal., 7-groove rifling
Furniture: iron, nosecap and wedge escutcheons, silver-plated
Patchbox: iron, 2-piece, hinged forward
Lockplate: flat
Markings: "JOHN KRIDER/ Philad[a]" forward of hammer

BL: 24¾"
Finish: "browned"
Configuration: octagonal with patent breech
Sights: rear—open "buckhorn" 6⅛" from breech; front—silvered brass blade
Fastenings: 2 wedges
Markings: none

This rifle with double-set triggers is typical of the fine-grade "Plains" rifle that was available from the Eastern rifle establishments of Krider or E. K. Tryon & Son of Philadelphia. This arm bears an 1852 silver presentation escutcheon on the cheekpiece on the left side of the buttstock. The barrel is somewhat shorter than the typical St. Louis "Plains" rifle, and the bore is considerably larger. Note that Tryon also sold furniture separately; the castings are stamped with the name "TRYON" inside. **(D)**

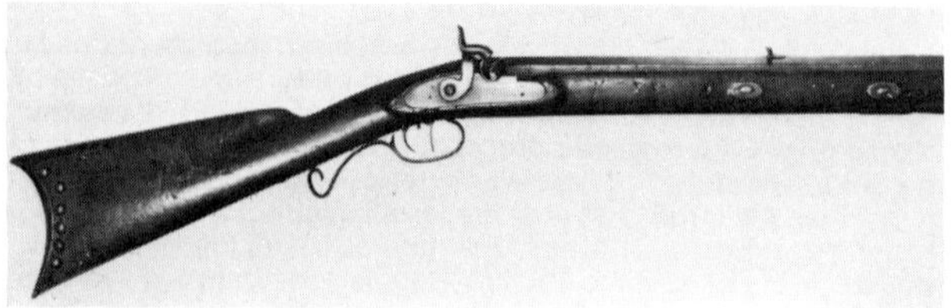

19-1

19-1 S. Hawken "Plains" Rifles

OL: 51½" (+1½")
BD: 48-55 cal., (usually .53), 7-groove rifling
Furniture: iron ("reverse scroll" triggerguard)
Patchbox: infrequent, special order; usually iron, 2-piece, hinged below
Lockplate: flat
Markings: (inside) "T. GIBBONS" "PSJ & Co.", or unmarked

BL: 36" (+1½")
Finish: "browned"
Configuration: octagonal
Sights: rear—open "buckhorn" c. 8" from breech; front—silvered brass blade dovetailed
Fastenings: 2 wedges
Markings: "S. HAWKEN/ST. LOUIS" or "S. HAWKEN ST. LOUIS" on top

The Hawken name was the most famous of the St. Louis makers of "Plains" rifles, In 1862 Samuel Hawken sold his shop to John P. Gemmer who briefly continued to use the Hawken stamp and barrels. **(D)**

19-2 H. E. Dimick "Plains" Rifles

OL: 49"-51"
BD: .48-.54 cal., 7-groove rifling
Furniture: iron ("reverse scroll" triggerguard)
Lockplate: flat
Markings: (inside) "T. GIBBONS" or unmarked

BL: 35"-36"
Finish: "browned"
Configuration: octagonal
Sights: rear—open "buckhorn" c. 8" from breech; front—brass blade dovetailed
Fastenings: 2 wedges
Markings: "H.E.DIMICK/ST LOUIS" or "H.E.DIMICK & CO./ST. LOUIS" on top

Rifles by H. E. Dimick are the best known and closest copies of the Hawken style. Other St. Louis makers, such as R. Beauvis and M. Friede, copied the basic style but modified the stocking or the furniture to suit their preferences. Dimick also made light sporting rifles. **(D)**

---

20 | American Percussion Target Rifles

Target shooting has long been a popular pastime in America. During the 19th century urban shooting clubs or associations were formed to acquire land where the competition could be held without detriment to others. Target competition first evolved in urban New England, and specialized guns were developed there for the sport. More emphasis was placed on the mechanical precision of the sport than its style. The shooter was permitted to assume the position he found most comfortable, utilizing whatever extraneous supports

that might be available. Thus, New England target rifles evolved without special consideration to the weight of the barrel. Indeed, some were truly massive guns that could only be fired from a bench rest. Most, however, were simply heavy barreled rifles, borrowing the English half-stock configuration with a reinforced rib underneath the exposed barrel. This "Yankee" style was brought to the Midwest by New Englanders and there evolved into the half-stock hunting rifle and, eventually, into the "plains" rifle.

To permit uninterrupted open sighting or the mounting of scope sights, many of the heavy bench rifles were made with the hammer underneath the barrel. This convenient method of "hiding" the hammer forward of the trigger assembly developed in the Connecticut River Valley as early as the 1830s, though it was not strictly an American invention. Mechanically, the underhammer guns were much simpler and more economical to make because they required fewer parts. For target shooting this was ideal. Making of the type was centered in New Hampshire and Vermont and took on a regional characteristic, even being adapted to hunting rifles. The influx of German immigrants during the late 1840s and '50s brought a new dimension to target competition. In the European German-speaking states, a style of off-hand target competition had evolved from the medieval crossbow "schuetzenfests." The shooter was required to stand with his rifle without any additional support. As a result, a type of longarm evolved in Europe that took full advantage of every possible body support by molding the stock and its fittings to the shooter. Like the bench rifle, the resulting arm was too awkward and heavy for anything but target competition, but German-American gunmakers in such cities as Philadelphia, Cincinnati, Milwaukee, and St. Louis soon discovered that there was a market for these "schuetzen" rifles and their more pragmatic derivative "light schuetzens."

20-O "Yankee Style" Percussion Target Rifles (color plate, above)

At first glance the "Yankee style" or target rifle looks no different from the half-stock hunting rifle. There are, however, minor differences. The barrel is usually heavier (too heavy for comfortable hunting) while the bores are relatively small (.35 to .45 cal.) in proportion to the barrel diameter. The muzzle itself is often either turned or the face drilled or cupped to accept either a brass bullet starter or a false muzzle. The latter insured that the cylindro-conical projectiles most frequently used in target competition would be properly seated in the rifling before the final ramming process took place. Finally, the rear sights are often more complex than found on the hunting rifle. Often either an open "V" or a short globe sight was mounted on a metal extension that fit the barrel or a peep sight was mounted to the tang of the frame where it joined the buttstock. Because these rifles were handmade, no dimensions can be generalized. Nearly all have doubleset triggers. The example depicted was made by Wells & Hale. **(B)**

Underhammer Target/Hunting Rifles (color plate, middle)

Two characteristics distinguish this rifle. Most evident is the hammer mounted in the frame underneath the barrel just forward of the trigger-guard. A second, less important distinction is the absence of a fore-stock to the relatively short (18"-27") barrel. Most bore diameters range from .39 to .44 caliber. The most prolific makers were D.H. Hilliard in New Hampshire and Nicanor Kendall of Windsor, VT. The latter used prison labor to make his guns to a relatively common style, including a repeating "harmonica" version. The maker of the illustrated example is unknown. **(C)**

"Early Style" American "Schuetzen" Target Rifles (color plate, below)

From the muzzle to the lock, the "Schuetzen" rifle resembles the "Yankee style" target rifle, including provisions for false muzzles and bullet starters. The 27"-30" long, heavy, octagonal barrels were generally cut in either .38, 42, or .44 ca. to the desire of the purchaser. The percussion ignition system was invariably of the "bar lock" type, usually with the improved spring catch. The distinctive characteristics are the intrically molded fingergrips cast into the triggerguard housing and the elongated crescent-shaped buttplate. Finally, the stock immediately forward of the triggerguard was adapted for a detachable extended palm rest. Noted makers include P.H. Klein of New York (depicted), John Wurfflein and Anschutz of Philadelphia, and a host of makers in Cincinnati, St. Louis, and Milwaukee, topped by John Meunier of the last city. The earlier products of these makers are distinguished from the later by the type of furniture employed. See 20-2 for additional furniture distinctions. **(C)**

20-1 New England Bench Match Rifles

Most such arms are distinguished by their heavy, octagonal barrels, usually varying in length only from 30"-33", but giving a total weight to the arm in excess of 15 pounds and not infrequently in excess of 20 pounds! Since this barrel rests on a bench support, no forestock was necessary or provided. Lock actions are either underhammer or more frequently backaction. Rear sights are either elaborate tang-mounted peeps or telescopic tubes running the full length of the barrel. Most were mitted at the muzzle with provision for a false muzzle by drilling four holes that mated four pegs on the face of the false muzzle. Bore diameters varied considerably, but .45-.50 was apparently the most popular based on surviving examples. **(B)**

20-2

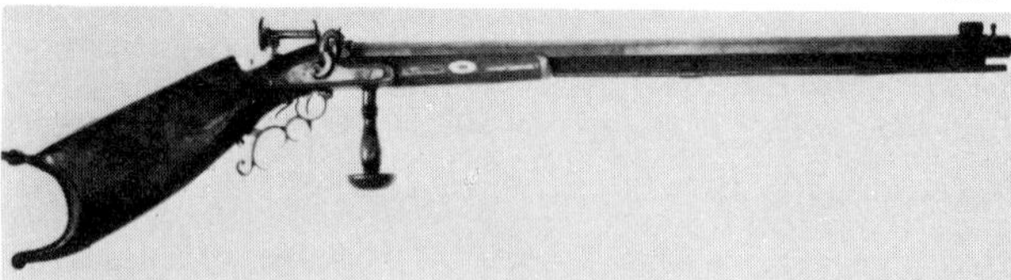

20-2 "Later Style" American "Schuetzen" Target Rifles

Basically the same as the earlier versions in characteristics and measurements, the later arms made in America may be distinguished by the type of buttplate and triggerguard employed. The later furniture was distinguished by a shortened pair of buttplate horns, one of which (the upper) was knobbed and detachable, and by a triggerguard that was more intricately formed for the individual fingers and stradled a setting trigger that dramatically slanted toward the butt. Similarities in the furniture from diverse makers indicate that these patterns were also manufactured for the commercial trade. **(C)**

20-3 Semi- or "Light Schuetzen" Target/Hunting Rifles

The semi- or "light Schuetzen" target rifle was a pragmatic attempt to combine an off-hand target rifle with one that was light enough for hunting. Most resemble half-stock sporting rifles, but the muzzles invariably have been adapted for bullet starters and less frequently for

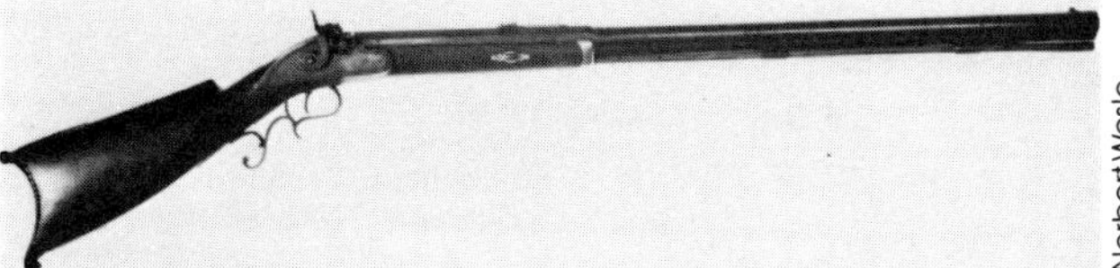
Norbert Wesle

false muzzles required for fine target competition. The buttplates usually have truncated horns in the "Schuetzen" style, and provision is made forward of the triggerguard for a detachable palm rest. The makers of these rifles were usually the same as those who made the "Schuetzen" rifles. Bore diameters are similar to these caliber ranges, but the barrels were made considerably smaller in diameter to lighten the overall rifle. **(C)**

---

21 Multi-Shot, Single-Barrel Muzzleloading Rifles

In April, 1777, Joseph Belton of Philadelphia proposed to the Continental Congress that the Army adopt his improvements in superimposed loaded firearms. Congress authorized him to alter 100 flintlock muskets, but it is not known if any were actually modified. When war with England again erupted in 1812, another Philadelphian, Joseph Chambers, proposed a slightly different superimposed loading and sliding flintlock system that was put into limited service, both with muskets and with multi-barreled swivel guns for ships' gunwhales. A decade later the state of New York pressed the federal government to provide U.S. M1817 "common" rifles altered to the sliding lock, superimposed repeating system that had been patented by Isaiah Jennings in 1821; 520 of these were delivered by Reuben Ellis in 1830. These arms, however, never saw combat service.

The government's final experimentation with superimposed rifles took place during the Civil War. John P. Lindsay had good reason to patent a superimposed loading system in 1860 after his brother had been killed by Indians while attempting to reload a muzzleloader. One thousand muskets based on that patent were ordered by the U.S. government in 1863 and were used in combat. They proved totally unreliable, however, and were quickly relegated to storage.

Although these were the only types of superimposed loading longarms produced in significant quantities to common specifications during the first sixty years of the 19th century, numerous gunmakers toyed with the idea and made individual rifles that incorporated this feature. These were one-of-a-kind, hand-made rifles. Some of these makers took out patents on their improvements, but, except for prototypes, no arms were produced conforming to their patent specifications. Most today are in museums.

21-O Lindsay Repeating Percussion Rifle-Muskets (color plate)

OL: 56"
BD: .58 cal., 3-groove rifling
Furniture: iron
Lockplate: none, mechanism is internal and behind breech
BL: 40"
Finish: "bright"
Configuration: round with patent breech terminating in two cones
Sights: rear—U.S. M1861 rifle-musket; front—iron block/blade
Fastenings: 3 iron bands
Markings: "LINDSAY/PATENT'D OCT. 9. 1860" on top of patent breech

A channel in the patent breech communicates the gases from the percussion cup to ignite the uppermost charge first. In 1863 the U.S. contracted for 1,000, these being delivered in 1864. **(D)**

21-1 I. Jenning/Reuben Ellis Repeating Flintlock Rifles, Types I & II

OL: varies according to charges
BD: .54 cal., 7-groove rifling
Furniture: iron
Patchbox: iron, oval, hinged below
Lockplate: flat, beveled edge; convex tail
Markings: "US/S.NORTH" forward of cock; "MIDD^{TN}/CONN/(date)" on rounded tail
BL: 36"
Finish: "bright"
Configuration: round
Sights: rar—open "V"; front—iron block/blade
Fastenings: 3 iron bands, the upper double strapped
Markings: "US/(inspector's initials —"A.H." or "J.M.")

Isaiah Jennings of New York City patented a superimposed, repeating rifle design in 1821. In 1828 the U.S. contracted with Reuben Ellis for 526 four-shot repeating Ellis rifles for the New York militia. These were assembled by R. & J. D. Johnson of Middletown, Conn. In addition to these 4-shot rifles (I), some were also made in 10-shot configuration (II), similarly utilizing the U.S. M1817 contract rifle as the basis for assembly. **(D)**

22 Multi-Barreled Muzzleloading Rifles and Shotguns

Although the attempts to achieve multiple fire when applied to single-barreled muzzleloaders proved unsuccessful, the goal was attained relatively simply by increasing the number of muzzleloading barrels attached to the same stock. Militarily, this resulted in a heavy weapon impractical for common usage; for sporting purposes, however, specialized needs occasionally permitted the practical use of multiple- (especially double-) barreled guns. The double-barrel muzzleloading percussion shotgun proved extremely popular in America, so it is surprising that so few were made here in the 19th century. A few gunmakers produced a small number of such arms, and at least two New England firms (Allen & Wheelock and Eli Whitney) briefly entered the commercial market. The cause for the disparity between production and demand lay in economics. American firms and gunsmiths (even with the 30% import tariff) could not successfully compete with the light, thin-walled

damascus barreled guns produced in Birmingham, England, and Liège, Belgium. In some instances, American makers simply imported whole guns from these two major sources and surcharged them with their own names.

Although few of these arms were made in the United States, the riflesmiths of New York and the Middle West created a type of double-barreled gun, which, judging from surviving examples, was widely produced (though only commercially by Allen & Wheelock). This was the double-barrel rifle and its cousin, the combination rifle-shotgun. These handmade longarms varied in characteristics from maker to maker. Two basic configurations, nevertheless, prevail in both types. In the most prevalent the two barrels are joined one over the other, invariably in the case of combination arms with the rifle barrel uppermost. In the other, rarer version, the barrels are joined side-by-side like the double-barreled imported shotguns. In their rarest form, three and infrequently four barrels were joined to a single stock. The weight of these arms, however, made them too heavy for hunting. While most of the makers used the conventional percussion lock, a few preferred underhammer mechanisms for over-under combinations.

22-O Side-by-Side Rifle/Shotgun Combinations (A.M. Hagadorn Example) (color plate, above)

OL: 47⅞″
BD: .48 cal. (right); 12 gal. (left)
Furniture: brass
Patchbox: 2-piece, brass, hinged to rear
Lockplate: flat
Markings: "A.M. HAGADORN" forward of hammer

BL: 32″
Finish: "browned"
Configuration: round with rib
Sights: rear—open "V" 7″ from breech; front—German silver blade inset in iron block
Fastenings: single wedge
Markings: "A.M. HAGADORN/ DETROIT, MICH." on rib

This arm typifies the better workmanship of the Midwestern gunsmiths who either were transplanted New Yorkers or who had apprenticed to, or otherwise been influenced by, the Hudson and Mohawk Valley gunsmiths. Side-by-side double rifles of this school are rarer than the combinations, the only prolific makers having been N. Lewis of Troy, N.Y. **(C)**

Over-Under, Rifle/Shotgun Combinations (W. & C. Ogden Example) (color plate, below)

OL: 47½″
BD: 41 cal.; 6-groove rifling (upper); 11 ga. (lower)
Furniture: German silver
Lockplate: backaction, flat
Markings: none

BL: 30″
Finish: "browned"
Configuration: both part round/ part octagonal
Sights: rear—open "V" on strap 6⅜″ from breech; front—brass blade set in dovetailed iron block
Fastenings: none
Markings: "W.&C. OGDEN/ OWEGO, N.Y." on top of upper barrel

The German silver furniture identifies this arm as being of high quality. Quite probably this furniture was commercially purchased from one of the major suppliers of gun parts and furnishings in New York, Philadelphia, or Pittsburgh. The balance of the gun, however, was made by the Ogdens. **(C)**

22-1 E. Allen Double Barrel Shotguns, Types I & II

OL: 49"-52" (I); 41½"-43½" (II)
BD: .12 ga.; .38 cal. if combination rifle/shotgun
Furniture: iron
Lockplate: internal, in iron frame (I); flat (II)
Markings: none (I); "E. ALLEN & CO. MAKERS" (II)

BL: 33¾"-36¾" (I); 26"-28" (II)
Finish: "damascus"
Configuration: round
Sights: rear—none (open "V" if combination); front—bead or blade
Fastenings: locking bolt (I) single wedge (II)
Markings: "ALLEN, THURBER & CO/WORCESTER" or "ALLEN & WHEELOCK/WORCESTER" (I); none (II)

From 1854-71 the successive firms of Allen, Thurber & Co., Allen & Wheelock, and E. Allen & Co. produced a limited number of double-barrel shotguns and combinations. The earlier production was marketed through the firm of William Read & Sons of Boston. **(D)**

22-2 Whitney Double-Barrel Shotgun

OL: 45½"
BD: 20 ga.
Furniture: iron
Lockplate: none, mechanism inside frame
Markings: none

BL: 30"
Finish: "blued"
Configuration: round
Sights: rear—none; front—bead
Fastenings: single wedge
Markings: "WHITNEY ARMS CO. WHITNEY-VILLE, CONN." and "HOMOGENEOUS WROUGHT STEEL" and serial no.

The mechanism was patented in 1866. Production commenced shortly afterward and 997 were made in 1867. Others may have been made before Whitney discontinued production of muzzleloading shotguns in 1869. A single-barrel version was also produced in small numbers utilizing reamed-out Civil War musket barrels. **(D)**

22-3

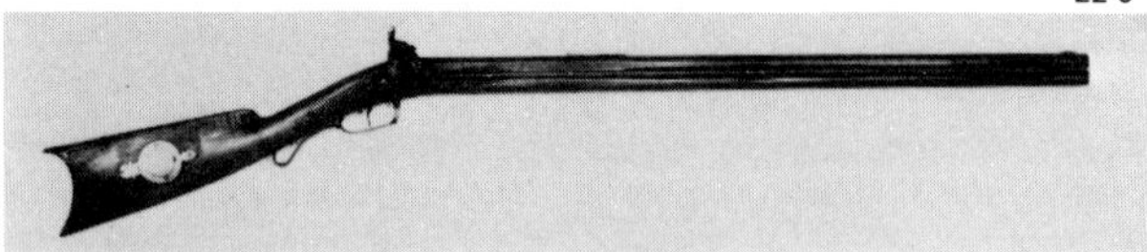

22-3 Over-Under, Rifle-Shotgun Combinations (Baker Example)

OL: 45½"
BD: .45 cal. (upper); 28 ga. (lower)
Furniture: brass
Lockplate: backaction, flat
Markings: "REMINGTON" behind each hammer

BL: 28½"
Finish: "bright"
Configuration: upper, part round/part octagonal; lower, round
Sights: rear—open "V" on strap 6" from breech; front—brass blade set in dovetailed iron block
Markings: "W H BAKER" and "MARATHON, N.Y." on top of rifle barrel

This arm by W. H. Baker represents the lower grade commonly manufactured. Although the barrels and stock were made by Baker, the furniture and locks were purchased commercially for assembly. This technique became increasingly common during the 19th century as commercial houses brought mass-produced components to the market at increasingly lower prices. **(B)**

22-4

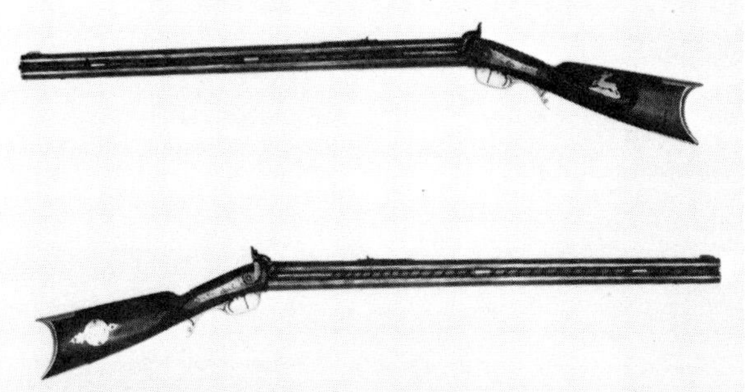

22-4 Over-Under Double Rifles (Schlegelmilch Example)

OL: 46½"
BD: .45 cal. (lower & upper)
Furniture: nickeled brass
Lockplate: backaction, flat
Markings: "G. GOULCHER" in a scroll behind both hammers

BL: 29⅞"
Finish: "bright"
Configuration: both round
Sights: rear—open sliding "V" 6" from breech; front—brass blade dovetailed
Fastenings: none
Markings: "H. SCHLEGELMILCH" and script "Eau Claire, Wis." on top of upper barrel

Although the illustrated piece shows earmarks of a slightly better grade hunting rifle in inlays and plating, this arm exemplifies the assembled longarm so common in the Midwest during the 19th century. "GOULCHER" locks were the most widely distributed available, both in backaction and barlock configurations, and were probably actually made near Birmingham, England. **(C)**

---

23 | Breechloading Flintlock Rifles

In May, 1811, John Hall of Portland, Maine, was issued a patent for a breechloading mechanism consisting of a pivoting breechblock at the rear of the barrel, the block being hollowed to bore diameter for a charge of powder and projectile. This breechblock was hinged on the back so that the forward face could pivot upward to permit loading the chamber with either loose powder and ball or with a prepared paper cartridge. A latch under the stock that interlocked with the block secured the chamber to the breech of the barrel for firing. In 1814 Hall was able to secure a limited test of his patent on several military rifles and muskets, and in 1817 the U.S. Ordnance Department ordered 100 of his rifles for further trials. These were successful, and in 1819 the government ordered 1,000 more rifles with

the provision that Hall was totally to supervise their production so as to insure perfect uniformity and interchangeability.

The latter concept was both the key to the successful implementation of Hall's invention and to the government's acceptance of the breechloading principle. High tolerances were required by Hall to insure that the junction between the breechblock and the barrel would so perfectly align that the escape of gases would be minimal. Hall promised to attain the goal of interchangeability by creating or modifying machinery to produce his rifles. Although he possessed little prior mechanical experience, Hall applied his inventive mind to the project at a special factory set up for him at Harpers Ferry, and by 1824 had assembled the appropriate machinery to deliver the 1,000 rifles. His contract was renewed, and he continued to produce his arms at Harpers Ferry until 1840. From this small beginning, the practice of machine production of interchangeable parts spread to other phases of American munitions making, and, after the Civil War, to other industries. It remains true, nevertheless, that Hall's breechloading device, even when made to the high tolerances he envisioned, was never so secure as to prevent total leakage of gas at the breech. Accordingly, the government pressed its search for a more effective breechloading system beginning in the late 1830s, but the advent of the percussion system would bring this search to an end.

23-O Hall's Patent U.S. M1819 Breechloading Flintlock Rifles, Types II (color plate), **& I**

OL: 52¾"
BD: .52 cal.; 16-groove rifling
Furniture: iron
Lockplate: none, mechanism within receiver
Markings: Top of receiver/breechblock, (I) "J.H. HALL/H. FERRY/(date)/U.S."; (II) either "J.H. HALL/H. FERRY/U.S. (date)" or "J.H. HALL/U.S. (date)"

BL: 32⅝"
Finish: "browned"
Configuration: round
Sights: rear—open, off-center "V" 1⅞" from breech; front—iron block/off-center blade
Fastenings: 3 iron bands, the upper double strapped
Markings: none

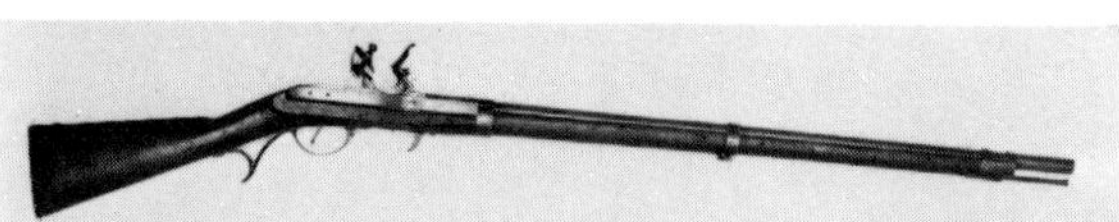

All early rifles (I—2,000, 1824-26) have the bands secured by spring bands forward of the bands (except the upper which has the band behind). Late rifles (II—17,680, 1828-40) have all the bands secured by wire pins. **(B-C)**

23-1 Early (1811-15) Hall Breechloading Rifles

OL: 46"-52½"
BD: .52-.58 cal.
Furniture: brass
Lockplate: none, mechanism within receiver
Markings: bronze (early) or iron receiver marked with serial no. and initials on right side

BL: 28"-34½"
Finish: "browned" (polished)
Configuration: octagonal; less frequently round
Sights: rear—open "V" c. 4" from breech; front—brass blade
Fastenings: pins
Markings: none

These are distinguished by an ungraceful cock and brass pans. Patchboxes (with one recorded exception) are not used and stocks tend to be thick in heft and generally not inletted under the forestock for cleaning rods. Up to 126 may have been made. **(F)**

23-2 Late (1816-18) Hall Breechloading Rifles

OL: 48″-55¾″
BD: .34-.38 cal. (infrequently .44 or .52 cal.)
Furniture: brass
Patchbox: brass, 4-piece, hinged forward; side pieces pierced
Lockplate: none, mechanism within receiver
Markings: iron breechblock receiver marked on top "JOHN H. HALL/PATENT" and on right side usually with serial no. and initials "RB" (occasionally other initials)
BL: 29½″-34½″
Finish: "browned"
Configuration: octagonal
Sights: rear—open "V" c. 6″ from breech; front—brass blade
Fastenings: wedges
Markings: none

These rifles are distinguished by delicate, reinforced gooseneck cocks. Stocks tend to be light and are usually inletted for a cleaning rod under the forestock. The 100 1817 deliveries are thought to follow this pattern with .52 cal. bores and octagonal muzzles turned for 3⅝″ to accept a socket bayonet that locked to a lug attached to the turning. Approximately 150 produced. **(E)**

23-3 Hall's Patent U.S. M1819 (North) Breechloading Rifle

OL: 52¾″
BD: .52 cal.; 16-groove rifling
Furniture: iron
Lockplate: none, mechanism within receiver
Markings: top of receiver/breechblock marked "U.S./S. NORTH/MIDL^{TN}./CONN./(date)"; government inspector's initials within cartouche should appear on stock
BL: 32⅝″
Finish: "browned"
Configuration: round
Sights: rear—open, off-center "V" 1⅞″ from breech; front—iron block/off-center blade
Fastenings: 3 iron bands, the upper double strapped
Markings: none

Simeon North delivered 5,700 of these rifles between 1830-36. All followed a Harpers Ferry pattern, Type I (with spring band retainers). Beware of Harpers Ferry receivers switched into North rifles to disguise them as rarer Harpers Ferry Type I rifles. **(C)**

---

24 | Breechloading Percussion Smoothbores

In 1833 Congress authorized the formation of the regiment of dragoons for service on the Western plains. To equip this mounted unit, the Ordnance Department sought a longarm easy to load in the saddle. Simeon North devised a model that employed John Hall's patented breechloading system and incorporated a percussion lock in

a short weapon. The U.S. M1833 Hall/North carbine was the first percussion arm to enter the U.S. service. The demand for it by the mounted militia units necessitated additional contracts with North. With the outbreak of hostilities in Florida, Congress authorized a second dragoon regiment, and for arms the Ordnance Department turned to Harpers Ferry to make a modified version of the U.S. M1833. Before it could be made, however, the 2nd Dragoons were sent to the Florida campaign, armed with North contract carbines.

The experience in combat with the arms was not widely satisfactory. Although most of the dragoon subordinate commanders favored a return to muzzleloading weapons (resulting in the prototype M1839 musketoons), the Ordnance Department championed Hall's system, instead making three relatively minor changes by which the breechblock was secured. North continued to produce Hall carbines for the militia as late as 1853 in spite of developments in breechloaders.

The Army did briefly toy with another breechloading system during the 1840s. It had already experimented with William Jenks's system in 1840-41. Consequent to extensive tests in 1842 with four Jenks carbines, the Army purchased an additional 40 carbines for field trials, half smooth and half rifled. These were in percussion and "like those making for the Navy." The Navy contracted with Jenks to provide 1,500 "long" and "short" smoothbore percussion breechloading carbines in 1841. Subsequent contracts in 1842, 1843, and 1844 called for the delivery of an additional 3,700 of the "short" carbines. All of these were manufactured by N.P. Ames, who had also contracted in 1843 with the Treasury Department for 144 short carbines for the U.S. Revenue Marine. With the contract to permit the use of 5,000 Maynard patented priming devices on U.S. arms, the Navy was apportioned 1,000 arms to be so designed. Because Ames did not consider the complex priming mechanism profitable, the 1845 contract was instead awarded to Remington. Like most of the later Hall carbines, these Jenks carbines were rifled and otherwise altered (see chapter 25) at the beginning of the Civil War to make them comparable to the breechloading rifled arms that had dominated arms production after 1851. It should be noted, however, that although most breechloaders produced in the 1850s were rifled, Sharps produced a limited number of breechloading shotguns between 1853-56 for civilian use.

24-O U.S. Hall/North M1840 Carbines, Types I & II (color plate, above)

OL: 40″
BD: .52 cal.
Furniture: iron, "browned"
Lockplate: none, mechanism within receiver
Markings: top of breechblock/receiver—"U.S./S.NORTH/MIDL^TN^/CONN./(date)", date being 1840 for type I, 1840-43 for II

BL: 21″
Finish: "browned"
Configuration: round with rod support lug below at muzzle
Sights: rear—open "V" 1 7/8″ from breech; front—iron block/blade
Fastenings: 2 iron bands
Markings: none

In 1840 North was advised to incorporate Patch's improved "elbow lever" catch as soon as possible into 500 of the carbines; other changes were adopted as well, including the 21″ barrel and a new "fishtail" catch (which distinguished type I from II). North delivered 500 of I and 6,001 of II. **(C)**

M1840 II

M1843

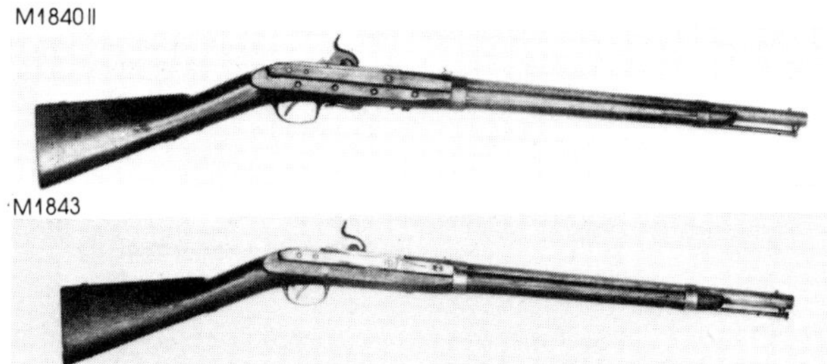

U.S. Hall/North M1843 Carbines (color plate, below)

OL: 40″
BD: .52 cal.
Furniture: iron, "browned"; sling ring and bar attached to left side of frame and lower band
Lockplate: none, mechanism within receiver
Markings: top of breechblock/receiver—"U.S./S.NORTH/MIDL^TN^/CONN./(date)"

BL: 21″
Finish: "browned"
Configuration: round with rod support lug below at muzzle
Sights: rear—open "V" 1⅞″ from breech; front—iron block/blade
Fastenings: 2 iron bands
Markings: beginning in Dec., 1848, "STEEL" on top of barrel flat behind rear sight; inspector's initials on right facet

The side lever mechanism for raising the face of the breechblock had been sugggested by Col. Twiggs of the 2nd Dragoons in 1840. North made 10,600 of these "side-lever" carbines between 1844-53. In 1861 5,000 were rifled and otherwise altered. (See section 25). **(B)**

24-1

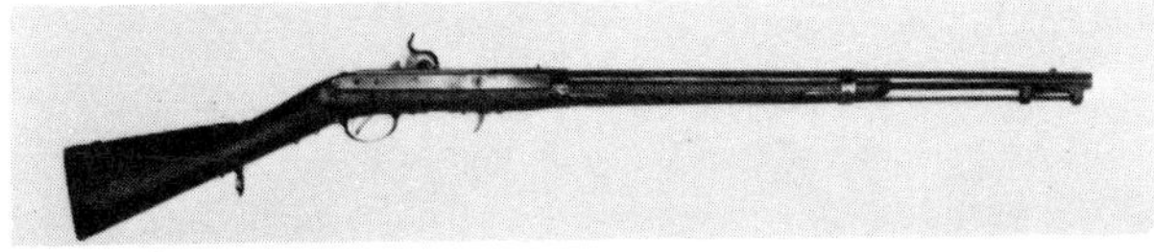

24-1 U.S. M1833 Hall/North Carbine, Types I & II

OL: 45″
BD: .58 cal. (I); .52 cal. (II)
Furniture: iron, "browned"; implement box concealed in buttstock
Lockplate: none, mechanism within receiver
Markings: top of receiver/breechblock—"U.S./S. NORTH/MIDLTN./CONN./(date)"

BL: 23″
Finish: "browned"
Configuration: round with ramrod bayonet locking mount brazed underneath muzzle
Sights: rear—open, off-center "V" 1⅞″ from breech; front—iron block/blade
Fastenings: 2 iron bands
Markings: inspector's initials on right frame facet

1,028 type I carbines were delivered in 1834 for the 1st Dragoons; 6,132 type II were delivered between 1836-39 under various agreements. Like the shorter M1836 Hall carbine, the distinguishing feature is the triangular ramrod bayonet. Note that the sling ring is attached to the triggerguard lower strap. **(C)**

24-2 II

24-2 U.S. M1836 Hall (Harpers Ferry) Carbine, Types I & II

OL: 42½"
BD: .64 cal.
Furniture: iron, "browned"; implement box concealed in buttstock (I only)
Lockplate: none, mechanism within receiver
Markings: top of receiver/breechblock—"J.H. HALL/U.S./(date)"

BL: 23"
Finish: "browned"
Configuration: round with ramrod bayonet locking mount brazed underneath muzzle
Sights: rear—open, off-center "V" 1⅞" from breech
Fastenings: 2 iron bands
Markings: none

A total of 2,020 of these arms were produced at Harpers Ferry between 1837-39. Minor differences in stocking and barrel diameter distinguish the pre-1839 (I) production from those made in 1839-40 (II), but the most evident in I is the absence of the implement box and its metal lid on the lower edge of the buttstock. The sling ring was attached to a metal bolt piercing the stock wrist. **(D)**

24-3 U.S. Hall (Harpers Ferry) M1842 Carbine

OL: 40"
BD: .52 cal.
Furniture: brass, except for iron ring bar attached to lower band and frame, on left
Lockplate: none, mechanism within receiver
Markings: top of breechblock/receiver—"H. FERRY/US/1842"

BL: 21"
Finish: "browned"
Configuration: round with rod support lug below at muzzle
Sights: rear—open "V" 1⅞" from breech; front—iron block/blade
Fastenings: 2 brass bands
Markings: none

Due to reports of field problems with earlier model Hall breechloaders, the Chief of Ordnance ordered Harpers Ferry to manufacture this improved model as soon as possible in 1842. Several small improvements were made, the most noticeable being the use of brass furniture and the "fishtail" catch. 1,001 made in 1842-43. **(D)**

24-4

24-4 Jenks (Ames) U.S. Navy "J" Long Carbines

OL: 52"
BD: .52 cal.
Furniture: brass
Lockplate: backaction, "mule-ear"; flat
Markings: "W^M^ JENKS" and "N.P. AMES/SPRINGFIELD/MASS." behind hammer

BL: 36" (35" bore)
Finish: "bright"
Configuration: round, bayonet lug below near muzzle
Sights: rear—none; front—brass blade on front band
Fastenings: 3 brass bands (screw fastened)

Markings: "W^M JENKS" and "USN/RP/P/1841" on top; "P" near breech

Although the Navy contracted for 1,000 of these arms in 1841, 200 of them were ordered made in the short version before completion of the contract. Many were rifled and otherwise altered in 1861. **(D)**

24-5 Jenks (Ames) U.S. Navy "J" Short Carbine

OL: 41"
BD: .52 cal.
Furniture: brass
Lockplate: backaction, "mule-ear"; flat
Markings: "W^M JENKS" and "N.P. AMES/SPRINGFIELD/MASS." behind hammer
BL: 25" (24" bore)
Finish: "bright"
Configuration: round
Sights: rear—none; front—brass blade on upper band
Fastenings: 2 brass bands (screw fastened)
Markings: "W^M JENKS" and "USN/RC/P/(date)" on top flat

The initial 1841 order called for 500 24" long-barreled carbines. Before completion, however, 200 of the long version were ordered delivered in this configuration. Subsequent orders in 1842-44 brought the total delivered to 4,400. Like the long version, many of these were rifled and otherwise altered in 1861. **(C)**

24-6 Jenks (Remington) U.S. Navy "J" Carbine

OL: 41"
BD: .52 cal.
Furniture: brass
Lockplate: backaction, "mule-ear"; flat
Markings: "REMINGTON'S/HERKIMER/N.Y." behind hammer; serial no. inside primer door
BL: 25" (24" bore)
Finish: "browned"
Configuration: round
Sights: rear—none; front—brass blade on upper band
Fastenings: 2 brass bands (screw fastened)
Markings: "W.JENKS" and "U.S.N./RP/P/(date)" and "CAST STEEL" on top flat

One thousand of these arms incorporating the Maynard tape primer (as designed for the "mule-ear" lock by Lt. Joseph Lanman, U.S.N.) were contracted for from Remington in 1845 through William Jenks. Most, if not all, were subsequently rifled and otherwise altered in 1861. **(D)**

---

25 | Breechloading Smoothbore and Rifled Alterations

The year 1861 found the suddenly divided United States in a scramble for weapons unparalleled since the Revolution. A number of obsolete arms were pressed into service after altering them to conform to the most "modern" systems, either as muzzleloading "Minie" rifled muskets or as rifled percussion breechloaders. The most plentiful of those that could be altered to percussion breechloading rifles were the Hall rifles and Hall/North smoothbore carbines. The former could be altered simply by reworking the receiver to percussion and replacing the flint cock with a percussion hammer. Because of

their notorious leakage of gas, even when percussioned, these Hall rifles were relegated to absolute emergency status (4th class arms) by the Ordnance Department. Nevertheless, the Union Defense Committee of New York purchased 1,575 of these (as well as 1,059 Hall percussion carbines) in August, 1861. Quantities had also been seized in Southern arsenals in 1861, and at least 1,000 of the 2,300+ seized at Baton Rouge in 1861 were in the process of alteration to percussion by Mississippi in mid-1861.

In addition to the Hall flintlock rifles in store in 1861, there were also several thousand unissued U.S. M1843 Hall/North carbines. In June, 1861, arms entrepreneur A.M. Eastman purchased 4,996 of these carbines for a mere $3.50 each and in turn sold them to Simon Stevens in August at a profit of $9 each! After reboring and rifling, Stevens sold the carbines to General Fremont in Missouri at the inflated price of $22.50 each. The government similarly disposed of 720 of the same carbines in April for $6 each, only to repurchase them (presumably unaltered) in July at $15. The same Eastman secured 2,800 Jenks percussion smoothbore carbines from the Navy and had them rifled and altered to rifles and carbines, the latter for mounted service. It is not known who eventually purchased these arms, which included both the Ames products in both lengths and the Remington/Maynard tape primer variants. Immediately prior to the War the Navy had had 240 of the Ames short carbines altered to rifled breechloaders on the Merrill patented system.

Not all of the alterations effected in this period were on breechloading arms. At least three patented breechloading systems were applied in small quantities to muzzleloading rifled arms. Prior to the War (in addition to the Naval carbine alterations) Merrill had contracted with the Ordnance Department to alter 100 each U.S. M1842 rifled muskets, U.S. M1841 rifles (altered to .58 cal.), and U.S. M1847 rifled dragoon musketoons. Most of these were delivered in 1860, and a few more were purchased in 1861. In addition to these arms, the government had also altered 400 rifles (presumably Harpers Ferry U.S. M1841) to the Mont Storm breechloading system during fiscal year 1859-60. All, however, were destroyed when the Harpers Ferry Arsenal was burned in April, 1861. Finally, Massachusetts had 103 Robbins & Lawrence U.S. M1841 contract rifles altered in 1861 to the Lindner breechloading system. None, however, were ever issued for use.

25-O Eastman Alterations of U.S. Navy Jenks/Remington Carbine
(color plate)

Eastman altered these arms by rifling the bore with 6 narrow grooves, enlarging the round loading hole to elliptical to accept the conical projectiles then in vogue, cutting a groove on the breechlock cover to serve as a rear sight, and by adding a sling ring to the triggerguard strap with a metal staple. Judging from surviving examples, nearly all 1,000 Remington-made "short" carbines were included in this alteration. **(C)**

25-1 Civilian Alterations to Percussion of Hall Flintlock Rifles

In 1857 all Hall breechloading arms in storage were declared obsolete and surplus. A considerable number were sold at prices seldom equal to one-tenth what the government had invested in them. The private speculators who purchased these altered the breechblocks by filling in the old pan and replacing the frizzen and its spring with a percussion cone and by substituting a new percussion hammer (similar to that used on the Hall/North carbine) for the old flint cock. **(C)**

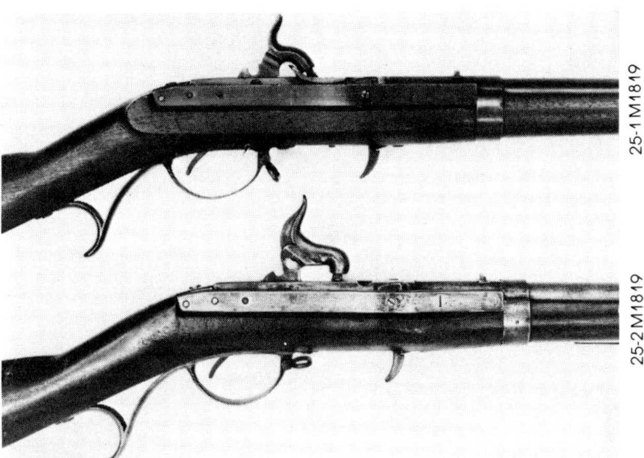

25-2 State of Mississippi Alterations to Percussion of Hall Flintlock Rifles

When the Baton Rouge Arsenal was captured by the forces of Louisiana in 1861, 2,287 flintlock Hall rifles were found among its inventories. One thousand of these were transferred to Mississippi in 1861, and were in the process of alteration during that year. The alteration was very similar to that employed on the same rifle in the North. Instead of substituting a new hammer, however, the old cock was altered by cutting away the jaws and welding a percussion head to the old shank (rather crudely). This type has erroneously been referred to as the "Fayetteville" alteration. **(D)**

25-3 Eastman/Stevens Alterations of U.S. M1843 Hall/North Carbines

Arthur M. Eastman and Simon Stevens subcontracted 4,000 of the 4,996 U.S. M1843 Hall/North carbines they had purchased from the U.S. in 1861 to W. W. Marston of New York City to be altered by reaming the chamber and barrel to .58 caliber and rifling the latter (with 6 narrow grooves). The balance purchased were subcontracted to the Taunton Locomotive Works, where the same work was effected. All were done on unissued carbines with cast steel barrels, which would date them between 1848-53. **(C)**

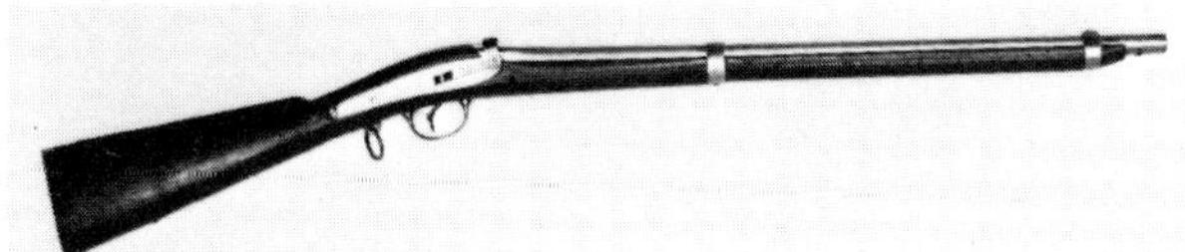

25-4

25-4 Eastman Alterations of U.S. Navy Jenks/Ames "Short" Carbines

Among the 2,800 Jenks arms that Arthur M. Eastman acquired from the U.S. Navy in 1861 were a significant number of the Jenks/Ames "short" carbines. These were altered in exactly the same manner as 25-0. **(C)**

25-5 Eastman Alterations of U.S. Navy Jenks/Ames "Long" Carbines

Those Jenks/Ames "long" carbines among the 2,800 Jenks smoothbore breechloaders that Eastman purchased of the Navy were altered in the same manner as the "short" and Remington carbines, but no sling ring was attached. **(D)**

25-6 Lindner (Allen) Alteration of U.S. M1841 Contract Rifles

Of the 4,000 Robbins & Lawrence U.S. M1841 contract rifles sent to Massachusetts from the Watertown Arsenal in 1861, 103 were set aside

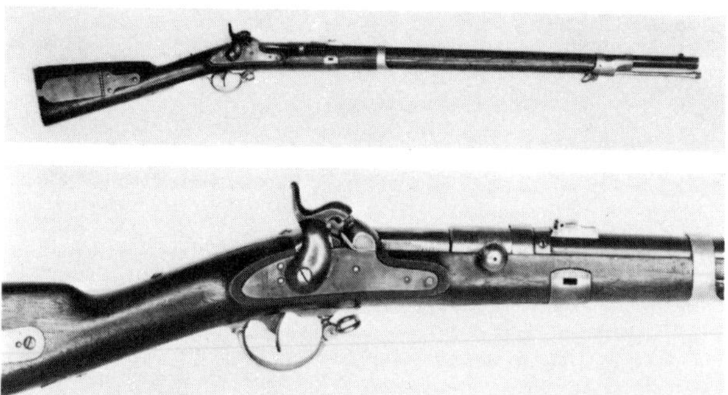

for alteration to breechloaders by Enos G. Allen. The alteration consisted of cutting away the breech section of the barrel and modifying it to accept the rotating sleeve marked on its top "PATENTED/Mar. 29, 1859", the date of Edward Lindner's patent on the system. The wood behind the barrel was inletted to accept a breech support that permitted the cut-away breech section to pivot upward when the sleeve bolt was rotated to the right of the rifle. A wedge-held reinforcement locked the barrel and sleeve in place. The sleeves are serially numbered on their lower side. Further alterations consisted of a new front and rear sight identical to those placed on the "Windsor" rifles that A. J. Drake had modified for Massachusetts. **(D)**

---

26 | Percussion Breechloading Rifles and Carbines

In 1855 Congress created two new mounted units for the Army—the 1st and 2nd Cavalry. Unlike the two regiments of dragoons and the regiment of mounted rifles which they supplemented, these two units were organized as a combat force that would fight solely from

the saddle. The prime arms for these two regiments were both muzzleloading: the U.S. M1855 rifle-carbine and the U.S. M1855 pistol-carbine with detachable shoulder stock. The arms assigned to one squadron (two companies, roughly 1/5th of the regiment) of each unit, however, were breechloading trial arms. Although the Army's previous experience with the Hall breechloading carbines had been unsatisfactory, the officials of the Ordnance Department were open-minded to novel developments in such arms. From 1855-60 limited quantities of nearly every conceivable breechloading percussion system were tried, either in limited board trials or in more extensive field trials. Of those that utilized paper or combustible linen cartridges, only the Sharps patent carbines found sufficient favor, and even these leaked gases at the breech until improved brass "obdurators" practically eliminated the problem. Many of these arms were offered commercially as well, but only Sharps met with any general success, the arm becoming the prime one furnished to "free state" immigrants to Kansas.

Although the Sharps rifle proved to be the most reliable percussion breechloading longarm prior to the invention of the metallic cartridge, the facilities of that firm were limited. As a result, when the Civil War erupted in 1861, the Ordnance Department was forced to turn to other firms to meet the needs of the volunteer cavalry units. The Confederacy felt the pressure for an effective breechloader for its mounted service as well. A number of different systems were produced on a limited basis, but none was found particularly effective. Finally, a direct copy of the Sharps was made in Richmond, first at a private establishment, but finally at a government arsenal. Even these were so poorly made (in terms of tolerances) that they frequently blew up in the field, causing the Confederacy to revert solely to muzzleloading arms in late 1863. The industrial Northeast, however, had little trouble meeting the manufacturing tolerances demanded of the patented breechloaders. Only the development of the self-contained copper rim-fire cartridge (with its total elimination of gas leakage of breech fouling) wrought the demise of the percussion breechloaders.

26-O Sharps M1869 (M1863/M1865) Military Rifles, Types I (color plate, above) **& II-III**

OL: 47⅜"
BD: .52 cal. (all types) and .58 cal. (III only), 6-groove rifling
Furniture: iron, "blued"
Patchbox: iron, 2-piece hinged forward
Lockplate: backaction; flat
Markings: R.S. LAWRENCE PAT./APRIL 15TH 1859" and "C. SHARPS' PAT./OCT. 5TH 1852" behind hammer. Serial no. on upper frame strap. Left side of frame marked: "C. SHARPS' PAT./SEPT. 12TH 1848"

BL: 29½" to frame (30" bore)
Finish: "blued"
Configuration: round, saber bayonet stud with 1" guide below near muzzle
Sights: rear—Lawrence M1859, 2¼" from frame; front—German-silver blade inset in iron block
Fastenings: 3 iron bands, "blued"
Markings: "SHARPS RIFLE/MANUFG. CO./HARTFORD, CONN." and either "NEW MODEL 1859", "NEW MODEL 1863", or "NEW MODEL 1865"

This rifle was first developed for the U.S. Navy with a saber bayonet, and 900 were purchased by that service between 1859-60 in .58 caliber. The Navy contracted for an additional 2,780 (type II) during the Civil War, but in .52 cal. Connecticut purchased at least 912 in this configuration, and the Ordnance Department accepted at least 1,000 in 1865 as well. The types most frequently purchased for the Army (I and II), however, used a socket bayonet that attached to the front sight base. In 1862, 2,000 were received, and another 5,000 were delivered in 1865. Part of the first 2,000 were equipped with double-set triggers (type II) and were especially made for the two units of U.S. Sharpshooters. Sharps rifles were secured by independent state action as well. **(B)**

Sharps M1853 (Sharps Rifle Manfg. Co.) Carbines, Types I (color plate, below) **& II-III**

OL: 32⅝", 35⅝", 37⅝", or 40⅝"
BD: .36, .44, .52, or .577 cal.; 6-groove rifling
Furniture: brass (infrequently iron), long iron swivel bar with ring on left side
Patchbox: brass, 2-piece, hinged forward
Lockplate: backaction; flat
Markings: "C. SHARPS/PATENT/1852" to rear of hammer; upper frame strap marked "C. SHARPS/PATENT/1852" and serial no.
BL: 15⅜", 18⅜", 20⅜", or 23⅜" to frame, (16½", 19½", 21½", 24½" bore)
Finish: "bright" (I); "browned" or "blued" (II, III)
Configuration: round
Sights: rear—folding leaf with slide, 2¼" from frame; front—brass blade
Fastenings: single brass band
Markings: "SHARPS RIFLE/MANUFG. CO./HARTFORD, CONN." on top

A total of 10,519 Sharps rifles of this sort were manufactured solely at Hartford, nearly all for the civilian market. The Egyptian government purchased the only 200 military versions (I) in .577 cal., the majority of this type being in .52 cal. for the U.S. contracts that totaled 4,440 from 1857-58. A significant number of the civilian (II) production was sold to abolitionists seeking to establish Kansas as a free state, these also being in .52 cal. Double-set triggers were optional (III). **(B)**

26-1 Allen & Wheelock Breechloading Percussion Rifles

OL: 43"
BD: .36 or .44 cal., 3- or 6-groove rifling
Furniture: iron; patchbox used early; later, buttplate contains door to cleaning rod pocket
Lockplate: none, mechanism within frame
Markings: top of breechblock—"ALLEN'S PATENT/JULY 3, 1855"
BL: 26⅛" to frame (26½" bore)
Finish: "blued"
Finish: "blued"
Configuration: part round/part octagonal
Sights: rear—open "V" on strap 3⅛" from frame; front—German-silver block/blade
Fastenings: forestock screwed to barrel
Markings: "ALLEN & WHEELOCK" and "CAST STEEL" and serial no. over "WORCESTER" on upper left facet; serial no. on left side of frame.

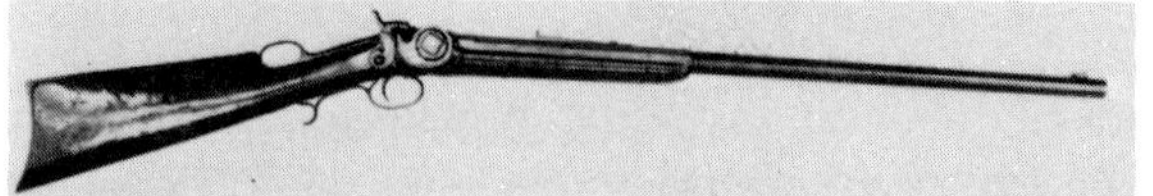

Based on surviving serial numbers, less than 300 of these rifles were produced by Allen & Wheelock in the period from 1856-60. Allen's patent of 1855 covered the faucet-like breechlock. **(D)**

26-2

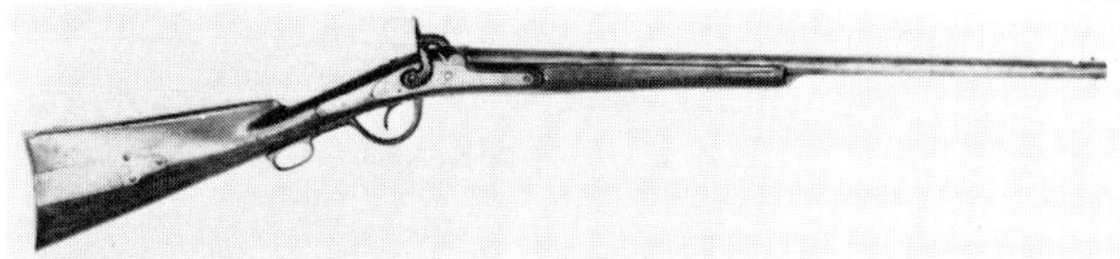

26-2 Gibbs (Lull & Thomas) "Baby" Carbines

OL: 37⅝″
BD: .42 cal. (.44 cal.)
Furniture: iron, sling ring on left
Patchbox: 2-piece, iron, hinged forward
Lockplate: extended back-action; flat
Markings: "LULL & THOMAS/ILION N.Y." forward of hammer; "L.H. GIBBS/PATENT JAN. 8 1856"; top of frame—"L.H. GIBBS/PATENT JAN. 8. 1856/N.Y." (same stamping on left of keyplate)

BL: 22⅛″
Finish: "browned"
Configuration: round
Sights: rear—block with leaf with slide 4″ from frame; front—brass blade, dovetailed
Fastenings: nosecap loops over barrel
Markings: none

Although small in caliber, the "Baby Gibbs" carbine shows evidence of having been made as a military arm. There is no record, however, of any purchases from Lull & Thomas by the U.S. during the period 1856-61, when that firm was in operation. Supposedly an ordnance board did test 20 Gibbs carbines in 1857, presumably those contracted for with G. Gay in 1855. **(F)**

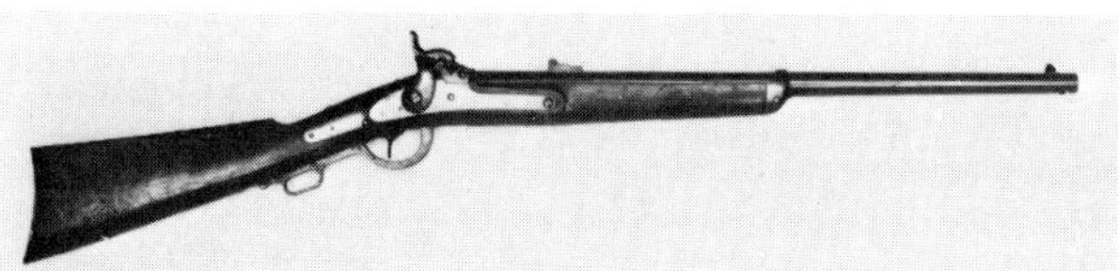

26-3 Gibbs (William F. Brooks) Carbines 26-3

OL: 38½″
BD: .52 cal., 6-groove rifling
Furniture: iron, "blued"; "U.S." on buttplate tang; no swivel ring or bar
Lockplate: extended back-action; flat
Markings: unmarked or eagle (behind hammer) and either "W.F. BROOKS/MANF^{R} NEW YORK" or "W^{M} F. BROOKS/MANF^{R} NEW YORK/1863"; top of frame—"L.H. GIBBS/PATENT JAN'Y 8 1856"

BL: 22″
Finish: "blued"
Configuration: round
Sights: rear—U.S. M1861 rifle-musket sight 2⅝″ from breech; front—German-silver blade inset in iron block, dovetailed
Fastenings: nosecap loops barrel
Markings: none

Although contracts called for more extensive deliveries, only 1,052

Gibbs carbines were delivered in 1863 before arson destroyed Brooks's plant during the 1863 New York Draft Riot. **(C)**

26-4 Greene (Mass. Arms Co.) Carbines, Type II

OL: 34⅜"
BD: .54 cal., 3-groove rifling
Furniture: iron, "blued"
Patchbox: iron, 2-pieced hinged forward
Lockplate: backaction; flat
Markings: on primer door—"MAYNARD'S PATENT (arced)" and "SEP. 22. 1845 (arced)"; to rear of hammer—"(crowned) V•R" and "MASS. ARMS CO/ CHICOPEE FALLS/U.S.A. 1856"; marked on top of frame—"GREENE'S PATENT./JUNE 27. 1854."

BL: 18" (bore)
Finish: "blued"
Configuration: round, stepped, with 16-sided stepped section
Sights: rear—folding leaf on base 4¾" from breech; front—iron blade, dovetailed
Fastenings: none, no forestock
Markings: British inspection marks and condemnation marks (e.g., two arrows, point to point, and "S")

The English government ordered 2,000 Greene patent breechloading percussion carbines in 1855 from the Massachusetts Arms Co. Because a suitable cartridge for them could not be found, all sat in storage until condemned. **(C)**

26-5 Greene (Waters) Bolt-Action Breechloading Rifles

OL: 52¾"
BD: .53/.54 cal., Lancaster oval bore
Furniture: iron, "blued"

BL: 39¾" (including receiver); 36" bore
Finish: "blued"
Configuration: round

Lockplate: none, underhammer lock
Markings: upper strap of frame—"GREENE'S PATENT/NOV. 17, 1857"

Sights: rear—2¼" long graduated block with slide leaf 4¼" from receiver; front—iron block/blade
Fastenings: 3 iron bands, "blued"
Markings: none

The U.S. War Department purchased 900 rifles based on James Durell Greene's 1857 patent in 1863. Although appearing to be smoothbore, these are actually rifled in accordance with Lancaster's English "oval-bore" patents. They are the only underhammer arms procured by the U.S. government. **(C)**

26-6 II

26-6 Gross (Cosmopolitan Arms Co.) Breechloading Carbines, Types I & II

OL: 39″
BD: .52 cal., 3-grade rifling
Furniture: iron, "blued"; either sling ring on left side of frame or sling swivel on buttstock lug
Lockplate: backaction; flat, beveled edge
Markings: "COSMOPOLITAN ARMS CO. (arced)/HAMILTON O. U.S./GROSS' PATENT" over, occasionally, either "1859" or substituting "UNION/RIFLE" for patent name and date; serial no. on bottom of barrel and frame
BL: 19⅛″ to frame (20″ bore)
Finish: "blued"
Configuration: part round/part octagonal
Sights: rear—2⅛″ block with folding leaf 1¼″-1½″ from frame; front—iron block/blade
Fastenings: none, no forestock
Markings: right side of frame occasionally marked "UNION RIFLE"

The earliest production pieces used a flat-sided double loop triggerguard/level assembly (I). Very quickly this was supplanted by the rounded "grapevine" design (II). A total of 1,140 carbines were delivered to the U.S. Ordnance Dept. in 1862. **(C)**

26-7 Gross (Gwynn & Campbell) Breechloading Carbines, Types I & II

OL: 39″ (I); 38½″ (II)
BD: .52 cal., 3-groove rifling
Furniture: iron, "blued"; sling ring and bar on left side
BL: (I) 19″ to frame (20″ to bore); (II) 18¾″ to frame (19¾″ to bore)
Finish: "blued"

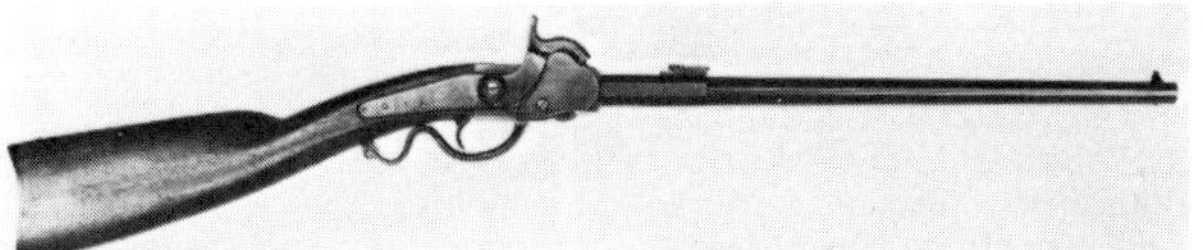
II

Lockplate: backaction; flat, beveled edge
Markings: "GWYNN & CAMPBELL (arced)/PATENT/1862/HAMILTON. O." behind hammer
Configuration: part round/part octagonal
Sights: rear—(see comments); front—iron block/blade
Markings: none; however, right side of frame marked "UNION RIFLE"; serial no. on bottom of frame and barrel

In 1863-64 Gwynn & Campbell delivered 8,202 carbines. Type I are little more than differently stamped Cosmopolitan carbines. Type II (and some transitional arms) used a shorter (1⁹⁄₁₆″) rear sight base located 1⅞″ from the frame, a flat-faced hammer, and newly-designed flat-sided triggerguard and lever catch. **(B)**

26-8

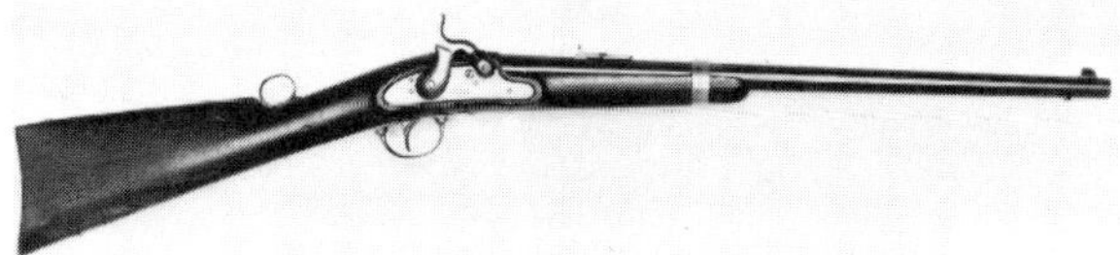

26-8 Joslyn (Waters) "Monkeytail" Breechloading Carbines

OL: 38⅞"
BD: .54 cal., 3-groove rifling
Furniture: brass, iron swivel ring and bar on left side
Lockplate: flat, beveled edge
Markings: "A.H. WATERS & C^O/ MILBURY MASS" forward of hammer; serial no. stamped into left side of breechlever; top of breechblock—"PAT^D BY/ B.F. JOSLYN/AUG. 28, 1855"

BL: 21⅛"
Finish: "browned"
Configuration: round
Sights: rear—single folding leaf with slide on base $2\frac{9}{16}$" from frame; front—iron blade, dovetailed
Fastenings: single brass band
Markings: none

Fifty Joslyn percussion carbines were ordered from William Freeman in 1857 by the U.S. Ordnance Dept. and were delivered in 1858. Successful trials led to an order for 1,000 more in 1860, but only 300 of these were delivered in 1861. After Freeman disassociated himself from Joslyn another 660 were delivered by the Joslyn Firearms Co. of Stonington, Conn., in 1862. In late 1861 Bruff Bros. & Seaver delivered 200 others to the state of Ohio. **(D)**

26-9 I

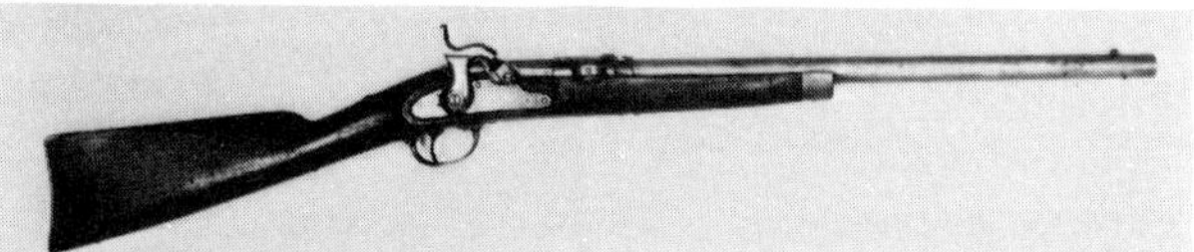

26-9 Lindner (Amoskeag) Breechloading Carbines, Types I & II

OL: 38½"
BD: .58 cal., 3-groove rifling
Furniture: iron, swivel ring and bar on left side (I); sling swivel on triggerguard bow (II)
Lockplate: flat, beveled edge
Markings: none (I) or "U. (eagle) S./AMOSKEAG M^FG C^O/MANCHESTER, N.H." foward of hammer; "1864" on tail; top of breechblock/chamber—"EDWARD LINDNER'S/PATENT/ MARCH 29, 1859"

BL: 18" to receiver (20" bore)
Finish: "bright"
Configuration: round
Sights: rear—pivoting "L" leaf on base on top of breech tang; front—iron block/blade
Fastenings: none
Markings: none

The U.S. Ordnance Dept. purchased 501 type I Lindner carbines from the Amoskeag Mfg. Co. in 1863. The 391 carbines delivered by Samuel B. Smith in 1861 are believed to be Austrian jäger rifles altered to the Lindner system. Amoskeag contracted for the delivery of 6,000 additional (II) carbines but these were refused by the War Dept., and 5,999 were sold to France in 1873. In addition to the markings and swivel variations, type II carbines have a flat-faced bolster without clean-out screw, use a 2-leaf rear sight on a base set upon the barrel forward of the sleeve, and an M1861 rifle-musket nosecap. **(D)**

26-10

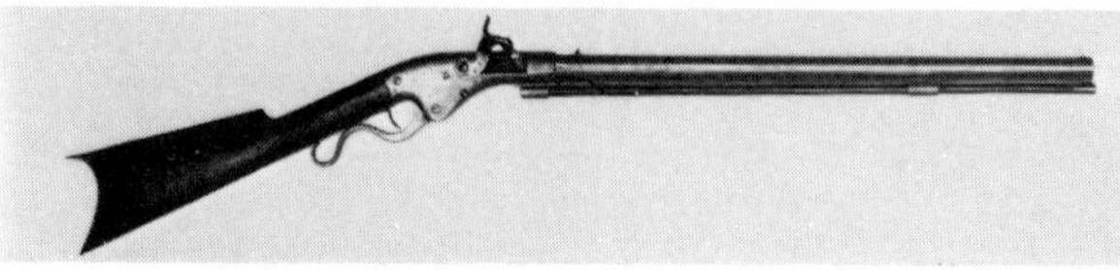

26-10 Marston Breechloading Sporting Rifles

OL: 43¾"
BD: .54 cal., 14-groove rifling
Furniture: iron
Lockplate: none, mechanism within frame
Markings: top of frame—"W.W. MARSTON PATENTED 1850 NEW YORK"; serial no. stamped in frame forward of triggerguard/lever

BL: 23" to frame (24" bore)
Finish: "bright"
Configuration: round
Sights: rear—open "V" ¾" from frame; front—German-silver blade
Fastenings: none, no forestock
Markings: none

An estimated 300 rifles (and a very few shotguns in the same configuration) were made by William Marston of New York from 1850-60. The triggerguard served as a lever, which, when activated, drew back a breechblock and exposed a port on the right side of the frame. The same action was used on a Marston single-shot pistol. **(F)**

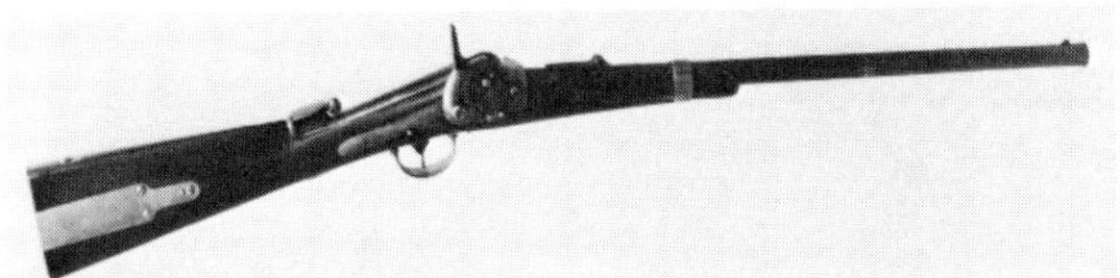

26-11 Merrill, Latrobe, & Thomas (Remington) Breechloading Carbines

OL: 38"
BD: .58 cal., 3-groove rifling
Furniture: brass, iron swivel ring and bar on left side
Patchbox: brass, 2-piece, hinged forward
Lockplate: backaction; flat
Markings: "S.REMINGTON/ILION, N.Y."; serial no. stamped in underside of breech lever; top of breech/lever—"MERRILL, LATROBE & THOMAS/BALTIMORE, MD./PATENT APPLIED FOR"

BL: 21" bore
Finish: "blued"
Configuration: round
Sights: rear—Sharps M1853 sight 2½" from frame; front—brass blade
Fastenings: single brass blade
Markings: none

A total of 170 of these carbines were ordered for military trials with the 1st U.S. Cavalry in 1855 and another 100 were ordered for the militia in 1860. It is not clear if the first 170 were actually delivered. **(E)**

26-12 Merrill (Merrill, Thomas & Co.) Breechloading Rifles, Types I & II

OL: 48½"
BD: .54 cal., 3-groove rifling
Furniture: (I) iron, except brass nosecap; (II) all brass buttplate, triggerguard bow
Patchbox: (I) iron; (II) brass
Lockplate: 2-piece, hinged forward; flat, beveled edge
Markings: J.L. MERRILL BALTO./PAT. JULY 1858/APR 9 MAY 21-28-61" forward of hammer; serial no. on tail; top of breech-

BL: 31" to receiver (32½" bore)
Finish: "browned"
Configuration: round, saber bayonet stud on right side
Sights: rear—1⅝" long base/latch lock with 2 "L" leaves; front—iron blade
Fastenings: 2 bands—(I) iron; (II) brass
Markings: none

block lever—"J.H.MERRILL BALTO./PAT JULY 1858"

II

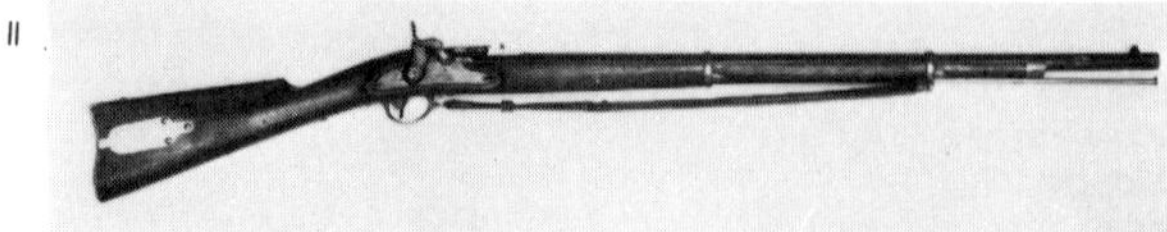

About 100 (I) Merrill rifles were privately purchased in 1861 by Co. K., 21st Indiana Vols. (and are marked with their owners' names on the triggerguard bow). To complete the armament of that unit uniformly, the Ordnance Dept. purchased 566 additional (II) in 1862. **(D)**

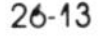
26-13

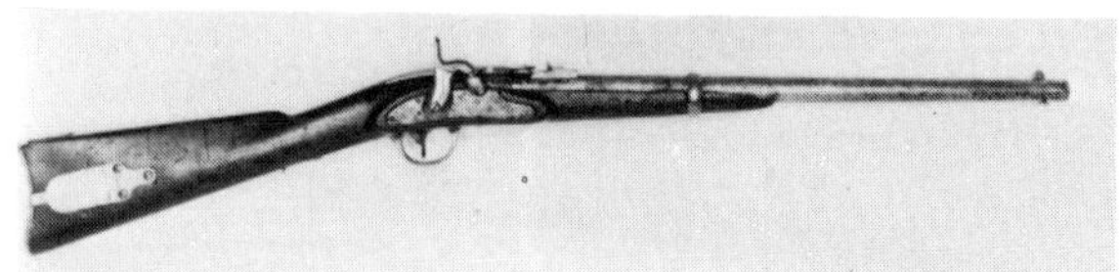

26-13 Merrill (Merrill, Thomas & Co.) Breechloading Carbines

OL: 37"
BD: .54 cal., 3-groove rifling
Furniture: brass
Patchbox: brass, 2-piece, hinged forward
Lockplate: flat, beveled edge
Markings: "J.H.MERRILL BALTO./PAT. JULY 1858/APR. 9 MAY 21-28-61" forward of hammer; serial no. on tail; top of breechblock—"J.H. MERRILL BALTO./PAT. JULY 1858"

BL: $19\frac{7}{8}$" to frame ($21\frac{1}{2}$" bore)
Finish: "bright"
Configuration: round
Sights: rear—$1\frac{5}{8}$" long base/latch lock with 2 "L" leaves; front—iron blade
Fastenings: single brass band
Markings: none

Between 1861-63 this firm delivered 9,835 carbines to the U.S. government under 10 contracts. A "fancy" grade was commercially available and was known to have been privately purchased by some Union cavalry officers. In addition to the patchbox, the most noticeable distinguishing characteristic of the Merrill production is the knurled long-latch release. **(B)**

26-14 Merrill (Merrill Pat. Firearms Co.) Breechloading Carbines

OL: 37"
BD: .54 cal., 3-groove rifling
Furniture: brass, "U S" on buttplate tang
Lockplate: flat, beveled edge
Markings: eagle and "J.H. MERRILL BALTO./PAT. JULY 1852/APR 9 MAY 21-28-61" forward of hammer; "1863" or "1864" on tail; top of breechblock—"J.H. MERRILL BALTO./PAT. JULY 1858" and serial no.

BL: $19\frac{3}{4}$" to frame ($21\frac{1}{4}$" bore)
Finish: "bright"
Configuration: round
Sights: rear—$1\frac{5}{6}$" long base/latch lock with 2 "L" leaves; front—iron blade
Fastenings: single brass band
Markings: "V", "P", and eagle head on left side near frame

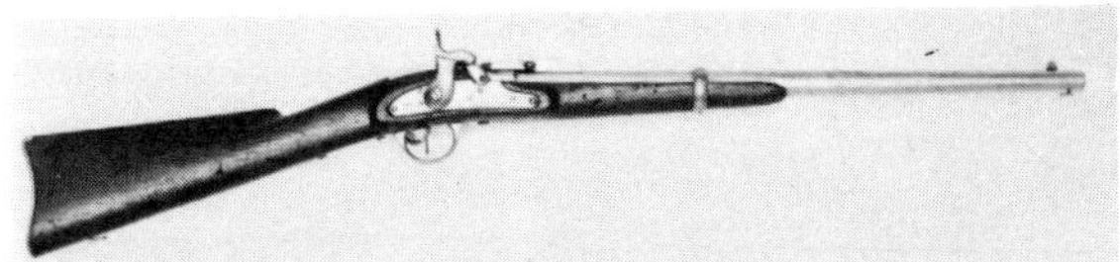

The U.S. Ordnance Dept. purchased 4,100 of these carbines between 1863-64. In addition to the markings and the absence of the patchbox, the button latch releases distinguish this carbine from the work of the Merrill Patent Firearms Co.'s predecessor. **(B)**

26-15 Mont Storm Breechloading Carbines

OL: 36¾"
BD: .57 cal.
Furniture: iron, "tinned"; swivel ring and bar on left side
Lockplate: flat
Markings: serial no. stamped into bottom of breechblock; top of breechblock marked—"W. MONT STORMS/PATENT JULY 1856"

BL: 18¾" to receiver (19½" bore)
Finish: "tinned"
Configuration: round
Sights: rear—1¾" base with folding leaf 1⅛" from receiver; front—iron block/blade
Fastenings: single, iron, "tinned" band
Markings: none

W. Mont Storm's patent covered a hinged breechblock that rotated up and forward. Based on surviving serial numbers, no fewer than 175 carbines were made conforming with this patent in the period 1856-65. Who actually manufactured these arms and to whom they were sold is not known. **(E)**

26-16 Nye-Terry (Tonks) Breechloading Carbines

OL: 36⅞"
BD: .54 cal., 6-groove rifling
Furniture: brass
Patchbox: brass, 2-piece, hinged forward
Lockplate: flat
Markings: "Joseph Tonks Maker/Boston" in script forward of hammer

BL: 24¼" incl. receiver (20½" bore)
Finish: "browned"
Configuration: round, octagonal receiver
Sights: rear—1⅝" base with folding ladder, 2" from receiver; front—iron blade
Fastenings: wedge plus single brass band
Markings: none

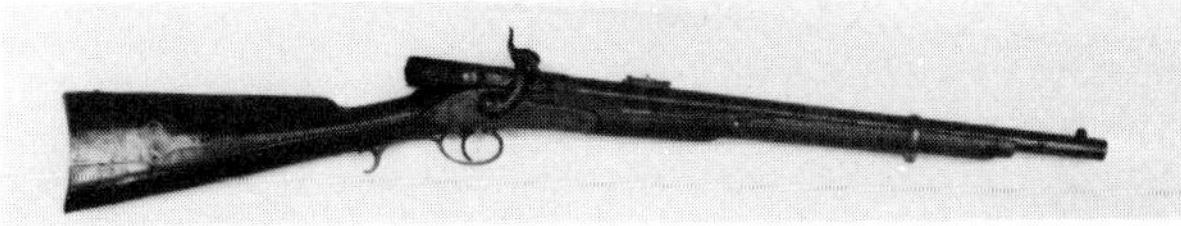

The basic breechloading action of this arm was patented by William Terry of Birmingham, England, in 1862, having been produced in limited quantities for the English government in 1858 (about 200 arms). John C. Nye of Cincinnati patented an improved latch to this system in 1862. Quantities produced by Tonks are not known. **(F)**

26-17 I

26-17 Perry (Perry Arms Co.) Breechloading Carbines, Types I & II

OL: 39⅜"
BD: .54 cal., 7-groove rifling
Furniture: iron; brass buttplates and patchboxes on early production
Patchbox: iron, 2-piece, hinged forward
Lockplate: none, mechanism within frame
Markings: top of breechblock—"A.D. PERRY/PATENTED" and also "PERRY PATENT ARM CO/ NEWARK, N.J."

BL: 20⅝" to frame (21½" bore)
Finish: "blued"
Configuration: round
Sights: rear—open "V" or short block with folding leaf ¾" from frame
Fastenings: single iron band
Markings: serial no. on top near frame, also on top of frame near barrel

The U.S. Ordnance Dept. ordered 200 Perry carbines in 1855 for trials with the newly-formed 2nd U.S. Cavalry. An unknown number of these arms (probably without swivel rings) were also purchased by the U.S. Navy prior to the Civil War for trials. On some of the cavalry carbines, the swivel ring attached to an eyelet on the left side. **(D)**

26-18 Perry (Perry Arms Co.) Breechloading Sporting Rifle

OL: 44¼"
BD: .44 cal., 7-groove rifling
Furniture: iron, engraved
Lockplate: mechanism within frame
Markings: top of breechblock—"A.D.PERRY/PATENTED" and also "PERRY PATENT ARM CO/ NEWARK, N.J./1855"; there are other variations recorded

BL: 25⅜" to frame (26¼" bore)
Finish: "browned"
Configuration: octagonal
Sights: rear—open "V" on strap 1⅜" from frame; front—German-silver blade inset in iron block, dovetailed
Fastenings: single wedge
Markings: serial no. (e.g., "630") on top near frame; also on top of frame near barrel

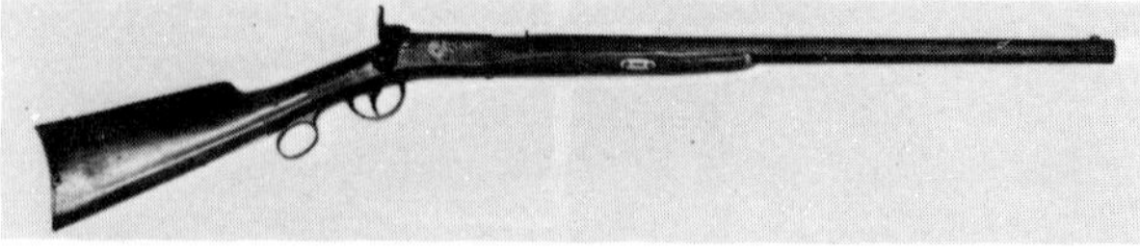

Alonzo Perry's patent covered a breechloading tilting block that not only permitted the insertion of a combustible cartridge in the chamber of the block, but also automatically affixed a percussion primer to the cone with each operation of the lever/triggerguard. The primers were stored in a tube loaded from the butt of the gun. Judging from existing serial numbers, up to 1,500 Perry arms of all types are believed to have been made between 1855-61. **(D)**

26-19 I

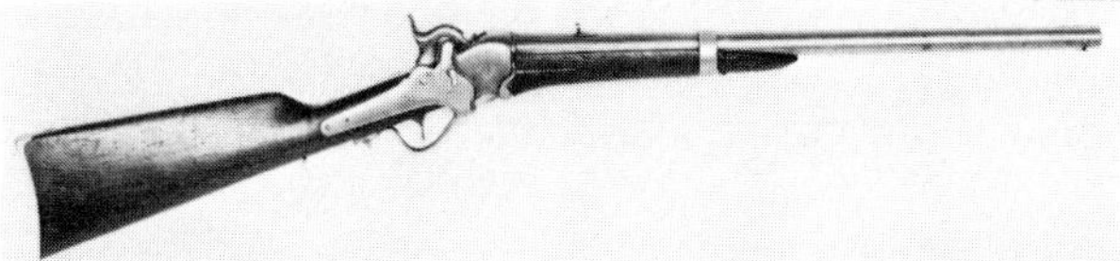

26-19 Sharps M1851 (Sharps R.M. Co./R. & L.) Carbines, Types I & II

OL: 37½"
BD: (I) .52 cal.; (II) .36, .44, or .52 cal.; 6-groove rifling
Furniture: brass
Patchbox: brass, 2-piece, hinged forward
Lockplate: backaction; flat
Markings: "EDWARD MAYNARD/PATENTEE/1845" on primer door forward of hammer; upper frame strap—"C. SHARPS/PATENT/1848" and serial no.
BL: 20¼" to frame (21½" bore)
Finish: (I) "bright"; (II) "browned" or "blued"
Configuration: round
Sights: rear—Sharps "squirrel ear" on 9/16" base 2¼" from frame; front—brass blade; tang and globe sights available
Fastenings: single brass band
Markings: "SHARPS' RIFLE/MANUF^G CO./HARTFORD, CONN." on top (II) or simply "U.S./S.K./P" on upper left surface

Of the 1,837 M1851 carbines produced by both the Sharps Rifle Manufg. Co. and Robbins & Lawrence, the vast majority were arms for the civilian market (II) with blued and occasionally engraved frames, and without the sling ring bar (on engraved grades). The U.S. Ordnance Dept. purchased 200 which were delivered in 1853 and another 25 in 1855. All of the U.S. military purchases have the long swivel ring bar on the left side (I). A few rare carbines (I) are known marked "U.S.N." on the buttplate tang. **(D)**

26-20 Sharps M1852 (Sharps R.M. Co./R. & L.) Carbines, Types I & II

OL: 34⅝" or 37⅝"
BD: .36, .44, or .52 cal. (I, .52 cal. only); 6-groove rifling
Furniture: brass, iron swivel and bar on left side
Lockplate: backaction; flat
Markings: "C. SHARPS/PATENT/1852" behind hammer; upper frame strap—"C. SHARPS/PATENT/1848" and serial no.
BL: 17½" or 20½" to frame (18½" or 21½" bore)
Finish: (I) "bright"; (II) "browned"
Configuration: round
Sights: rear—9/16" base 2¼" from frame; front—brass blade
Fastenings: single brass band
Markings: either "ROBBINS &/LAWRENCE" or "SHARPS' RIFLE/MANUF^G CO/HARTFORD CONN." on top (II) or "U.S./J.H. (or) S.K.P."

Of 4,997 M1852 Sharps carbines made between 1853-55, nearly all were supplied for the civilian trade (I) and were available with optional tang and globe sights. The Ordnance Dept. ordered 50 (I) in 1852 and another 200 in 1854. The M1852 Sharps model is distinguished from the M1853 by the use of a band spring in the right forestock to hold the key lever on the frame. **(C)**

26-21 Sharps M1853 (Sharps R.M. Co.) Sporting Rifles

OL: 39¾"-49¾"
BL: 24"-34" bore (27" most

BD: .36, .44, or .52 cal.
Furniture: brass (early) or iron (late)
Patchbox: brass or iron, 2-piece, hinged forward
Lockplate: backaction; flat
Markings: "SHARPS/PATENT/1852" behind hammer; upper frame strap—"C. SHARPS/PATENT/1848" and serial no.

common)
Finish: "bright," "browned," or "blued"
Configuration: octagonal (most common), round, or (infrequently) part round/part octagonal
Sights: rear—folding leaf on base 2¼" from frame; front—brass blade, dovetailed
Fastenings: forestock screwed to barrel
Markings: "SHARPS RIFLE/MANUFG. CO./HARTFORD, CONN." on top

Between 1854-59, 2,970 Sharps M1853 sporting rifles were produced at Hartford. The models are distinguished from their nearly identical predecessors by the use of a pin on the frame to retain the key lever in lieu of the spring band in the forestock. The rifles were available in four grades of finish. Tang and globe sights optional. **(C)**

26-22 I

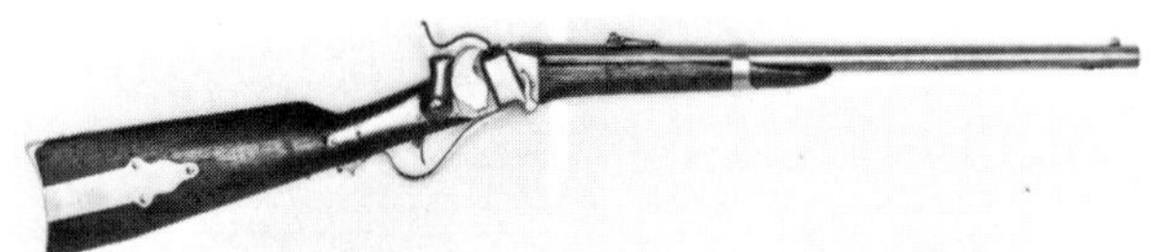

26-22 Sharps M1855 (Sharps R.M. Co.) Carbines, Types I & II
OL: 37⅝"
BD: .52 cal., 6-groove rifling
Furniture: brass, iron swivel bar and ring on left side (short)
Patchbox: brass, 2-piece, hinged forward
Lockplate: backaction; flat
Markings: on primer door—"EDWARD MAYNARD/PATENTEE 1845"; upper frame strap—"C. SHARPS/PATENT/1848" and serial no.
BL: 20⅜" to frame (21½" bore)
Finish: "bright" or "blued"
Configuration: round
Sights: rear—Sharps folding leaf on base 2⅜" from frame; front—brass blade
Fastenings: single brass band
Markings: "SHARPS RIFLE/MANUFG. CO./HARTFORD, CONN." on top; "US/J.H.P." on upper left surface (I only)

The prime purchaser of the M1855 series was the military, only 95 with the Maynard primer that distinguishes the M1855 having gone to the civilian market (II). The U.S. Ordnance Dept. purchased 600 between 1855-57. The U.S. Navy ordered 101 of the martial (I) version as well. None of the 12 M1855 sporting rifles with 27" barrels made in 1856-57 have survived. **(D)**

26-23 Sharps M1855 (Sharps R.M. Co.) Carbines, Types III & IV
OL: 37⅝" (III); 35⅜" (IV)
BD: .577 cal., 3-groove rifling
Furniture: brass, iron swivel bar
Patchbox: brass, 2-piece, hinged forward
Lockplate: backaction; flat
BL: 20⅜" to frame (III); 18" to frame (IV); (21½" bore, III); (19⅛" bore, IV)
Finish: "blued"
Configuration: round
Sights: rear—block with 4 folding

Markings: on lid of primer door—"EDWARD MAYNARD/PATENTEE 1845"; upper frame strap—"C. SHARPS/PATENT/1848"

leaves, 2 on each side of open "V" c. 6" from frame; front—iron block blade

Fastenings: single brass band

Markings: "SHARPS RIFLE/MANUFG. CO./HARTFORD, CONN." on top and British proof marks

Types III and IV were manufactured solely for the British government, the initial contract of 1855 calling for 1,000. This was increased to 6,000, half of which were to have 18" barrels and half 21" barrels. Sharps subcontracted production to Robbins & Lawrence, who failed to make deliveries in time. Sharps renegotiated the contract but delivered only 900 before penalty clauses were invoked. Many of the 6,000 were issued in India. **(C)**

26-24 I

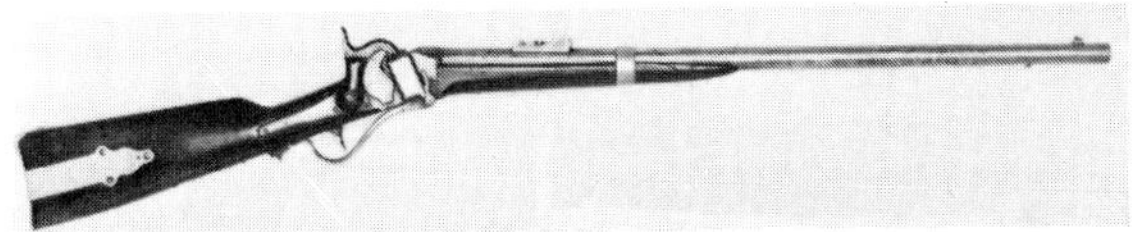

26-24 Sharps M1855 (Sharps R.M. Co.) Military Rifles, Types I-III

OL: 44" (I & II); 56" (III)

BD: .52 cal., 3-groove rifling

Furniture: brass (I & II); iron (III)

Patchbox: brass, 2-piece, hinged forward (I & II)

Lockplate: backaction; flat

Markings: on primer lid—"EDWARD MAYNARD/PATENTEE 1845"; upper frame strap—"C. SHARPS/PATENT/1848"

BL: (I & II) .27" to frame (28¼" bore); 39" (III)

Finish: "blued"

Configuration: round; saber bayonet stud below near muzzle (I & II)

Sights: rear—3" long base with folding ladder with slide 2³⁄₁₆" from frame; front—iron block/blade

Fastenings: single brass band (I & II); 3 iron bands (III)

Markings: "SHARPS RIFLE/MANUFG. CO./HARTFORD, CONN." on top and occasionally an anchor (I & II)

The U.S. Navy ordered 150 of these military rifles (I) in 1856. Rollin White's patented cocking device was added to the final 50 of these (II), but it was found ineffective and removed from all but 12. These 50 bear the additional lock marking "R. WHITES/PATENT/1855" behind the hammer. Twelve rifles were contracted for by the Army (III) with 39" barrels and full forestocks. **(E)**

26-25 Sharps M1859/M1863/M1865 Carbines, Types I-III

OL: 39"

BD: .52 cal.

Furniture: brass (early), iron (late); iron swivel bar and ring on left

Patchbox: brass or iron, 2-piece, hinged forward

Markings: "R.S. LAWRENCE PAT./APRIL 15TH 1852" behind ham-

BL: 21⅜" to frame (22" bore)

Finish: "blued"

Configuration: round

Sights: rear—Lawrence M1859 2¼" from frame; front—brass blade inset in iron block

Fastenings: single band, brass (early) or iron (late)

Markings: "SHARPS RIFLE/MANU-

mer; left side of frame marked —"C. SHARPS' PAT./SEPT. 12TH 1848"; serial no. on upper frame strap

FG. CO./HARTFORD, CONN." and either "NEW MODEL 1859", "NEW MODEL 1863", or "NEW MODEL 1865" on top

I

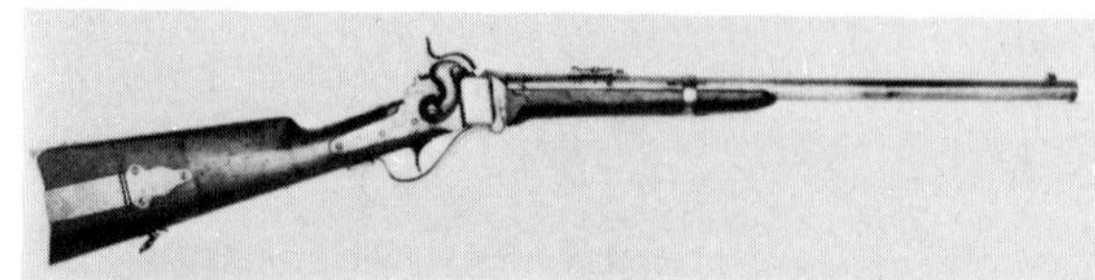

Beginning with a contract for 2,500 carbines granted in 1859, this arm was produced exclusively for the military, with an estimated 93,000 being made in all three models. The earliest production (I) was brass-mounted, but this was changed to iron (II) near the end of the 1859 series. In 1863 the patchbox was eliminated (III). **(D)**

26-26 S.C. Robinson/Richmond Armory Sharps Confederate Carbines, Types I & II

OL: (I) 38¾"; (II) 38½"
BD: .52 cal., 6-groove rifling
Furniture: brass, iron sling swivel on buttstock and iron swivel bar and ring on left side
Lockplate: backaction; flat
Markings: (I) "S.C. ROBINSON./ ARMS MANUFACTORY/RICHMOND VA/1862" and serial no. behind hammer; (II) serial no. only behind hammer, and on upper frame strap

BL: 21" to frame (21⅝" bore)
Finish: "bright"
Configuration: round
Sights: rear—open "V" 2⅜" from frame; front—iron blade, dovetailed
Fastenings: single brass band
Markings: (I) "S.C. ROBINSON/ ARMS MANUFACTORY" and "RICHMOND VA/1862"; (II) "RICHMOND VA." on top

About 1,900 of these arms were made in 1862-63 (I) before the Richmond manufactory was purchased outright by the Confederate government. The latter made approximately 3,300 more before the complaints about its poor reliability caused the government to revert to muzzleloading carbines. **(D)**

26-27

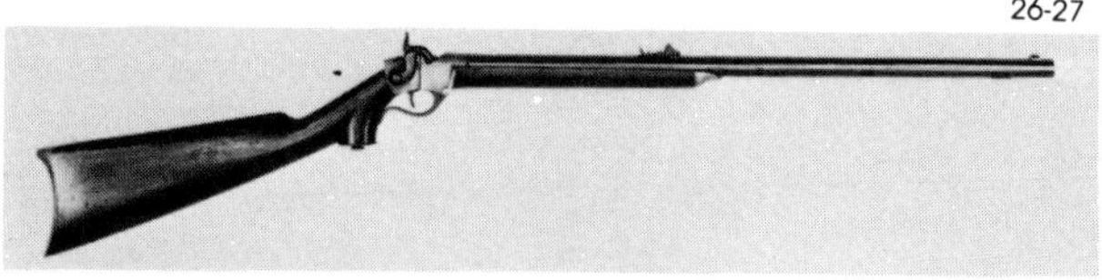

26-27 Sharps (C. Sharps & Co.) Pistol-Rifles

OL: 39¾"-45¾"
BD: .36 or .38 cal., 6-groove rifling
Furniture: brass
Patchbox: brass, 2-piece, hinged forward (not always present)
Lockplate: none, mechanism within frame

BL: 23"-29" to frame (24"-30" bores)
Finish: "browned"
Configuration: round, rarely octagonal
Sights: rear—globe (early) or patented elevating leaf 7¾" from frame; front—iron block/ blade

Markings: "C. SHARPS/PATENT/ 1848-1852" on left side plate, or serial no. on upper frame strap; "C. SHARPS/PATENT/1852" with "C. SHARPS & CO'S/RIFLE WORKS/PHILA. PA." on alternate sides

Fastenings: forestock screwed to barrel

Markings: "C. SHARPS & CO. PHILAD^A^ PA." on top

Judging from surviving serial numbers, Christian Sharps made about 500 of these pistol-rifles after disassociating himself from the Sharps Rifle Mfg. Co. and relocating in Philadelphia. One is known with bayonet lug on the barrel's right side. **(D)**

26-28

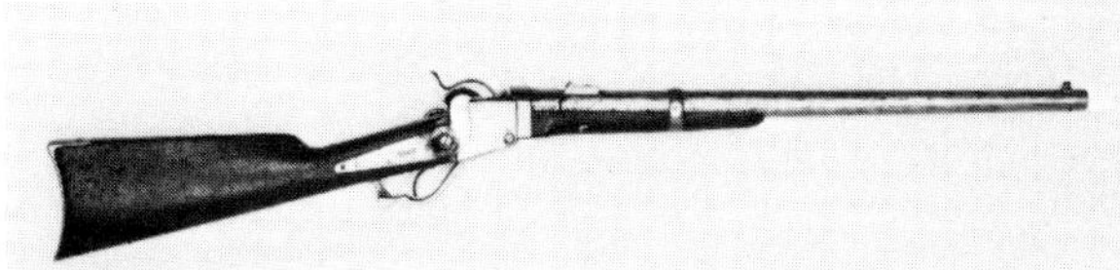

26-28 Starr Breechloading Percussion Carbines

OL: 37⅝"

BD: .54 cal., 5-groove rifling

Furniture: brass

Lockplate: backaction; flat

Markings: "STARR ARMS CO./ YONKERS, N.Y." behind hammer; upper frame strap—"STARR'S PATENT./SEPT. 14TH 1858"

BL: 20" to frame (21" bore)

Finish: "blued"

Configuration: round, stepped

Sights: rear—1½" long base with pierced "L" leaf 1¼" from frame; front—iron block/ blade

Fastenings: single brass bands

Markings: "STARR ARMS CO YONKERS, N.Y." on top

Ebenezer T. Starr delivered 20,001 of his patented breechloading carbines between 1863-64. He had previously sold another 600 to the U.S. government. His subsequent government contract called for cartridge carbines. **(A)**

26-29

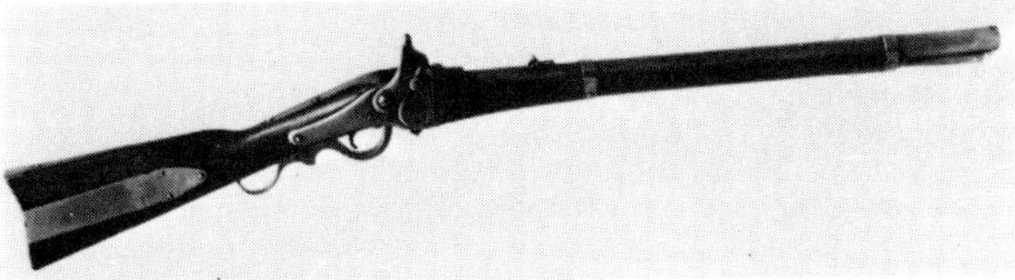

26-29 Symmes Breechloading Carbines

OL: 38⅜"

BD: .54 cal., pentagonal rifling

Furniture: brass

Patchbox: brass, 2-piece, hinged forward

Lockplate: backaction; flat with rounded edges

Markings: upper frame strap—"LT. SYMMES PATENT"; inspector's initials in buttstock

BL: 21⅞" (bore)

Finish: "blued"

Configuration: round

Sights: ½" long block with pivotint pierced "L" leaf 3½" from frame; front—iron blade

Fastenings: 2 brass bands

The triggerguard/lever causes the chamber/breechblock to pivot upward for loading. A Maynard tape primer is incorporated into the right side of the lock. Although up to 200 carbines were contracted for in 1856, only 20 were delivered, and no more were ordered when tests determined that the breech mechanism leaked excessive amounts of gas. **(F)**

---

27 Patented Breechloading Percussion/Cartridge Rifles and Carbines

The Ordnance Department continued to seek an effective means of eliminating the gas leakage problem with the Sharps patented carbines and other arms. Four individuals devised improved cartridges which, while not self-contained (i.e., a separate percussion cap still had to be affixed to the cone with each loading sequence), were very close to the metallic cartridge breechloader that would evolve after 1860. In each case the cartridge patent was for a patented breechloading military carbine.

The first patent granted in March, 1856, was to Ambrose E. Burnside. His carbines were little different from those of the Hall system; they contained an upward pivoting breechblock with chamber, activated first by a side lever and later by a triggerguard latch that permitted the triggerguard to swing the chamber open. Burnside prevented the gas leakage by using a tapering brass cartridge pierced with a small hole or vent at its back end. The cartridge proved successful, and after initial government tests with 200, sizeable numbers were ordered. Burnside was followed shortly by the indomitable Washington, D.C. dentist, Edward Maynard. His cartridge patent, issued in June, 1856, covered a brass cylinder with large attached rim, similarly pierced in the rear with a small vent. Maynard's carbine was a simple tilting barrel, activated by the triggerguard/lever. During the Civil War, a similar operating carbine patented in July, 1860, by Mahlon J. Gallager, used a straight brass cylindrical cartridge without the rim, but pierced with a vent in the rear like the Burnside model. In December, 1863, two ordnance officers, Rodman and Crispin, were issued a patent that substituted brass foil and paper composition for the drawn brass. This permitted easier extraction of the casings, a major problem with the rimless Gallager brass cartridge. This same principle was also applied to the Smith cartridge, heretofore made of gutta-percha. Gilbert Smith had been issued a patent for this in 1857, but the Ordnance Department waited to order 300 in July, 1860, and war broke out before they could be delivered.

Were it not for the exigencies of the Civil War, most of these patented carbines and corresponding cartridges would have died an early death. The pressing need for cavalry arms, however, prompted the Ordnance Department to purchase significant quantities of each type mentioned despite the confusion these varying types would wreak upon the ammunition supply system. The Maynard rim-fire cartridge was eventually the only one to survive for long.

27-O Burnside Breechloading Carbines, Types V (color plate, above), **III & IV**

OL: 39⅛"
BD: .54 cal., 5-groove rifling
Furniture: iron, "blued"; iron sling swivel on buttstock; swivel bar and ring on left side
Lockplate: backaction; flat
Markings: behind hammer—"BURNSIDE RIFLE CO./PROVIDENCE R.I."; top of frame—"BURNSIDE PATENT/MARCH 25TH 1856./(serial no.)" early, or "BURNSIDE PATENT/MODEL OF 1864/(serial no.)" late

BL: 19⅝" to frame (21" bore)
Finish: "blued"
Configuration: round
Sights: rear—1" long block with pierced "L" leaf 9/16" from frame; front—iron blade, dovetailed
Fastenings: single iron band
Markings: "CAST STEEL" and date (1862-64)

Early production was marked with "G.P.FOSTER PAT./APRIL 10TH 1860" on lever release. During 1861-65 Burnside delivered 51,291 type III-V carbines. Type III incorporates a forestock; types IV and V use a jointed level mechanism, the last with frame screw guides. **(A)**

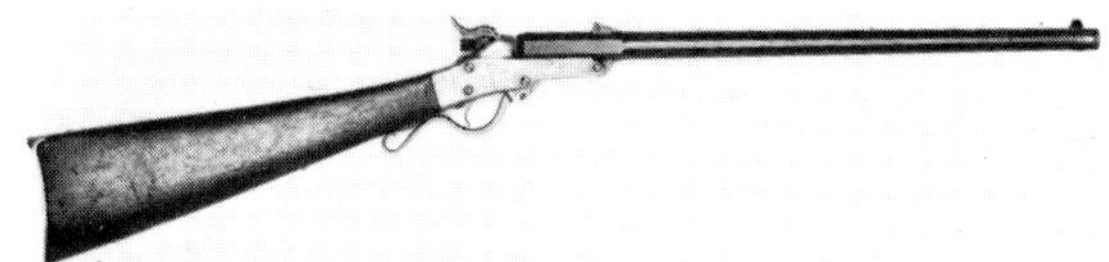

Maynard "M1864" Breechloading Cartridge Carbines (color plate, middle)

OL: 36¾"
BD: .50 cal., 3-groove rifling
Furniture: iron: "blued"; swivel bar and ring on left side
Lockplate: none, mechanism within frame
Markings: left side of frame—"EDWARD MAYNARD/PATENTEE/ MAY 27, 1851/DEC. 6, 1859"; right side of frame—"MANUFACTURED BY/MASS. ARMS. CO./CHICOPEE FALLS."

BL: 20"
Finish: "blued"
Configuration: part round/part octagonal
Sights: 11/16" long block with 2 leaves 2⅝" from breech; front—iron blade
Fastenings: none, no forestock
Markings: inspectors' initials on left side; serial no. under barrel

The Massachusetts Arms Co. delivered 20,002 of these carbines between 1864-65. Due to their late delivery date, few saw combat service in the Civil War. **(A)**

Gilbert Smith Breechloading Carbines, Type I (color plate, below) **& II, III**

OL: 39"
BD: .50 cal., 3-groove rifling

BL: 20⅛" to frame (21½" bore)
Finish: "blued"

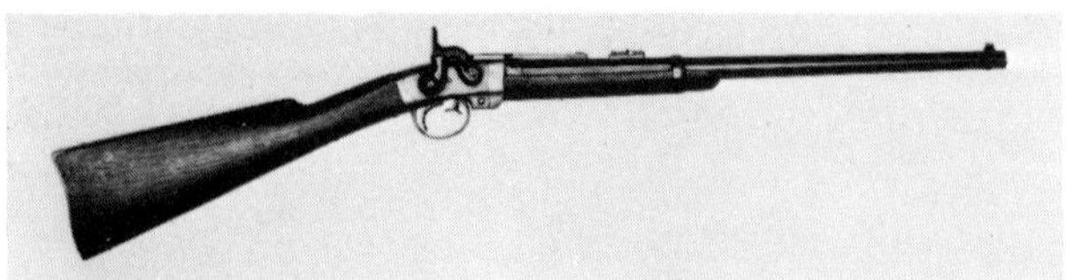

Furniture: iron, swivel bar and ring on left side (I); sling swivels on stock and band (II)
Lockplate: none, mechanism within frame
Markings: left side of frame—"ADDRESS/POULTNEY & TRIMBLE/ BALTIMORE, U.S.A." over "SMITH'S PATENT/JUNE 23, 1857" in conjunction with either "MANUFACTURED BY/MASS. ARMS CO./CHICOPEE FALLS", or "MANUFACTURED BY/AM'N M'CH'N WKS/SPRINGFIELD, MASS" or "AMERICAN ARMS CO./CHICOPEE FALLS
Configuration: part round/part octagonal
Sights: rear—1½" long block with folding leaf with slide 3⅝" from frame; front—German-silver blade inset in iron block
Fastenings: single iron band, "blued"
Markings: none

To complete their contract of 1863 for 20,000 Smith carbines, Poultney & Trimble subcontracted the work to three New England machine shops and armsmakers. 500 Smith carbines were also sold to New York in 1863. **(A)**

27-1 Burnside Breechloading Carbines, Type I
OL: 40"
BD: .54 cal., 5-groove rifling
Furniture: iron
Lockplate: backaction; flat
Markings: top of frame near breech—"BURNSIDE'S PATENT/ MARCH 25TH/1856/(serial no.)"
BL: 22" (bore)
Finish: "blued"
Configuration: round
Sights: rear—Sharps M1853 type block and folding ladder ¾" from frame; front—iron blade
Markings: none

A total of 200 were delivered in 1858 to the U.S. Ordnance Dept. Another order for 1,000 was withdrawn, and instead Burnside's "Bristol Firearms Co." was permitted to deliver up to $25,000 worth of their weapons. This should have covered 709 carbines, but only 690 were delivered in 1860-61. These carbines incorporated the Maynard primer. **(D)**

27-2

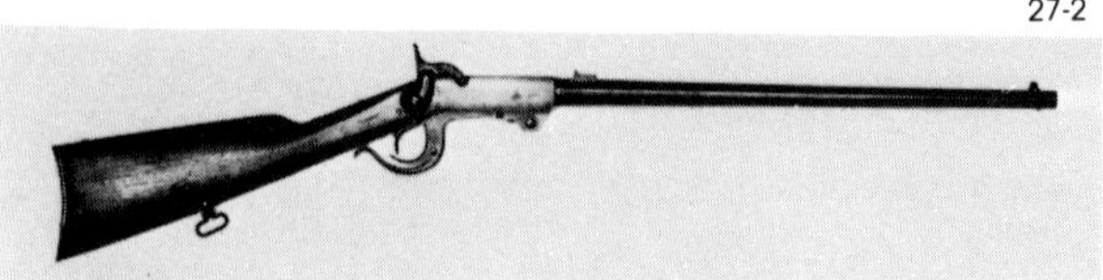

27-2 Burnside Breechloading Carbines, Type II
OL: 39⅛"
BD: .54 cal., 5-groove rifling
Furniture: iron, iron sling swivel
BL: 19⅝" to frame (21" bore)
Finish: "blued"
Configuration: round

on buttstock; swivel bar and ring on left side
Lockplate: backaction; flat
Markings: either "BRISTOL FIRE-ARMS CO." or "BURNSIDE RIFLE CO. PROVIDENCE R.I." behind hammer; top of frame—"BURN-SIDE PATENT/MARCH 25TH 1856/(serial no.)"

Sights: rear—1" long block with pierced "L" leaf ⅜" from frame; front—iron blade
Fastenings: none, no forestock
Markings: "CAST STEEL 1861" on top; serial no. on bottom

The company delivered 1,640 carbines during 1861-62. These are distinguished by the separate lever release within the triggerguard marked on its right side: "G.P. FOSTER PAT./APRIL 10TH1860". **(C)**

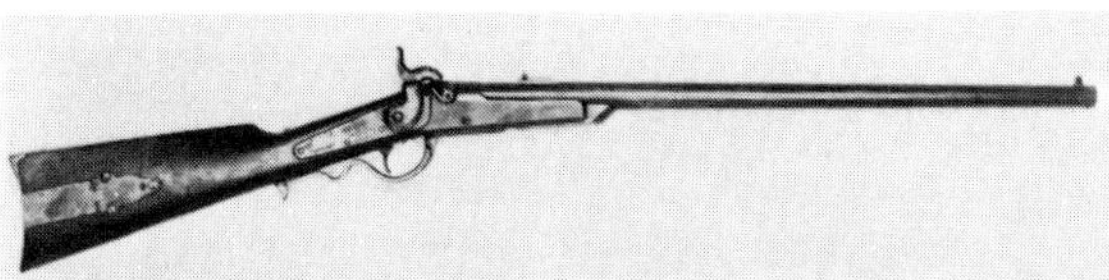
27-3 II

27-3 Gallager (Richardson & Overman) Breechloading Percussion Carbines, Types I and II

OL: 39⅛"
BD: .52 cal., 5-groove rifling (I); 6-groove rifling (II)
Furniture: iron, swivel bar and ring on left side
Lockplate: backaction; flat
Markings: "GALLAGHER/PAT-ENTED JULY 17TH 1860/(serial no.)" (I) or "MANUFACTD BY/RICHARDSON & OVERMAN/PHIL-ADA/(serial) no.)" and "GALLA-GER'S PATENT/JULY 17TH 1860 (II) behind hammer

BL: 22¼" (barrel and bore)
Finish: "blued"
Configuration: round
Sights: rear—(I) 1" long block with 2 "L" leaves 2" from frame, (II) 1¼" long block with pierced "L" leaf 1⅜" from frame; front—iron blade, dovetailed
Fastenings: none
Markings: none

Richardson & Overman of Philadelphia delivered 17,878 of Gallager's patented carbines during the early 1860s. The 5,000 carbines of a later contract (1865) were metallic cartridge models (see chapter 36). **(A)**

27-4 Maynard "M1859" Breechloading Patent Cartridge Carbines, Types I & II

OL: 36½"
BD: (I) .35 cal., (II) .50 cal., 3-groove rifling
Furniture: iron
Patchbox: iron, 2-piece, hinged to rear
Lockplate: none, mechanism within frame
Markings: right side of frame—"MAYNARD ARMS CO./WASH-INGTON"; left side of frame—"MANUFACTURED BY/MASS ARMS CO./CHICOPEE FALLS"; patchbox (primer box) lid—

BL: 20"
Finish: "blued"
Configuration: part round/part octagonal
Sights: rear—tang sight and open "V" 3" from breech; front—iron blade
Fastenings: none, no forestock
Markings: none

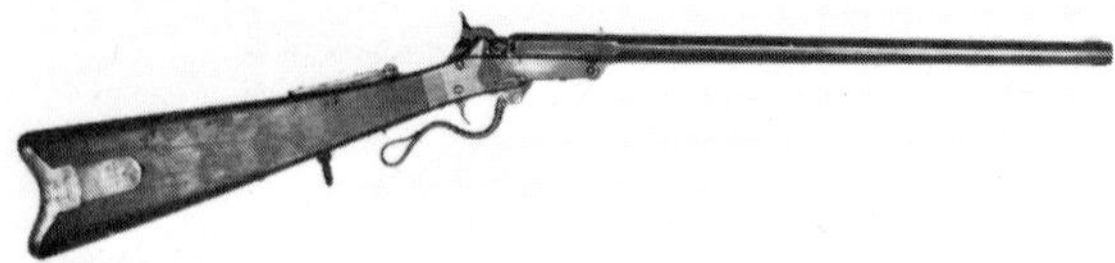

"MAYNARD PATENTEE/MAY 27,
1851/JUNE 17, 1856"

Four hundred type I were delivered to the U.S. Ordnance Dept. in 1859. Presumably these should bear standard U.S. inspection marks. Under an 1861 contract, Mississippi purchased 325 type I and 300 type II. **(D)**

27-5 Maynard "M1865" Breechloading Cartridge Sporting Rifles

OL: 36¾", 40¾", or 42¾"
BD: .35, .40, .50 cals., also available in .55 and .64 cal. shot
Furniture: iron, "blued"
Lockplate: none, mechanism within frame
Markings: left side of frame—"EDWARD MAYNARD/PATENTEE/MAY 27, 1851/DEC. 6, 1859"; right side of frame—"MANUFACTURED BY/MASS. ARMS CO./CHICOPEE FALLS"
BL: 20", 24", or 26"
Finish: "blued"
Configuration: part round/part octagonal
Sights: rear—tang sight and open "V" c. 3" from breech; front—iron blade
Fastenings: none, no forestock
Markings: none

Unknown quantities of the M1865 sporting rifles were made from excess frames of the M1864 carbine production. In 1873 the M1865 was virtually supplanted by a center-fire cartridge version, which, in turn, was supplanted in 1882 by an improved version. **(C)**

28 Percussion Muzzleloaders Altered to Cartridge Breechloaders

The Civil War, with its outpouring of technological arms inventiveness, greatly influenced the development of the military breechloader. The sheer number of breechloading mechanisms patented within the short span of that conflict is almost overwhelming. Yet the war also negatively effected the adoption of the best possible military breechloading system by the U.S. Army. The war was fought primarily with muzzleloading rifle-muskets, and, at its close, the government was left in possession of more than a million-and-a-half obsolete muzzleloading weapons. To utilize these surpluses, the U.S. Ordnance Department compromised. It did not seek the best possible breechloading system, but rather the best system by which this huge surplus might be altered to breechloading single-shot cartridge rifles.

The system first adopted was that devised by Master Armorer E. S. Allin of the Springfield Armory. In some respects this system, utilizing a hinged breechblock milled into the top of the old muzzleloading barrel that swung up and forward to expose the breech for a

metallic cartridge, resembled that patented by W. Mont Storm prior to the Civil War. (So much so, in fact, that Mont Storm later sued the government for patent violations.) At first the old .58 cal. barrels were used intact. The large caliber, however, was found inconvenient, and the next group of rifle-muskets altered were first reamed out and then sleeved with a new .50 cal. bore. When even this was found unsatisfactory, new shorter barrels were made in .50 cal. and installed on the modified stocks of the old arms. Finally, in full commitment to the Allin system, the government adopted an entirely new rifle for the breechloading system.

Between 1865-72 there were numerous attempts on the part of private inventors to adapt the muzzleloading rifle-musket to a practical breechloading cartridge arm. The fiscal conservatism that caused the War Department to settle on the Allin system prompted these inventors and their backers to look elsewhere for buyers. Their attempts to sell altered arms to the states met with little success except in Reconstruction South Carolina. The Franco-Prussian War in 1870-71 provided an excellent outlet. But that some outlet drained American supplies of surplus muzzleloading rifle-muskets to alter; more than a quarter-million were sold to France during her hour of need.

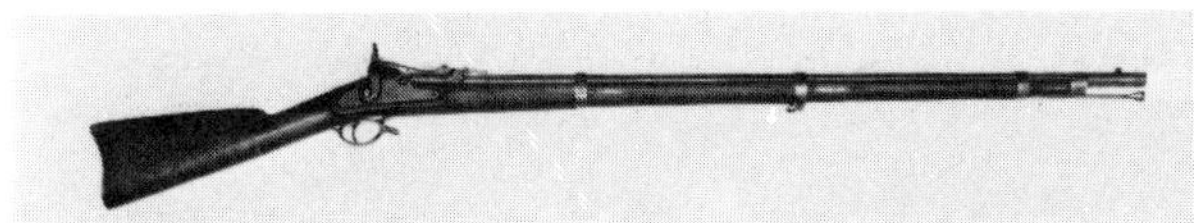

28-O Allin (Springfield Armory) M1865 Alterations of M1863 Rifle-Muskets, Type II (color plate, above)

OL: 55¾"
BD: .58 cal., 3-groove rifling
Furniture: iron
Lockplate: flat, beveled edge
Markings: eagle and "U.S./SPRINGFIELD" forward of hammer; "1865" on tail

BL: 40" (3/8" bore)
Finish: "bright"
Configuration: round
Sights: rear—M1861 rifle-musket base with single pierced "L" at receiver; front—iron block/blade
Fastenings: 3 iron bands, flat-M1861 type
Markings: eagle head usually remains

A total of 5,005 of these alterations were done at Springfield. The actual work was begun in late 1865 but not completed until 1866. The large caliber was found unsatisfactory, and the extraction process too complex, resulting in the M1866 alterations. **(B)**

Allin (Springfield Armory) M1866 Alterations of M1863 Rifle-Muskets, Type II (color plate, below)

OL: 55¾"
BD: .58 cal., 3-groove rifling
Furniture: iron
Lockplate: flat, beveled edge
Markings: eagle and "U.S./SPRINGFIELD" forward of hammer; date on tail, usually "1864"; top of breechblock—

BL: 40" (36½" bore)
Finish: "bright"
Configuration: round
Sights: rear—M1861 rifle-musket base with double peep "L" leaf, reversed; front—iron block/blade
Fastenings: 3 iron bands

M1865

M1866

"1866/(eagle head)" near hinge

Markings: none

Between 1867-69 Springfield altered 52,349 muzzleloading rifle-muskets, principally Springfield-made M1863 type II arms, to this improved Allin system. First the barrels were bored smooth to .64 cal. Then a new steel sleeve of .50 cal. inner diameter was brazed into the bore and rifled as before. A slightly different sight leaf, pierced with two peeps, was substituted on a reversed sight base forward of the hinge. **(A)**

28-1 G. Merrill (Brown Mfg. Co.) Alterations of P1853 English Rifle-Muskets

OL: 54¾"

BL: 33½" to receiver (35" bore)

BD: .577 cal., 3-groove rifling

Finish: "blued"

Furniture: brass, except for iron bands
Lockplate: removed and filled with wood
Markings: bolt—"BROWN MFG. CO. NEWBURYPORT, MASS./ PATENTEE OCT. 17, 1871"
Configuration: round
Sights: rear—Enfield P1853 base with folding ladder at receiver; front—iron block/blade
Fastenings: 3 iron bands, "blued"
Markings: none

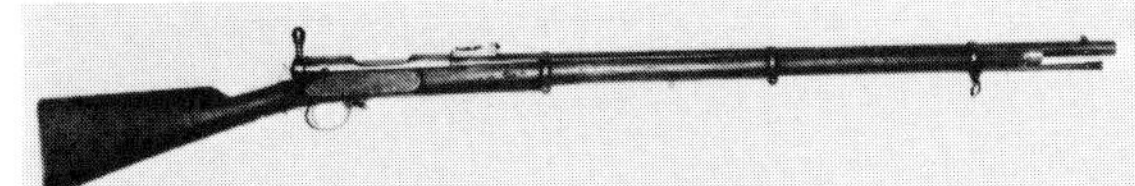

The Brown Mfg. Co. was only in existence from 1869-73, primarily making Ballard action breechloading rifles. Quantities of this straight pull bolt action alteration based on George Merrill's 1871 patent must not have exceeded 1,000, given the year-and-a-half production time before the firm closed. **(D)**

28-2

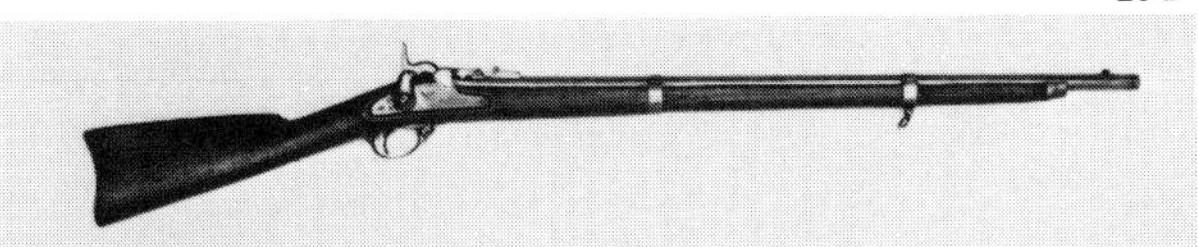

28-2 Miller (Meriden Mfg. Co.) Alterations of M1861 Rifle-Muskets

OL: 48¼"
BD: .58 cal., 3-groove rifling
Furniture: iron, "US" on buttplate tang
Lockplate: flat, beveled edge
Markings: usually "(eagle)/U.S." and "PARKERS' SNOW & CO./ MERIDEN, CONN." forward of hammer; date ("1863" or "1864") on tail; top of breechblock—"W.H. & G.W. MILLER/ PATENT MAY 24, 1865" over "MERIDEN MANFG. CO./MERIDEN, CONN."
BL: 31¼" (barrel and bore)
Finish: "bright"
Configuration: round
Sights: rear—U.S. M1861 rifle-musket type ⅜" from breechblock; front—iron block/blade
Fastenings: 2 iron bands
Markings: none

Quantities of this side-swinging breechblock design of the Miller brothers is unknown. Production was probably restricted to the period 1866-68, with probable numbers altered under 5,000. **(C)**

28-3 Needham (Jenks/Bridesburg) Alterations of M1861 Rifle-Muskets

OL: 55¾"
BD: .58 cal., 3-groove rifling
Furniture: iron, "US" on buttplate tang
Lockplate: flat, beveled edge
Markings: usually "(eagle—partially obscured)/BRIDESBURG" forward of hammer; date on tail
BL: 36" to receiver (36¾" bore)
Finish: "bright"
Configuration: round
Sights: rear—2⅞" long base with tall folding ladder ¼" from receiver; front—iron block/blade
Fastenings: 2 iron bands
Markings: none

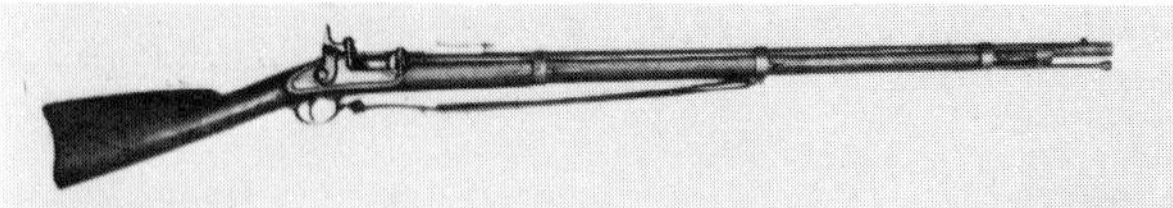

The alteration was patented by George and Joseph Needham of London in 1867 and covered a laterally swinging breechblock hinged on the right side. It is believed that they were made for about one year at the Jenks Bridesburg Machine Works, primarily using muskets formerly made under government contract. Quantities are unknown. **(C)**

28-4

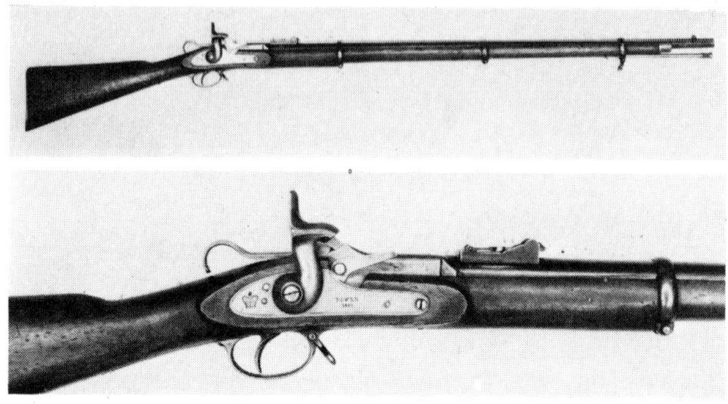

28-4 Peabody (Providence Tool Co.) Alterations of P1853 English Rifle Muskets

OL: 55¼"
BD: .577, 3-groove rifling
Furniture: brass, except iron bands
Lockplate: flat, beveled edge
Markings: forward of hammer—various P1853 lock markings, e.g., "TOWER/(date)"; British crown on tail; left side of receiver—"PEABODY'S PAT./ JULY 22, 1862"

BL: 35¾" to receiver (36¼" bore)
Finish: "browned"
Configuration: round
Sights: rear—Enfield P1853 base with folding ladder at receiver; front—iron block/blade
Fastenings: 3 iron bands, "blued"
Markings: none

The Peabody alteration apparently was affected primarily on surplus rifle-muskets and rifles imported during the Civil War, most of which were disposed of during the late 1860s. The alteration was not listed, however, in the 1865 and '66 Peabody catalogues. **(A)**

28-5 Remington-Rider Alterations of U.S. M1863 Rifle-Muskets, Type II

OL: 54⅝"
BD: .58 cal., 3-groove rifling
Furniture: iron, "US" on buttplate tang (plus "S.C." for South Carolina purchase)
Lockplate: none, mechanism within frame
Markings: upper frame strap—

BL: 37½" to frame (39" bore)
Finish: "bright"
Configuration: round
Sights: rear—U.S. M1861 rifle-musket type ¼" from frame; front—iron block/blade
Fastenings: 3 iron bands
Markings: none

"REMINGTONS ILION N.Y. U.S.A./
PAT. MAY 30 NOV 15TH 1864
APRIL 17TH 1866"

Of these Remington alterations, 5,000 were sold to the Reconstruction government of South Carolina in 1868. More than 63,000 were also supposedly sold to France during the Franco-Prussian War, but using M1863 (type I) rifle-muskets as the basis of alteration. These purportedly have 39⅜" bores and overall lengths of 55⅞". **(B)**

28-6

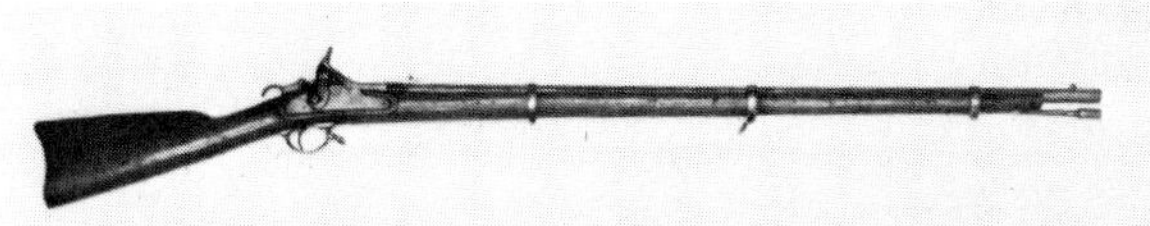

28-6 Roberts Alterations of U.S. M1863 Rifle-Muskets, Type I

OL: 56"
BD: .58 cal.
Furniture: iron, "US" on buttplate tang
Lockplate: flat, beveled edge
Markings: (usually) forward of hammer—"U.S./SPRINGFIELD"; date on tail, e.g., "1864"; left side of receiver—"ROBERT'S PAT./JUNE. 11, 1867"
BL: 36¾" to receiver (37¾" bore)
Finish: "bright"
Configuration: round
Sights: rear—M1865 base with pierced leaf ¼" from receiver; front—iron block/blade
Fastenings: 3 iron bands
Markings: none

The Roberts breechloading action is nearly identical to that of the Peabody, and both were manufactured at the Providence Tool Co. 5,000 were sold to the Reconstruction government of South Carolina in 1868 to arm its black militia. It was recommended also for adoption by New York, but alterations made for that state are believed to have been diverted to France during the Franco-Prussian War. **(B)**

28-7 Roberts Alterations of English P1853 Rifles and Rifle-Muskets

OL: 49-49½"
BD: .577 cal., 3-groove rifling
Furniture: brass, except iron bands
Lockplate: flat
Markings: forward of hammer—various contractors, such as "BARNETT/LONDON" or "(date)/TOWER"; crown on tail; number struck into lower band; left side of receiver—"ROBERT'S PAT. JUNE. 11. 1867"; "PB" struck into stock, left side, opposite lockplate together with
BL: 29¾" to receiver (30¾" bore)
Finish: "blued"
Configuration: round, some with stud on right
Sights: rear—English P1853 rifle-musket type ⅛"-½" from receiver; front—iron block/blade
Fastenings: 2 iron bands
Markings: none

number; number struck behind lockplate

The meaning of the various numbers struck into the stock and bands is not clear since none match one another on the same gun. These numbers are not found on Springfield M1863 alterations. **(A)**

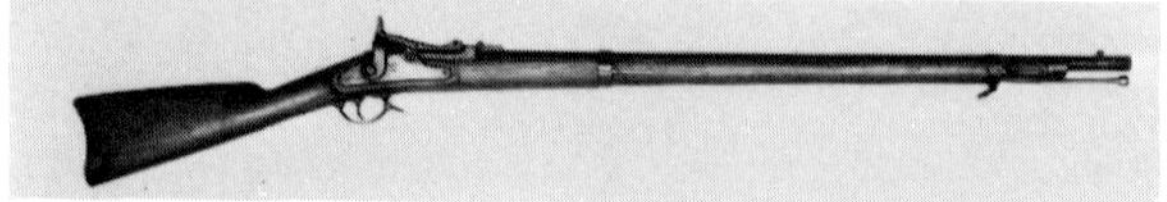
28-8

28-8 Allin (Springfield Armory) M1865 "Cadet" Alteration Rifles

OL: 51¾"
BD: .58 cal., 3-groove rifling
Furniture: iron, "blued"
Lockplate: flat, beveled edge
Markings: eagle and "U.S./ SPRINGFIELD" forward of hammer; "1865" on tail

BL: 35¾" overall (33½" bore)
Finish: "blued"
Configuration: round
Sights: rear—M1865 base at receiver; front—iron block/ blade
Fastenings: 2 iron bands, M1861 type
Markings: none remain, milled away

There are no actual documents verifying the alterations of the M1865 of this type by Springfield. The current thought is that these rifles were made after the disposal of the M1865 arms as surplus. **(B)**

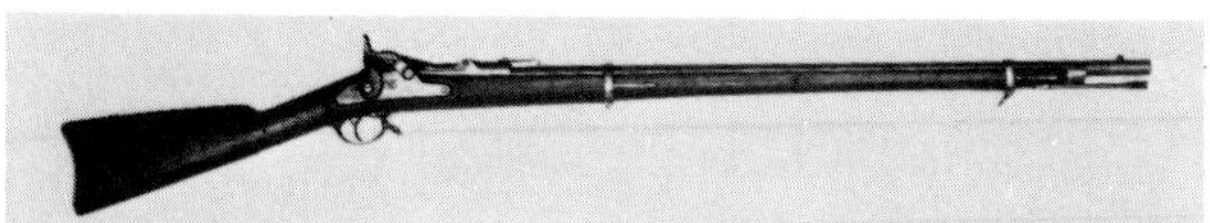

28-9 Allin (Springfield Armory) M1868 Alterations of M1863 Rifle-Muskets, Type II

OL: 51⅞"
BD: .50 cal., 3-groove rifling
Furniture: iron
Lockplate: flat, beveled edge
Markings: eagle and "U.S./ SPRINGFIELD" forward of hammer "1863" or "1864" on tail; top of breechblock marked: "1869/(eagle-arrows)/ U.S."; serial no. on receiver on left side

BL: 30½" to receiver (32½" bore)
Finish: "bright"
Configuration: round
Sights: rear—1$\frac{5}{16}$" long base with folding ladder with slide at receiver; front—iron block/ blade
Fastenings: 2 iron bands
Markings: serial no. on left side

During the fiscal years 1869-71 Springfield altered 52,149 type II rifle-muskets to M1868 breechloaders. Because the linings on many of the M1866 alterations had separated in service, the M1868 was given a totally-new shorter barrel with Allin-type receiver attached. **(A)**

28-10 Allin (Springfield Armory) M1869 Cadet Alteration Rifles

OL: 51⅞"
BD: .50 cal.
Furniture: iron, no sling swivels

BL: 28½" to receiver (29½" bore)
Finish: "bright"
Configuration: round

Lockplate: flat, beveled edge
Markings: eagle and "U.S./ SPRINGFIELD" forward of hammer; "1863" or "1864" on tail; "1869/(eagle-arrows)/U.S." on top of breechblock; serial no. on left side of receiver
Sights: rear—M1868 rifle sight; front—iron block/blade
Fastenings: 2 iron bands
Markings: serial no. on left side

A total of 3,403 of these rifles were assembled between 1869-71. For some reason another 20 were produced in 1876. **(B)**

28-11 Allin (Springfield Armory) M1870 Alterations of M1863 Rifle-Muskets, Type II

OL: 51⅞"
BD: .50 cal., 3-groove rifling
Furniture: iron
Lockplate: flat, beveled edge
Markings: eagle and "U.S./ SPRINGFIELD" forward of hammer; "1863" or "1864" on tail; top of breechblock—"1870/(eagle-arrows)/U.S."
BL: 31⅛" to receiver (32½" bore)
Finish: "bright"
Configuration: round
Sights: rear—M1868 rifle sight, but 7/16" forward of receiver; front—iron block/blade
Fastenings: 2 iron bands
Markings: none, no serial nos.

The only major difference between this arm and the M1868 is the use of a shorter receiver on the former. 11,513 alterations were produced between 1870-73. **(A)**

28-12

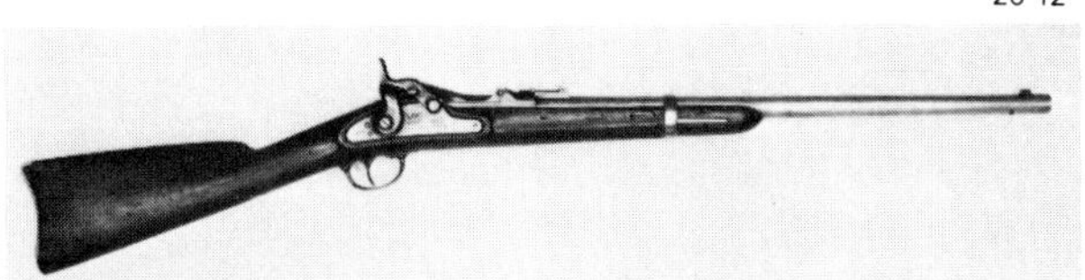

28-12 Allin (Springfield Armory) M1870 Carbines

OL: 41¼"
BD: .50 cal., 3-groove rifling
Furniture: iron
Lockplate: flat, beveled edge
Markings: eagle and "U.S./ SPRINGFIELD" forward of hammer; "1864" on tail; top of breechblock—"1870/(eagle-arrows)/U.S."
BL: 20½" to receiver (22½" bore)
Finish: "blued"
Configuration: round
Sights: rear—M1868 rifle type at receiver; front—brass blade inset in iron block
Fastenings: single iron band
Markings: none

Only 341 M1870 carbines were produced during 1871 at Springfield, primarily being intended as test samples. **(D)**

28-13 Sharps (Springfield Armory) M1871 Alteration Rifles

OL: 52"
BD: .50 cal., 3-groove rifling
Furniture: iron, "US" on buttplate
Lockplate: none, mechanism within frame
Markings: right side of frame—
BL: 34¼" to frame (35" bore)
Finish: "bright"
Configuration: round, stepped
Sights: rear—M1868 rifle sight 2⅞" from frame; front—iron block/blade

"R.S. LAWRENCE. PAT./APRIL 12TH 1859" and "C. SHARPS' PAT./OCT. 5TH 1852"; left side of frame—"C. SHARPS' PAT./SEPT. 12TH 1848"; Sharps serial no. on upper frame strap

Fastenings: 2 iron bands
Markings: none

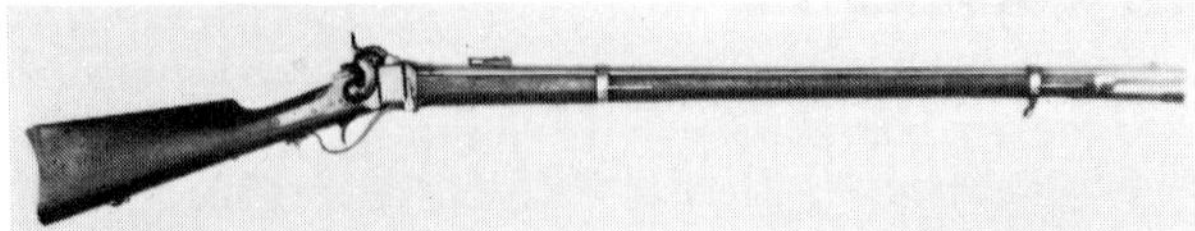

Springfield made 1,000 of these rifles in 1871-72 by rebarreling Sharps carbine frames with a new .50 cal. barrel and restocking the same for a rifle. New actions and levers were furnished by the Sharps Rifle Co. The distinguishing characteristic of these arms vs. the altered M1859-M1863-M1865 rifles is the original .50 cal. barrel with 3-groove rifling. **(C)**

28-14 Sharps M1859/M1863/M1865 (Sharps Rifle Mfg. Co.) Alterations from Percussion to Cartridge Carbines

In 1867 the U.S. Ordnance Dept. instructed Sharps to alter from percussion to cartridge as many carbines and rifles as the government had in surplus from previous Sharps contracts. The first type (M1867 Sharps alteration) was made to 1,900 carbines of different models, but principally the M1863 and M1865. This alteration utilized a new breechblock with a spring-retracted firing pin. A much simpler cam-operated retractor was substituted in 1868 (Sharps M1868 alteration). Because many of the bores were badly worn from service, it was necessary to reline all of those that gauged more than .5225 calibler. These were lined with .50 caliber brazed liners like the M1866 Allin alterations, except 2,300 which only had the chambers relined. A total of 28,298 carbines were altered by Sharps on the M1868 principle. After the end of the Franco-Prussian War, arms dealer Herman Boker of New York approached Sharps to alter 5,000 percussion Sharps carbines that he had bought in Europe. These were altered in the same manner, but all were relined to .50 cal. Barrels were usually refinished in the Boker work, obliterating previous manufacturing markings. **(A)**

28-15 Sharps M1859/M1863/M1865 (Sharps Rifle Mfg. Co.) Alteration from Percussion to Cartridge Rifles

In addition to the carbines forwarded by the government for alteration from percussion to cartridge, Sharps agreed to alter Sharps percussion rifles in the government's possession at the same price that applied to the carbines. As a result 1,186 rifles were similarly altered, all on the M1868 Sharps, and all in 1869. Deliveries of carbines and rifles were made in 1868-69. **(B)**

29 Single-Shot, Martial Breechloading Rifles

In 1872 a U.S. Army trial board held extensive tests to determine the best possible breechloading system for newly manufactured arms. Not surprisingly the system adopted was that which was already familiar—the Allin "trap door" mechanism. This was adapted the following year to the three basic needs of the service—a rifle for the infantry, a shortened and lighter version of the same for the U.S. Military Academy cadets, and an even shorter version for the cavalry. All three arms were reduced in bore size from the old .50 cal. to .45 cal., though it was necessary to chamber the cavalry carbine for a shorter cartridge to reduce its recoil. These arms were produced at Springfield Armory only, and almost immediately underwent a number of small improvements, including the addition of a stacking swivel to the rifle and carbine in 1874, and the adoption of an improved breechblock in 1878. The year before, an implement compartment in the buttstock was added to the carbine. In 1879 a new rear sight was adopted for all three arms, producing the "M1879" series. The following year a special test run of 1,000 rifles was made, incorporating a triangular "ramrod"/cleaning rod under the barrel and stock as a means by which the detachable socket bayonet might be eliminated. The tests were inconclusive, and when another improved model was adopted in 1884, Springfield was authorized to incorporate a revised, rounded "ramrod"/cleaning rod bayonet in 1,000 rifles of the new model. The 1884 model differed from its predecessors most visibly in the sighting. The new rear sight incorporated the Buffington adjustable wind gauge. The supply of Civil War triangular socket bayonets having become nearly exhausted by 1888, the military at last adopted a slightly modified version of the "ramrod"/cleaning rod bayonet in 1890. By 1893, however, production of the .45 cal. Allin system rifle had ceased, as the Army had finally adopted a magazine breechloader.

The cadet and cavalry arms basically kept pace with the changes that were incorporated into the infantry rifles, both having been adapted to the 1879 and 1884 sights. Although the cavalry experimented with an arm with a triangular "ramrod"/cleaning rod bayonet in 1882, there was really little practical need for such a weapon in the mounted service, and the concept was restricted to infantry weaponry. The cavalry weapons did receive an improved front sight protector in 1884, and after 1890 those carbines sent for repair or renewal were equipped with a new front band that gave added protection to the Buffington rear sight.

29-O Springfield U.S. M1873 Rifles (color plate, above)

OL: 51¾"
BD: .45 cal., 3-groove rifling
Furniture: iron, "blued"; after 1874 with stacking swivel marked "PAT. MAR. 1874"
Lockplate: flat
Markings: eagle and "U.S./SPRINGFIELD/1873" forward of

BL: 31⅛"; receiver (32½" bore)
Finish: "blued"
Configuration: round
Sights: 2⅜"; long base with folding ladder 2¼" from receiver; front—iron block/blade
Fastenings: 2 iron bands, "blued"

hammer; serial no. on top of receiver; top of breechblock—either (early) "MODEL 1873/ (eagle head and arrows)" or "U.S./MODEL/1873"

Markings: "V", "P", and eagle head

Between 1873-79 Springfield produced 71,700 rifles of this pattern for the Army. The breechblock (when raised) is distinguished by the high arc to the interior cutout, a feature eliminated after March, 1878. Production after 1877 incorporated a compartment well in the buttstock for implements and cleaning rod. **(B)**

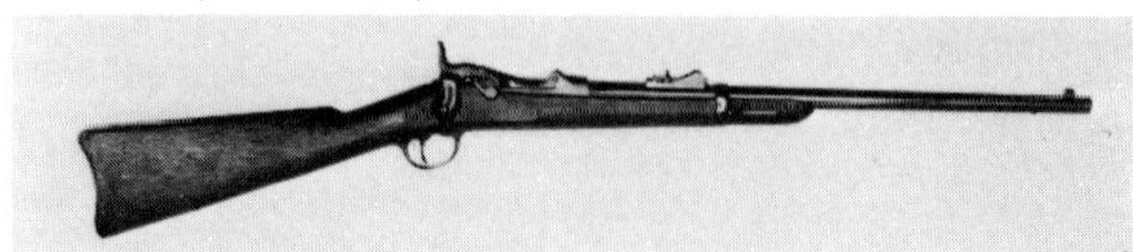

Springfield U.S. M1879 Carbines (color plate, below)

In size this arm is identical to the M1873 carbine. The most apparent changes are identical to those made on the M1879 rifle (29-3). 15,385 were made between 1879-81. Many were subsequently altered by the substitution of the "Buffington" M1884 carbine rear sight. **(A)**

29-1

29-1 Springfield U.S. M1873 Cadet Rifles

OL: 48¾"
BD: .45 cal., 3-groove rifling
Furniture: iron; not equipped with stacking ring
Lockplate: flat
Markings: eagle and "U.S./ SPRINGFIELD/1873" forward of hammer; serial no. on receiver top; breechblock top—"U.S./ MODEL/1873"
BL: 28¼" to receiver (29½" bore)
Finish: "blued"
Configuration: round
Sights: rear—2⅜" base with folding ladder 2¼" from receiver; front—iron block/blade
Fastenings: 2 iron bands, "blued"
Markings: "V", "P", and eagle head

Production of the cadet rifle totalled 3,072. **(B)**

29-2 Springfield U.S. M1873 Carbines

OL: 41¼"
BD: .45 cal., 3-groove rifling
Furniture: iron, "blued," with stacking ring on band marked "Pat. MAR. 1874"
Lockplate: flat
Markings: eagle and "U.S./ SPRINGFIELD/1873" forward of hammer; serial no. on receiver
BL: 20½" to receiver (21¾" bore)
Finish: "blued"
Configuration: round
Sights: 2⅜" long base with folding ladder 2¼" from receiver; front—iron block/blade
Markings: "V", "P", eagle head

top; breechblock top—"U.S./MODEL/1873"

From 1873-79 Springfield produced 18,024 M1873 carbines. The last 4,496 incorporate an implement and cleaning rod in their buttstocks and have a thinner wrist. These are sometimes referred to as "M1877" carbines. **(B)**

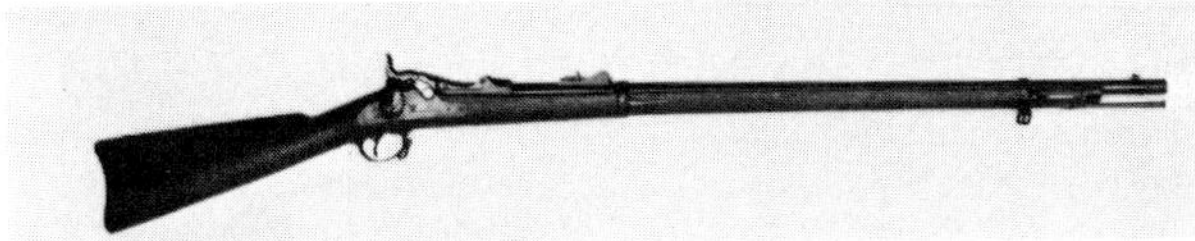

29-3

29-3 Springfield U.S. M1879 Rifles

This arm is identical in dimensions to the M1873 rifle. Four major differences are visible 1) the breechblock is the "low-arch" type; 2) the date "1873" is eliminated from the lockplate; 3) an implement compartment (accessible through the buttplate) is inletted into the buttstock; 4) a new-style rear sight, whose base and distance from the receiver remain the same, is on the barrel. The new sight is distinguished by its higher side walls and the presence of a "buckhorn" upon the ladder slide. 144,161 of these rifles were produced between 1879-84. **(A)**

29-4 Springfield U.S. M1879 Cadet Rifles

This arm is identical in dimensions to the M1873 cadet rifle. The changes effected by 1879 are the same as applied to the M1879 rifle except no implement/cleaning rod container was inletted into the buttplate. Between 1879-84, 1,021 were made. **(B)**

29-5 Springfield U.S. M1884 Rifles, Type I

The most evident change is the addition of the "Buffington" rear sight with wind gauge. This sight, on a 2⅞" base, is still located 2¼" from the receiver, but its additional length causes the leaves to overlap the rear band. The breechblock marking was changed to reflect the new model, and reads "U.S./MODEL/1884". There had been no dating change in the M1879 series from those of 1873. Springfield produced 236,560 between 1884-90. **(A)**

29-6 Springfield U.S. M1884 Cadet Rifles, Types I & II

The 3,500 arms made in 1884 and 1887 are identical to the M1879 Cadet rifles, except that they incorporate the new "Buffington" rear sight and a newly-marked breechblock. These rifles have been referred to as "type I" to distinguish them from the 10,500 produced between 1890-93 which also incorporate two features from the M1888 rifle: the single-piece triggerguard and, for the first time on cadet arms, stacking swivels on the upper band. **(B)**

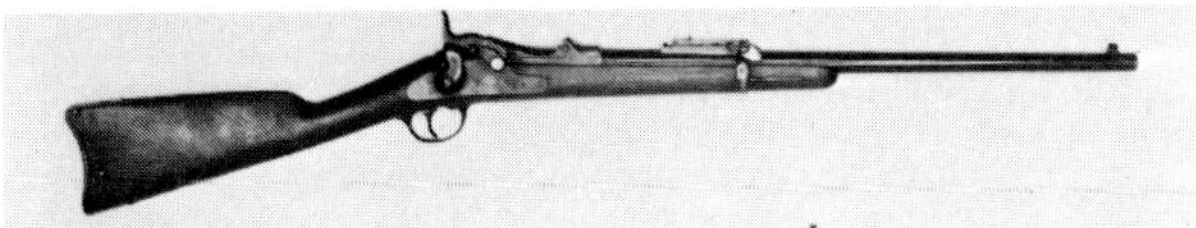

29-7 II

29-7 Springfield U.S. M1884 Carbines, Types I & II

The same changes that were incorporated in the M1884 rifle were also effected on carbines produced between 1886-89 (21,003 total) to create the M1884 carbine, type I. No carbines were produced after 1889. A significant number, however, were returned to the arsenal for reconditioning. As part of that process, a new front band with a large swell at its top was affixed. This swell gave the projection of the rear sight added protection. At the same time a detachable front sight hood was added to the muzzle (removed in illustration). These features distinguish the type II M1884 carbine, erroneously dubbed by collectors "M1890". **(A)**

29-8 Springfield U.S. M1888 Rifles

With the exhaustion of Civil War socket bayonets (whose sockets had been reforged to fit the M1873 series rifles and its derivatives from 1873-88, ramrod bayonet types excepted), the Army in 1888 finally adopted a slightly modified round "ramrod" bayonet similar in all characteristics to the M1884 type II rifle bayonet but with a slightly longer nosepiece. Only three were made in 1888, with full production beginning in 1890 and continuing until 1893 for a total of 64,825 rifles in this configuration. The production items incorporate two other features —a solid, one-piece triggerguard, and a protective hood over the front sight. **(A)**

29-9 Springfield U.S. "M1890" Carbines

See comments under 29-7.

---

30 | Special Arsenal Production of Martial Breechloaders

In addition to the three standard Springfield arms (the rifle, cadet rifle, and carbine) produced between 1875-85, the armory manufactured a limited number of special-purpose and trial weapons. Best known are the high-grade M1875 officer's rifles. The first of these were made between 1875-79 and incorporated the features of the M1873 rifle. Those manufactured in later years incorporated the improvements adopted in 1879. Lesser known is a special shotgun for foraging in the field for wild fowl. The armory also produced two versions of the M1879 rifle specially modified for long-range target competition in 1881. (It should be noted, however, that many Allin 1873 actions were adapted for sporting purposes during the 20th century, and that the collector should regard any M1881 Long-Range rifle offered for sale with reservations.) Lastly, a limited number of trial cavalry rifles or long carbines were made in 1882 and 1886 in the continuing search for a more powerful cavalry arm; the trials, unfortunately, were not successful.

In addition to these limited production single-shot breechloading weapons, a number of patented breechloading devices were specially fitted to barrels, stock, and furniture specially made at Spring-

field for their incorporation. These include the designs of Joslyn, Lee, Rider, Sharps, and the Ward-Burton system. The Rider design was first applied to arms specifically made for the Navy at Springfield, but then also produced on a large trial run for the Army. Most of these special patent breech manufactures were constructed prior to the decision of the Terry trial board of 1872 to adopt the Allin system for newly-made arms. As late as 1875, however, a limited trial was made with James P. Lee's breechloading system. After that date, breechloading systems made on patented designs were restricted to repeating actions.

3O-O Springfield Armory M1875 Officer's Rifles, Types II (color plate) **& I**

OL: 45¼"
BD: .45 cal., 3-groove rifling
Furniture: iron, with fancy nickeled nosecap or (late) brass nosecap
Lockplate: flat
Markings: engraving and eagle and "U.S./SPRINGFIELD" and "1873" (early) forward of hammer; serial no. on top of receiver; breechblock top—"U.S. /MODEL/1873"
BL: 24½" to receiver (25⅞" bore)
Finish: "blued"
Configuration: round
Sights: rear—M1873 (I) or M1879 (II) sight 2¼" from receiver and tang vernier sight; front—folding loop/blade, brass
Fastenings: single iron band
Markings: "V", "P", and eagle head

Type I officer's rifles have straight stocks, but are checkered at the wrist and firearm. Type II has either an integral or detachable pistol grip as part of the stock and incorporates the improvements of 1879 (low-arch breechblock, M1879 rear sight, implement-cleaning rod compartment in buttstock). A total of 285 of these rifles (I) were made between 1875-78. Of II, 187 were made in 1879, 1882, and 1885. **(D)**

3O-1 Springfield Armory M1881 Shotgun

OL: 45¼"
BD: .63 cal. (20 ga.)
Furniture: iron, "bright"; "US" on buttplate tang
Lockplate: flat
Markings: eagle and "U.S./SPRINGFIELD/1873" forward of hammer; serial no. on receiver top; breechblock top—"1881"
BL: 24½" to receiver (26" bore)
Finish: "blued"
Configuration: round
Sights: rear—none; front—brass band
Fastenings: stock screwed to barrel
Markings: none

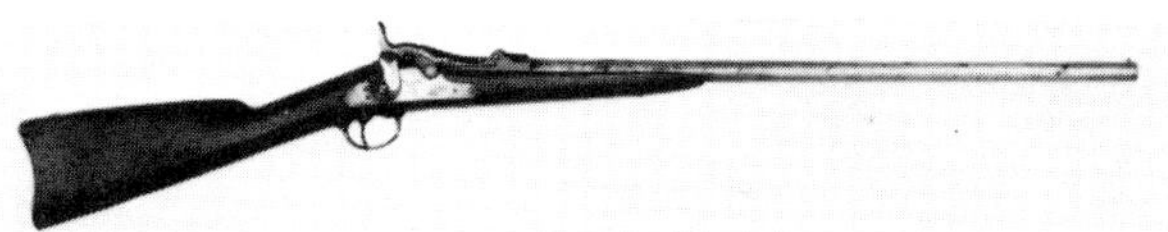

Only 1,378 of these shotguns were produced between 1880-84. They were intended for foraging wild fowl while on the march. As late as 1906, a few were issued to troops in Alaska. **(D)**

30-2 II

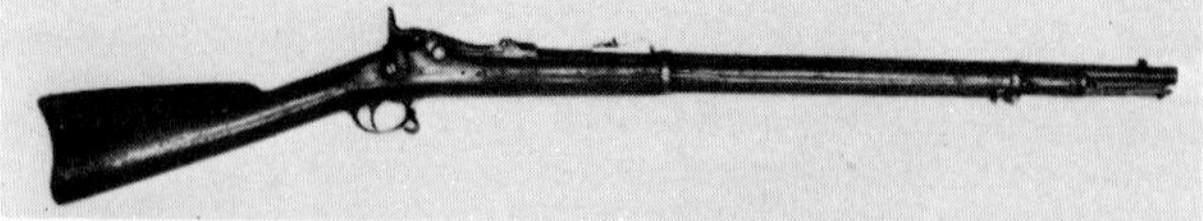

30-2 Springfield Armory U.S. M1882 Rifle-Carbines, Types I & II

OL: 47¼"
BD: .45 cal., 3-groove rifling
Furniture: iron, "blued"; "US" on buttplate tang
Lockplate: flat
Markings: eagle and "U.S./SPRINGFIELD/1873" forward of hammer; serial no. on receiver top; breechblock top—"U.S./MODEL/1873"
BL: 26½" to receiver (27⅞" bore)
Finish: "blued"
Configuration: round
Sights: rear—M1879, 2¼" from receiver; front—iron block/blade
Fastenings: 2 iron bands
Markings: "V", "P", and eagle head

Type I rifle-carbines are distinguished from II by the bayonets employed; I uses the standard socket bayonet and II employs the triangular "ramrod"/cleaning rod bayonet of the U.S. M1880 rifle. A total of only 52 of both types were made. **(E)**

30-3 Joslyn (Springfield Armory) Breechloading Rifles, Types I & II

OL: 52"
BD: .58 cal. (I), .50 cal. (II)
Furniture: iron, "US" on buttplate tang
Lockplate: flat, beveled edge
Markings: "U.S./SPRINGFIELD" forward of hammer; "1864" on tail; breechblock back—"B.F. JOSLYN'S PATENT/OCT. 8 1861 JUNE 24, 1862"
BL: 34½" to breechblock (35½" bore)
Finish: "bright"
Configuration: round
Sights: rear—M1865 1¾" from breechblock; front—iron block/blade
Fastenings: 3 iron bands
Markings: none

II

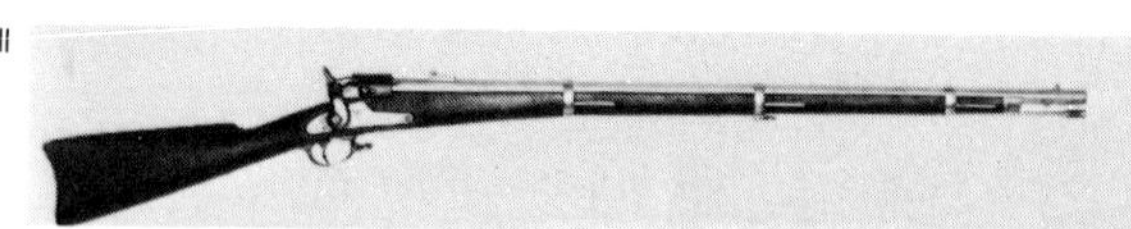

A total of 3,007 of these rifles were made in 1864-65 in .58 cal. rimfire (I). Of these, 1,600 were later altered at the Armory to .50 cal. (II) by sleeving the barrels. **(C)**

30-4

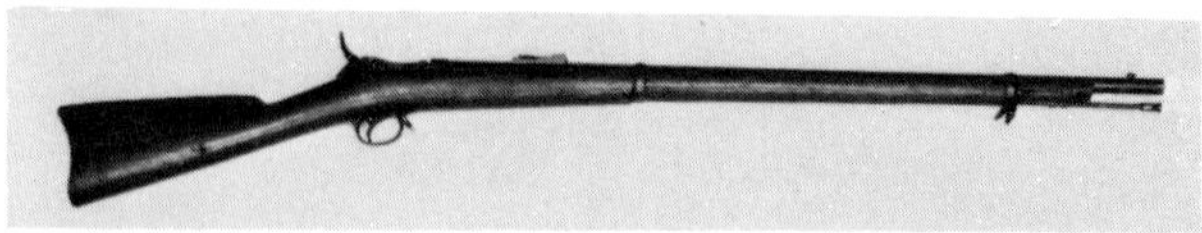

30-4 J. P. Lee (Springfield Armory) Breechloading Rifles

OL: 49¼"
BD: .45 cal., 3-groove rifling
Furniture: iron, "blued"; "US" on
BL: 31¾" to receiver (32½" bore)
Finish: "blued"
Configuration: round

buttplate tang
Lockplate: none, mechanism within frame
Markings: upper frame strap—"U.S." and "PAT. MAR. 17 1875"
Sights: rear—M1873 rifle 2⅞" from receiver; front—iron block/blade
Fastenings: 2 iron bands, "blued"
Markings: none

Only 143 of these rifles were manufactured in 1875. The breechblock pivots down to expose the chamber. **(D)**

30-5 Rider (Springfield Armory) U.S. Navy M1870 Rifles, Types I & II
OL: 48½"
BD: .50 cal., 3-groove rifling
Furniture: iron, "US" on buttplate tang
Lockplate: none, mechanism within frame
Markings: right side of frame—"(eagle)/USN/SPRINGFIELD/1870"; upper frame strap—"REMINGTONS PATENT/PAT. MAY 3D NOVTH 1864 APRIL 17TH 1869"
BL: 31" to frame (32½" bore)
Finish: "blued"
Configuration: round with saber bayonet stud with guide below barrel at muzzle
Sights: (I) reversed M1861 rifle-musket 3⅛" from frame and (II) M1868 rifle; front—iron block/blade
Fastenings: 2 iron bands
Markings: none

II

After the 1869 decision of the U.S. Navy trial board to adopt the Remington/Rider "rolling block" action for all new arms, the Navy ordered 10,000 from Springfield. These were completed in 1870-71, but for obscure reasons the wrong rear sight was applied (I). These were quickly sold to a Baltimore dealer who in turn sold them all to France, and, with the proceeds, 12,000 more were made with the proper sight (II). **(A)**

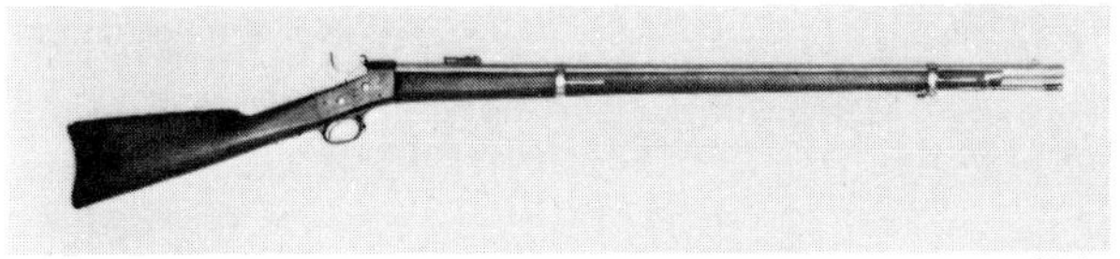

30-6

30-6 Rider (Springfield Armory) U.S. M1871 Rifles
OL: 51¾"
BD: .50 cal., 3-groove rifling
Furniture: iron, "bright"; "US" on buttplate tang
Lockplate: none, mechanism within frame
Markings: right side of frame—"(eagle)/U.S./SPRINGFIELD/(date)"; left side of frame—"MODEL 1871"; upper frame strap—"REMINGTONS PATENT/
BL: 34½" to frame (36" bore)
Finish: "bright"
Configuration: round
Sights: rear—M1868 3⅛" from frame; front—iron block/blade
Fastenings: 2 iron bands, "bright"
Markings: none

PAT. MAY 3D NOV 15TH 1864,
APRIL 17TH 1868"

A total of 10,001 were made in 1872-73. **(B)**

30-7

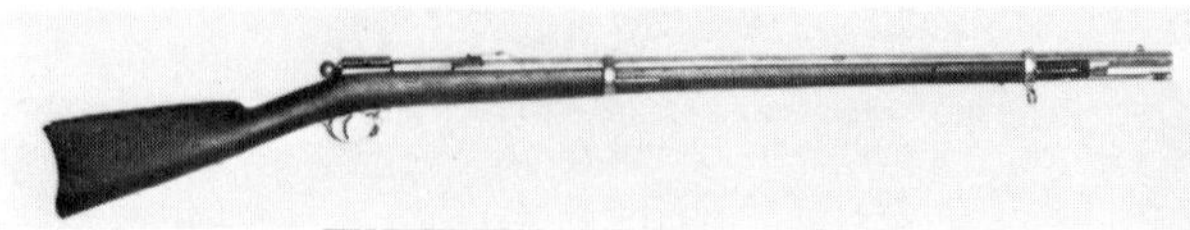

30-7 Ward-Burton (Springfield Armory) M1871 Rifles

OL: 51¾"
BD: .45 cal., 3-groove rifling
Furniture: iron, "bright"; "US" on buttplate tang
Lockplate: none, mechanism within stock
Markings: left side of receiver—eagle and "U.S./SPRINGFIELD 1871"

BL: 31½" to receiver (32½" bore)
Finish: "bright"
Configuration: round
Sights: rear—U.S. M1868 against receiver; front—iron block/blade
Fastenings: 2 iron bands
Markings: none

Springfield manufactured 1,011 of these rifles based on the Ward-Burton bolt action. **(C)**

30-8

30-8 Ward-Burton (Springfield Armory) M1871 Carbines

OL: 41⅛"
BD: .45 cal., 3-groove rifling
Furniture: iron, "blued"; "US" on buttplate tang
Lockplate: none, mechanism within stock
Markings: left side of receiver—eagle and "U.S./SPRINGFIELD 1871"

BL: 21" to receiver (22" bore)
Finish: "bright"
Configuration: round
Sights: rear—U.S. M1868 against receiver; front—iron block/blade
Fastenings: single iron band
Markings: none

Only 316 of these carbines were manufactured in 1871 for field trials. They were not found to be superior to the M1870 carbines and, accordingly, were soon turned in. **(D)**

30-9

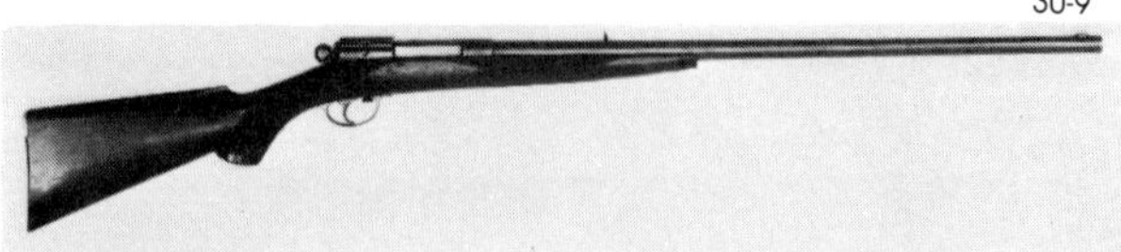

30-9 Ward-Burton (Springfield Armory) Sporting or Officer's Rifles

OL: 45"
BD: .45 cal., 3-groove rifling

BL: 25¼" to receiver (26¼" bore)
Finish: "browned"

Furniture: nickeled brass, except for horn nosecap
Lockplate: none, mechanism within stock
Markings: left side of receiver—eagle and "U.S./SPRINGFIELD 1871"
Configuration: round
Sights: rear—open "V" 4½" from receiver; front—dovetailed brass blade
Fastenings: stock screwed to barrel
Markings: none

The records are mute as to when this pattern was manufactured or the quantities produced; however, 1871 or 1872 is the probable date. Note the screw adjustment within the triggerguard to adjust trigger pull. **(F)**

---

31 Patented Breechloading, Single-Shot Cartridge Rifles

The advent of the successful self-contained metallic cartridge sparked a resurgence in longarms invention unparalleled in American history. From 1860-75, mechanics nationwide (but primarily in industrial New England) patented ingenious techniques to seal the breech of cartridge longarms and handguns. Some patent designs (primarily military longarms) were produced in significant quantities during the early stages of the single-shot era. Despite advances in repeating cartridge arms, the single-shot cartridge weapon retained its popularity, especially for sporting and long-range target competition and were the mainstay of such famous firms as the Sharps Rifle Co., the Marlin Arms Co., and Remington.

While the earliest of the self-contained single-shot breechloaders date before the Civil War, the impetus for their development was that conflict. The difficulty of loading and capping even the improved percussion carbines while mounted promoted the search for an effective cartridge breechloader. Although several designs were tested and ordered in quantity, they were soon superseded by the Spencer magazine carbine. Nevertheless, a myriad of designs was tested again by the Army during trials in 1865 and 1872, including several percussion types that had been modified to the self-contained cartridge. When the military decided to economize, first by adopting the modified Sharps carbine in conjunction with the surplus Spencer carbines and then by adopting the Allin breechloading mechanism, the inventors of other breechloading systems and their manufacturers turned for sales to foreign and the civilian markets. Depending on the acceptance of their designs by the American public, the sporting arms vary in availability from common to quite rare. In spite of some popularity, however, few of the patented sporting arms could stand up to the competition posed by the makers of the Ballard (Marlin), Sharps (Sharps Rifle Co.), and Rider (Remington) patented mechanisms.

31-O Holden "Ring Hammer" or "Open Frame" Sporting Rifles (color plate, above)
OL: 42½" or 46½"
BD: .44 cal., 5-groove rifling
BL: 22⅞" to frame (24" or 28" bore)

Furniture: iron, with iron frame or occasionally with bronze frame
Lockplate: none, mechanism within frame
Markings: serial no. stamped into right side of trigger and triggerguard
Finish: "blued"
Configuration: octagonal
Sights: rear—leaf with slide on base 2⅜" from frame; front—iron blade, dovetailed
Fastenings: none
Markings: "HOLDEN'S PATENT/ APRIL 1862" on top

Although data is limited, these rifles are believed to have been made by Arsby & Harrington of Worcester, Mass. Holden's design (patented April, 1862) employs a pair of interlocking sliding blocks within an open (right-side) frame. The forward block serves as a breechblock; the rear is the hammer. The triggerguard serves as a lock. Serial numbers as high as 168 survive. **(D)**

Howard (Whitney) "Thunderbolt" Breechloading Rifles (color plate, below)
OL: 43¼"
BD: .44 cal., 6-groove rifling
Furniture: iron, "blued"
Lockplate: none, mechanism within receiver
Markings: serial no. stamped on inner level mechanism
BL: 27¼" to frame (24" bore)
Finish: "blued"
Configuration: round
Sights: rear—pivoting leaf with sliding peep ⅛" from frame; front—iron blade, dovetailed
Fastenings: none, no forestock
Markings: on right side—either WHITNEY ARMS CO-WHITNEY-VILLE CONN." or "MANF'D FOR HOWARD BROS. BY WHITNEY ARMS CO., WHITNEYVILLE CONN."; on left side—either "C. HOWARD. PATENTED. SEPT 25 & OCT. 10.1865-OCT. 28. 1862" or "CHARLES HOWARD'S PATENTS OF SEPT. 26. AND OCT. 10 1865. AND MAY. 16.1866"

Approximately 1,500 Howard arms were made by Whitney between 1866-70, including 20 ga. shotguns with 25"-25¾" bores. **(C)**

II

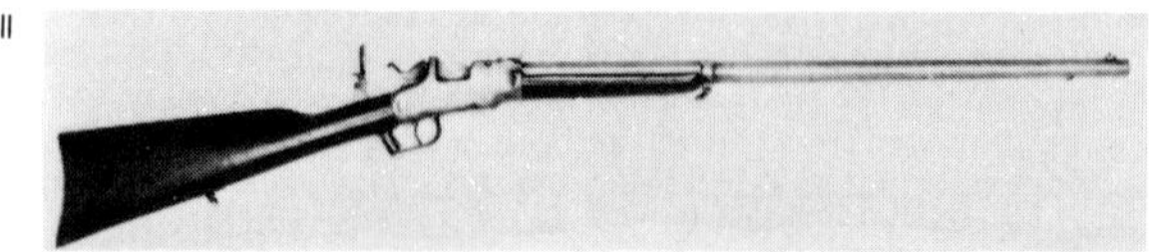

31-1 Allen & Wheelock (incl. E. Allen & Co.) Breechloading Rifles, Types I & II
OL: 41½"-44⅝" (42⅜")
BD: .31, .32, .35, .38, .41 or .44 cal. (.41)
Furniture: iron; (early) without nosecap; sling swivels optional
Lockplate: none, mechanism within frame
Markings: left side of frame—graduation numbers from "1"
BL: 23¾"-26¼" bores; (24" to frame; 26" bore)
Finish: "blued"
Configuration: part round/part octagonal
Sights: rear—pivoting leaf on frame top and tang peep sight; front—brass blade on iron block, dovetailed

through "0" (for 10) for pivoting leaf sight; serial no. stamped into lower triggerguard tang

Fastenings: forestock screwed to barrel
Markings: "ALLEN & WHEELOCK/ ALLEN'S PAT. SEP. 18 1860" on top

Based on surviving serial numbers, no fewer than 1,500 were made by Allen & Wheelock and its successors in two frame styles, flat-sided (I) and convex-sided (II) between 1860-71. Production was continued by E. Allen & Co.'s successor, Forehand & Wadsworth, from 1871-90. Examples with the later barrel marking are rare, however, suggesting limited production. **(C-E, according to marking).**

31-2 Beals (Remington) Breechloading Rifles, Types I & II

OL: 39½", 40½", 41½", or 43½"
BD: .32 or .38 cal.
Furniture: (I) brass, including frame; (II) iron
Lockplate: none, mechanism within frame
Markings: serial no. stamped on triggerguard/lever assembly and triggerguard tang

BL: 24,", 25", 26", or 28"
Finish: "blued"
Configuration: part round/part octagonal
Sights: rear—block with single sliding peep on leaf 3⅛" from breech; front—German-silver blade, dovetailed
Fastenings: none, no forestock
Markings: "BEALS PATENT JUNE 28 1864, JAN. 30, 1866/E. REMINGTON & SONS ILION N Y" on top near breech

I

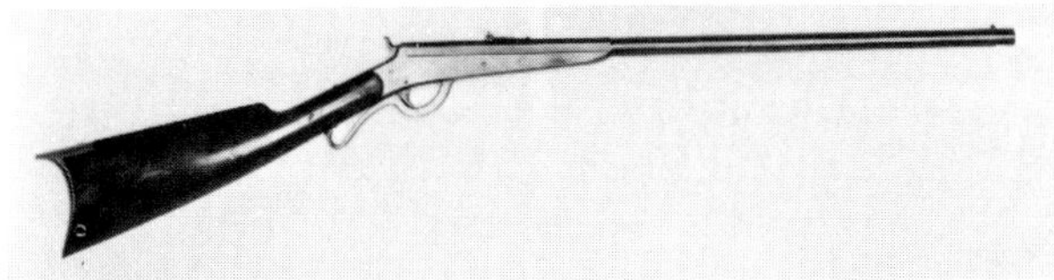

The triggerguard serves as a lever, which when swung forward slides the barrel to permit loading the chamber. Based on highest serial numbers observed, at least 865 of these rifles were produced by Remington between 1866-68. **(D)**

31-3 Bullard Breechloading Single-Shot Rifles, Types I-III

OL: varies according to type and barrel
BD: .32, .38, .45, or .50 cal.
Furniture: iron
Lockplate: none, mechanism within frame
Markings: top of frame—"BULLARD REPEATING ARMS COMPANY/SPRINGFIELD, MASS. USA PAT. JULY 6, 1886"

BL: (I) 24"-28"; (II) 30"; (III) 32"
Finish: "blued"
Configuration: (I & III) round; (I & II) part round/part octagonal
Sights: rear—variety available; front—iron block/blade
Fastenings: forestock screwed to barrel
Markings: none

These rifles were manufactured between 1883-90 in three basic configurations: the simple target/hunting rifle (I), the specialized "Schuetzen" target rifle with elongated prongs on the buttplate (II), and a quasi-military rifle (III). I and II buttstocks incorporate a pistol grip below the lever that forms part of the triggerguard assembly. **(B)**

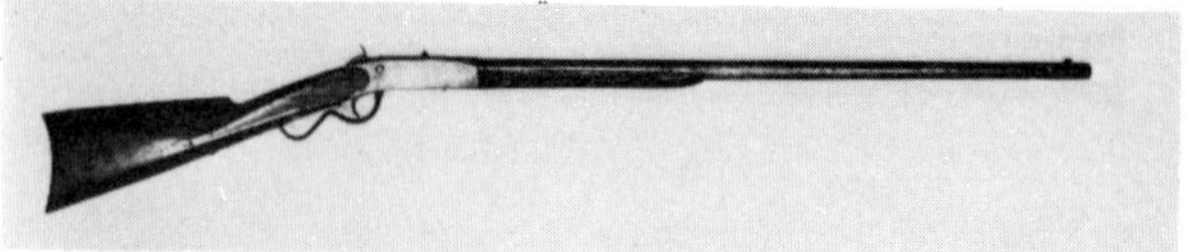

31-4 Cochran (Whitney) Breechloading Rifles

OL: 45½"
BD: .44 cal., 6-groove rifling
Furniture: iron
Lockplate: none, mechanism within frame
Markings: top of breechblock—"J.W. COCHRAN. N.Y. PAT'D./ APRIL 4, 1865 & FEB'Y 20, 1866"

BL: 26½" to frame (28" bore)
Finish: "blued"
Configuration: round
Sights: rear—"L" leaf pierced with 2 peeps on top of block; front—iron blade, dovetailed
Fastenings: single half-band screwed to forestock
Markings: none

Cochran rifles were loaded by lowering the lever/triggerguard which in turn pivoted the breechblock in the frame upward, thereby permitting insertion of a cartridge through a cavity in the underside of the frame. An estimated 50 rifles were made by Eli Whitney, Jr., and one carbine with 22" bore was submitted to the 1865 Army breechloading trials. **(E)**

31-5 Hopkins & Allen Breechloading Rifles, Types I-III

OL: varies according to type and barrel
BD: (I) .22 or .32 cal.; (II) .22, .25, .32, or .38 cal.; (III) .22 or .25 cal.
Furniture: iron
Lockplate: none, mechanism within frame
Markings: none

BL: (I) 20"; (II) 24", 26", or 28"; (III) 26"
Finish: "blued"
Configuration: (I & II) round; (II & III) octagonal
Sights: rear—open "V" or sliding "V" on strap; front—iron blade, dovetailed
Fastenings: forestock screwed to barrel
Markings: "MADE BY THE HOPKINS & ALLEN MANFG. CO., NORWICH, CONN. U.S.A." together with various patent markings and occasional Merwin & Hulbert agent marks

Between 1888-1917 Hopkins & Allen produced three variations, all of which utilized a dropping breechblock activated by the triggerguard/lever. I has a full grip ring behind the triggerguard to facilitate leverage; II and III use a simple triggerguard bow as the lever. III is a "schuetzen"-style target rifle. Pistol grips were optional on all. **(A)**

31-6 Howard (Whitney) "Thunderbolt" Breechloading Carbines

OL: 37½"
BD: .44 cal., 6-groove rifling
Furniture: iron, "blued"
Lockplate: none, mechanism within receiver
Markings: serial no. stamped on inner lever mechanism

BL: 21½" to frame (18½" bore)
Finish: "blued"
Configuration: round
Sights: rear—pivoting leaf with sliding peep ⅛" from frame; front—iron blade, dovetailed
Fastenings: none, no forestock
Markings: on right side—"WHIT-

NEY ARMS. CO-WHITNEYVILLE CONN." or "MANF'D FOR HOWARD BROS. BY WHITNEY ARMS CO. WHITNEYVILLE CONN."; on left side—"C. HOWARD. PATENTED. SEPT. 26 & OCT. 10 1865-OCT. 28. 1862" or "CHARLES HOWARD'S PATENTS OF SEPT. 26 AND OCT. 10. 1865. AND MAY. 15. 1866"

Although tested by the state of New York in 1867, no Howard carbines were adopted by the military. They were used for sporting purposes; serial numbers are in the same series as rifles and shotguns. **(D)**

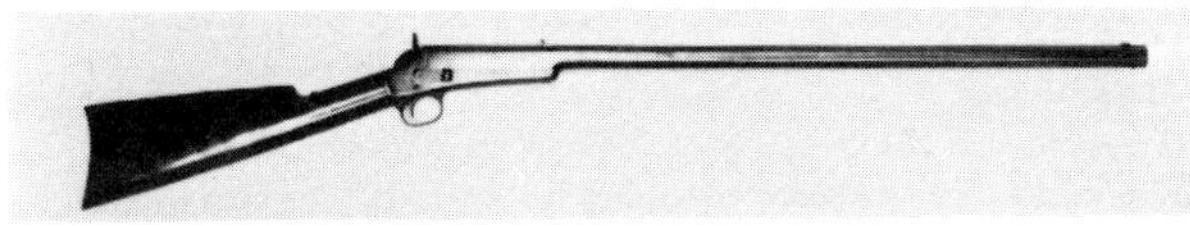
31-7

31-7 Lee Firearms Co. Sporting Rifles

OL: 42½"-45¾"
BD: .32 (rarely), .38, or .44 cal., 6-groove rifling
Furniture: iron
Lockplate: none, mechanism within frame
Markings: serial no. (ranging from 1000 through 2300) stamped on flat of frame below barrel

BL: 27¾"-31" (one noted with 25¼")
Finish: "blued"
Configuration: octagonal
Sights: rear—open "V" 4⅞" from breech; front—iron block/blade, dovetailed
Fastenings: none, no forestock
Markings: "LEE'S FIRE ARMS CO. MILWAUKEE WIS./PAT^{D} JULY 22^{D} 1862" on top

Between 1866-68 James Paris Lee assembled the unfinished parts from his U.S. government carbine contract into three types of sporting rifles based on his 1862 patent: a .44 cal. "light" (28" barrel) sporting rifle, and two (.38 cal., 28" barrel or .44 cal., 31" barrel) grades of "heavy" sporting rifles. Total production did not exceed 1,500. **(C)**

31-8 No. 16
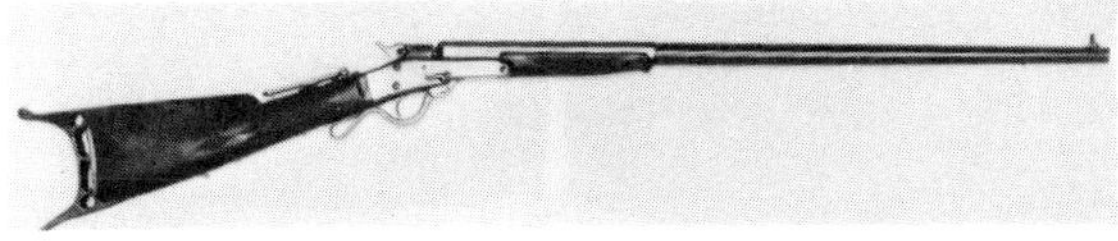

31-8 Maynard M1873 and M1882 Breechloading Cartridge Rifles

OL: varies according to type and barrels
BD: .22, .32, .35, .38, .40, .45, or .50 cal., rifled (also smooth in .55, .64 cal., and 20 ga.)
Furniture: iron
Lockplate: none, mechanism within frame
Markings: on left side of frame—

BL: 20", 24", 26", 30", or 32"
Finish: "blued"
Configuration: part round/part octagonal
Sights: vary according to type; rear—tang vernier sights common; front—globe in conjunction with tang sights
Fastenings: no forestock, except

"EDWARD MAYNARD/PATENTEE/ MAY 27 1861/DEC. 6 1859" and either "1873" or "1882"

No. 15 and 16 rifles which are screwed to barrel
Markings: none

The 1873 and 1882 models were available in sixteen different grades, each with various options. Usually variations in caliber, barrel lengths, sights, stocking, and furniture defined the grades, with many of the lower-numbered grades having the option of taking a patented device that permitted the use of rimfire cartridges as well. Three smoothbore shotgun grades were also made, two with 26" barrels in the small calibers, and one with 28", 30", or 32" barrels in the two larger calibers. **(B)**

31-9

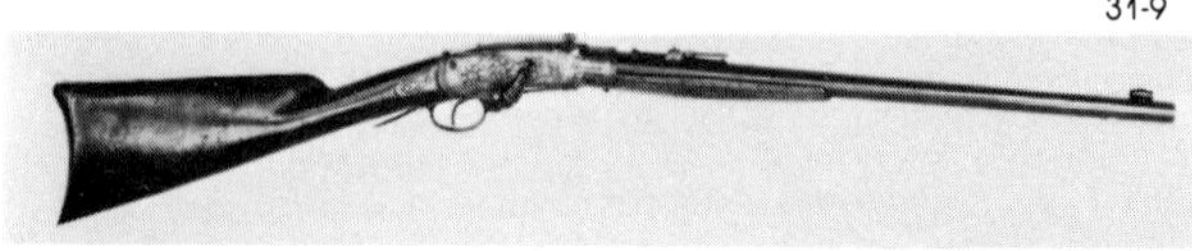

31-9 Morse (Muzzy) Breechloading Cased Sets

OL: 40½" (carbine), 48½" (rifle), 50½" (shotgun)
BD: .54 cal., 12 ga., 5-groove rifling
Furniture: iron, engraved
Lockplate: none, mechanism within frame
Markings: top of breechblock—"MORSE'S PATENT/OCT. 20, 1858"

BL: 20½" to frame (22" bore), carbine; 28½" to frame (30" bore), rifle; 30½" to frame (32" bore), shotgun
Finish: rifle and carbine—"blued,"; shotgun—"damascened"
Configuration: round (carbine and shotgun); octagonal (rifle)
Sights: rear—folding leaf with slide on base ¾" from frame; front—globe sight, dovetailed
Fastenings: single wedge
Markings: "MUZZY & CO./WORCESTER" on top

One hundred cased sets were made by Muzzy for Morse in 1859. Measurements vary from set to set; those given apply to set no. 98. **(E)**

31-10

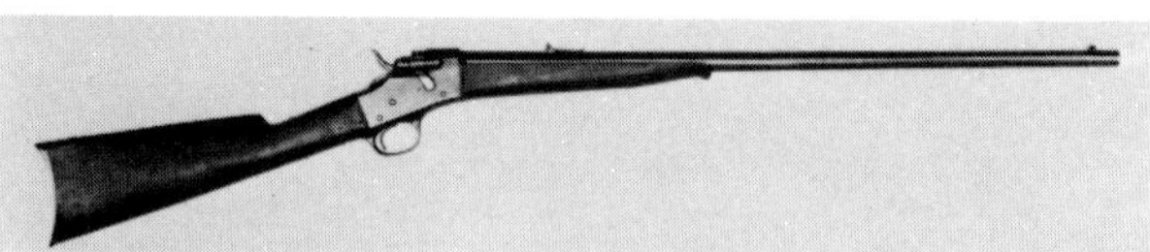

31-10 "Phoenix" (Whitney) Breechloading Sporting Rifles

OL: 47"-51"
BD: .22, .32, .38, .40, .433 (11 mm), .45, and .50 cal.
Furniture: iron, "blued"
Lockplate: none, mechanism within frame
Markings: none

BL: 26", 28", 30", or 32"
Finish: "blued"
Configuration: round or part round/part octagonal
Sights: rear—vary according to type; front—iron blade, dovetailed
Fastenings: forestock screwed to barrel
Markings: "PATENT MAY. 26, 74.

PHOENIX" on top forward of sights; cartridge size on top near frame

Probably about 5,000 of the 25,000 Phoenix breechloaders made by Whitney between 1874-81 were sporting rifles. Another approximately 5,000 were shotguns utilizing the same side swinging breechblock principle patented in May, 1874. Shotguns came in round barrels only. **(B)**

31-11 Stevens Breechloading Rifles, Types I-III

OL: varies according to type and barrels
BD: (I & II) .22, .25, .32, .38, or .44; (III) .22 or .25
Furniture: iron, either "blued" or nickeled
Lockplate: none, mechanism within frame
Markings: none
BL: 24", 26", 28", 30"; (III) only .24-.26"
Finish: "blued"
Configuration: octagonal and part round/part octagonal
Sights: varies according to type
Fastenings: some with forestock screwed to barrel
Markings: "J. STEVENS & CO., CHICOPEE FALLS, MASS. PAT' SEPT. 6, 1864" (early); "J. STEVENS A & T CO./CHICOPEE FALLS, MASS. U.S.A. PAT. SEPT. 6 1864" on top of barrel (later)

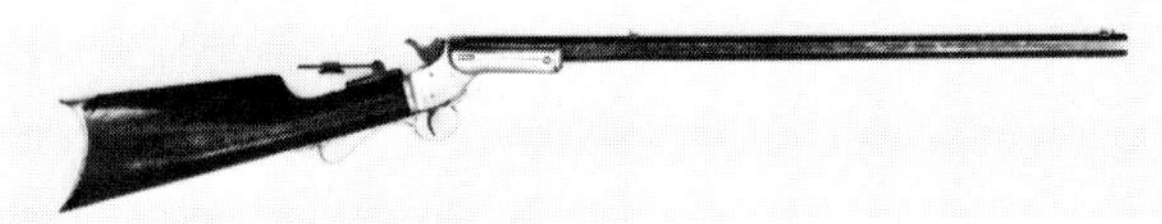

The Stevens "tip-up" single-shot cartridge rifles were introduced about 1870 and continued in production until replaced by the lever-action "Ideal" models in 1894. **(A)**

31-12 Frank Wesson "Tip-Up" Breechloading Rifles, Types I-V

OL: 39¼"-49¼"
BD: .22, .32, .38, .41, and .44 cal. (one example, .56 cal.)
Furniture: iron, occasionally nickeled and rarely engraved
Lockplate: none, mechanism within frame
Markings: serial no. stamped on triggerguard grip
BL: 24", 25½", 28", 32", or 34"
Finish: "blued"
Configuration: (I-IV) octagonal; (V) part round/part octagonal
Sights: rear—varies according to type; front—varies
Fastenings: none
Markings: "FRANK WESSON WORCESTER MASS/PATD. OCT. 25, 1859 (I); "& NOV. 11, 1862" (added on II and III); "& APR. 9, 1872" (added on IV & V)

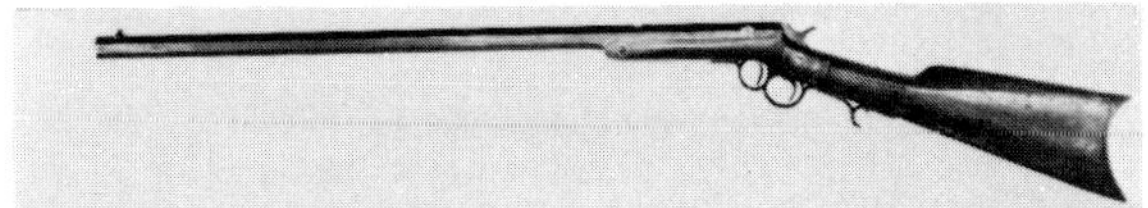

The most distinctive features are the separate tandem triggers and housings. The forward trigger releases the tipping barrel. Type I rifles (1859-62) permit the barrel to swing freely; Type II (1862-64) incorporate a patented pivot stop on the right side, this being moved to the left side on Type III (1864-72) to incorporate an extractor on the right; IV & V incorporate a selector on the hammer for rim- or center-fire. **(A)**

31-13 "M1887" Winchester Single-Shot Breechloading Rifles, Types I-III

OL: 29"-45"; "schuetzen" rifles longer
BD: available in nearly every caliber made
Furniture: iron, "blued"
Lockplate: none, mechanism within frame
Markings: frames occasionally engraved

BL: 25"-30", "schuetzen" rifles longer
Finish: "blued"
Configuration: round, octagonal, or part round/part octagonal
Sights: rear and front—varies according to type
Fastenings: forestock screwed to barrel
Markings: (early) "BROWNING BROS., OGDEN, UTAH, U.S.A.", (caliber), and "PAT. OCT. 7 '79"; (late) "—MANUFACTURED BY THE WINCHESTER REPEATING ARMS CO. NEW HAVEN, CONN. U.S.A.—"

This rifle was based on John Browning's patent of October, 1879, purchased by Winchester in 1883. Three frame sizes (I, II & III) were produced to accommodate the multiplicity of cartridges and resulting barrels. 85,086 were made until 1900. **(A)**

---

32 Ballard Action Breechloading, Single-Shot Cartridge Rifles

When Charles H. Ballard received his patent for an "improved breechloading firearm" in 1861, he had no problem finding a manufacturer. The witnesses to his patent, Hartley Williams and Richard Ball, owned a woodworking machine factory where Ballard was employed as a machinist. Precisely how Joseph Merwin and Edward P. Bray of New York City became sole agents for this patent is not clear, but since the very early products bear this agency name, they may have been major stockholders in the project from the beginning. Surprisingly, in view of the state of war at the time, the majority of the first 500 or so arms produced were sporting rather than military arms. Except for the first few, none of these incorporated the automatic extraction device. Probably for economy, a manual extractor was adopted, first with a short hooked pull and later with a more substantial rounded knob. The more easily machined brass frames found within the first 250 or so produced soon gave way to cast iron, probably to meet the requirements of the military.

During the critical winter of 1861-62 Union officials in Kentucky ordered at least 3,000 military carbines from Merwin & Bray and

ordered the following year 1,600 carbines and 1,000 rifles in the same .44 cal. These orders, in conjunction with one from New York for 500 similar carbines as well as other contracts, kept the Ball & Williams plant in full operation. The close of the war did not deter Merwin & Brya from promoting the Ballard action. In January, 1864, they patented an alternate rim-fire/percussion ignition device. When Williams disassociated himself from Ball in 1865, Merwin & Bray determined to take over production entirely. At Newburyport, Mass., they constructed the Merrimack Arms & Mfg. Co., and from 1866-69 this firm produced about 2,000 sporting and martial rifles as well as a very few shotguns. In 1869 Merwin & Bray's partnership terminated and the Newburyport plant was sold to the Brown Manufacturing Co., together with Ballard's patent rights. Only about 2,000 additional Ballard sporting arms were produced before the Panic of 1873 forced the closing of Brown's doors.

The Ballard machinery was purchased from Brown by J.M. Marlin and removed to New Haven. Marlin redesigned the arm to incorporate a mechanical ejector and also patented a reversable center-fire/rim-fire firing pin. The Ballard line became the major single-shot produced by that company (reorganized as the Marlin Firearms Co. in 1881) during the 19th century. For sporting purposes it was one of the most respected actions on the market. Its reliability is attested by its frequent use in conjunction with specially-made high-quality target barrels.

32-O Ballard (J. M. Marlin/Marlin Firearms Co.) No. 6 Off-Hand "Schuetzen" Rifles (color plate, above)

The "off-hand schuetzen" model is distinguished from the No. 6 "schuetzen" and No. 6½ "off-hand mid-range" by having a full octagonal barrel in either 30" or 32" lengths (bore). The long, pronged "schuetzen" buttplate, double-set triggers, and distinctive spurred triggerguard/lever are common with the No. 6 "schuetzen." Standard calibers are .38, .40, and .44. Production began in the mid-1870s and continued through most of the '80s. **(C)**

Ballard (J. M. Marlin/Marlin Firearms Co.) No. 5 "Pacific" Rifles (color plate, below)

These rifles are distinguished from the No. 2 and No. 4 sporting rifles by the presence of two thimbles or tubes or a cleaning rod attachment forward of the forestock underneath the barrel. All have double-set triggers and a triggerguard/lever terminating in the two-finger loop. Produced from 1876-91, the arm was available in three barrel (bore) lengths: 28", 30", and 32", always octagonal in configuration. Calibers are: .38, .40, .44, and .45 center-fire only. 28" barrels and .38 cal. bores are rarely encountered. **(C)**

32-1 Ball & Williams-Produced Ballard Sporting Rifles

All frames, whether faceted or rounded, are of the tanged type and measure 1$^{11}/_{16}$" from the breech to the barrel juncture. Faceted frames predominate for sporting rifles until the 16,000 serial range. Serial nos. are struck into the top of the frame near the juncture. Markings appear on the barrel through about the 8,000 serial range, consisting of three lines: "BALL & WILLIAMS/Worcester, Mass." on the top facet, "BALLARD'S PATENT/NOV. 5, 1861" on the upper right facet, and "MERWIN & BRAY AGT'S/NEW YORK" on the upper left facet. From about serial no. 8,500 through 16,500 these markings were removed to the frame, the right side being marked: "BALLARD'S PATENT/NOV. 5, 1861", and the left side being marked: "BALL & WILLIAMS/Worcester, Mass." over "MERWIN & BRAY AGT'S/NEW YORK". The final 1,000 or so eliminated the Ball & Williams marking entirely.

32-1a

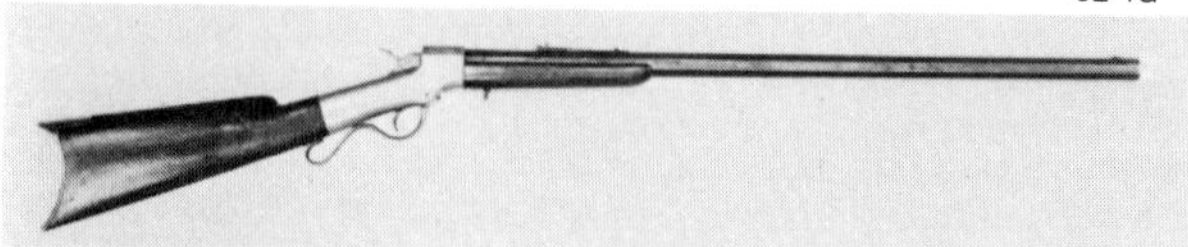

32-1a Ballard (Ball & Williams) Sporting Rifles, Brass Frame Type

A substantial portion of the production of the first 200-250 rifles were made with brass (bronze) frames. These arms use the earliest type (hooked handle) extractors. Although advertised only with 24" barrels (bores), this arm was made in 24", 26", 28", and 30" bore lengths. Octagonal barrels predominate, but half-round, half-octagonal barrels were available on special order. Overall lengths are correspondingly 39⅛", 41⅛", 43⅛", or 45⅛". Cartridge sizes are .32, .38, and .44. **(F)**

32-1b

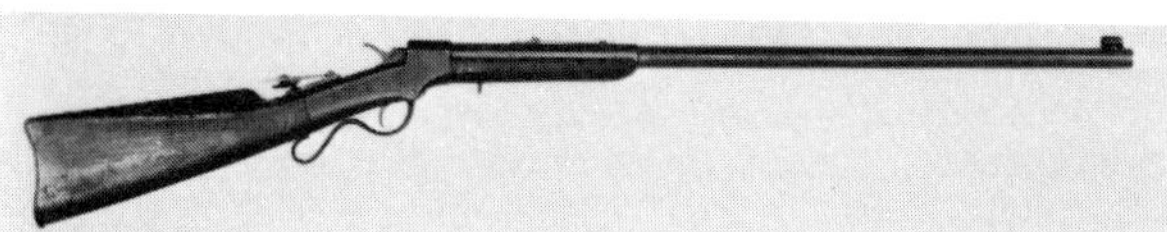

32-1b Ballard (Ball & Williams) Sporting Rifles, Iron Frame, Types I-IV

Beginning with serial no. about 200-250, all frames are cast iron, faceted on top like the brass. The type I iron-frame model duplicates the brass (bronze) frame type. The difference is the small, hooked manual extractor handle. Tang and globe sights were optional. Type II exchanges the hooked extractor handle for a larger, rounded knob, as do III & IV. The distinguishing characteristic of III is the use of the Merwin & Bray alternate rim-fire/percussion breechblock and hammer. Type IV has a rounded instead of the usual faceted type frame. **(D-E)**

32-2 Merrimack Arms & Mfg. Co.-Produced Ballard Sporting Rifles

All frames, whether faceted (infrequent) or rounded, are tangless, and all measure 1⁹⁄₁₆" from breech to barrel juncture. Serial nos. are struck into the frame top near the barrel juncture. Markings (except for serial no. and calibration) all appear on the frame's left side and read: "MERRIMACK ARMS & MFG. CO./NEWBURYPORT MASS./BALLARD'S PATENT/NOV. 5, 1861". The left side of the hammer is marked "PATENTED JAN. 5, 1864", but unlike Ball & Williams incorporates a two-piece rimfire striker, with a floating striker in the breechblock and a floating hammer attachment screwed to the hammer top. Serial ranges are in sequence after the Ball & Williams production, beginning with about 18,000 and terminating at 20,000.

32-3 Brown Manufacturing Co.-Produced Ballard Sporting Rifles

Barrel markings remain identical to Merrimack production. Only the left-side marking was changed to "BROWN MFG. CO. NEWBURYPORT MASS/BALLARD'S PATENT/NOV. 5, 1861". The hammer (left side) continued to be marked "PATENTED JAN. 5, 1864", but the screwed-on floating hammer attachment was eliminated in favor of a solid hammer, the floating striker remaining in the breechblock. From the number of martial stocks used in Ballard-Brown sporting rifles, it is evident that Brown endeavored to utilize surpluses. Serial ranges are in a sequence after Merrimack, from about 20,000 to 22,000.

32-3a Ballard (Brown Manufacturing Co.) Sporting Rifles

Brown-made sporting rifles are identical to those of Merrimack with the exceptions noted previously. Barrel lengths of 24", 26", 28", and 30" were standard in all three configurations, but most commonly either octagonal or round. Calibers are .22, .32, .38, .44, and .46. Special sights (front and rear) were optional as was engraving on the frame. **(D)**

32-4 Marlin/Marlin Arms Co.-Produced Ballard Sporting Rifles

J. M. Marlin introduced a new frame to the Ballard action when he moved the machinery to New Haven. This new frame incorporates a mechanical ejector and is 1/8" shorter than the Merrimack and Brown frames, measuring 1 7/16" from breech to barrel juncture. Like Merrimack and Brown frames, the Marlin is tangless. Unlike the earlier production, however, the frames only have faceted tops. The exact frame configuration differs from type to type. Markings are found on the frame's left side, and (depending on whether the arm incorporates Marlin's patented reversible center-fire, rim-fire firing pin) include the patent date. Prior to 1881 these marking are either "J.M. MARLIN. NEW HAVEN, CONN. U.S.A./BALLARD'S PATENT NOV. 5, 1861" or "J.M. MARLIN NEW HAVEN, CONN. U.S.A./PATENTED. FEBRUARY 9, 1875/BALLARD'S PATENT NOV. 5, 1861." After the 1881 reorganization, "MARLIN FIREARMS CO." was substituted for the "J.M. MARLIN" section of the first line in either alternative marking. Overall length is dependent on buttstock type and buttplate type ordered with the rifle, and consequently this varies considerably within the same grade. Front and rear sights were optional, and vary considerably within the same grade; generally, however, the finer grade target rifles were equipped with tang sights. The serial no. is struck into the frame immediately forward of the triggerguard/lever. A separate serial range was begun with the Marlin production. About 40,000 rifles were made in all grades.

32-4a Ballard (J.M. Marlin) No. 1 "Hunter's" Rifles

The No. 1 sporting rifle was manufactured during the period 1875-80 and incorporates the patented firing pin (and was marked accordingly on the frame). The "blued" rounded barrel was available in 26", 28", and 30" lengths (bores) in .44 cal. Open sights were most frequent. Probably 4,000 made. **(B)**

32-4b Ballard (J. M. Marlin/Marlin Firearms Co.) No. 2 Sporting Rifles, Types I & II

The No. 2 sporting rifle is virtually identical to the No. 1 (32-4a) except that its "blued" barrel is octagonal instead of round. Standard barrel (bore) lengths are 24", 26", 28", and 30"; most common calibers are .32, .38, and occasionally .44, with the patented firing pin optional. Those so equipped have a triggerguard terminating in a two-finger loop, while those without it terminate in a simple curl. Type I rifles have a single triggerguard; type II, double-set triggers and a longer corresponding triggerguard bow. .22 cal. rifles were made. Production spanned 1876-91. **(B)**

32-4c Ballard (J. M. Marlin) No. 3½ Target Rifle

This arm differs from the No. 2 sporting rifle by having a straight, checkered stock with straight (shotgun) buttplate and vernier tang rear and globe front sights. Its 30" "blued" octagonal barrel is only chambered for the .40/65 cal. cartridge. Production ceased by 1880. **(C)**

32-4d Ballard (J. M. Marlin/Marlin Firearms Co.) No. 4 "Perfection" Rifles

The No. 4 was the center-fire only equivalent of the No. 2 sporting rifle. Barrel lengths (bore) are 28" and 30" in octagonal configuration only. Calibers available included .32, .38, .40, and .44. Open stepped sights were standard. Production began in 1876 and lasted until 1891. **(C)**

32-4e Ballard (J. M. Marlin) No. 4½ "Mid-Range" Target Rifles, Types I & II

The 4½ was a better quality rifle than the 3½, having a pistol grip incorporated into the buttstock and the corresponding full-hand triggerguard/lever loop. The "blued" 30" long (bore) barrel is turned part octagonal/part round, and vernier tang sights are standard. The arm was available in center-fire cartridge chambers only, either .38 or .40 cal.

II

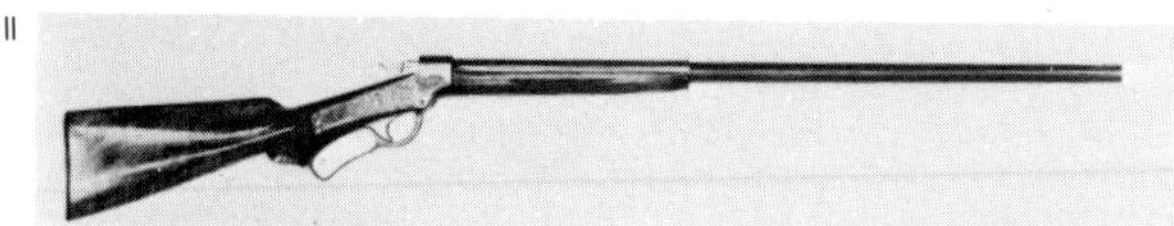

Type I has a plain frame; II ("A-1") has an engraved frame reading "BALLARD A-1" on the left side and "MID-RANGE" on the right side. The 4½ grade was discontinued by 1881 in favor of the 6½ series. **(B)**

32-4f

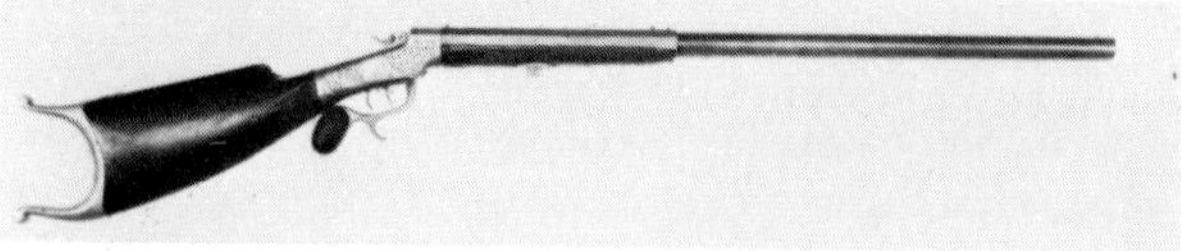

32-4f Ballard (J. M. Marlin/Marlin Firearms Co.) No. 6 "Schuetzen" Rifles

The No. 6 is readily distinguished by the long pronged buttplate, spurred triggerguard/lever, and double-set triggers. Although the 1881 Marlin catalog lists it only available in 32"-long half round/half octagonal configuration in either .32 or .38 cal., many "schuetzen" actions were rebarreled by local gunsmiths. The triggerguard is found with or without a wooden handle insert. Tang sights are standard. The arms were made from the mid 1870s-90. **(B)**

32-4g Ballard (Marlin Firearms Co.) No. 6½ Rigby "Off-Hand" Rifles

By 1883 the short-lived No. 6½ Rigby "Off-Hand Mid-Range" rifle had been standardized to the No. 6½ Rigby "Off-Hand." The round barrels were made only in 28" and 30" lengths (bore), and advertised only in .32 and .38 cal. The "schuetzen"-style buttplate is standard. Both pistol grip and forestock are checkered. Production continued until 1891. **(C)**

32-4h Ballard (Marlin Firearms Co.) No. 8 "Union Hill" Rifles

The No. 8 was introduced in 1884 and continued in production until 1890. It is basically similar to the No. 6½, "Rigby Off-Hand" in that it was available only in 28" and 30" barrels (bores) in .32 or .38 cal. The barrel, however, is part round/part octagonal, and double-set triggers are standard, along with a "schuetzen"-style buttplate and pistol grip. **(C)**

32-4i Ballard (Marlin Firearms Co.) No. 9 "Union Hill" Rifles

Identical to the No. 8 in almost every way, but this arm has a single instead of double-set triggers. **(C)**

32-4j Ballard (Marlin Firearms Co.) No. 10 "Schuetzen-Junior" Target Rifles

This arm is also identical to the No. 8 rifle except that the barrel is heavier and 32" in length (bore). It was produced from 1885-91. **(C)**

---

33 Remington/Rider-Action Breechloading, Single-Shot Cartridge Rifles

In 1863 Leonard Geiger of Hudson, New York, was issued a patent for a breechloading cartridge mechanism that secured the breechblock in place by means of the design of the internal portions of the hammer. E. Remington & Sons secured the patent rights, and their master armorer, Joseph Rider examined the action for potential improvements. His first improvement was patented in December, 1863, and was incorporated into a Remington pistol. This was followed by successive innovations patented in 1864-65, all directed to the mechanism incorporated on a carbine, for which the Remingtons and their close associate, Samuel Norris, had contracted with the U.S. government. Rider patented further modifications in 1866, 1868, and 1873. The perfected action, best titled the "Geiger-Rider-Remington," was nicknamed the "rolling-block" to describe its hammer/breechblock interaction. Remington's initial sales were primarily martial. Samuel Remington, the firm's chief sales executive, displayed the new rifles at the 1867 Imperial Exposition in Paris, winning a silver medal for the design. While the French were then uninterested in the mechanism, the Danish government gave Remington a contract for 42,000 martial rifles. This order lifted the company out of the post-Civil War doldrums and further stimulated orders from the combined kingdoms of Sweden and Norway for an additional 30,000 rifles. Spain ordered 10,000 for Cuba in 1869, Egypt ordered 60,000 the same year, and the French soon followed.

Despite the expansion of their production facilities, Remington was unable to satisfy the needs of more than the French during the

1870-71 War. To satisfy other European customers the firm granted foreign licenses to produce the rolling-block action overseas. With the collapse of France, the effect of these licenses became apparent—the lucrative foreign export market disappeared. To compensate for the production loss, Remington turned to the American hunting and sporting trade. The first rifle, the No. 1 sporting rifle, had been introduced in 1870. Within the next three years Remington introduced both modifications of this rifle for target shooting and a lighter-weight and small-caliber version. In 1880 a new modification was adopted, utilizing the side lever patented by Remington's chief of design, Lewis Hepburn. Variants of this "No. 3" rifle were also quickly put into production for target competition. But as Sharps had already learned, the target rifle and single-shot hunting rifle trade was not sufficient to maintain steady profits. In 1888 E. Remington & Sons declared bankruptcy. The company's assets were purchased mainly by Marcellus Hartley, owner of the Union Metallic Cartridge Co. Redesignated "The Remington Arms Co.", the firm continued to manufacture "rolling-block" action rifles well into the smokeless powder era, substantiating the claim often advanced that the action is one of the strongest ever devised.

33-O Rider (Remington) No. 1 "Rolling-Block", "Mid-Range" Target Rifles, Types II (color plate) **& I**

Introduced in 1875, this rifle is nearly identical to the No. 1 "long-range" except that the barrel was available in 28" or 30" (bore) lengths. Calibers optional were .40, .44, .45, and .46. Two stock configurations, either straight (I) or with a pistol grip buttstock (II) were offered, the latter with either crescent or flat, straight "Creedmoor" buttplate. **(C)**

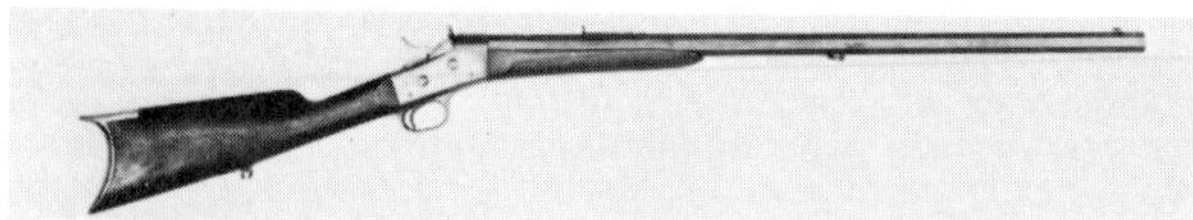

33-1 Remington "Rolling-Block" Sporting and Target Rifles.

Markings on these arms vary considerably over the production span of 1868-1910. From 1868-88 the barrel top is usually marked "E. REMINGTON & SONS. ILION, N.Y." After 1888 this was changed to "REMINGTON ARMS CO." The earliest patent markings appear on the upper frame strap and read: "REMINGTON'S ILION, N.Y. U.S.A./PAT. MAY 3D NOV. 15TH 1864 APRIL. 17TH 1866". This marking appears on the No. 1 sporting rifles during their earliest production. Later production added an extra line of patent dates to cover additional improvements. The No. 1 series target rifles are marked on the frame, left side: "PATENTS/MAY 3 1864/MAY 7 JUNE 11/NOV 2 DEC 24/DEC 3, 1872/SEPT. 10 1873". No. 3 (Hepburn) rifles simply are marked "HEPBURN'S PAT/OCT 7TH 1879" on the frame's left side.

33-1a Rider (Remington) No. 1 "Rolling-Block" Sporting Rifles, Types I & II

The arm was produced from 1868-1902. Type I, "Hunter's Rifle," was originally available only with its octagonal barrel in 30" (as shown), 32", and 34" lengths and in .38 or .46 rim-fire cartridges. By 1877 three shorter barrel lengths (24", 26", and 28") had been added and the calibers increased to include .22, .44, .45, and .50 cartridges, both rim- and center-fire. In 1877 a round-barreled version was introduced (II), known as the "Black Hills" rifle, but only with a 28" long (bore) barrel in .45 cal. This was discontinued in 1882 as uneconomical. Both used straight buttstocks with a crescent buttplate standard (adding 16¾" to the barrel length). **(A)**

33-1b Rider (Remington) No. 1½ "Rolling-Block" Sporting Rifles

This arm was introduced by Remington in 1888 to provide for smaller caliber bullets. Made only with octagonal barrels in 24", 26", and 28" lengths, it was available in .22, .25, .32, .38, and .44 cal. Discontinued in 1897. **(B)**

33-1c Rider (Remington) No. 2 "Rolling-Block" Sporting Rifles

Made from about 1877-1910, this arm is distinguished by its diminutive frame and fishbelly buttstock. It was primarily designed for small caliber ammunition, and was offered in .22, .32, .38, and .44 cal. The octagonal barrels were standard in 24" and 26", but optional lengths were available at extra cost. **(A)**

33-1d

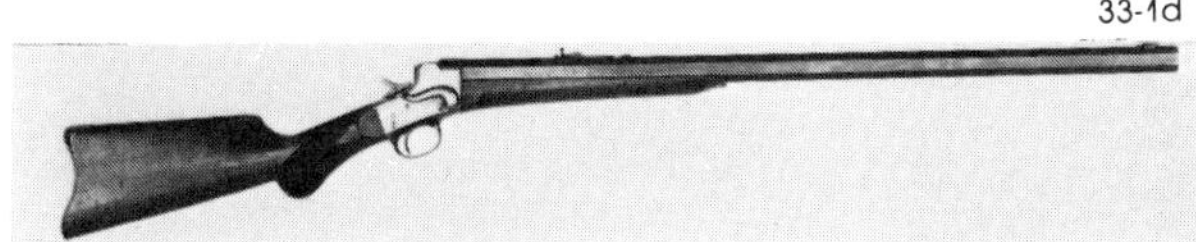

33-1d Remington-Hepburn No. 3 Sporting and Target Rifles

This arm was produced in nearly every caliber for which a cartridge was available from roughly 1880-1907. All three barrel configurations (round, octagonal, or part round/part octagonal) were available in three basic barrel (bore) lengths: 26", 28", or 30". Illustrated is a 30" octagonal barrel; overall length is 45¾". **(A)**

33-1e Rider (Remington Arms Co.) No. 4 "Rolling-Block" Rifles

Not introduced until 1890 (and not discontinued until 1933), the No. 4 "rolling-block" action rifle was the last model to be adopted before the general switch to smokeless powder cartridges (the end date for this guide). The 22½" or 24" octagonal barrels were chambered for .22, .25, and .32 rim-fire cartridges only. The frame is smaller than the No. 2 rifle, which this model generally replaced. Rear sights are simple open "V"'s on strap, and the front were simple iron blades. Note, however, that a substantial portion of the production took place during the 20th century, and only the earliest serial nos. fall within the range of this guide. **(A)**

---

34 | Sharps Single-Shot Cartridge Rifles

The Sharps Rifle Manufacturing Co. of Hartford, Conn., devoted its full energies during the Civil War to the production of percussion

breechloading military weapons. Following the war, the company was suddenly bereft of a market for its products. The government contracts for alterations pulled the firm through the doldrums of 1868-69, but the long-term prospects looked dismal. Indeed, from 1869-71 sales were barely sufficient to maintain the work staff in spite of Richard Lawrence's redesign and lightening of the lock action that yielded the M1869 series rifles and carbines. Finally in 1871 the sales slump broke. The reopening of the West and revived interest in the East in long-range target competition as a result of the establishment of the Creedmoor range on Long Island by the recently-formed National Rifle Association promoted this new prosperity, but the orders that came in were at first for special one-of-a-kind products that disrupted the company's operations and organization. To rectify the latter problem, the company, reorganized in 1874 as the Sharps Rifle Co., began a widespread advertising campaign, and hired Nelson King from Winchester to supervise production, which shortly afterward was moved to a new plant in Bridgeport, Conn. King reorganized production by standardizing the line and limiting the potential options available. King's tenancy, however, was brief. An unauthorized change he instigated in the company's chamber gauges led to his dismissla, and he was replaced by Hugo Borchardt.

A new model breechblock had been designed in 1871 by Lawrence for the Springfield Armory alterations utilizing old Sharps carbine frames, and, after the coompany reorganized, this was called the "Model 1874" (though in fact it had been in production since 1871). Another model was introduced in 1877, but this was quickly superseded by a new Borchardt design having a totally internal firing mechanism and designated by the company "Model 1878," though it, too, had been in production slightly earlier. Economic woes, principly connected with an insufficient cash flow caused the company to cease production in 1880, but arms were assembled from existing parts as late as 1883.

34-O Sharps (Sharps Rifle Co.) M1874 Mid-Range Target Rifles (color plate)

179 of these arms were produced at Bridgeport. Except for two in round configuration, all barrels were octagonal and "blued." Bore diameter was standardized at .40 cal., but a few special orders were accepted for different calibers. Barrel length (bore) was also standardized at 30" but 28 were processed in 28", 32", or 34" lengths. **(D)**

34-1 M1869 Series Rifles and Carbines

All locks were backaction, flat-surfaced, and marked "SHARP'S RIFLE MFG. CO./HARTFORD, CONN." All barrels were marked on their top "SHARP'S RIFLES/MANUFG. CO./HARTFORD, CONN." forward of the sights; "NEW MODEL 1869" to the rear of the sights; and "CALIBRE (figures)" at the frame. Serial nos. were stamped on the upper frame tang, with the letter "C" or "CL" preceeding the figures indicative of either 100,000 or 150,000. Sights were available in a multiplicity of styles. Buttstock and buttplate design were also subject to special order. Accordingly, overall length is not an important criterion.

34-1a Sharps (Sharps Rifle Mfg. Co.) M1869 Carbines

About 500 were made between 1869-71 in either .40, .45, or .50 cal.

(6-groove rifling). Barrel (bore) lengths were 22", 24", or 26", and the round barrels were "blued." **(D)**

34-2 M1871/"M1874" Series Rifles and Carbines

All locks are backaction, flat-surfaced, and unmarked. Frames are marked on the left side, first (1871-75)—"C. SHARPS' PAT./SEPT. 12TH 1848", and later (1875-80)—"SHARPS' RIFLE CO./PAT. APR. 1869". During the transition period both marks were applied. All barrels are marked on their top: "SHARPS RIFLE/MANUFG. CO./HARTFORD CONN." or "SHARPS RIFLE MANUFG. CO/HARTFORD, CONN." (1871-74) and finally "SHARPS RIFLE CO. BRIDGEPORT. CONN." (1874-80) in conjunction with "Old Reliable" and "CALIBRE (figures)" at the frame. Serial nos. are stamped on the upper frame tang prefixed by a "C" (for 100,000) until about 154,000. Sights were available in a bewildering multiplicity of styles. Buttstock and buttplate design were limited, and as this affects overall length, these measurements are not given except in the illustrated examples.

34-2a

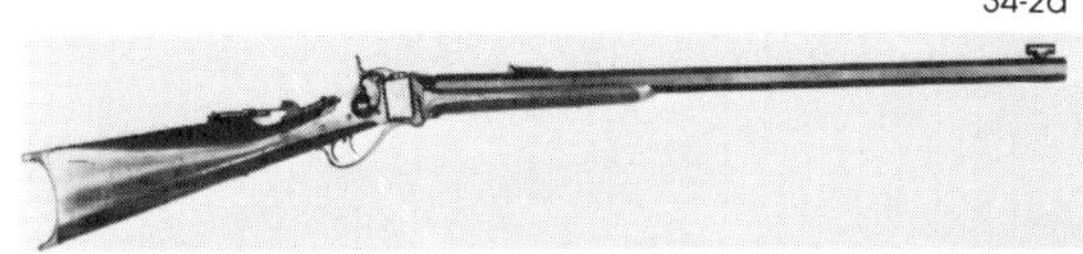

34-2a Sharps (Sharps Rifle Mfg. Co./Sharps Rifle Co.) M1874 Sporting Rifles

A total of 6,441 were made at Hartford and Bridgeport between 1871-80. The round, part round/part octagonal, or full octagonal barrels were available in any specified length between 21½" and 36", with any variation in sighting specified. Calibers, however, were limited to .44 or .45, but special bores could be prepared. Double-set triggers were optional, as were pistol-grip buttstocks or "schuetzen"-style buttplates (light "schuetzen" style illustrated). **(B)**

34-2b

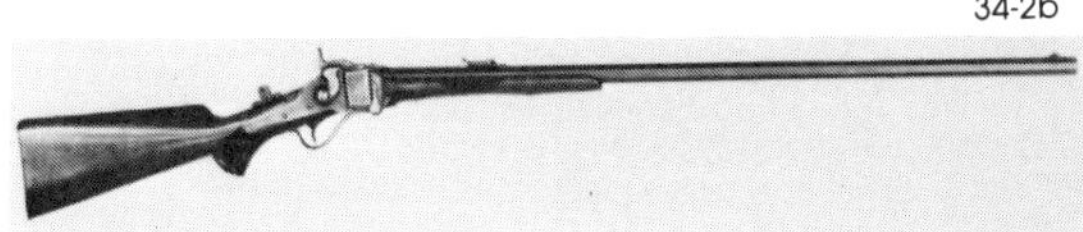

34-2b Sharps (Sharps Rifle Co.) M1874 Long-Range Target Rifles

A total of 429 were made at Bridgeport in four grades. Calibers were limited to .40, .44, or .45. Until 1877 the barrel was only available in octagonal configuration and 34" length; that shown has a 50⅞" overall length. In 1876 a decision was made to change the length to 32" and offer the rifle only with part round/part octagonal barrel. Due to customer complaints the 34" barrel was reintroduced in late 1879 and the last 106 were made with 34" part round/part octagonal barrels. **(D)**

34-2c Sharps (Sharps Rifle Mfg. Co./Sharps Rifle Co.) "Business" Rifles

This arm has a model name coined by Sharps for the simplest, least expensive product destined for the general hunting trade. Hartford and

Bridgeport produced 1,604 of these arms in the M1874 style. 28" long round barrels are standard, although ten were made in octagonal configuration, and 100 26" and 30" barrel (bore) rifles were also made. Caliber was restricted to either .40 or .45, but six were specially ordered in .50. Double-set triggers are the only luxury item on these arms. **(C)**

34-3 M1877 Series Rifles

All locks are backaction, flat-surfaced, and unmarked, although some are engraved. If the lock is engraved, the frame is also. The left side of the frames are marked: "SHARP'S RIFLE CO./PAT. APR. 6TH 1869". All barrels are marked on their top "Old Reliable" together with "SHARPS RIFLE CO. BRIDGEPORT, CONN." and "CALIBRE (figures)" near the frame. Like all Sharps rifles made between 1869-80, a multiplicity of sights was available.

34-3a Sharps (Sharps Rifle Co.) M1877 Long-Range Target Rifles

This arm was an unsuccessful attempt to supplant the popular M1874 long-range. It met with so little favor in America that sales were sought in England. Nevertheless, only 98 were produced between 1877-79.

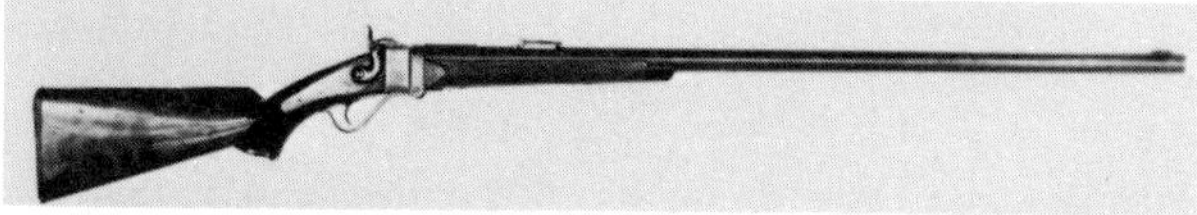

The arms were made only in round "blued" barrels of .45 cal. Barrel lengths of either 32" or 34" were optional. Checkered pistol grip and vernier tang comb sights are standard, but special sights could be ordered (as on the arm shown—34" barrel (bore) length, for an overall length of 50½"). **(D)**

34-4 M1878 Series Rifles

All barrels are marked on the top "Old Reliable" and "SHARPS RIFLE CO. BRIDGEPORT, CONN." together with the cartridge caliber. Unless the frame is engraved, the left side is marked "BORCHARDT PATENT/ SHARPS RIFLE CO. BRIDGEPORT CONN./U.S.A." Sights and buttstocks/ buttplates were available in a number of options although the M1859-type Lawrence patent rear sight predominates.

34-4a Sharps-Borchardt (Sharps Rifle Co.) M1878 Sporting Rifles

The 1,610 arms of this type made in Bridgeport were available in only two calibers, .40 or .45. The "blued" barrels were available either in octagonal configuration (in lengths between 24"-32" bore) or in round configuration (in lengths between 21"-36"). This internal hammer rifle was not particularly popular among target shooters, althoughthe Borchardt action is reputedly one of the strongest ever made. **(C)**

35 | Patented, Single-Shot Breechloading Martial Cartridge Rifles

When George W. Morse, and later Smith and Wesson, patented their cartridge innovations in the period 1856-60 for what would become center-fire and rim-fire self-contained ammunition, they sparked a revolution in the firearms industry. These innovations effectively eliminated the main problem of all percussion breechloaders—gas leakage that either so fouled the mechanism as to eventually make it inoperable or so disconcerted the shooter as to make the arm inoperable. The Army experimented with alterations of muskets and possibly rifles utilizing the Morse cartridge and his patented breechloading system prior to the Civil War, but in 1861 his machinery was captured by Virginia forces, who loaned it to Tennessee. Morse followed its fortunes until it came to rest in Columbia, S.C. in 1863, where he manufactured arms for the Confederacy. The center-fire cartridge remained in limbo during the Civil War as a result.

Such was not the case with the rim-fire cartridge. Smith and Wesson had devised the cartridges primarily for thei revolvers based on Rollin White's patent. Other firms, however, quickly recognized the adaptability of the missile to different arms, especially repeating breechloaders. From the Henry and Spencer repeating breechloaders, the concept quickly spread to single-shot breechloaders as well, first in the smaller .44 cal. of the Henry and later to the larger Spencer ammunition. At least ten different patented mechanisms were adapted for self-contained cartridges during the War, primarily for cavalry carbines.

The close of the War permitted a return to experimentation with the center-fire cartridge. In an economy move the U.S. government adopted the .50 cal. center-fire cartridge and altered large numbers of muzzleloading rifle-muskets and breechloading carbines, an action which closed the patented breechloading market to the American military. To compensate for this loss, most inventors and their sponsoring firms turned to both the civilian and the foreign military markets. Since the latter was more lucrative in terms of capitalization of of machinery, most of the effort was devoted to those sales.

35-O Sharps & Hankins "M1861" Military Rifles, Type II (color plate)

OL: 42⅝"
BD: .52 cal., 6-groove rifling
Furniture: brass buttplate
Lockplate: none, mechanism within frame
Markings: left side of frame—"SHARPS/PATENT/1859"; right side of frame—"SHARPS/&/HANKINS/PHILADA."; serial no. on upper frame tang
BL: 27"
Finish: "browned"
Configuration: round
Sights: rear—S. & H. patented elevating sight; front—small iron blade
Fastenings: none, no forestock
Markings: none

Quantities produced are not recorded, but all serial numbers are under 500, suggesting limited production for a Philadelphia volunteer militia organization in 1861. **(D)**

35-1 Ballard (Dwight & Chapin) Military Carbines

OL: 37¾"
BD: .54 cal., 5-groove rifling
Furniture: iron
Lockplate: none, mechanism within frame
BL: 20$\frac{15}{16}$" to frame (22" bore)
Finish: "bright"
Configuration: round
Sights: rear—½" long base with folding leaf 1" from frame;

Markings: left side of frame—"MERWIN & BRAY/AGT'S. N.Y./(serial no.)"; right side of frame—"BALLARD'S PATENT/NOV. 5. 1861"

front—iron blade, dovetailed
Fastenings: single iron band
Markings: none

Kentucky purchased 1,000 of these arms during 1863-64. They have long been erroneously attributed to a non-extant "Ballard Arms Co." of Fall River, Mass., but no such marking appears on them. A very few bear the actual maker's name on the frame, "DWIGHT & CHAPIN/BRIDGEPORT, CONN." over the left frame agency markings. **(C)**

35-2 Ballard (Ball & Williams) Military Carbines, Types I & II

OL: (I) 37⅜"; (II) 37¼"
BD: .44 cal.
Furniture: iron, sling swivels on buttstock and band.
Lockplate: none, mechanism within frame
Markings: serial no. on top of faceted frame; inspector's initials on barrel left side; left side of breechblock, top of comb, and buttplate tang, and in script in cartouche on left side of stock; late production marked on frame—"BALL & WILLIAMS/Worcester, Mass." over "MERWIN & BRAY AGTS/NEW YORK" on left side; "BALLARD'S PATENT/NOV. 5, 1861" on right side
BL: (I) 20$\frac{5}{16}$" to frame (22$\frac{1}{16}$" bore); (II) 20¼" to frame (22" bore)
Finish: "blued"
Configuration: part round/part octagonal
Sights: rear—½" long block with pierced "L" leaf 1" from frame; front—dovetailed iron blade
Fastenings: single iron band
Markings: (early) serial no. near breech and "BALL & WILLIAMS/Worcester, Mass." on top; "MERWIN & BRAY AGTS/NEW YORK" on upper left facet, and "BALLARD'S PATENT/NOV. 5, 1861" on upper right facet

II

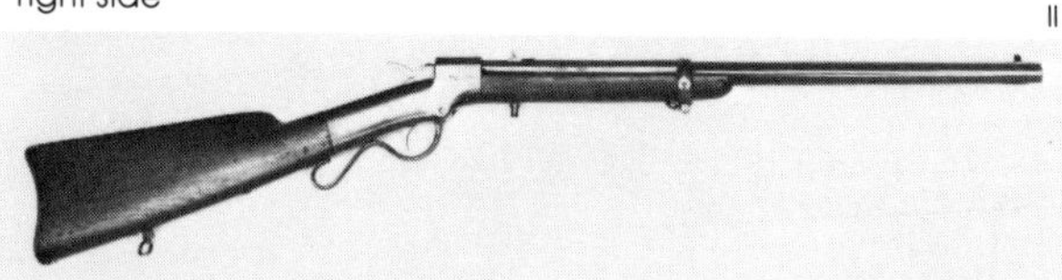

Kentucky was the first to purchase Ballard carbines (3,000) prior to November, 1863. In the succeeding fiscal year 1,600 more were purchased. New York also purchased 500 in 1863. In 1864 Merwin & Bray delivered 1,500 of 5,000 type II military carbines ordered by the U.S. Ordnance Dept. Early production carbines utilize a solid breechblock; later, a split breechblock. Both use the faceted frame of the early sporting rifles. **(B)**

35-3 Ballard (Ball & Williams) .44 cal. Military Rifle

OL: 45⅜"
BL: 28$\frac{7}{16}$" to frame (30⅛" bore)

BD: .44 cal., 5-groove rifling
Furniture: iron, "blued"
Lockplate: none, mechanism within frame
Markings: serial no. on top of of faceted frame
Finish: "blued"
Configuration: part round/part octagonal
Sights: rear—½" long base with pierced "L" leaf 1" from frame; front—dovetailed iron blade
Fastenings: single iron band
Markings: serial no. near breech, "BALL & WILLIAMS/ Worcester, Mass." on top, "MERWIN & BRAY AGTS/NEW YORK" on upper left facet, "BALLARD'S PATENT/NOV. 5, 1861" on upper right facet, "KENTUCKY" on top

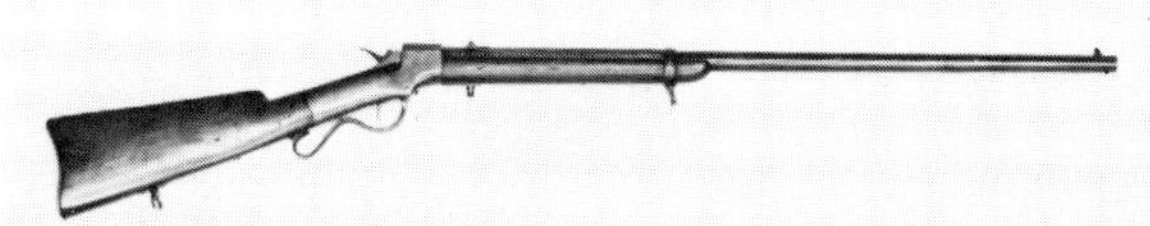

One thousand of these rifles were delivered to Kentucky in 1863-64. All use the same ammunition as the .44 cal. early military carbines. (35-2). All use solid breechblocks typical of early production. Serial numbers are in the same series as the carbines in the range 7,200 to 8,500. **(C)**

35-4 Ballard (Ball & Williams) .46 cal. Military Rifles, Types I & II
OL: (I) 45¼"; (II) 45⅜"
BD: .46 cal., 5-groove rifling
Furniture: iron, sling swivels on buttstock and middle band
Lockplate: none, mechanism within band
Markings: left side of frame—"BALL & WILLIAMS/Worcester, Mass./MERWIN & BRAY AGT'S/ NEW YORK"; right side of frame —"BALLARD'S PATENT/ NOV. 5, 1861"; top of frame—serial no. and "KENTUCKY" (type I only)
BL: (I) $28\frac{5}{16}$" to frame (30" bore); (II) $30\frac{1}{6}$" bore)
Finish: "blued"
Configuration: round
Sights: rear—½" long base with pierced "L" leaf, 1⅛" from frame; front—dovetailed iron blade
Fastenings: 3 iron bands
Markings: serial no. on top near frame

In 1863-64 Kentucky ordered an additional 3,000 .56 cal. military rifles from Merwin & Bray. Before any deliveries commenced, the state ordered the bore size reduced to .46 cal. to conform with newly-adopted Federal standards. The first 2,200 were delivered prior to Nov., 1864, the balance in 1865. Type II rifles have the alternative percussion hammer marked on its left side "PATENTED JAN. 5.1864" **(B)**

35-5 Berdan (Colt Pt. Fire Arms Co.) Military Rifles, Types I & II
OL: 52⅞"
BD: .42 cal. or .45 cal.
BL: 29⅝" to receiver (32½" bore)
Finish: "blued"

Furniture: iron, "blued"
Lockplate: none, mechanism within receiver
Markings: none

Configuration: round, bayonet lug on right side near muzzle
Sights: rear—folding ladder with slide on base mounted on receiver; front—iron block/blade
Fastenings: 2 iron bands
Markings: "-COLT'S P^{T} FIREARMS M^{FG} C^{O} HARTFORD C^{T}-" (rare) or the equivalent on top in Cyrillic letters

I

About 100 rifles with English marks (including 20 in .45 cal.) were made based on Berdan's patents of Feb., 1866 and Mar., 1869. 30,000 were made for the Russian government on contract after 1870. **(B & D)**

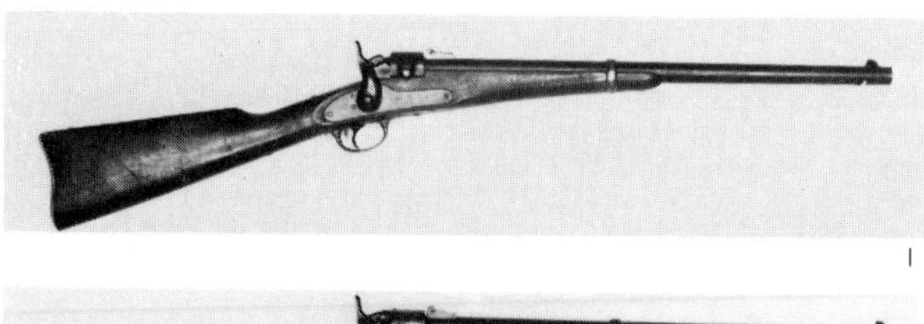

I

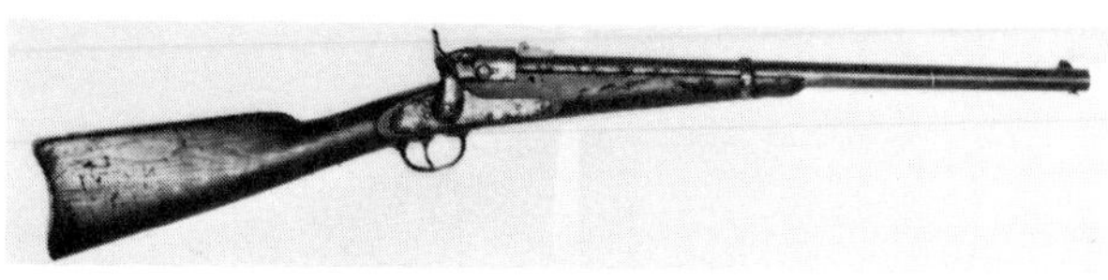

II

35-6 Joslyn Breechloading Cartridge Carbines, Types I & II

OL: (early) 38½"; (late) 38¾"
BD: .52 cal., 3-groove rifling
Furniture: (I) brass; (II) iron
Lockplate: flat
Markings: (I-early)—"JOSLYN FIRE ARMS C^{O}/STONINGTON/ CONN."; (late I and II)—"JOSLYN FIRE ARMS Co/STONINGTON CONN./1864" forward of hammer; serial no. on breechblock top (I & II); breechblock—"B.F. JOSLYN'S PATENT/OCTOBER 8TH 1861/JUNE 24TH 1862" on top with serial no. (I) or on back of breechblock (II)

BL: 21⅛" to breechblock (22" bore)
Finish: "blued"
Configuration: round
Sights: rear—U.S. M1861 rifle-musket sight ⅛" from block; front—dovetailed iron blade
Fastenings: single band, brass (I), iron (II)
Markings: inspector's initials on upper left side

10,200 Joslyn breechloading cartridge carbines were delivered during the Civil War under four contracts, the first 3,200 as type I with the hook rather than the plunger (II) breechblock release. **(A)**

35-7 Laidley (Whitney) Breechloading Military Rifles, Types I & II

OL: 50" (also 47½" in .50 cal.)
BD: .433, .44, .45, and .50 cal.
Furniture: iron; top band (I) marked—"PAT. NOV 8, 1874"
Lockplate: none, mechanism within frame
Markings: upper strap of tang (I) —"WHITNEYVILLE ARMORY CO. PATENTED/OCT. 17'65, RE-IS-D JUNE 25'72, DEC 26'65. RE-IS'D OCT 1'67, MAY 15'66, JULY 16'72." or (II) "WHITNEY ARMS CO./NEW HAVEN, CT. U.S.A."
BL: 33¼" to frame (34⅞" bore)
Finish: "blued"
Configuration: round
Sights: rear—2½" long block with folding ladder 2¼" from frame; front—iron block/blade
Fastenings: 3 (or 2) iron bands
Markings: caliber of cartridge, e.g., ".44 RF"; serial no. on triggerguard strap

It is estimated that between 1874-88 Whitney produced about 39,000 type I (using Laidley's May, 1866, 4-piece breechblock action) and 30,000 type II (using a 2-piece breechblock that virtually copied Remington's successful Rider rolling-block action). **(A)**

35-8 Laidley (Whitney) Breechloading Carbines, Types I & II

OL: 35⅞"
BD: .433, .44, .45, .50 cal.
Furniture: iron
Lockplate: none, mechanism within frame
Markings: upper frame strap—(I) "WHITNEY VILLE ARMORY CO. PATENTED/OCT. 17'65 RE-IS'D JUNE 25'72, DEC 26'65. RE-IS-D OCT 1'67, MAY 15'66, JULY 16'72" or (II) "WHITNEY ARMS CO./NEW HAVEN, CT. U.S.A."
BL: 18⅞" to frame (20¼" bore)
Finish: "blued"
Configuration: round
Sights: rear—1⅛" long base with "L" leaf 1⅚" from frame; front—dovetailed iron blade
Fastenings: single iron band
Markings: caliber on top; serial no. on triggerguard strap

II

Whitney manufactured approximately 10,000 of both types I and II Laidley carbines, though, like the rifles, type II did not truly use his four-piece patented breechblock. Serial nos. run consecutively in the same series as the rifles. **(B)**

35-9 Palmer (Lamson & Co.) Breechloading Carbines

OL: 37¼"
BD: .50 cal., 5-groove rifling
Furniture: iron, "blued"; swivel and ring on left side
Lockplate: flat, beveled edge
Markings: "U.S./E.G. LAMSON & CO./WINDSOR, VT." forward of hammer; "1865" on tail
BL: 23¾" (incl. receiver) (20" bore)
Finish: "blued"
Configuration: round
Sights: rear—⅝" long base with pierced folding leaf ½" from port; front—iron blade
Fastenings: single iron band
Markings: "W^M PALMER/PATENT/

DEC. 22,1863" on top behind loading port; inspectors' initials "MM" on various parts

One thousand arms conforming to William Palmer's bolt action patent of Dec., 1863, were ordered as trial arms by the U.S. Ordnance Dept. in 1864. All were delivered in 1865, too late to see any combat during the war and were later disposed of as surplus. **(C)**

35-10 Peabody (Providence Tool Co.) Breechloading Carbines

OL: 38¾"
BD: .433, .45, and .50 cal.
Furniture: iron, "blued"; South Carolina purchases have "S.C." on buttplate tang
Lockplate: backaction; flat
Markings: left side of frame—"PEABODY'S PAT./JULY 22, 1862/MAN'F'D BY/PROVIDENCE TOOL CO./PROV. R.I."
BL: 19¼" to frame (20" bore)
Finish: "blued"
Configuration: round
Sights: rear—⅜" long base with ladder with slide 1⅝" from frame; front—iron block/blade
Fastenings: single iron band
Markings: none

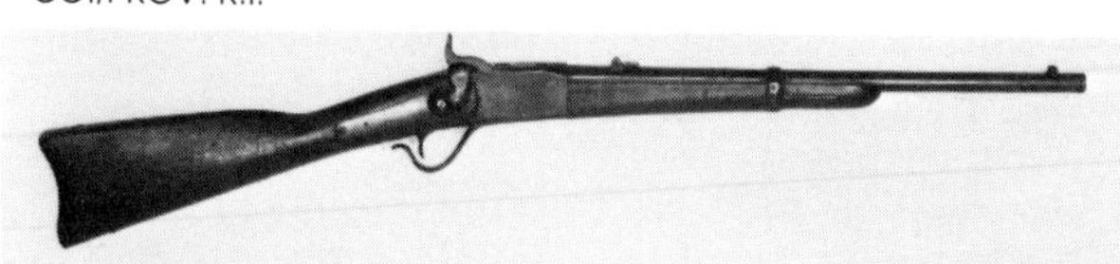

Exact quantities are not recorded. The arm was listed as early as the 1864 catalogue, and 350 were sold to South Carolina as late as 1877. France purportedly purchased a quantity in .50 cal. **(C)**

35-11 Peabody (Providence Tool Co.) Breechloading Rifles, Types I & II

OL: (I) 51¾"; (II) 53"
BD: .41, .433, .45, and .50 cal.
Furniture: iron, "blued"
Lockplate: backaction; flat
Markings: left side of frame—"PEABODY'S PAT./JULY 22, 1862/MAN'F'D BY/PROVIDENCE TOOL CO./PROVID. R.I."
BL: (I) 32¼" to frame (33" bore); (II) 34¼" to frame (35" bore)
Finish: "blued"
Configuration: round
Sights: rear—2½" long base with folding ladder 1⅛" from frame; front—iron block/blade
Fastenings: 2 iron bands
Markings: none

I

This military rifle, first offered in 1865, was purchased in limited numbers by the Connecticut, New York, and Massachusetts state militias, all in .433 (11 mm) bore size. Most military rifle sales were abroad. **(A)**

35-12 Peabody-Martini (Providence Tool Co.) Breechloading Rifles

OL: 49″
BD: .45 cal.
Furniture: iron, the upper band with a saber bayonet stud on right side
Lockplate: none, mechanism within frame
Markings: Ottoman sultan cypher over Arabic numbers stamped into frame right side; frame left side—"PEABODY & MARTINI PATENTS/MAN'F'D BY/ PROVIDENCE TOOL CO./PROV. R.I. U.S.A."
BL: 32½″ to frame (33⅛″ bore)
Finish: "blued"
Configuration: round
Sights: rear—2¼″ long base with folding ladder with slide 6¼″ from frame; front—iron block/ blade
Fastenings: 2 iron bands
Markings: usually Turkish "star-/-in-crescent" proofs

After the British adopted this action with Henry-type rifling as their standard military arm, their ally, Ottoman Turkey, followed suit, purchasing over 600,000 rifles of this type after 1872. **(A)**

35-13 Peabody-Martini (Providence Tool Co.) Breechloading Carbines

OL: 38″
BD: .45 cal.
Furniture: iron
Lockplate: none, mechanism within frame
Markings: left side of frame—"PEABODY & MARTINI PATENTS/ MAN'F'D BY/PROVIDENCE TOOL CO./PROV. R.I. U.S.A."; "PTC"/ cypher sometimes found in stock
BL: 21⅜″ to frame (22″ bore)
Finish: "blued"
Configuration: round
Sights: rear—⅜″ base with folding ladder 1½″ from frame; front—iron block/blade
Fastenings: single iron band
Markings: none

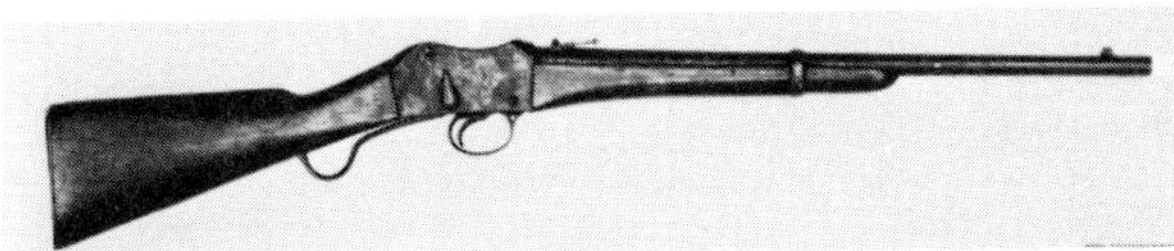

In addition to the rifles, Ottoman Turkey is purported to have bought carbines (quantities unknown) of this pattern. Others may have been sold on a limited basis to American militias. **(B)**

35-14 "Phoenix" (Whitney Arms Co.) Breechloading Carbines

OL: 36″
BD: .433, .44, .45, and .50 cal.
BL: 19″ to frame (20½″ bore)
Finish: "blued"

Furniture: iron, "blued"
Lockplate: none, mechanism within frame
Markings: upper frame strap—"PATENT MAY. 26. 74"
Configuration: round
Sights: rear—1⅛" long base with two "L" leaves 1⅝" from frame; front—dovetailed iron blade
Fastenings: single iron band
Markings: serial no. stamped on triggerguard strap

An estimated 25,000 "Phoenix" longarms of all types were made by Whitney between 1874-81; about 5,000 were probably carbines. **(B)**

35-15

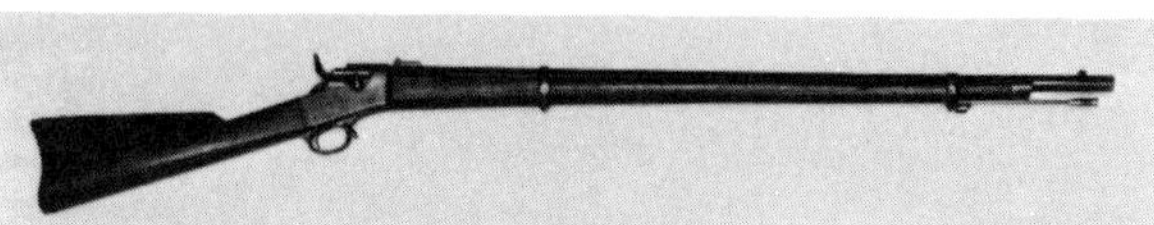

35-15 "Phoenix" (Whitney Arms Co.) Breechloading Military Rifles

OL: 50½"
BD: .433, .44, .45, and .50 cal.
Furniture: iron, "blued"
Lockplate: none, mechanism within frame
Markings: upper strap of frame —"PATENT MAY.26,74"
BL: 34½" to frame (35" bore)
Finish: "blued"
Configuration: round
Sights: rear—1¼" base with pierced "L" leaf ¼" from frame; front—iron blade, dovetailed
Fastenings: 3 iron bands
Markings: serial no. on triggerguard strap

From 10,000-15,000 of the "Phoenix" arms made between 1874-81 were military rifles. **(B)**

35-16 Rider (Remington) "Split-Breech" .50 Cal. Carbines

OL: 34"
BD: .50 cal., 3-groove rifling
Furniture: iron, "US" on buttplate tang
Lockplate: none, mechanism within frame
Markings: upper frame strap—"REMINGTON'S ILION. N.Y./PAT. DEC. 23, 1863, MAY 3 & NOV. 16, 1864"
BL: 18¼" to frame (20" bore)
Finish: "blued"
Configuration: round
Sights: rear—1¼" base with pierced "L" leaf 2 3/16" from frame; front—iron blade
Fastenings: single iron band
Markings: none

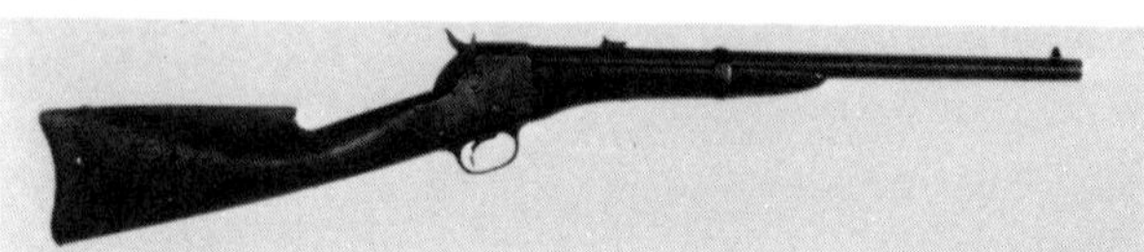

Remington contracted in 1864 for these arms based on Rider's patents and Leonard Geiger's designs; all deliveries were made by May, 1866. Five years later Remington purchased most of them back for resale to France. France recorded receiving 21,117, including some modified for bayonets. **(C)**

35-17 Rider (Remington) "Rolling-Block" N.Y. State Contract Rifles

OL: 52"
BD: .50 cal., 3-groove rifling
Furniture: iron "blued"
Lockplate: none, mechanism within frame
Markings: upper frame strap—"REMINGTON'S ILION, N.Y. U.S.A./PAT. MAY 3D. NOV 15TH 1864. APRIL 17TH 1866/AUG 27TH 1867. NOV 7TH 1871"
BL: 34½" to frame (36" bore)
Finish: "blued"
Configuration: round
Sights: rear—2½" long base with folding ladder 2¼" from frame; front—iron block/blade
Fastenings: 3 iron bands
Markings: "P" on right, "S" on left near frame ("B" on frame)

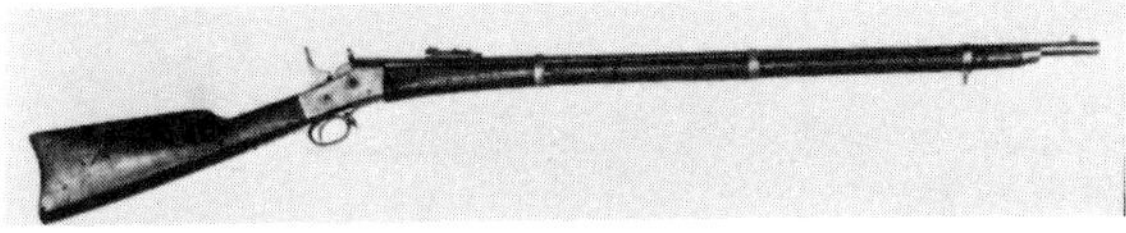

New York purchased approximately 10,000 for the national guard, c. 1872. On the right side of the buttstock a cartouche bears the script initials "S.N.Y.", while the other side of the stock bears script inspectors' initials, also in a cartouche. **(A)**

35-18 Rider (Remington) "Rolling-Block" Foreign Contract Rifles, Types I-III

OL: (I & II) 50⅜"
BD: .433 cal. (11 mm)
Furniture: iron, "blued" or case hardened
Lockplate: none, mechanism within frame
Markings: upper frame strap—"REMINGTON'S ILION, N.Y. U.S.A." over two or three line patent dates
BL: (I & II) 33¾" to frame (35⅛" bore); (III) 34⅝" to frame (36" bore)
Finish: "blued"
Configuration: round
Sights: rear—2½" long base with folding ladder 2⁵⁄₁₆" from frame; front—iron block/blade
Fastenings: 3 iron bands
Markings: various inspection marks of accepting governments; III marked on top facet "MODELO ARTENTO 1879 E.N."

Types I, the "Spanish Model," II, the "Egyptian Model," and III, the "Argentine Model" represent the most commonly manufactured foreign contract rifles produced by Remington on the Rider patents. Since Remington also licensed foreign governments to produce this action, arms without the Remington mark on the strap should be examined carefully. Types II and III have a saber bayonet stud with guide on the right side. **(A)**

35-19 Sharps & Hankins U.S. Navy Contract Carbines

OL: 38⅝"
BD: .52 cal., 6-groove rifling
Furniture: brass buttplate, single
BL: 23⅝"
Finish: covered with leather
Configuration: round with band

iron sling swivel on buttstock
Lockplate: none, mechanism within frame
Markings: left side of frame—"SHARPS/PATENT/1859"; right side of frame—"SHARPS/&/HAWKINS/PHILADA."
at muzzle to secure leather
Sights: rear—S.&W. patented elevating sight; front—iron blade
Fastenings: none, no forestock
Markings: leather occasionally found with U.S. Navy inspection marks

The Navy purchased 6,986 during 1862-67. After mid-1863 all were of the "New Model" with floating firing pin (not attached to hammer). **(B)**

35-20 Starr Breechloading Metallic Cartridge Carbines

OL: 37¾"
BD: .53 cal., 5-groove rifling
Furniture: iron, swivel bar and ring on left side
Lockplate: backaction; flat
Markings: "STARR ARMS CO/YONKERS, N.Y." behind hammer; upper frame strap—"STARR'S PATENT/SEPT. 14TH 1858"
BL: 20⅛" to frame (21" bore)
Finish: "blued"
Configuration: round
Sights: rear—1¼" long base with pierced "L" leaf 1¼" from frame; front—iron blade
Fastenings: single brass or iron band
Markings: "STARR ARMS CO YONKERS, N.Y." on top; serial no. on right side

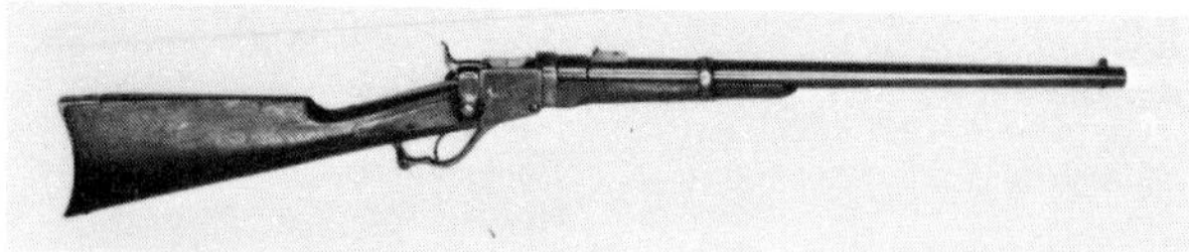

Except for caliber and the substitution of a striker for the old percussion cone, this arm is nearly identical to Starr's earlier U.S. carbine. A total of 5,002 were purchased in accordance with an 1865 contract. None saw combat. **(B)**

35-21 Warner Breechloading Carbines, Types I & II

OL: 37¾"
BD: .50 cal., 3-groove rifling
Furniture: brass, iron swivel ring set into left side of brass frame; iron band
Lockplate: none, mechanism within frame
Markings: left side of frame—"JAMES WARNER. SPRINGFIELD, MASS./WARNER'S/PATENT" or "GREENE RIFLE WORKS/WORCESTER, MASS./PAT. FEB. 1864"
BL: 19" to brass frame (20" bore)
Finish: "bright"
Configuration: round
Sights: rear—1⅛" long base with leaf pierced twice 2¼" from frame; front—iron block/blade
Fastenings: single iron band
Markings: none except inspector's initials

The cylindrical brass breechblock swings to the side when the iron latch on the left side of the hammer is depressed. 4,001 Warner carbines were purchased during 1864. 2,492 of these were disposed of to Schuyler, Hartley, & Graham, who sold them to France in 1870-71. **(C)**

35-22 Frank Wesson "Tip-Up" Breechloading Rifle/Carbine, Type II

OL: 39¼"
BD: .44 cal.
Furniture: iron, including sling swivel; serial no. on trigger-guard trip
Lockplate: none, mechanism within frame
Markings: none
BL: 24⅜"
Finish: "browned" or "blued"
Configuration: octagonal
Sights: rear—1½" long base with folding ladder with slide 4" from breech; front—iron block/blade
Fastenings: none, no forestock
Markings: "FRANK WESSON WORCESTER MASS/PATD. OCT. 25. 1859 & NOV 11, 1862"; on military purchases—"B. KITTREDGE & CO./CINCINNATI, O."

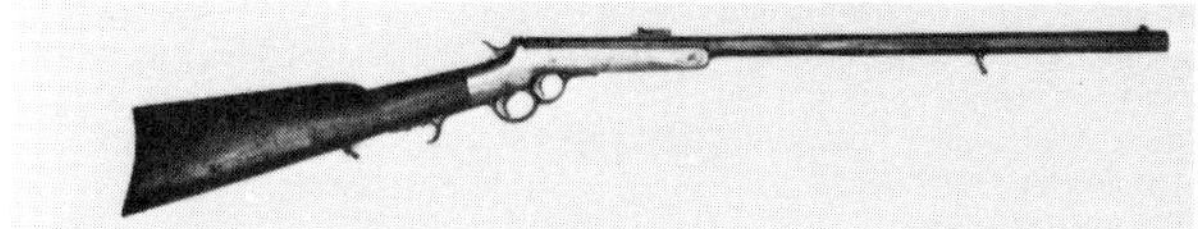

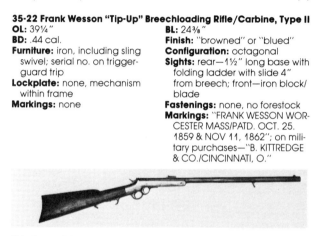

151 of these 24" long barreled rifles (carbines) were purchased in 1863 to supplement the 220 purchased privately by the 11th Ohio Cavalry. Indiana also purchased 760 for her militia, and others were privately purchased by Kansas volunteers. **(C)**

---

36 | Flintlock, Repeating Magazine Longarms

On April 12th and 26th, 1756, the Boston Gazette ran the following advertisement:

> **Made by John Cookson and to be sold at his house in Boston a handy gun of nine pound and a half weight having a place convenient to hold nine bullets and powder for nine charges and nine primings; the said gun will fire nine times distinctly, as quick, or as slow as you please; with one turn of the handle of said gun, it doth charge the gun with powder and bullet and doth both prime and shut the pan and cock the gun. All these motions are performed immediately at once, by one turn with the said handle. Note there is nothing put into the muzzle of the gun, as we charge other guns.**

Cookson was active in gunmaking and importing in Boston from 1704-62. The "Berselli" or "Lorenzoni" action that he copied was essentially a crank-operated brass cylinder situated in the frame behind the barrel. Two channels were partially cut through the round cylinder surface, and two separate magazines, one for loose powder and one for loose balls, were located in the frame behind the cylinder. Rotating the crank counterclockwise brought the two channels into alignment with the magazine chambers, causing one ball and a charge of powder to be deposited into each channel. Rotating the crank or lever clockwise caused first the ball and then the powder to be deposited into the barrel. A separate chamber near the "pan" held priming powder, and another cylinder with channel similarly filled the pan with each turn of the same lever. While the principle was ingenious, it required precise tolerances to prevent gas leakage around the cylinder and the consequent explosion of the entire powder magazine. Cylinder wear inherent with repeated firings increased that danger, and eventually caused the demise of the system.

Very little experimentation was again made with magazine repeating breechloaders until the invention of the metallic self-contained cartridge. The breechloading percussion rifles made by Nicanor Kendall in Windsor, Vt., in the late 1830s are the sole exceptions (aside from the Winchester predecessors covered in chapter 41). Kendall's sporting (quasi-military) rifles utilized a sliding "harmonica" magazine block containing five separate chambers. Although not terribly successful, more than 100 were made.

36-O Cookson Breechloading, Magazine Repeating Longarms
(color plate)

OL: 48"-50"; 41" on illustrated example, cut-back barrel
BD: .54-.55 cal.
Furniture: iron, engraved
Lockplate: convex, banana-shaped
Markings: IOHN COOKSON" behind rounded, gooseneck cock

BL: 31"-33"; 24" on cut-back illustrated example
Finish: "bright"
Configuration: part round/part octagonal
Sights: rear—none; front—iron, crescent-shaped blade
Fastenings: none, no forestock
Markings: "IOHN COOKSON FECIT" on top flat near breech

Fewer than a half-dozen of these Cookson-marked "Berselli/Lorenzoni" system magazine breechloaders survive in this country. Although all exhibit the styling characteristic of the late 17th/early 18th centuries, it is possible that the elder Cookson passed on not only the mechanism design to his son but the styling as well. **(F)**

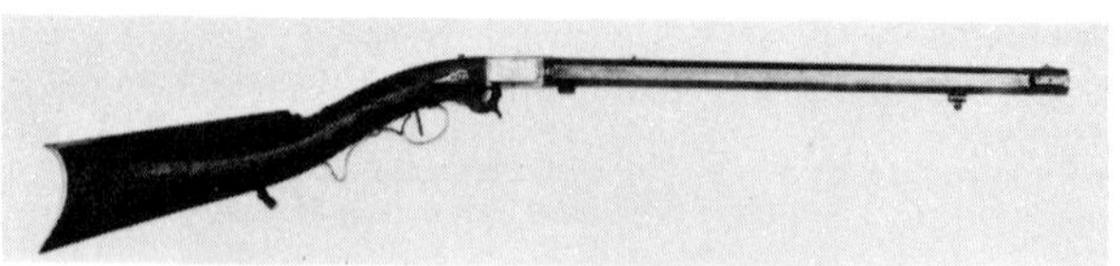

36-1 Kendall "Harmonica" Breechloading Magazine Rifles

OL: 38¾"
BD: .45 cal., 6-groove rifling
Furniture: brass

BL: 19½" (20" bore)
Finish: "bright"
Configuration: octagonal with

Lockplate: underhammer; flat
Markings: serial no. struck into underside of barrel, front sight base, frame bottom, and magazine back face
rectangular open lug on right side for square-sided bayonet
Sights: rear—open "V" dovetailed 3" from frame; front—iron block/blade, dovetailed
Markings: "N. KENDALL/WINDSOR, VT./PATENT" on top facet

Based on surviving serial nos., at least 110 of these "harmonica" rifles were made between about 1837-42, all using William B. Smith's patented underhammer as well as Fisher and Chamberlain's magazine. This magazine has a series of pairs of indentations on its upper surface that engage a spring lever on the frame to secure the magazine between firing. Nicanor Kendall produced these and single-shot muzzleloading underhammer rifles between 1835-42. **(E)**

---

37 Percussion, Revolving Cylinder Repeating Longarms

Artemus Wheeler, Elisha Collier, and Cornelius Coolidge invented a revolving mechanism in 1818 utilizing the flintlock ignition system incorporating a powder reservoir for the priming powder. In addition to the patent model, however, only two longarms were made in America, both by Wheeler, and both failed U.S. Navy tests. The prime reasons for the failure of these arms to gain acceptance lies in the ignition system. With the dissemination of the percussion ignition system, however, the revolving cylinder magazine concept was revived, first by two Rochester, N.Y., brothers, James and John Miller. In June, 1829, they patented a revolving cylinder magazine firearm one of whose principal features was a locking mechanism forward of the cylinder and under the barrel that insured correct alignment between the individual cylinder chambers and the barrel bore. The cylinder was still manually turned, but it was equipped with the pill-type percussion ignition system. Although the Millers made a number of rifles on this principle, the greatest number of these was produced by one of their apprentices, William Billinghurst. In turn, Billinghurst's apprentices (as well as other Miller apprentices) carried the idea into the Great Lakes and Ohio Valley (as well as throughout New York State) during the 1830s and '40s. No fewer than eighteen gunsmiths are associated with the Miller revolving mechanism.

In 1836 Samuel Colt was issued a patent that revolutionized the Miller design. He made two basic improvements—first, the cylinders' chambers were bored through to accept a regular percussion cone on their rear faces (instead of on the cylindrical rounded surface), and, second, (and most important) the cylinder was mechanically turned and locked into proper alignment by the hammer's cocking action. Colt's first venture in armsmaking under this patent was with the Patent Arms Mfg. Co. of Paterson, N.J. The Panic of 1837 and its aftermath so curtailed sales, however, that the firm collapsed. To add insult to injury, the government rejected a few hundred trial arms. In 1848, after re-establishing in Hartford, Colt introduced a new series of revolving longarms incorporating E. K. Root's patented side

hammer. Although moderately successful, the invention of more effective and less expensive repeating system caused the eventual demise of the Colt series. Allen & Wheelock and Remington also produced revolving longarms after Colt's patent rights expired in 1857, but neither firm achieved great acceptance of sales.

37-O Colt-Paterson (Patent Arms Mfg. Co.) M1839 Carbines, Types III (color plate) **& I & II**

OL: 41¾" standard
BD: .525 cal., smooth
Furniture: iron, "blued"
Lockplate: none, mechanism internal
Markings: serial no. struck internally on various parts and buttplate

BL: 24", standard; 28" and 32" special order
Finish: "blued"
Configuration: part round/part faceted
Sights: rear—open "V" 1⅛" from cylinder face; front—iron bead
Fastenings: none, no forestock
Markings: "•Patent Arms M'G Co. Paterson, N.J.—Colt's Pt.•" on left or right barrel side

III

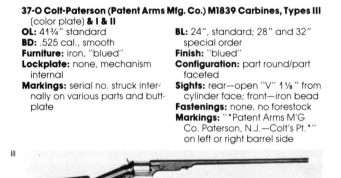

Approximately 950 of these carbines were produced from late 1838-45. The first are without a loading lever (I), and have straight-backed cylinders. About 1841 a loading lever was added to the frame's right side (II). During the 1841-42 Dorr Rebellion in Rhode Island, the state purchased 100 of type II; these were repurchased by Colt at Hartford in 1849 and a new cylinder (bright and ungrooved) was substituted (type III). The type I & II cylinder is "blued" with an engraved scene rolled between two pairs of grooves circumventing the cylinder. **(D)**

37-1 Colt (Colt Pt. F.A. Mfg. Co.) "First Model" Sporting Rifles

OL: 33⅝"-48⅝"
BD: .36 cal.
Furniture: iron, "blued"
Lockplate: none, mechanism within frame
Markings: serial no. stamped into triggerguard strap and bottom of frame

BL: 13¾"-28¾" to frame (15", 18", 21", 24", 27", 30" bores)
Finish: "blued"
Configuration: part round/part octagonal
Sights: rear—Colt brass folding leaf with 3 peeps on frame top; front—brass blade inset on iron block, dovetailed
Fastenings: none, no forestock
Markings: top of barrel facet—"COLT'S PT./1856" and "AD-

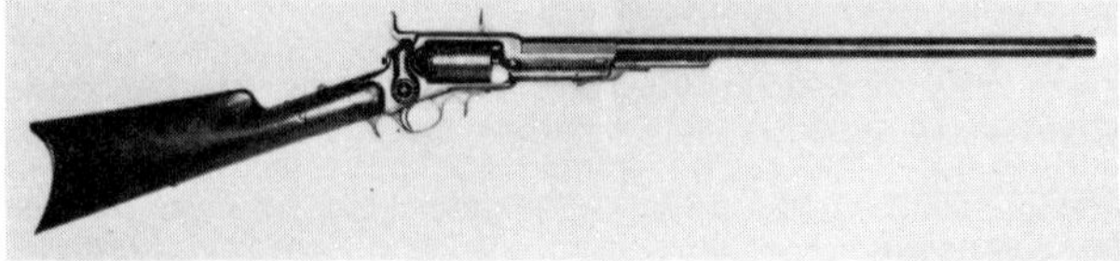

DRESS COL. COLT./HARTFORD CT. U.S.A."

About 1000 were produced at Hartford from about 1856-59. In addition to the lack of a forestock and the spurs on each triggerguard side, the arm is distinguished by the patented Colt oiler attached (usually) on the frame's left side. **(D)**

37-2 Colt (Colt Pt. F.A. Mfg. Co.) Half-Stock Sporting Rifles, Types I & II

OL: 42¼", 45¼", or 48¼"
BD: .36, .44, or .56 cal.
Furniture: iron, "blued", except for German-silver nosecap
Lockplate: none, mechanism within frame
Markings: serial no. stamped into frame bottom; top of frame—"COLT'S PT./1856" and "ADDRESS COL. COLT./HARTFORD CT. U.S.A."
BL: 22¾", 25¾", or 28¾" to frame (24", 27", or 30" bores)
Finish: "blued"
Configuration: part round/part octagonal
Sights: rear—Colt patented elevating sight ¼" from frame; front—iron blade, dovetailed
Fastenings: single wedge
Markings: cylinder—"PATENTED SEPT. 10th 1850"

I

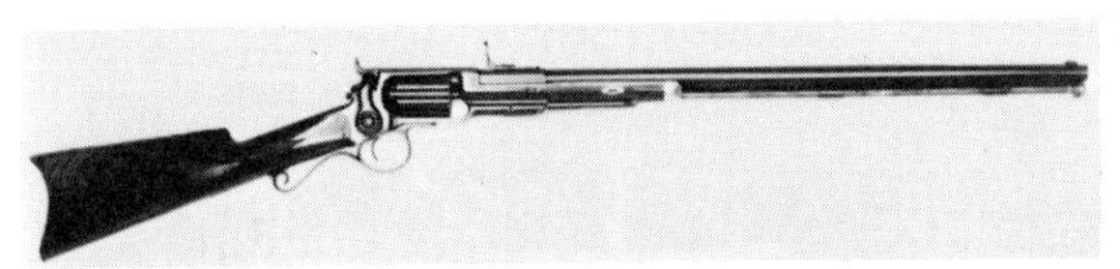

An estimated 1,000-1,500 of these rifles were made at Hartford between 1857-64. Type I rifles have the English-style triggerguard with reverse scroll strap; type II have standard Colt full-stock sporting rifle triggerguards. Sights vary. **(D)**

37-3 Colt (Colt Pt. F.A. Mfg. Co.) Full-Stock Sporting Rifles, Types I & II

OL: 39⅝"-48⅝"
BD: .36, .40 (rare), .44, .50, and .56 cal.
Furniture: iron, except for brass nosecap
Lockplate: none, mechanism within frame
Markings: serial no. struck into triggerguard strap and frame bottom; each cal. has its own serial range coinciding with martial production; top of frame—same as 37-2
BL: 19¾"-28¾" to frame (21", 24", 27", and 30" bore)
Finish: "blued"
Configuration: part round/part octagonal
Sights: rear—Colt 2-leaf 13/16" from cylinder face; front—German-silver blade inset in iron block
Fastenings: 2 iron, "blued" blades
Markings: none

II

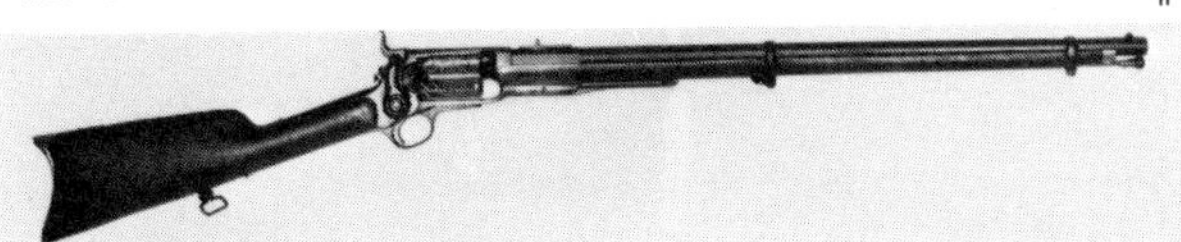

Type I uses the double-spur triggerguard; II, a plain spurless triggerguard. Due to overlapping serial nos. with the martial production, quantities produced between 1856-64 are not known; probably only a few hundred were made. **(D)**

37-4 Colt (Colt Pt. F.A. Mfg. Co.) Military Carbines, Types I-III

OL: 36½" or 39½"
BD: (I & II) .44 cal., (III) .56 cal.
Furniture: (I & II) iron, (III) with brass triggerguard
Lockplate: none, mechanism within frame
Markings: serial no. struck into frame bottom and triggerguard strap
BL: 16⅝" or 19⅝" to frame (18" and 21" bores)
Finish: "blued"
Configuration: part round/part octagonal
Sights: rear—Colt 2-leaf ⅞" from frame; front—brass blade
Fastenings: none, no forestock
Markings: top of frame—"COLT'S PT./1856" and "ADDRESS COL. COLT/HARTFORD CT. U.S.A." (I & II) or "COL. COLT HARTFORD CT. U.S.A."; left frame side—"COLT'S PATENT/NOV. 24th 1857"

Type I differs from II by the use of the double-spurred triggerguard. Both I and II use sling swivels in addition to the swivel ring found only on III. Four samples were purchased by the U.S. prior to the Civil War; Virginia bought 76 (II) in 1860. III is often seen with British proofs. **(D)**

37-5 Colt (Colt Pt. F.A. Mfg. Co.) Military Rifle-Muskets

OL: 56"
BD: .56 cal.
Furniture: brass except for iron bands
Lockplate: none, mechanism within frame
Markings: left frame side—"COLT'S PATENT/NOV. 24th 1857"; serial no. stamped into frame bottom and triggerguard strap
BL: 36⅛" to frame (37½" bore)
Finish: "blued"
Configuration: part round/part octagonal
Sights: rear—Colt 2-leaf sight ⅞" from frame; front—iron block/blade
Fastenings: 2 iron bands
Markings: top of frame—same as 37-4

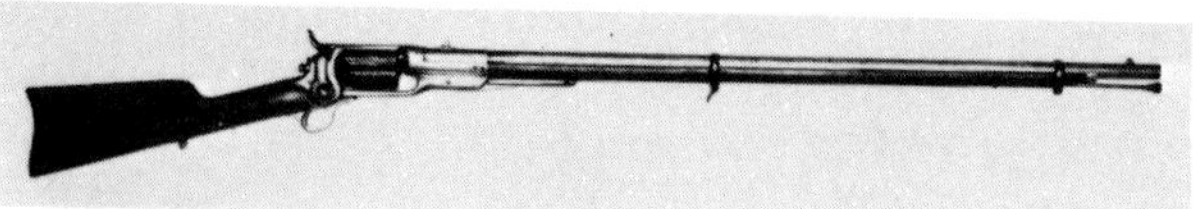

Evidently all 3,125 arms delivered by Colt to the U.S. government in 1862-63 were of this configuration. The first 1,000 were for the 1st U.S. Sharpshooters. 768 rifles purchased of Kettridge and 70 of Brockway in 1861 are believed to have been type II military rifles. **(D)**

37-6 J. & J. Miller (Billinghurst) Revolving Rifles

OL: 48¼"
BD: .41 cal., 6-groove rifling
Furniture: brass, except pewter nosecap
Lockplate: backaction; flat
Markings: none
BL: 29¼"
Finish: "browned"
Configuration: part round/part octagonal
Sights: rear—open "V" 6¾" from cylinder face; front—brass bead
Fastenings: single wedge
Markings: "W. BILLINGHURST/ROCHESTER, N.Y."

Billinghurst

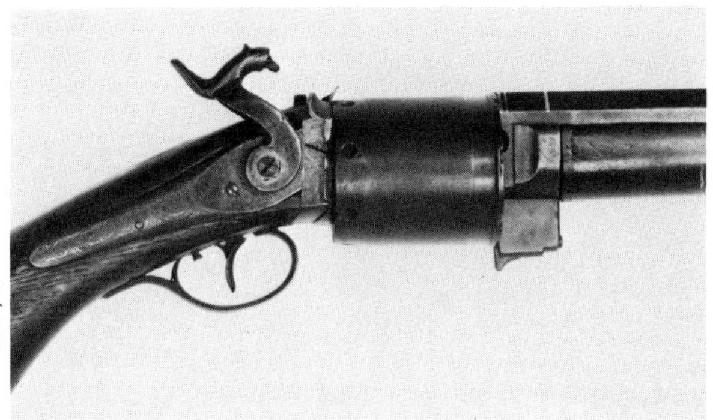
Van Dyke

This rifle, based on the joint patent of James and John Miller, exemplifies the type produced by them and their apprentices, of whom Billinghurst was the most famous. All dimensions on these handmade arms are different. Other known makers include: C. E. Bunge, T. P. Cherrington, Benjamin Bigelow, G. A. Brown, Jonathan Browning, Anrrobias Edwards, R. Holmes, Calvin Miller, L. F. Munger, E. S. Orsby, H. V. Perry, A. S. Sizer, Patrick and W. H. Smith, Elijah Snell, A. P. Spies, and O. Van Dyke. The depicted example has provision for cleaning rod underneath the barrel. **(C)**

37-7 Remington Revolving Rifles

OL: 41⅜"-45⅜"
BD: .36 or .44 cal.
Furniture: brass
Lockplate: none, mechanism within frame
Markings: none

BL: 22⅜"-26⅜" to frame (24", 26", 28" bores)
Finish: "blued"
Configuration: octagonal; rarely part round/part octagonal
Sights: rear—folding leaf on base 2½" from frame: front—iron blade, dovetailed
Fastenings: none, no forestock
Markings: either "REMINGTON/ CAST STEEL" on left side or "PATENTED SEPT. 14, 1858 E. REMINGTON & SONS, ILION,

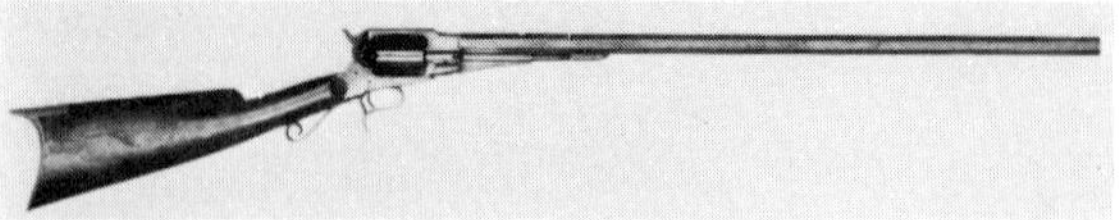

NEW YORK, U.S.A/NEW MODEL" on barrel top

Less than 1,000 of these were made between 1866-72. A very few were altered to rim-fire cartridge revolving rifles. **(C)**

37-8
II

37-8 James Warner (Springfield Arms Co.) Revolving Rifles, Types I-III

OL: 38¾"-48¾"
BD: .40 cal.
Furniture: iron, "blued"
Patchbox: (occasionally): 2-piece brass, hinged to rear
Lockplate: none, mechanism within frame
Markings: right side of frame—"WARNER'S PATENT" and "JAN. 1851" (I) or "JAMES WARNER/ SPRINGFIELD MASS." (II) in conjunction with "WARNER'S PATENT" on left frame side or on top strap; same on top strap (III)

BL: 18¾"-28¾" to frame; (20"-30" bores)
Finish: "blued"
Configuration: part round/part octagonal
Sights: rear—open "V" on frame top; front—brass blade or brass blade inset in iron block
Fastenings: none, no forestock
Markings: top of frame—SPRINGFIELD ARMS CO. (I only)

Earliest production used mechanical rotating cylinders (I). After about 250 were made, Warner was sued by Colt, forcing him to change to a manually rotating cylinder (II & III). **(D)**

---

38 | Percussion, Revolving Turret Magazine Repeating Longarms

Colt's re-emergence after 1848, and the popularity of his revolvers, instigated a number of attempts to circumvent the letter of Colt's

1836 patents. Most of these endeavors were directed at producing the financially lucrative revolving pistols. Colt responded by seeking injunctions against the perpetrators. His successful suit against the Massachusetts Arms Co. and the precedent it wrought for similar actions against less prolific pistol and rifle makers caused the copyists to seek more circuitous means to avoid infringement. The mechanical turning of the cylinder, however, proved an insurmountable problem. In April, 1837, John W. Cochran devised a rotating "turret" or radial cylinder that was affixed horizontally at the breech of the rifle. Only about 200 were made in the United States, but the system found greater favor in Europe, the major gunmaking house of A. Francotte listing it in its catalogue in the 1860s. In the early 1850s, another attempt was made to circumvent the Colt mechanical cylinder rotation by Patrick W. Porter, a Memphis, Tenn., mechanic. His device also used a radial cylinder or turret, but the "turret" was mounted vertically through the frame. Not only was this rifle mechanically rotated, but a mechanical capper was built into the right side of the frame on the earlier models. Over 1,200 were made before the inherent danger caused by having some of the chambers always poointed toward the shooter caused its demise.

James Warner (see chapter 37) and others endeavored to devise workable solutions, but the mechanisms they patented would not stand up in court to Colt's challenges. Alexander Hall's revolving rifle patent of 1856 was the last attempt at circumvention. Although manually turned, the Hall firearm did have the cones in the rear of the chambers and parallel to them. The chambers, however, were drilled into the periphery of the rim of a cylindrical wheel rather than a solid cylinder. Hall's invention was so cumbersome and unpopular that Colt never needed to challenge it in the courts, and after a very limited production it disappeared.

38-O Porter Revolving Turret Repeating Rifles, Types II (color plate), **I, & III**

OL: 40¼"-46¼"
BD: .44 and .50 cal.
Furniture: iron
Lockplate: none, mechanism within frame
Markings: serial no. on frame bottom

BL: 20⅛"-26⅛" to frame (22"-24" and 26"-28" bores)
Finish: "blued"
Configuration: octagonal
Sights: rear—open off-center "V" on strap 2¼" from frame; front—off-center iron blade, dovetailed
Fastenings: none, no forestock
Markings: upper left facet—"ADDRESS/P.W.PORTER/NEW-YORK" and "P.W. PORTER'S/PATENT/1851"

A total of about 1,225 of these arms were made by G. P. Foster of Taunton, Mass., during the 1850s. The first 300 have squared-off magazine covers (I) and are 9-shot; the succeeding 400 are also 9-shot but use a circular primer magazine cover (II). The last 550 are 9-shot but are without the primer magazine. **(D)**

38-1 Alexander Hall Revolving Wheel "Cylinder" Rifles

OL: 45¼"
BD: .38 cal., 6-groove rifling
Furniture: brass, engraved

BL: 23" to frame (24½" bore)
Finish: "bright"
Configuration: round

Lockplate: none, mechanism within frame
Markings: round face of 15-shot cylindrical wheel—"Hall's/Repeating Rifle/Patented June 10/1856" (in script)
Sights: rear—open "V" 1½"from frame; front—brass bead
Fastenings: none, no forestock
Markings: none

The patented magazine is actually in an open cylinder or wheel form with fifteen chambers located in the rim periphery. The wheel is manually rotated, the release being a hook-shaped lever partially enclosed by the wheel. The cocking lever is housed within the triggerguard forward of the actual trigger. **(F)**

38-2 Cochran Revolving Turret Repeating Rifles, Types I-III

OL: varies according to buttstock utilized
BD: .36 or .40 cal.
Furniture: iron, occasionally with brass 2-piece patchbox, hinged forward in butt
Lockplate: none, mechanism within frame
Markings: none
BL: 21"-32" (bores)
Finish: "browned"
Configuration: octagonal
Sights: rear—open "V" c. 4" from frame; front—iron or brass blade
Fastenings: none, no forestock
Markings: either "COCHRAN'S PATENT" (rare) or none; top of frame—"COCHRANS/MANY CHAMBERED/&/NON RECOIL/RIFLE." and "C.B. ALLEN/SPRINGFIELD/MASS."

Approximately 30 type I 9-shot rifles were made, distinguished by the circular plate over the turret top. On the succeeding (II) arm this was replaced by a straight, rectangular top plate conforming to the frame width. At about serial no. 155 a new 7-shot cylinder was introduced, the triggerguard eliminated, and the top plate hinged (III). About 45 of III made. **(E)**

---

39 | Metallic Cartridge, Revolving Magazine Repeating Longarms

All percussion cylindrical magazine repeating arms had one major flaw—the seal was never so tight as to prevent gas leakage at the joint of the cylinder (or turret) and the bore. With a handgun this was not terribly inconvenient since the gases were all directed away from the shooter. With longarms, however, the left arm of the shooter usually held the barrel (or forestock) and the gases would frequently scorch the shooter's wrist and hand. A greater danger than the occasional minor powder burns was caused by this defect—the hot gases might blow back into the face of the cylinder and inadvertently ignite all or some of the other charges. If the cylinders did not explode, the shooter was minimally endangered by the discharge of those chambers not aligned with the bore. With the invention of the metallic self-contained cartridge, however, the danger of premature ignition was virtually eliminated. Allen & Wheelock attempted to capitalize on this by manufacturing a revolving rifle utilizing their patented lip-fire cartridge, but they were sued by Smith & Wesson for patent infringement and returned to making percussion revolvers. Although Remington would eventually alter some of his percussion revolving rifles to cartridge, the public had totally soured on the concept by 1871.

One of the few armsmakers to continue with the production of these mechanisms in the post-Civil War period was Sylvester H. Roper. In 1866 he patented a mechanism that utilized a cylindrical 4-shot magazine. Unlike the previous percussion cylindrical magazine arms, the magazine did not serve as a chamber for the ignition. Instead a plunger, activated by the cocking of the hammer, extracted spent (special) cartridge cases from the single chamber in the barrel and forced another cartridge into the chamber. Roper manufactured a limited number of both rifles and shotguns with interchangeable barrels with limites success. The cylindrical magazine for cartridge arms was revived briefly just before the turn of the century. A New Yorker, John H. Blake, patented a bolt-action military rifle using a 7-shot magazine in 1898. Although the rifle was very successful in trials, the United States had already decided to adopt the Krag system, and very few were actually produced.

39-O Roper Cylindrical-Magazine Repeating Shotguns (color plate)

OL: 46⅜"-49⅜"; other sizes possible

BD: 16 ga. or 12 ga.

Furniture: iron, except for pewter nosecap

Lockplate: none, mechanism within frame

Markings: none

BL: 25¾"-28¼" to frame (26¼"-29¼" bores)

Finish: "blued"

Configuration: round

Sights: rear—none; front—brass or iron bead

Fastenings: forestock screwed to barrel

Markings: at least one barrel marked "MADE BY THE HOPKINS & ALLEN MANFG. CO. NORWICH CONN U.S.A." is known; magazine loading lid top—"ROPER REPEATING RIFLE CO./AMHERST MASS./PATENTED APRIL 10, 1866" or (later) "ROPER. SPORTING ARMS CO./HARTFORD, CONN./PAT. APR 10. 1866, JULY 14, 1868"

The company was established at Amherst in 1866 and moved to Hartford in 1868. It was reorganized there as "Billings & Spencer Co." Quantities unknown. **(D)**

39-1 Blake Bolt-Action, Cylindrical-Magazine Repeating Rifles, Types I & II

OL: 50"
BD: .30 cal.
Furniture: (I) brass, (II) iron)
Lockplate: none, mechanism within receiver and frame
Markings: left frame side near extremes of cut-off lever—"SINGLE" and "RAPID"; serial no. stamped into triggerguard strap
BL: 29" to frame (30" bore)
Finish: "blued"
Configuration: round
Sights: rear—1¾" long base with folding ladder with slide ¾" from frame; front—iron block/blade
Fastenings: 3 bands, (I) brass, (II) iron
Markings: none

II
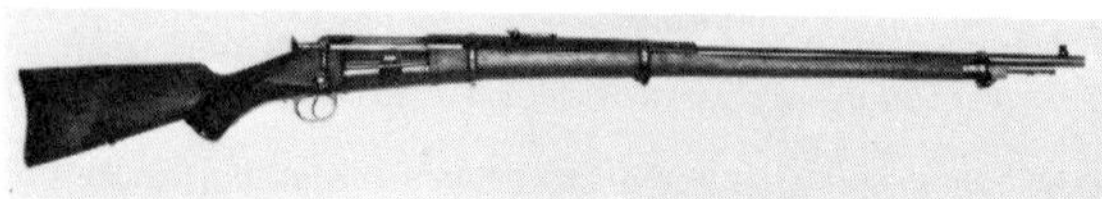

Based on surviving serial nos., probably not more than 300 were manufactured. The first half have brass (darkened) mountings, distinguishing I from those with iron (II) mountings. **(D)**

39-2 Roper Cylindrical-Magazine Repeating Rifles

OL: 48"
BD: .41 cal.
Furniture: iron, except pewter nosecap
Lockplate: none, mechanism within frame
Markings: none
BL: 26¾" to frame (27¾" bore)
Finish: "blued"
Configuration: octagonal
Sights: rear—½" long base with folding ladder 4" from frame; front—folding globe/blade
Fastenings: forestock screwed to barrel
Markings: magazine loading lid top—"ROPER. SPORTING ARMS CO./HARTFORD, CONN./PAT. APR. 10, 1866, JULY 14, 1868"

Roper rifle barrels were usually made along with shotgun barrels as a set and could be interchanged with the shotgun barrel on the same frame. The cylindrical magazine cover was removed with the barrel. Quantities are unknown. **(E)**

---

40 | Lever-Action, Tubular Magazine Repeating Rifles and Carbines

The year 1860 was propitious for the development of the repeating magazine rifle, especially the lever-action, tubular magazine variety. April, 1860, saw the patenting of the rim-fire self-contained metallic cartridge by Smith & Wesson, which made the tubular magazine rifle a practical success. 1860 also saw the patenting of two im-

portant mechanisms utilizing this cartridge. Christopher M. Spencer was issued a patent for a cartridge breechloading repeating arm that held the reservoir of bullets in a tubular magazine that pierced the length of the buttstock. The triggerguard served as a lever to advance these cartridges beyond the breechblock into the barrel chamber. Benjamin Tyler Henry was granted a patent for another lever-action, tubular magazine cartridge rifle. In Henry's design, however, the tubular magazine was located beneath the barrel, and the lever served to activate a carrier within the frame that elevated the cartridges singly to align with the barrel chamber. A piston breechblock activated by the same lever served to extract empty cartridges and force new ones into the chamber. Both designs had some minor flaws, but both proved eminently successful.

Spencer was a more aggressive salesman than Henry and successfully petitioned the Lincoln administration to contract for a significant quantity of his rifles. After an initial test that proved the arm totally suited for military service, the War Department ordered a carbine version, eventually purchasing nearly 100,000. Although only 1,730 of the Henry rifles were purchased by the U.S. government, most of the balance of the wartime production was privately purchased, primarily by soldiers in the field who had seen or heard of the exploits of the Henry. After the war, Spencer was never able to secure a significant share of the civilian sporting market or compete with the supply of surplus Spencer carbines on the market; the company failed by 1870 and was taken over by Winchester. Henry, on the other hand, first as the Henry Repeating Arms Co. and after 1866 as the Winchester Repeating Arms Co. of New Haven, totally dominated the postwar repeating arms market. The success of the Henry/Winchester during the 1870s prompted such other firms as Colt, Whitney, and Marlin to bring out similar arms. Warren Evans sought to improve the tubular magazine and produced the largest capacity magazine—four parallel tubular magazines with a rotating action—until the adoption of the long box magazines of the 20th century.

40-O Ball (Lamson & Co.) Repeating Carbines (color plate, above)

OL: 37½″
BD: .56 cal.
Furniture: iron, "blued"; sling bar and ring on left side
Lockplate: none, mechanism within frame
Markings: frame left side—"E.G. LAMSON & CO./WINDSOR.VT./U.S./BALLS PATENT./JUNE. 23. 1863/MAR. 15.1864"

BL: 20½″ to frame (22″ bore)
Finish: "blued"
Configuration: round
Sights: rear—⅝″-long base with pivoting "L" leaf 1″ from frame; front—iron blade
Fastenings: 2 iron bands
Markings: none

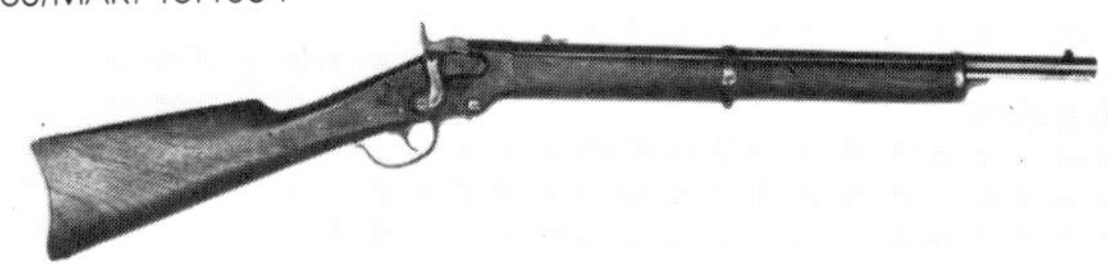

1,000 of these arms having a tubular magazine in the wooden forestock were delivered to the U.S. Ordnance Dept. in 1865. None saw Civil War combat service. **(C)**

Spencer (Spencer Rep. Rifle Co./Burnside Rifle Co.) Carbines, Types II (color plate, below) **& I**

OL: (I) 39", (II) 37"
BD: (I) .56 cal., 3-groove rifling; (II) .50 cal.
Furniture: iron, "blued"; swivel ring and bar on left side
Lockplate: backaction; flat
Markings: none

BL: (I) 20¼" to frame (22" bore), (II) 18⅜" to frame (20" bore)
Finish: "blued"
Configuration: round
Sights: rear—½" long base with spring-locked folding leaf 1⅝" from frame; front—iron block/blade
Fastenings: single iron band
Markings: top of frame—"SPENCER REPEATING/RIFLE CO. BOSTON MASS/PAT'D MARCH 6,1860" and serial no. behind ejection port; (II) "M1865" and top of frame either "SPENCER REPEATING/RIFLE CO. BOSTON MASS/PAT'D MARCH 6,1860" or "MODEL/1865" and "SPENCER REPEATING RIFLE/PAT'D MARCH 6,1860/MANUFD AT PROV. R.I./BY BURNSIDE RIFLE CO."

Beginning in Oct., 1863, and through 1866, Spencer delivered 64,683 carbines in both lengths. The Burnside Rifle Co. delivered another 30,496 (II) in 1865. **(A)**

40-1 Burgess (Colt Pt. F.A. Co.) Repeating Rifle

OL: 44½"
BD: .44 cal.
Furniture: iron
Lockplate: none, mechanism within frame
Markings: lever bottom—"+BURGESS PATENTS+"; serial no. on frame strap bottom

BL: 25½" bore
Finish: "blued"
Configuration: round, octagonal, or part round/part octagonal
Sights: rear—open "V" on strap; front—iron block/blade
Fastenings: forestock secured by nosecap
Markings: "COLT'S PT. F.A. MFG. CO. HARTFORD, CT.U.S.A./PAT. JAN. 7,73,OCT.19,75,APR. 1,79 DEC.7,80,DEC.13,81,JAN. 3,82+"

3,810 Burgess arms were produced by Colt between 1883-85. **(B)**

40-2
I
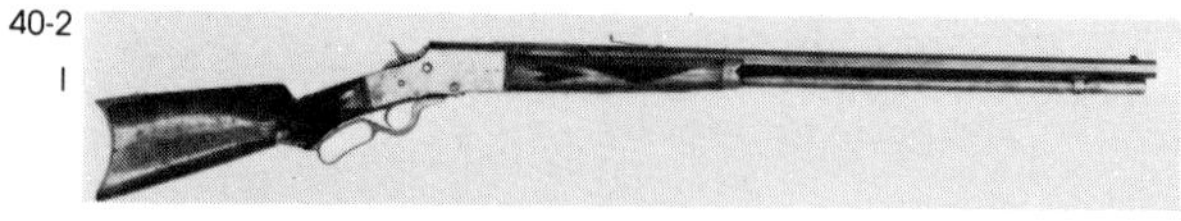

40-2 Bullard Repeating Rifles, Types I & II

OL: (I) 47¼", (II) 49¼"
BD: (I) .32, .38 cal., (II) .40, .45 cal.
Furniture: iron
Lockplate: none, mechanism within frame
Markings: upper left section of

BL: (I) 25¼" to frame (26" bore), (II) 27¼" to frame (28" bore)
Finish: "blued"
Configuration: octagonal
Sights: rear—open "V" on strap 1" from frame; front—German-

frame—"BULLARD REPEATING ARMS COMPANY/SPRINGFIELD MASS.U.S.A. PAT. AUG. 16.1881"

silver blade inserted on iron block

Fastenings: forestock secured by nosecap

Markings: none

10,000-12,000 of these rifles were made between 1886-90. Two frame sizes (small and large) were available (I & II) with full or truncated magazine tubes. **(B)**

40-3 Bullard Repeating Carbines

OL: 41"

BD: .45 cal.

Furniture: iron

Lockplate: none, mechanism within frame

Markings: upper left frame section—"BULLARD REPEATING ARMS COMPANY/SPRINGFIELD MASS.U.S.A. PAT. AUG. 16.1881"

BL: 20¼" to frame (22" bore)

Finish: "blued"

Configuration: round

Sights: rear—open "V" on strap 1" from frame; front—German-silver blade inset in iron block

Fastenings: forestock secured by noscap

Markings: none

These carbines were produced at the same time as the Bullard repeating rifles. Frame size is the same as Type II rifles. **(B)**

40-4
I

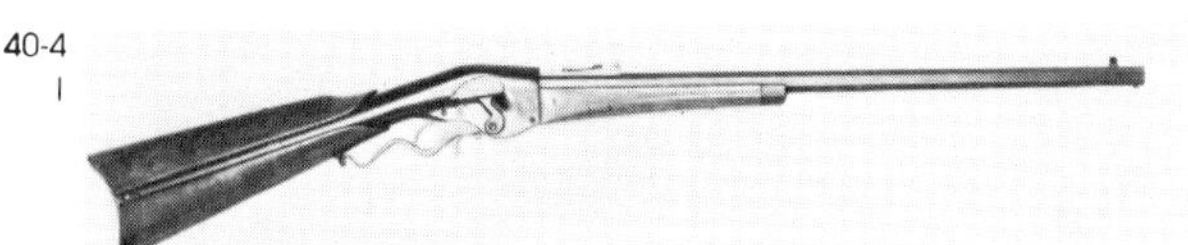

40-4 Evans (Evans Rifle Mfg. Co.) Repeating Rifles, Types I & II

OL: 43½"-47½"

BD: .44 cal.

Furniture: iron, "blued"

Lockplate: none, mechanism within frame

Markings: none

BL: (I) 24⅛"-28⅛" to frame; (II) 24½"-28½" to frame (26", 28", 30" bores)

Finish: "blued"

Configuration: round or octagonal

Sights: rear—3½"-long base with folding ladder against frame; front—blade

Fastenings: forestock screwed to barrel; 2 iron bands on martial rifle

Markings: (I) "EVANS REPEATING RIFLE/PAT. DEC 8, 1868 & SEPT 16, 1871"; (II) "EVANS SPORTING RIFLE" or "EVANS REPEATING RIFLE MECHANIC FALLS ME./ PAT. DEC. 8 1868 & SEPT.16 1871" on top

Approximately 7,500 arms were manufactured between 1873-79. Type I (earlier) is distinguished by a single-piece buttstock only over the magazine and a frame that extends over the barrel. II uses a split stock and straight front. **(B)**

40-5 Marlin (Marlin Firearms Co.) M1881 Repeating Rifle

OL: 43½", 45½", 47½", 49½"

BL: 19⅜"-25⅜" to frame (24",

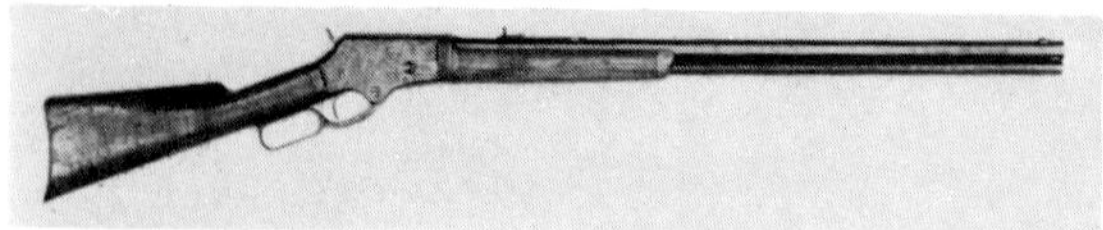

BD: .32, .38, .40, .45 cal.
Furniture: iron
Lockplate: none, mechanism within frame
Markings: serial no. stamped into frame bottom

26", 28", or 30" bores)
Finish: "blued"
Configuration: octagonal, rarely round
Sights: rear—stepped "buck-horn" 1⅞" from frame; front—German-silver blade
Fastenings: forestock locked by nosecap
Markings: top of barrel—"MARLIN FIRE-ARMS CO. HEW HAVEN, CT.U.S.A. [/] PAT'D FEB.7'65, JAN.7'73,SEPT.14'75, NOV.19 & 26 '78, JUNE 3 '79, NOV. 9'80/ (RE ISSUE NOV.9 1880)" and caliber

Between 1881-92 the company produced almost 20,000 of these rifles in two frame sizes. Three marking variations were used, the earliest with all in single line and eliminating reissue date, the second in two lines but without reissue date, and the last as shown. The first 600 produced substituted "J. M. MARLIN" in the name. **(A)**

40-6 Marlin (Marlin Firearms Co.) M1888 Rifles, Types I & II

OL: 43½", 45½", 47½"
BD: .32, .38, .44 cal.
Furniture: iron
Lockplate: none, mechanism within frame
Markings: none

BL: 19⅜"-23⅜" to frame (24", 26", 28" bores)
Finish: "blued"
Configuration: round, octagonal, or part round/part octagonal
Sights: rear—stepped "buck-horn" c. 2" from frame; front—German-silver blade
Fastenings: forestock secured by nosecap
Markings: "MARLIN FIREARMS CO. NEW HAVEN, CT. U.S.A./ PATENTED OCT. 11,1887" on top; cal. near frame on top

Marlin produced 4,814 of these arms between 1888-92 in full-length magazine style (I) or with a shorter magazine beneath the barrel (II). **(B)**

40-7 Marlin (Marlin Firearms Co.) M1889 Repeating Rifles and Carbines

OL: 24½"-59½"
BD: .25 (rare), .32, .33, .44 cal.
Furniture: iron
Lockplate: none, mechanism within frame
Markings: frame top—"MARLIN SAFETY"

BL: 15", 20", 24" (standard), 26", 30", 32", and 40" bores
Finish: "blued"
Configuration: octagonal or round

Sights: rear—"buckhorn" c. 2" from frame; front—German-silver blade, dovetailed
Fastenings: forestock, locked by nosecap
Markings: top of barrel—"MARLIN FIRE-ARMS CO. NEW-HAVEN, CT. U.S.A./PATENTED OCT. 11, 1887. APRIL 2, 1889" and cal.

From 1889-99 55,072 of these arms were made. 15" and 20"-barrel lengths were for the carbine version and have a swivel ring on the left side of the frame. 8,685 were carbines. **(A)**

40-8 Marlin (Marlin Firearms Co.) M1891 Repeating Rifles, Types I & II

OL: 40½"-44½"
BD: (I) .22 cal., (II) .22 and .32 cal.
Furniture: iron
Lockplate: none, mechanism within frame
Markings: top of frame—"MARLIN SAFETY"; frame tang—"MODEL/1891" after serial no. 112,000
BL: 24", 26", or 28" bores
Finish: "blued"
Configuration: octagonal, round, or part round/part octagonal
Sights: rear and front—sights vary
Fastenings: forestock secured by nosecap
Markings: "MARLIN FIRE-ARMS CO. NEW-HAVEN CT., U.S.A./PAT'D NOV. 19, 1878, APRIL 2, 1889, AUG. 12, 1890" (I) on barrel top; (II) addition of "MARCH 1, 1892"

18,642 of these arms were made from 1891-97. Type I is made with a loading port on the frame's right side and a short magazine; II is loaded through a full-length tubular magazine housed under the barrel. Pistol grip buttstocks were optional, as were a variety of tang sights. **(A)**

40-9 Marlin (Marlin Firearms Co.) M1892 Repeating Rifles

OL: 40½"-44½"
BD: .22 or .32 cal.
Furniture: iron
Lockplate: none, mechanism within frame
Markings: frame top—"MARLIN SAFETY"; frame tang—"MODEL/1892"
BL: 23⅜"-27⅜" to frame (24", 26", or 28" bores)
Finish: "blued"
Configuration: octagonal, round, or part round/part octagonal
Sights: rear—stepped "buckhorn" 1⅞" from frame; front—German silver blade set in iron block

This arm is identical to 40-8, type II, except for the addition of the model designation to the frame tang. Approximately 45,000 made between 1895-1916; serial nos. over 120,000 should be considered 20th-century production. **(A)**

40-10 Marlin (Marlin Firearms Co.) M1893 Rifles and Carbines

OL: varies according to buttplate design
BL: 15" and 20" (carbine) (24", 26", 30", 32" bores)

BD: .25, .30, .32, and .38 cal.
Furniture: iron, "blued"; carbine with swivel ring on left side of frame
Lockplate: none, mechanism within frame
Markings: upper frame tang—"MODEL 1893"
Finish: "blued"
Configuration: octagonal or round
Sights: rear and front—varies according to type
Fastenings: forestock secured by nosecap on rifle and by single iron band (carbine and musket)
Markings: top of barrel—same as 40-7 with addition of AUG. 1, 1893" and cal.

More than 750,000 M1893 rifles were made between 1893-1936 in three basic configurations—a rifle with 24"-32" barrel, a carbine with 15" (rare, only 61 made) or 20" barrels, and a military musket with 30" round barrel, of which only 31 were made. Serial nos. after 125,000 should be considered 20th-century production. Rifles made after 1904 are for smokeless powder and are so marked. **(A)**

40-11 Marlin (Marlin Firearms Co.) M1894 Rifles and Carbines

OL: varies according to buttplate design
BD: .25, .32, .38, and .44 cal.
Furniture: iron, "blued"; carbines with swivel ring on left side of frame
Lockplate: none, mechanism within frame
Markings: top of frame—"MARLIN SAFETY"; most upper frame tangs—"MODEL 1894"
BL: 14", 15", 20" (carbine) and 24", 26", 28", 30", 32" bores
Finish: "blued"
Configuration: round or octagonal
Sights: rear and front—vary according to type
Fastenings: forestock secured by nosecap on rifle and by single iron band on carbine and musket
Markings: top of barrel—same as 40-10

Between 1894-1917, about 250,000 of these arms were made in three basic configurations, sporting rifles, carbines in three barrel lengths, and as a military musket (152 manufactured, mainly for prison guards), marked "BUREAU COUNTY" on the frame. **(A)**

40-12 Marlin (Marlin Firearms Co.) M1895 Rifles and Carbines

OL: 38" (carbines) or 42"-48"
BD: .33, .38, .40, and .45 cal.
Furniture: iron, "blued"; carbines with swivel ring on left side of frame
Lockplate: none, mechanism within frame
Markings: top of frame—"MARLIN SAFETY"; upper frame tang—"MODEL 1895"
BL: 22" (carbines) (26", 28", 30", or 32" bores)
Finish: "blued"
Configuration: octagonal or round
Sights: rear—stepped "buckhorn" c. 3" from frame; front—German-silver blade
Fastenings: forestock secured by nosecap
Markings: on barrel top—same as 40-10

About 18,000 were made between 1895-1917. Those made after 1896 are marked on their barrels, "SPECIAL SMOKELESS STEEL." Pistol-grip buttstock was optional. **(A)**

I

II

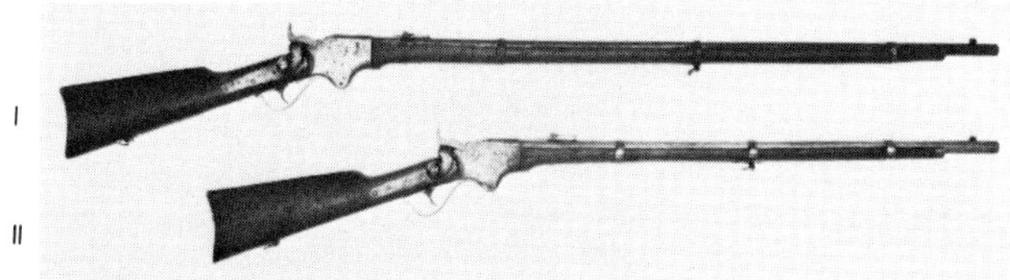

40-13 Spencer (Spencer Rep. Rifle Co.) Rifles, Types I & II, and Rifle-Muskets

OL: 47″ (rifles) and 55⅞″ (rifle-muskets)
BD: .56 and .50, 6-groove rifling
Furniture: iron, "blued"; saber bayonet stud with guide on first 709 type II rifles for U.S. Navy
Lockplate: backaction; flat
Markings: none

BL: 28⅜″ and 37⅜″ to frame (30″ and 38¾″ bores)
Finish: "blued"
Configuration: round
Sights: rear—½″ long base with spring-locked folding leaf 1⅝″ from frame; front—iron block/blade
Fastenings: 3 iron bands
Markings: top of frame—"SPENCER REPEATING/RIFLE CO. BOSTON MASS/PAT'D MARCH 6, 1860"; serial no. behind ejection port.

Between 1862-64 the U.S. government purchased 11,471 of these arms. 2,000 of these are believed to be the rifle-musket length (serial no. 9179 depicted), originally ordered by Massachusetts. 500 rifles were finally secured by Massachusetts in 1865 in .50 cal., and have "M1865" upon the barrel top near the breech as well as 6-groove rifling. **(B)**

40-14 Whitney-Kennedy (Whitney Arms Co.) Rifles and Carbines, Types I & II

OL: varies according to butt-plate type
BD: .32, .38, .40, .44, .45, and .50 cal.
Furniture: iron, "blued"
Lockplate: none, mechanism within frame
Markings: upper frame tang—various Burgess, Kennedy, or Kennedy-Tiesling patents of Jan. 7, 1873, Apr. 1, 1879, May 13, 1879, Aug. 12, 1879

BL: 20″ or 22″ bores (carbines), 24″, 26″, 28″ (rifles), 32½″ (muskets)
Finish: "blued"
Configuration: round, octagonal, or part round/part octagonal
Sights: rear and front—vary according to type
Fastenings: forestock secured by nosecap (rifle); single iron band (carbine); or 2 iron bands (musket)
Markings: top of barrel—"WHITNEY ARMS CO./NEW HAVEN, CONN. U.S.A." or "WHITNEY KENNEDY MF'D BY WHITNEY ARMS CO./NEW HAVEN, CONN. U.S.A."

Type I rifles and carbines are distinguished by a reverse scroll triggerguard/lever; type II use a full-hand loop triggerguard/lever. An estimated 15,000 were made of all types between 1879-86. **(B)**

41 The Predecessors of the Winchester Longarms

In late 1847 Walter Hunt submitted a model to the U.S. Patent Office for a tubular magazine repeating "Volution Rifle" adapted to a separately primed, but otherwise self-contained, cartridge called a "Rocket Ball." Hunt's description was apt, for the cartridge consisted of a cylindro-conical projectile with a hollow base that was filled with powder and sealed with a thin cork disc. This disc was perforated in its center to permit ignition via the mechanical primer built into the frame mechanism. Hunt did not have sufficient resources to exploit his invention, and, after selling the rights to George A. Arrowsmith, Lewis Jennings was assigned to perfect the design for mass production. In 1850 Robbins & Lawrence of Windsor, Vt., contracted to produce 5,000 of the modified rifles. In actual production it was found that the Jennings mechanism proved so unreliable as a repeater that most were completed as single-shot breechloaders.

In 1851 Horace Smith of Norwich, Conn., patented an improvement to the Jennings design that permitted the mechanism to function more smoothly, though fouling remained a significant problem. The next year Smith and ex-Robbins & Lawrence employee Daniel Wesson obtained a patent for a new totally self-contained cartridge that eliminated the problem. Their improvement added to the cork washer a steel cup that incorporated the fulminate primer into the base of the bullet. Smith and Wesson had entered into partnership to produce a handgun based on revisions of the Jennings and Smith patents. These pistols were produced under their own names for a short duration. Soon, however, the men were forced to recapitalize, and the Volcanic Repeating Arms Co. of New Haven was founded with Wesson as plant superintendent, and rifles and carbines were added to the line. The new company was dissolved in February, 1856, but, after a brief period, it was reorganized as the New Haven Arms Co., producing the same line of arms, with a former minor shareholder, Oliver F. Winchester, as its president and major subscriber. Between 1857-60 this firm manufactured the Volcanic pistols, carbines, and rifles, but the arms continued to be plagued by two problems: continued fouling from the poor breech seal, and insufficient bullet penetration due to the smaller powder charge. Winchester hired B. Tyler Henry as plant superintendent, and in 1860 Henry not only altered the action but also adapted it to the newly devised rim-fire cartridge that Smith & Wesson had patented the same year. The new cartridge effectively eliminating the problems, the Henry rifle went on to win laurels during the Civil War.

41-O Henry (New Haven Arms Co.) Repeating Rifles, Types II (color plate), **I & III**

OL: (I & II) 43⅛", (III) 43½"
BD: .44 cal.
Furniture: (I) iron, (II & III) brass; iron sling swivel on left side (on martial version)
Lockplate: none, mechanism within frame
Markings: none

BL: 23¼" to frame (24¼" bore)
Finish: "blued"
Configuration: octagonal
Sights: rear—folding leaf with slide 1" from frame; front—iron blade
Fastenings: none, no forestock
Markings: serial no. on top near frame; top—"HENRY'S PATENT

OCT. 16, 1860/MANUFACT'D BY THE NEW HAVEN ARMS CO. NEW HAVEN CT."

Approximately 13,000 arms were manufactured between 1860-65, the first 100-150 with iron frames and furniture (I). Brass was substituted for the balance of the production. I and II rifles use a rounded buttplate; III use a sharper-angled "crescent" buttplate. **(B)**

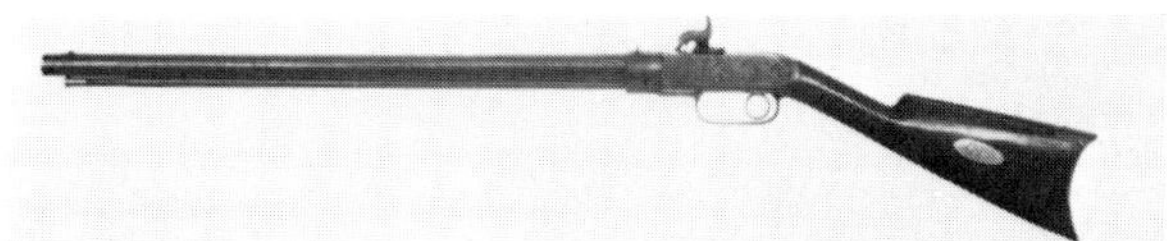

41-1 Jennings (Robbins & Lawrence) Repeating Rifles

OL: 44"
BD: .54 cal., 7-groove rifling
Furniture: iron, engraved
Lockplate: none, mechanism within frame
Markings: left side of frame—"ROBBINS & LAWRENCE/MAKERS /WINDSOR VT." and "C.P.DIXON AGENT/NEW YORK/PATENTED 1849"; serial no. located on lower frame strap

BL: 24½" to frame (26¼" bore)
Finish: "browned"
Configuration: round
Sights: rear—open "V" on frame top; front—brass blade
Fastenings: none, no forestock
Markings: none

Although nominally repeaters, most of these arms left the factory as single-shot breechloaders. In 1852-53 the firm even assembled the surplus parts into single-shot muzzleloaders distinguished by the indented triggerguard. **(E)**

41-2

41-2 Jennings/Smith (Robbins & Lawrence) Repeating Rifles

The specifications are practically the same as 41-1 with the barrel length being ⅛" less; a serial no. appears on the barrel top near the frame and on the lower frame strap. **(E)**

41-3 Volcanic (Volcanic Repeating Arms Co./New Haven Arms Co.) Rifles, Types I & II

OL: (I) 38⅞", (II) 42⅞"
BD: .38 or .40 cal.
Furniture: brass, occasionally silver-plated and engraved
Lockplate: none, mechanism within frame
Markings: none

BL: (I) 20⅛" to frame (21" bore), (II) 24⅛" to frame (25" bore)
Finish: "browned"
Configuration: octagonal
Sights: rear—open "V" on strap screwed to frame; front—German-silver blade
Fastenings: none, no forestock
Markings: top of barrel (early Volcanic production)—"THE

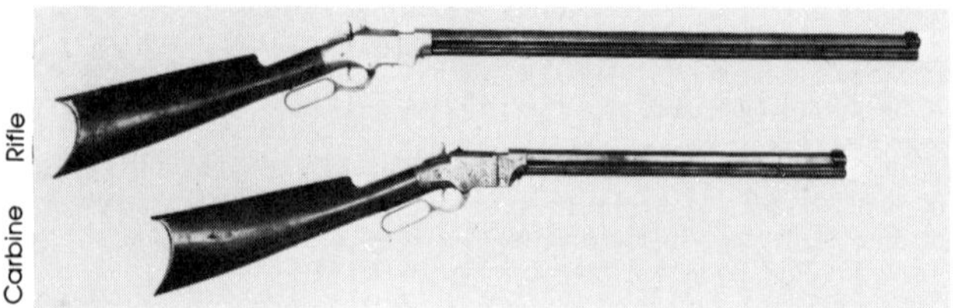

VOLCANIC/REPEATING ARMS CO./PATENT NEW HAVEN CONN. /FEB. 14, 1854"; (later New Haven production)—either "PATENT. FEB. 14,1854/NEW HAVEN, CONN." or "NEW HAVEN CONN. PATENT Feb. 14, 1854" or "NEW HAVEN, CONN. CAST-STEEL PATENT/NEW HAVEN CONN. FEB. 14,1854"

The rifles are distinguished by the two basic bore lengths, 21" and 25". **(D)**

41-4 Volcanic (Volcanic Repeating Arms Co./New Haven Arms Co.) Carbines

The carbine and rifle differ in overall and barrel length, bore diameter and bore length. The carbine is 34⅜"-long overall with a barrel length of 15⅝" to frame (16½" bore). The bore diameter is .38 or .40 cal. These carbines were produced in 1857-60 along with the two lengths of rifles.

---

42 Winchester, Lever-Action, Tubular Magazine Repeating Rifles

In 1865 Major J. S. Baker, commanding one of the few Union cavalry regiments to be issued the Henry repeating rifle, the 1st District of Columbia Cavalry, provided the New Haven Arms Co. with a testimonial. He qualified his praise, however, by stating:

> **. . . But notwithstanding my high opinion of this arm when in the hands of dismounted men, I do not think it a suitable weapon for cavalry. I consider it too long for the mounted service; the coil spring used in the magazine is also liable in the cavalry to become foul with sand and mud, and this, for the time being renders the arm unserviceable.**

The last objection to the Henry rifle was the most problematic. In the New Haven Arms Co.'s 1865 catalogue, Winchester indicated that a new model carbine had been adopted "enclosing the spring in a closed tube." The carbine to which he referred was the M1866, including Nelson King's improvement consisting of a loading gate or port on the frame's right side that permitted loading the tubular magazine from the breech.

In 1865 the New Haven Arms Co. was reincorporated as the Henry Repeating Arms Co.; however, this title was short-lived as the charter actually granted was to call the firm the "Winchester Repeating Arms Co." By 1871 the firm had moved back to New Haven. Firmly entrenched there, and with increasing demand from the developing cattle kingdoms of the Great Plains, Winchester brought out a new model, the M1873. In addition to having an iron instead of a less durable brass frame, the new series was chambered for a center-fire cartridge that could be interchanged with the .45 Colt revolver cartridge. The M1873 was followed by new models in 1876, 1886, 1892, and 1894 as well as a lever-action shotgun in 1887 and a lever-action box magazine rifle in 1895. Others endeavored to imitate Winchester's success, but none came close to the sales that Winchester enjoyed.

42-O Volcanic Lever-Action, Tubular Magazine Repeating Rifles
(color plate, above)

See 41-3.

Winchester M1873 Repeating Rifles, Types I (color plate, below), **& II**

OL: with crescent buttplate, straight stock, 43"; various buttplate options and pistol-grip buttstock available. "Blued" octagonal (most frequent), round, or part-round/part-octagonal barrel with either (I) full-length magazine or (II) half-magazine underneath. 24¼" barrels (BL to frame, 23½") standard, but also available in special-order bore lengths of 20¼", 26¼", 28¼", and 30¼". In addition to .22, .32, .38, and .44 cal. center-fire bore diameters, .22 cal. rim-fire was also offered. .22 cal. rifles are without the loading gate on the right side of the frame. A small number of engraved frame rifles were also made and are marked on the barrel top ("1 of 100" or "1 of 1000"). These rifles are usually equipped with tang sights. **(A)**

General comments on Winchester Lever-Action Longarms, 1866-1900

Winchester models are marked on the upper frame tang from the M1873 on with the "MODEL" followed by the year the design was introduced. Exceptions or additions to this are noted under each model. The barrel top, beginning in about 1869, is also marked: "WINCHESTER'S REPEATING ARMS. NEW HAVEN. CT./KING'S IMPROVEMENT-PATENTED MARCH 29 1866. OCTOBER 17 1860" (Connecticut was later abbreviated "CONN." and "U.S.A." was added after it.) Beginning with the M1866 series, this was changed to "-MANUFACTURED BY THE-/-WINCHESTER REPEATING ARMS CO. NEW HAVEN, CONN. U.S.A.-" Caliber markings were usually placed on the barrel top near the frame juncture. Each series usually has three variations—sporting rifle with the forestock secured to the nosecap, a carbine with the forestock secured by a single band, and a military muskėt with the forestock secured by two bands. Carbines differ further from short versions of the sporting rifles by having a swivel ring attached to the left side. While the military musket and the carbine usually come with only a standard buttplate, the sporting rifles of each series were available in three buttplate types—the standard sharp crescent, the lesser arced military, or the straight shotgun style. Pistol-grip buttstocks were also special-order items that could change the overall length slightly, although straight stocks were standard. Both rear and front sights vary within each model. The stepped "buckhorn", however, was the most common rear sight for sporting rifles, while the dovetailed iron blade on a wide base was the most common front sight. Tang sights were rarely used.

42-1 M1866 Series

Although the first 39,300 were manufactured at Bridgeport, the markings reflect the New Haven headquarters. A total of 156,000 of all types were made between 1867-98. Serial numbers begin with the end of the Henry rifle range, about 13,500, and continue until 170,100. These numbers usually are located on the upper frame tang left side. At about 20,000 the number was relocated to the exterior of the lower tang, first beneath the lever and later near its tail end. Early production used a flat-faced loading gate and was referred to as "Old Model"; the "New Model" uses a loading gate with a concave indentation. The same "Old Model" has a two-line barrel marking, viz: "HENRY'S PATENT-OCT. 16.1860/KING'S PATENT-MARCH 29.1866".

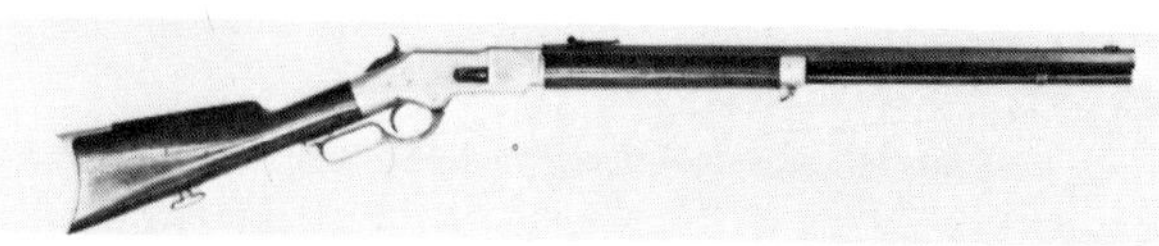

42-1a Winchester M1866 Repeating Sporting Rifles, Types I & II

OL: 43¾", with crescent buttplate. Barrels are "blued," 24¼" long (bore, 23½" to frame), either octagonal (early) or round. The rifle was produced only in .44 cal. rim-fire. Types distinguished by loading gate. **(B)**

42-1b (Winchester M1866 Repeating Carbins, Types I & II

OL: 39¼" (20¼" bore, 19½" to frame). Round, "blued" barrel, only in .44 cal. rim-fire. Types distinguished by loading gate. A half-magazine variation made of this carbine. **(C)**

42-2 M1873 Series

This series is distinguished from the M1866 series by use of iron in place of brass frames. Initially introduced only in .44 cal., center-fire in 1873, a .38 cal. variety was offered in 1880, .32 cal. in 1882, and .22 center-fire in 1885. A total of 55,250 of all three types was produced from 1873-1900. Production continued until 1919 for an additional 20,000.

42-2a Winchester M1873 Repeatng Carbines

OL: 39¼", with 20¼" long (bore), round barrel, "blued". .44 cal. is the most common, but .38 and .32 were also manufactured. **(A)**

42-3 M1876 Series

This series was introduced in the centennial year to provide a stronger action for larger cartridges. Although very similar in appearance to the M1873 series, the marking on the upper frame tang clearly indicates which model is represented. 63,871 made until 1898.

42-3a Winchester M1876 Repeating Sporting Rifles, Types I-III

OL: 48½", with crescent buttplate, straight stock. I is a standard sporting rifle with 28" long (bore, 27¼" to frame) barrel in either octagonal,

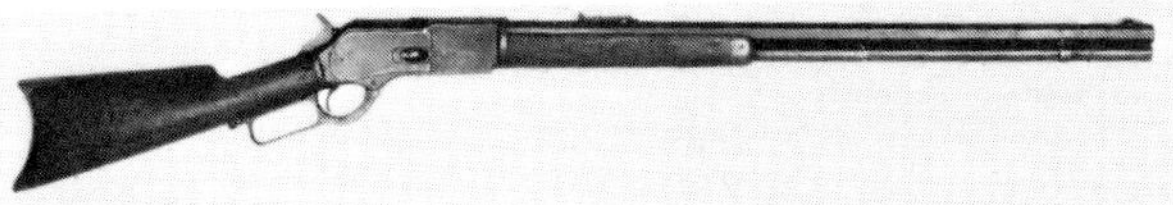

round, or, rarely, part-round, part-octagonal configuration. It is "blued" in either .40 or .45 cal. II is a special "Express" rifle with standard 26"-long (bore, 25¼" to frame), barrel, usually round but also in the other two forms, chambered for .50 cal. cartridges. Half-magazines were common in II rifles. Other options on both I and II are pistol-grip buttstocks and shotgun buttplates. III is a special target version of I that incorporates the pistol grip as standard and includes a tang-mounted vernier sight. 48 "1 of 1000" (marked on barrel top, in script, "One of One Thousand") and 8 "1 of 100" rifles were produced in this type. **(A)**

42-4 M1886 Series

This series evolved as an improved version of the M1876 rifles. The impetus was the development of and popularization of long, high-power cartridges. The action was patented by John M. and Matthew S. Browning in 1884 and slightly improved by William Mason of Winchester. Some M1886 rifles will be found with standard Winchester late barrel marks with the added line, "PAT. OCT. 14 1884 JAN. 20, 1885", and others will bear the additional marking, "BROWN BROS. OGDEN, UTAH". Those made after 1895 may also bear the marking, "NICKEL STEEL BARREL/ESPECIALLY FOR SMOKELESS POWDER." 159,994 rifles, carbines, and muskets were produced between 1886-1935, 122,826 of these prior to 1900.

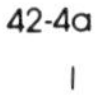

42-4a
I

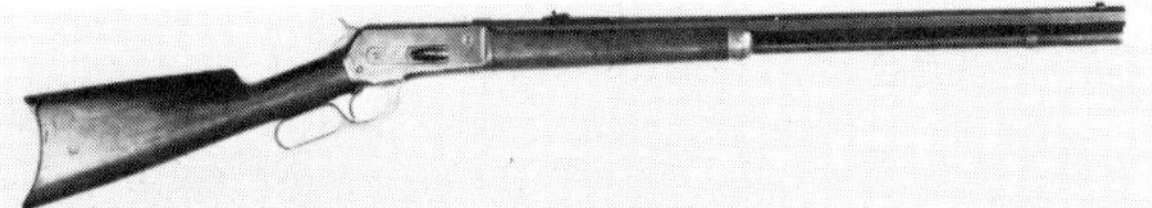

42-4a Winchester M1886 Repeating Sporting Rifles, Types I-III

OL: 44½", with crescent buttplate, straight stock. 26" long (bore, 25¼" to frame) barrel, either octagonal or round (rarely, part-round/part-octagonal), chambered for .38, .40, .45, .50, and .33 WCF cartridges. I has a standard straight buttstock and crescent buttplates; II has a pistol grip and shotgun buttplate; III has a straight buttstock, shotgun buttplate, and half-length magazine. **(A)**

42-4b Winchester M1886 Repeating Carbines, Types I & II

OL: 41". 22" long (bore, 21¼" to frame), round, "blued" barrel, usually chambered in .40 or .45 cal. I produced from 1886-89 with full-length forestock like the M1876 carbine. In 1889 the old-style short forearm was readopted, distinguishing II. **(B)**

42-4c Winchester M1887 Lever-Action Shotgun

OL: either 37½" (with 20" riot-gun barrel) or 47¼"-49¼" (if 30" or 32" regular barrels). "Blued" round barrels with single brass-bead front sight in either 10 ga. or 12 ga. Iron furniture, "blued"; forestock screwed to magazine and barrel junction. Left side of frame marked

with Winchester cypher (W R A Co.), and bottom of frame tang, lower, marked, "MANUFACTURED BY/WINCHESTER REPEATING ARMS CO./-NEW HAVEN, CONN. U.S.A.-/PAT. FEB. 16 & JULY 20, 1886". "10" or "12" on barrel top. Between 1887-1901, 64,855 M1887 shotguns produced. **(A)**

42-5 M1892 Series

This series was basically developed as a lighter replacement for the M1873. The longarms are distinguished by the marking on the upper frame tang; first, "MODEL 1892/-WINCHESTER-/PAT. OCT. 14. 1884", and later, "MODEL 1892/-WINCHESTER—/TRADE MARK". After 1909 a registration warning was added to the second marking.

42-5a Winchester M1892 Repeating Sporting Rifles

OL: dependent on buttplate type and buttstock (either straight or with pistol grip). 24-24½" (bore), octagonal or round barrels (rarely part-round/part-octagonal), chambered for .25, .32, .38, or .44 cal. Production was discontinued in 1932, most production being in smokeless powder era. **(A)**

42-5b Winchester M1892 Repeating Carbines, Types I & II

OL: about 37". 20" long (bore) round barrel standard, but shorter versions (down to 14") available on special order. Chambered in .32, .38, or .44 cal. Type I carbine has full-length magazine; II has half-magazine under barrel. Production ceased in 1941. **(A)**

42-6 M1894 Series

The series was specially designed on Browning's patent of 1894 to accept the newly developed smokeless-powder cartridges. Due to slow release of the new product, Winchester's first arms were chambered for black-powder .32/40 and .38/55 cartridges. Earliest production marking is stamped into the upper frame tang: "-MODEL 94-WINCHESTER NICKEL STEEL/TRADE MARK-". Although the M1894 continues in production with more than three million made, only the earliest serial nos. fall into the 19th century.

42-6a Winchester M1894 Repeating Sporting Rifles, Types I & II

Since made in a variety of buttplate and buttstock (straight or pistol-grip) configurations, overall length will vary considerably. While the 26" long (bore) barrel is standard, 24" is quite common, and 22" was made in a lightweight frame version. Round or octagonal barrels are most frequent, but half-round/half-octagonal were available. Type I rifles have full-length magazines; II utilize half-magazines. Although the only two black-powder calibers were .32 and .38, the rifle was made in a wide variety of smokeless-powder cartridges as well, .30/30 being the most popular. **(A)**

42-6b Winchester M1894 Repeating Carbine

Virtually the same as the round-barreled, straight-stock rifle, but with 20" long (bore) barrel, and a single iron band securing the forestock.

Chamberings same as rifle. Special barrel lengths (14", 16", 18") available. **(A)**

42-7 M1895 Series

With the new smokeless cartridges proving to be long and relatively short in cross section, Winchester introduced its 1895 lever-action box magazine series rifle, carbine, and, eventually, a military musket. The first 5,000 were made with flat frames that distinguish type I rifles from the balance of the production which terminated in 1931, a total of 425,881 having been made.

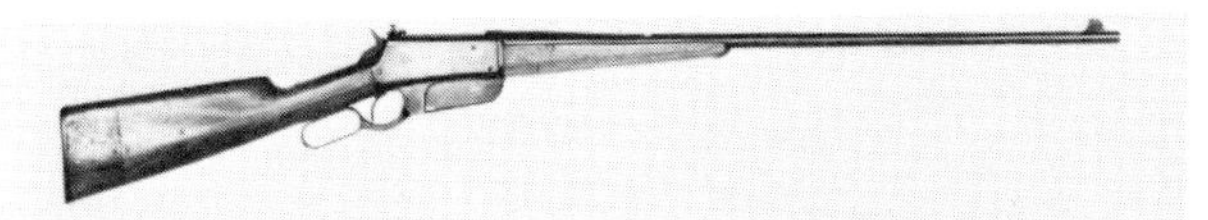

42-7a Winchester M1895 Repeating Sporting Rifles, Types I & II

26" and 28" barrel lengths (bore, respectively 25¼" and 27¼") were standard in either octagonal or round, but special-order lengths were available until 1908 up to 36". Until 1900 the rifle was available in four calibers: .30/40, .303 British, .38/72, and .40/72. More calibers were added later. **(B)**

---

43 | Slide-Action, Tubular Magazine Repeating Rifles and Carbines

The success of the Winchester lever-action repeating rifles and carbines during the 1870s and '80s caused considerable envy among the other arms manufacturers. Many introduced their own copies. Colt, in an attempt to diversify from the handgun trade, followed suit with the Burgess patent lever-action rifles. These arms, however, were no great commercial success. Still seeking some part of the longarms market, Colt attempted a different route, one that would improve upon the basic principle and awkwardness of reloading the lever-action rifle. Colt turned to patents that permitted reloading with the less critical left hand. The action determined most effective had been patented in 1883 by W. H. Elliot. Carl J. Ehberts set about to enhance that action, and between May, 1885, and November, 1887, was issued five patents for improvements. In the same time span, F. F. Knous was issued four patents that were also incorporated by Colt into the design. At least three other individuals patented elements that were also used in the Colt product. The result of these inventions was the Colt "Lightning" magazine rifle and carbine. First issued in a "medium" frame size for the most popular cartridges prevalent in 1884, the gun became so popular as to warrant the creation of two other frame sizes, one for large cartridges (the "large" frame model), and one for the increasingly popular .22 rimfire cartridge (the "small" frame model), both in production by 1888. Colt's success with this last size caused Winchester to enter the slide-action magazine rifle field as well. In 1890 Winchester introduced a

new rifle based on a Browning patent. Like the Colt, this rifle met with significant sales success, resulting in a multitude of copies. The slide-action copies of the Colt and Winchester rifles, however, were all manufactured after the turn of the century, and therefore fall outside the scope of this study.

43-O Colt "Lightning" "Medium Frame" Rifles and Carbines, Types II (color plate, carbine) **& I**

OL: (rifles) 43¼" standard, (carbines) 37" standard
BD: .32, .38, or .44 cal.
Furniture: iron, "blued"; carbine with swivel ring on left side of frame
Lockplate: none, mechanism within frame
BL: (rifles) 25½" to frame (26" bore); (carbines) 19½" to frame (20¼" bore)
Finish: "blued"
Configuration: round or octagonal (carbines, round)
Fastenings: forestock screwed

(A)

43-1 Colt "Lightning" Slide-Action Rifles and Carbines

Until 1887 (when the breech cover was added to the "medium-frame" rifles and carbines, distinguishing type II), the barrel top was marked with the caliber (near the frame) and "COLT'S PT. F.A. MFG. CO. HARTFORD CT. U.S.A./ELLIOTS PATENTS MAY 29, 1883, SEPT. 18, 1883." After the addition of the cover (post serial no. 22950) the marking was: "COLT'S PT. F.A. MAY 26,85, JUNE 15,86, FEB. 22,87." The serial nos. are consecutive in each frame size and are stamped into the triggerguard strap with the exception of a special serial no. for 401 "medium-frame" type II round-barreled (26" bore) rifles delivered in 1898 to the San Francisco Police Dept. Until 1900, 85,800 "medium-frame," 6,496 "large frame," and 42,800 "small frame" rifles and carbines were produced. The standard rifle sight is a stepped "buckhorn," c. 2" from the frame in conjunction with a German-silver blade inset into a dove-tailed iron block. The carbine, however, uses a 1¾"-long base with folding ladder with slide ¾" from the frame. The "small frame" model uses a simple open "V" as standard. There were, however variant sight options. Buttplates of various configurations were also available as well as special barrel lengths.

43-1a Colt "Lightning" "Large Frame" Rifles and Carbines

OL: (rifles) 45¼" standard
BD: .38, .40, .45, or .50 cal.
Furniture: iron, "blued"; carbine with swivel ring on left side
BL: (rifles) 28" bore, (carbines) 22" bore
Finish: "blued"
Configuration: round (carbines) or octagonal (rifles)
Fastenings: forestock screwed

(B)

43-1b Colt "Lightning" "Small Frame" Rifles

OL: 41½"
BD: .22 cal.
Furniture: iron, "blued"
BL: 24" bore
Finish: "blued"
Configuration: octagonal
Fastenings: forestock screwed

(A)

43-2 Winchester M1890 Slide-Action Magazine Rifles, Types I & II

OL: 40½"
BD: .22 cal.
BL: 23¾" to frame (24¼" bore)
Finish: "blued"

Furniture: iron, case-hardened; "blued" after Aug., 1901
Lockplate: none, mechanism within frame.
Markings: upper frame tang—"WINCHESTER/-MODEL 1890-/ PAT. JUNE 25-88. DEC. 6-92"

Configuration: octagonal
Sights: rear—open "V" on strap 4¾" from frame; front—iron blade, dovetailed
Fastenings: forestock screwed to slide
Markings: top of barrel—"MANUFACTURED BY THE-/-WINCHESTER REPEATING ARMS CO. NEW HAVEN. CONN. U.S.A.-" and "22 SHORT" (or other .22 caliber) on top near frame

The M1890 was designed to replace the poor-selling M1873 sporting rifle in .22 rim-fire. The design was patented by John M. Browning and Matthew S. Browning in 1888. Although more than 849,000 were made between 1890-1932, probably only a small portion were made prior to 1900. Type I has a solid frame; II is "takedown." Serial nos. were inscribed on the lower triggerguard strap during early production. **(A)**

Slide-Action, Tubular Magazine Repeating Shotguns

While the slide-action rifle was slow to gain in popularity except in the small caliber target and varmint grades, the 1890s saw a proliferation of the action as applied to shotguns. Since the target (fowl) was usually moving, it was exceedingly important that the person firing a shotgun retain an eye on the target at all times, especially if a second shot was to be attempted. The slide-action not only permitted rapid reloading of the chamber, but it did not disrupt the hold of the arm or its sighting.

No practical American shotgun had been made on the slide-action principle until Christopher M. Spencer and his associate Sylvester Roper patented a mechanism in April, 1882. They purchased tooling and set up a plant at Windsor, Conn. Manufacturing was underway when their toolmakers foreclosed, and the plant was sold to Francis Bannerman of New York, who moved it to Brooklyn. While Bannerman was re-establishing the plant, Andrew Burgess had invented a different slide-action system wherein the pistol grip rather than the forestock slid to activate the mechanism. In 1892 the Burgess Gun Co. was established at Buffalo, N.Y., to manufacture these arms. Winchester, sensing a market for the slide-action shotgun, introduced its M1893 repeating model which, like the Spencer and Roper design, used a sliding forearm. To protect his investment, Bannerman sued Winchester in 1894 over a claimed patent infringement. The suit was drawn out through appeals until 1897, when the courts decided in favor of Winchester, basing their decision partly on a technicality that the patent never belonged to one individual and also on tool room mockups of earlier French patents. The court's decision effectively opened the market for the free production of slide-action repeating shotguns. Winchester almost immediately introduced its M1897 model, and Marlin followed suit by announcing its M1898. These early developments were to anticipate a prolifera-

tion of slide-action shotgun models in the first quarter of the 20th century.

44-O Winchester M1897 Slide-Action Shotgun, Types I (color plate, above) **& II**

OL: 49⅛"
BD: 16 ga. (II) or 12 ga.
Furniture: iron, "blued"; rubber buttplate
Lockplate: none, mechanism within frame
Markings: left side of slide—"MODEL 1897/-WINCHESTER-/TRADE MARK"; serial no. on trigguard strap

BL: 28¾" to frame (30⅛" bore)
Finish: "blued"
Configuration: round
Sights: rear—upper frame recessed; front—brass bead
Fastenings: forestock screwed to slide
Markings: top of barrel—"MANUFACTURED BY THE WINCHESTER REPEATING ARMS CO./NEW HAVEN, CONN. U.S.A. PAT. NOV. 25,80, DEC. 6, 92, JULY 21,96" and later production, "FEB. 22,98, JUNE 14,98, OCT. 16,1900"

This arm was a replacement for the M1893 shotgun, so made to withstand smokeless powder loads. Over one million were produced until 1957, and only the earliest can be classified as "antiques." Initially offered only in solid frame (I), in 12 ga., a take-down version was added in 1898; this was followed by a 16 ga. take-down in 1900. **(A)**

Spencer (Spencer Arms Co./Francis Bannerman) Slide-Action Shotguns (color plate, below)

OL: 48¾"
BD: 12 ga.
Furniture: iron, except for rubber buttplate
Lockplate: none, mechanism within frame
Markings: left side of frame—(late) "F. BANNERMAN MNFG. NEW-YORK. U.S.A./MODEL 1890"

BL: 29½" to frame (30" bore)
Finish: "damascus"
Configuration: round
Sights: rear—frame top recessed; front—brass bead
Fastenings: rubber forestock molded around slide
Markings: early—"SPENCER ARMS CO., WINDSOR, CT U.S.A. PAT. APR. 1882."; late—"SPENCER RPTG. SHOT GUN PAT. APL. 1882" on top

About 3,000 shotguns were produced before the firm was foreclosed by Pratt & Whitney. Bannerman purchased the machinery and made about 17,000 more between 1890-1900. The U.S. Army bought 240 in 1885-86. **(B)**

44-1 Burgess (Burgess Gun Co.) Slide-Action Shotguns, Types I & II

OL: c. 39¼"-49¾"
BD: 12 ga.
Furniture: iron, "blued"
Lockplate: none, mechanism within frame
Markings: frame bottom has various patent dates

BL: (I) 28" or 30" bores; (II) 19½" bore
Finish: "blued"
Configuration: round
Sights: rear—none; front—iron blade
Fastenings: nosecap secures forestock
Markings: top of frame—"BURGESS GUN CO./BUFFALO N.Y. U.S.A."

This arm is distinguished by its sliding pistol grip. Type I is solid frame; II has a hinged frame that permits the arm to fold to about 20" overall length. A small number of rifles were also made in .30 and .45 cal. of the Type I design. Only a few thousand shotguns were made between 1892-99 when the firm was purchased by Winchester. **(C)**

44-2 Marlin (Marlin Firearms Co.) M1898 Slide-Action Shotguns

OL: 44½"-50½"
BD: 12 ga.
Furniture: iron, "blued", rarely engraved
Lockplate: none, mechanism within frame
Markings: none
BL: 26" to 32" (bores)
Finish: "blued"
Configuration: round
Sights: rear—none; front—brass bead
Fastenings: forestock circumvents slide
Markings: "MARLIN FIREARMS CO., NEW HAVEN CT. U.S.A./ (patent dates for 1894 and 1896).", and serial no.

The arm was produced from 1898-1905. Quantities exceed 55,000. **(A)**

44-3 Winchester M1893 Slide-Action Shotguns

OL: 49" or 51"
BD: 12 ga.
Furniture: iron, "blued"; rubber buttplate
Lockplate: none, mechanism within frame
Markings: left side of slide—"MODEL 1893/-WINCHESTER-/ TRADE MARK"
BL: 30" or 32" (bore)
Finish: "blued"
Configuration: round
Sights: rear—none; front—brass bead
Fastenings: forestock screwed to slide
Markings: top of barrel—"MANUFACTURED BY THE WINCHESTER REPEATING ARMS CO./NEW HAVEN CONN. U.S.A. PAT. NOV. 25.90," DEC. 6. 92."

Between 1893-97 34,050 of these arms were made. It was superseded by the M1897 because the barrel was unsuitable for smokeless powder cartridges. **(B)**

---

45 Bolt-Action, Tubular Magazine Repeating Sporting Rifles

By the 1870s the bolt-action was nothing novel. It has been used with qualified success in Europe as well as America since the 1840s. In the 1870s, however, a new application was made of it in conjunction was tubular magazine rifles, and in each case the patented improvements were backed by one of the two major longarms manufacturers—Remington and Winchester. The patentees of these two rifles were Benjamin Berkely Hotchkiss and John W. Keene. Hotchkiss's patents considerably predate those of Keene, the first having been issued in 1869; however, he was still perfecting the design and adapting it to a tubular repeating system as late as November, 1876, the year before he sold all patent rights to Winchester.

The Hotchkiss bolt-action magazine rifle was somewhat of an odd-

ity for Winchester to seek since it was loaded from the buttstock tubular magazine, and Winchester's tubular magazines heretofore had always been located beneath the barrels. There is a strong suspicion that Winchester may have known of Hotchkiss's ability to influence the military as a result of his other martial developments (the machine gun) and purchased the rights with both that and the Act of 21 November 1877 (appropriating money for the selection of a military magazine rifle) in mind.

Conversely, the arm that was championed by Remington did have the tubular magazine beneath the barrel like the Winchester lever-action repeaters. Keene's patents only spanned the three-year period from February, 1874, until March, 1877, but, during that time, he secured no fewer than eight different patents of various aspects. Like Winchester, Remington's motives for producing this arm seem to have been prompted by the hope of securing a substantial martial contract. In this respect the firm was frustrated, and most of the Keene production was devoted to the sporting and hunting trade.

45-O Keene (Remington) Repeating Sporting Rifles (color plate)

OL: 44.¼"

BD: .45 cal., also .40 and .433 cal.

Furniture: iron, "blued"

Lockplate: none, mechanism within receiver

Markings: left side of frame—cartridge size on back

BL: 23⅞" to receiver (24⅜" bore)

Finish: "blued"

Configuration: round or part round/part octagonal

Sights: rear—2⅝" base with folding ladder with slide ⅛" from receiver; front—iron blade

Fastenings: nosecap secures stock

Markings: top of bolt—"E. REMINGTON & SONS ILION, N.Y./PAT. FEBY 24, MCH 17, 1874 JAN. 18/SEPT 26 1876, MCH 20, JULY 31, 1877"

Approximately 5,000 of these arms were produced between 1880 and the demise of Remington & Sons. A limited number 24" barrel rifles were purchased by the U.S. Dept. of the Interior to arm Indian police; these bear U.S. inspection marks and the initials "U.S.I.D." **(B)**

45-1 Hotchkiss (Winchester) M1878 Repeating Rifles, Types I & II

OL: 45⅞"

BD: .45 cal.; .40, rare

Furniture: iron, "blued"; horn or ebony nosecap

Lockplate: none, mechanism within receiver

Markings: upper left side of receiver—"MANUFACTURED BY THE WINCHESTER REPEATING ARMS CO., NEW HAVEN, CONN. U.S.A./-PATENTED OCT. 16. 1860, JUNE 25, 1872, JULY 23, 1872, AND: UNDER-/B.B. HOTCHKISS' PAT'S AUG. 17, 1869, FEB. 15, 1870, NOV. 5, 1875, NOV. 15, 1876, JAN. 23, 1877."; serial no. on left receiver top flat

BL: 25" to receiver (26" bore)

Finish: "blued"

Configuration: octagonal or round, rarely part round/part octagonal

Sights: rear—folding ladder on base c. 2" from receiver; front—iron blade

Fastenings: forestock screwed to barrel

Markings: none

Type I differs from II by the "cut-off" pattern that permits single-shot loading. I uses a circular knob on the stock's right side just below the receiver. II has small switches on either side of the receiver top. Around 5,000 were made between 1879-80. **(C)**

45-2 II

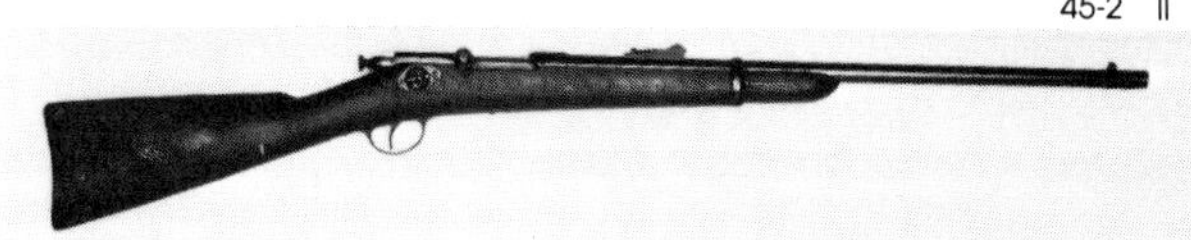

45-2 Hotchkiss (Winchester) M1878 Repeating Carbines, Types I & II

OL: 42⅜" or 43⅜"
BD: .45 cal.
Furniture: iron, "blued"; swivel ring on left side
Lockplate: none, mechanism within receiver
Markings: very similar to 45-1
BL: 21½" or 23" to receiver (22" or 22½" bores, respectively)
Finish: "blued"
Configuration: round
Sights: rear—U.S. M1877 carbine rear sight 2¼" from receiver; front—iron block/blade
Fastenings: single iron band
Markings: none

Type I carbines differ from II by the selector switch pattern. **(C)**

45-3 Hotchkiss (Winchester) M1883 Repeating Sporting Rifles

OL: 46"
BD: .45 cal., .40 also advertised
Furniture: iron, horn or ebony nosecap; frame case-hardened
Lockplate: none, mechanism within receiver
Markings: upper frame strap—"-(MODEL OF 1883)-"; trigger-guard strap—"PAT. OCT. 16, 1860, JUNE 25, 1872, JULY 23, 1878/-AND UNDER B.B. HOTCHKISS' PAT'S AUG. 17, 1869-/FEB. 15, 1870, NOV. 9, 1875, NOV. 14, 1876, JAN. 23, 1877."
BL: 25" to frame (26" bore)
Finish: "blued"
Configuration: usually round but also octagonal and part round /part octagonal
Sights: rear—folding ladder on base 2" from frame; front—iron blade
Fastenings: forestock screwed to barrel
Markings: "-MANUFACTURED BY THE-/WINCHESTER REPEATING ARMS CO. NEW HAVEN CONN. U.S.A.-" on top; serial no. on bottom of frame

This rifle continued in production until 1899. **(B)**

45-4 I

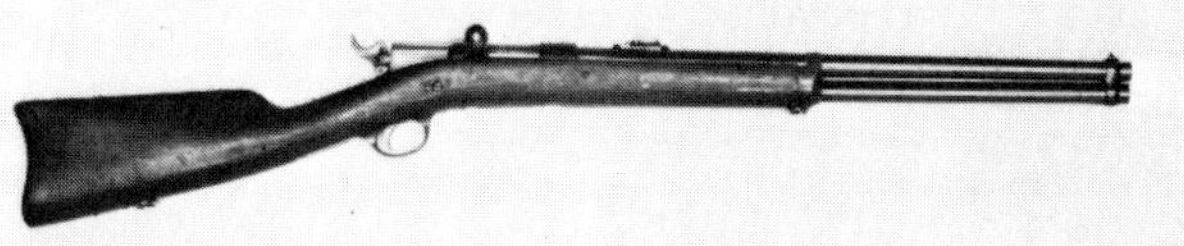

45-4 Keene (Remington) Repeating Carbines, Types I & II

OL: (I) 39¼", (II) 41¼"
BD: .45 cal.
Furniture: iron, "blued"; sling swivels on nosecap and butt-stock
Lockplate: none, mechanism within receiver
BL: 19⅜" or 21⅜" to frame; (20" or 22" bores)
Finish: "blued"
Configuration: round
Sights: rear—2" long base with folding ladder 1¼" from receiver; front—iron blade

Markings: left side of receiver—cartridge size at back

Fastenings: (I) stock secured by nosecap, (II) two iron bands, full forestock

Markings: top of bolt—same as 45-0

Type I differs from II in the forestock, one resembling that used on a sporting rifle, and the other, martial style. Quantities unknown. **(C)**

---

46 | Bolt-Action, Tubular Magazine Repeating Martial Rifles

In September, 1878, a U.S. Ordnance Department board decided, after tests on 27 different systems, including two Sharps designs, that only one design, that of B. B. Hotchkiss, was suitable for production as a military arm. Accordingly, the entire $20,000 Congressional appropriation for trial guns was expended at Springfield Armory in the manufacture of these Winchester rifles and carbines. In the next year the U.S. Navy also ordered the Hotchkiss rifle. As a result of dissatisfaction with the decision, however, a new trial board was established in 1881. At the completion of that board's work in the fall of 1882, it was recommended that the $50,000 Congress had then appropriated for trial magazine rifles be spent on the purchase of three patented mechanisms: the Chaffee-Reece, an improved version of the Hotchkiss tried earlier, and the Lee. Of these, all were bolt-action, and the first two were tubular magazine. There being no facilities for the manufacture of the Chaffee-Reece rifle, these were made at the Springfield Armory in 1884. The other two types were purchased from the firms holding the patent rights—Winchester and Remington. Among the 40 designs tested by this later trial board was that of J. W. Keene. Although the Keene action was deemed unsuitable for Army use, the U.S. Navy conducted separate tests and concluded that both the Lee action and the Keene action were suitable, and ordered small quantities of these two designs from Remington.

46-O Hotchkiss (Winchester) U.S. M1883 Magazine Rifles (color plate)

OL: 48¼"

BD: .45 cal.

Furniture: iron, "blued"; "US" on buttplate tang; frame is case-hardened

Lockplate: none, mechanism within frame

Markings: left side of frame—"U.S./D.F.C."; on bolt—"D.F.C."; upper frame tang—"-(MODEL OF 1883)-"; serial no. on frame bottom; lower triggerguard strap—"PAT. OCT. 16, 1860, JUNE 25, 1872, JULY 23, 1878/ AND UNDER B.B. HOTCHKISS' PAT'S AUG. 17, 1869/FEB. 15, 1870, NOV. 9, 1875, NOV. 15, 1876, JAN. 23, 1877"

BL: 27¼" to receiver (28¼" bore)

Finish: "blued"

Configuration: round

Sights: rear—US.. M1877 rifle sight 2¼" from receiver; front—iron block/blade

Fastenings: 2 iron bands, "blued"

Markings: "U.S./VP (circled)/ D.F.C." on upper left surface; on top—"-MANUFACTURED BY THE-/-WINCHESTER REPEATING ARMS CO. NEW HAVEN, CONN. U.S.A."

The U.S. Ordnance Dept. purchased 200 of these rifles during fiscal year 1883-84, and 550 more the succeeding fiscal year. **(C)**

46-1 Chaffee-Reece (Springfield Armory) U.S. M1882 Magazine Rifles

OL: 49″
BD: .45 cal.
Furniture: iron, "blued"
Lockplate: none, mechanism within receiver
Markings: upper left flat of receiver—"US -SPRINGFIELD.-1884"; cartouche on left side of buttstock bears inspector's initials "SWP/1884"
BL: 27⅛″ to receiver (28″ bore)
Finish: "blued"
Configuration: round
Sights: rear—U.S. M1877 rifle sight 2¼″ from receiver; front—iron block/blade
Fastenings: 2 iron bands, "blued"
Markings: "V", "P", and eagle head

This design was patented in 1879 by Reuben S. Chaffee of Springfield, Mass., and J.N. Reece. Approved by the 1882 Brooke trial board, 753 were made at Springfield during fiscal year 1883-84. **(D)**

46-2

46-2 Hotchkiss (Springfield Armory) Army and Navy Rifles, Types I & II

OL: (Army) 52″; (Navy) 48⅝″
BD: .45 cal.
Furniture: iron, "blued"
Lockplate: none, mechanism within receiver
Markings: upper left side of receiver—"MANUFACTURED BY THE WINCHESTER REPEATING ARMS CO. NEW HAVEN, CONN. U.S.A./PATENTED OCT. 18.1860, JUNE 25, 1872, JULY 23, 1878, AND UNDER/B.B. HOTCHKISS PAT'S AUG. 17,1869, FEB. 15, 1870, NOV. 9, 1875, NOV. 14, 1876, JAN. 23, 1877"
BL: (Army) 31¼″ to receiver (32¼″ bore), (Navy) 27⅝″ to receiver (28⅝″ bore)
Finish: "blued"
Configuration: round
Sights: rear—U.S. M1877 2¼″ from receiver; front—iron block/blade
Fastenings: 2 iron bands, "blued"
Markings: "V", "P", and eagle head on upper left surface; "(inspector's initials/US" on top

Type I differs from II by the magazine cut-off pattern, I being on the right side, II being on the receiver top. 513 type I Army rifles, 1,474 type I Navy rifles, and 999 type I Navy rifles were made at Springfield between 1879-80. **(C)**

46-3 Hotchkiss (Springfield Armory) Carbines, Types I & II

OL: 43¾″
BD: .45 cal.
Furniture: iron, except for pewter nosecap
BL: 23″ to receiver (24″ bore)
Finish: "blued"
Configuration: round
Sights: rear—U.S. M1877 rifle

II

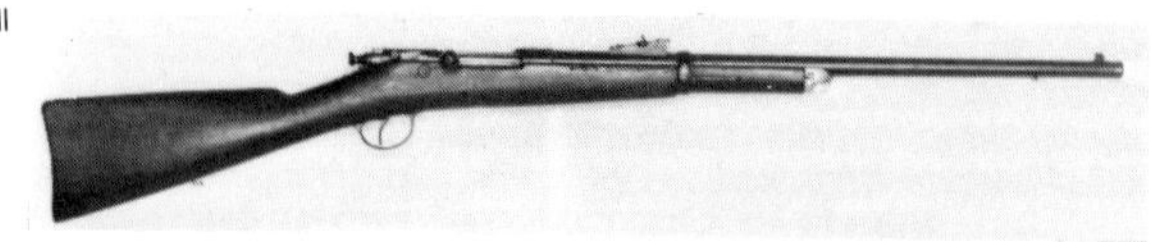

Lockplate: none, mechanism within frame
Markings: upper left side of receiver—same as 46-2
sight 2¼" from receiver; front—iron block/blade
Fastenings: single iron band, "blued"
Markings: "U.S." and "V", "A", and eagle head

513 type I carbines were made in 1879; 400 type II were manufactured at a later date; all bear "HN" on the bolt and selector switches. **(D)**

46-4

46-4 Keene (Remington) U.S. Navy Contract Rifles

OL: 48⅝"
BD: .45 cal.
Furniture: iron, "blued"
Lockplate: none, mechanism within receiver
Markings: top of bolt—"E. REMINGTON & SONS. ILION, N.Y./ PAT. FEBY 24, MCH 17, 1874, JAN 18/SEPT 26, 1876, MCH 20, JULY 31, 1877"
BL: 28⅝" to receiver (29¼" bore)
Finish: "blued"
Configuration: round
Sights: rear—2½"-long base with folding ladder 2⅜" from receiver; front—iron block/blade
Fastenings: 2 iron bands, "blued," marked "U"
Markings: "US/(anchor)" and "P/W.W.K."

250 Keene rifles were purchased by the Navy in 1880. It should be noted that Remington produced an "Army" version of this rifle. **(D)**

---

47 | Other Tubular Magazine Repeating Rifles and Carbines

While the two most common methods of chambering tubular magazines were by means of either a lever-activated or a bolt-activated device, and only later by means of slide-action, a few inventors stretched their ingenuity to devise other means. Louis Triplett of Columbia, Ky., patented one such device in 1864. His chambering mechanism worked on a frame that not only secured the barrel, but rotated to the right approximately 120 degrees to align the chamber with a tubular magazine that protruded through the buttstock. The cartridges were pushed forward by means of a coil spring and individually fed into the chamber with each turn of the frame. The arm was awkward to handle, and the torque caused by the swinging of the barrel and frame often caused the magazine tube to split the

buttstock which held it. Nevertheless, Kentucky purchased no fewer than 5,000 of these arms, only to dispose of them in 1868 when the Civil War crisis had passed. The only other significant attempt was made by Orvil M. Robinson of Upper Jay, N.Y. Robinson held a total of three patents, and essentially his action was a modification of the bolt-action. It, too, met with little success and was discontinued after its manufactory was purchased by Winchester in 1874.

47-O Triplett & Scott (Meriden Mfg. Co.) Repeating Rifles (color plate)

OL: 46⅛"
BD: .50 cal., 3-groove rifling
Furniture: iron, "blued"
Lockplate: none, mechanism within frame
Markings: left side of frame—"MERIDEN MANFG. CO./MERIDEN, CONN."; upper frame strap—"TRIPLETT & SCOTT/PATENT DEC. 6, 1864"; serial no. on frame right side
BL: 27½" to receiver (30" bore)
Finish: "blued"
Configuration: round
Sights: rear—1$\frac{5}{16}$" long base with folding leaf with slide ⅜" from receiver; front—iron block/blade
Fastenings: single iron band
Markings: left side of receiver—"KENTUCKY"

Kentucky purchased 3,000 for her Union Militia in about 1865 or 1866. By 1868 negotiations were under way to dispose of all of them. **(B)**

47-1 Triplett & Scott (Meriden Mfg. Co.) Repeating Carbines

Specifications are almost identical to the rifles, with the differences being an overall length of 38⅛" and a barrel length of 19½" to receiver (22" bore). 2,000 of these arms were bought by Kentucky at the same time as 47-0. They met the same fate. **(B)**

---

48 Bolt-Action, Box Magazine Repeating Rifles and Carbines

As early as 1875 the Sharps Rifle Co. was seeking a suitable commercial magazine rifle. The company approached several inventors before finally coaxing J. P. Lee away from Remington to produce a bolt-action, box magazine repeating rifle under his later patents. Although a few prototypes were made using modified Sharps M1873 barrels, the arm was not ready for the national 1878 magazine trial board, and the firm closed its factory before the arms could be completed. To complete a small U.S. Navy contract, Lee, through his newly-formed Lee Arms Co., turned to his former employer and shortly afterward gave Remington sole manufacturing and agency rights to his invention. Having had abyssmal luck promoting the Keene tubular magazine rifle as a martial shoulder arm, Remington readily adopted the more promising design. Although the 1882 trial

board found more favor with the Lee (Remington) submission, only 750 were purchased by the Army. Nevertheless, Remington had made extensive contacts abroad as a result of its sale of rolling-block action single-shot rifles, and the firm exploited this advantage. While the United States would eventually adopt a foreign design for a magazine rifle, the Lee, ironically, was adopted by several European powers, including England. Although only the black-powder arms are covered herein, the Lee M1899 series was produced from that year through 1907 in a variety of smokeless powder chamberings.

None of the magazine arms recommended by the 1882 trial board sufficiently impressed the U.S. Army to warrant their general adoption. As the 19th century neared its close, however, most European powers had recognized the superiority of the magazine repeating rifle. Moreover, the perfecting of heretofore unreliable smokeless powder had also caused most of these countries to adopt the higher velocity propellent and correspondingly smaller bored projectiles. Impressed by these developments, the War Department created a third magazine trial board in late 1890 to examine not only domestic magazine repeaters but foreign designs as well. In 1891 this board tested 50 repeating systems. It recommended that the Army adopt the magazine design then in use by Denmark and which had been devised by Captain C. Krag (director of the Norwegian Royal Manufactory of Arms) and E. Jörgensen. This selection caused such an uproar in the American arms community that another board was convened in 1893 to review American designs, but this group also found that none was better than the Scandinavian. Production of the Krag model continued until 1904 when the U.S. M1903 Springfield rifle came into being.

48-O Krag (Springfield Armory) U.S. M1898 Rifles (color plate, above)

OL: 49¼″
BD: .30 cal.
Furniture: iron, "blued"
Lockplate: none, mechanism within receiver
Markings: upper left receiver surface—"U.S./MODEL 1898 SPRINGFIELD ARMORY./(serial no.)"

BL: 30″ (bore)
Finish: "blued"
Configuration: round
Sights: rear—3⅛″-long base with elevating leaf 3½″ from breech; front—iron blade in iron block
Fastenings: 2 iron bands, the upper double strapped with knife bayonet stud on lower surface

Springfield made 262,548 of these arms between 1898-1904; 152,670 prior to 1900. Nearly all made before 1901 were subsequently modified to accept the 1901-1902 rear sights. **(A)**

Lee (Remington "M1882" U.S. Contract Magazine Rifles (color plate, below)

OL: 42⅛″
BD: .45 cal.
Furniture: iron, "blued"; "U.S." on buttplate tang
Lockplate: none, mechanism within receiver
Markings: "D.E.C." on bolt; top receiver flat—"THE LEE ARMS

BL: 31⅞″ to receiver (32½″ bore)
Finish: "blued"
Configuration: round
Sights: rear—U.S. M1884 rifle sight, 2¼″ from receiver; front—iron block/blade
Fastenings: 2 iron bands, "blued"

CO. BRIDGEPORT, CONN. U.S.A. /PATENTED NOV. 4TH 1879" and serial no.; left receiver side—"E. REMINGTON & SONS, ILION, N.Y. U.S.A./SOLE MANUFACTURERS AND AGENTS/US"

Markings: "US" and "V"/"P" on left side; "D.E.C." on top

During fiscal year 1884-85 the U.S. Ordnance Dept. purchased 750 of these rifles upon recommendation of the Brooke 1882 board. **(D)**

48-1 Krag (Springfield Armory) U.S. M1892 Magazine Rifles, Types I & II

OL: 49⅛"
BD: .30 cal.
Furniture: iron, "blued"
Lockplate: none, mechanism within receiver
Markings: upper left surface of receiver—"U.S./(date) SPRINGFIELD ARMORY" and serial no.

BL: 30" (bore)
Finish: "blued"
Configuration: round
Sights: rear—2½"-long base with folding ladder with slide 3½" from breech; front—iron blade inset into iron block
Fastenings: 2 iron bands, the upper wide and solid (I) or double strapped (II) with knife bayonet stud on lower surface
Markings: none

The most distinctive feature of this arm is the cleaning rod in the forestock, first with brass tips, later with iron (except for 300). 24,562 were made between 1894-96, the first 1,500 of which were type I with a solid front band. **(B)**

48-2 Krag (Springfield Armory) U.S. M1896 Magazine Rifles and Carbines

OL: (rifle) 48⅞", (carbine) 40⅞"
BD: .30 cal.
Furniture: iron "blued"
Lockplate: none, mechanism within receiver
Markings: upper left surface of receiver—"U.S./MODEL 1896 SPRINGFIELD ARMORY (serial no)"

BL: (rifle) 30" (bore); (carbine) 22" (bore)
Finish: "blued"
Configuration: round
Sights: 2½"-long base with folding ladder with slide c. 3½" from breech; front—iron blade inset into iron block
Fastenings: (rifle) 2 iron bands, the upper double strapped with knife bayonet stud on lower surface; (carbine) single iron band with top projection sight protector
Markings: none

The principal difference between the M1896 and the M1892 rifles is the relocation of the cleaning rod to a butt trap on the former and the adoption of a slightly different rear sight. 62,000 were produced between 1896-98; 19,133 carbines were produced at the same time. It should be noted, however, that during the Spanish-American War a significant number of carbines were altered to incorporate improvements of the M1898 and M1899 carbines. **A (rifle); C (carbine)**

48-3 Krag (Springfield Armory) U.S. M1899 Carbines, Types I & II

OL: 40⅞"

BL: 22" (bore)

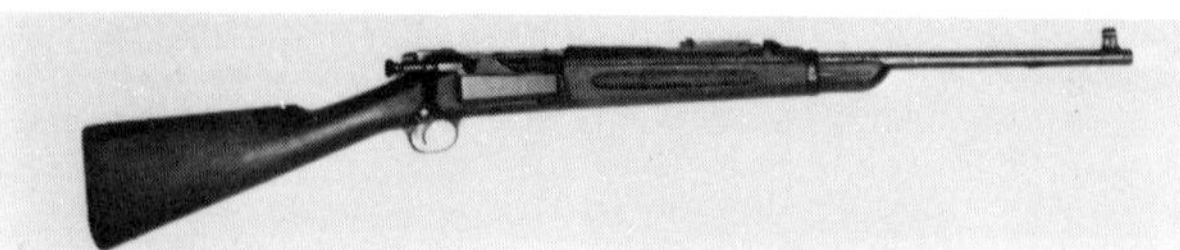

BD: .30 cal.
Furniture: iron, "blued"; swivel ring and bar on left side
Lockplate: none, mechanism within receiver
Markings: upper left surface of receiver—"U.S./MODEL 1899 SPRINGFIELD ARMORY (serial no.)"
Finish: "blued"
Configuration: round
Sights: rear—various sightings, M1898, M1901 or M1902; front—iron blade inset into iron block
Fastenings: single iron band, no projection
Markings: none

The distinctive feature is the elongated forestock (increased 2" over former carbine models) with its simple iron band 2" further forward of the rear sight and a wooden cap between with a "hump" in the earlier sighting variations (I) and flat with the M1902 rear sight alteration (II). 35,951 manufactured between 1899-1902. **(A)**

48-4

48-4 Lee (Remington) "M1879" U.S. Navy Contract Rifles
OL: 48½"
BD: .45 cal.
Furniture: iron, "blued"
Lockplate: none, mechanism within receiver
Markings: inspector's initials on bolt, "HN"; upper left flat of receiver—serial no. and "THE LEE ARMS CO. BRIDGEPORT, CONN. U.S.A./PATENTED NOV. 4TH 1879" and inspector's initials
BL: 28½" to receiver (29⅛" bore)
Finish: "blued"
Configuration: round
Sights: rear—U.S. M1877 rifle sight 2¼" from receiver; front—iron block/blade
Fastenings: 2 iron bands, "blued," marked "U"
Markings: "W.W.K/US/(anchor)" on upper left surface

The U.S. Navy order for 300 rifles was subcontracted by Lee to Sharps. When Sharps failed to fulfill it, Lee transferred the completed receivers to Remington for fitting up into complete arms, using Remington-made parts. Another 1,000 may have been ordered by the Navy. **(D)**

---

49 | Quasi-Bolt-Action, Box Magazine Repeating Rifles

Through more than 30 years of perseverance, James Paris Lee rose to the forefront of American arms design. Beginning with his 1862 patents for a laterally swinging, single-shot breechloader, Lee had sought to interest the military, but all for nought. His 1862 patent had

elicited a government contract for military carbines, but a misinterpretation of the instructions had caused a refusal of the completed arms. Another single-shot breechloader, patented in 1871 while Lee was still attempting to salvage what he could of his Milwaukee, Wis., operation, was tested unconclusively at Springfield Armory in 1874. His limited career with Sharps and Remington is covered in the previous chapter. With Remington's failure in 1888, the company's assets were acquired by the Union Metallic Cartridge Co. and Winchester. Lee moved to the latter, and during the early 1890s developed yet another box magazine rifle, a modified bolt-action "straight-pull" design that would finally be accepted by the American military in significant quantities. At first glance the repeater appears to be a standard bolt-action rifle. Unlike the standard, however, Lee's design was not contingent upon a rotating piston secured by a handle lug that locked into the receiver or frame. The piston traveled back and forth within the receiver without any turning motion. Instead of a lug-like handle, a knob on the right side of the receiver locked into a milled recess. Pulling this handle up and back released the piston and closed the breech for reloading the chamber and reversing its direction. Although the mechanism was both strong and simple, only the U.S. Navy adopted it, and only for a brief interlude. The true bolt-action so dominated martial ordnance circles as to preclude general acceptance of any other design until the development of the semi-automatic gas-operated rifles of the 20th century.

49-O Lee (Winchester Rpg. Arms Co.) "Straight-Pull" M1895 U.S. Navy Contract Rifles (color plate)

OL: 47¾"
BD: .236 cal. (6 mm)
Furniture: iron, "blued"
Lockplate: none, mechanism within receiver
Markings: left side of frame—"-MANUFACTURED BY THE WINCHESTER REPEATING ARMS CO-/NEW HAVEN. CONN. U.S.A. PAT. OCT. 10.93. JAN. 30.94.OCT.8. 95"
BL: 27¼" to receiver (28¼" bore)
Finish: "blued"
Configuration: round
Sights: rear—2½"-long base with folding leaf with slide 2⅛" from receiver; front—iron block/blade
Fastenings: two iron bands, the upper wider, with bayonet stud below
Markings: top of receiver forward of loading port—"U.S.N.-/(anchor)/N^{O} (serial no.)/inspector's initials)."

A total of 14,658 arms were delivered to the U.S. Navy from 1896 to 1900. The final 1,245 of these were immediately declared surplus and disposed of. Winchester also manufactured approximately 1,700 sporting rifles on this same pattern after the turn of the century. These have straight buttplates, a more pronounced pistol grip, a short forestock without bands, and utilize a stepped "buckhorn" rear sight. **(A)**

50 American Double-Barrel, Breechloading Shotguns

Although the American arms industry had made great strides in the

mass production of firearms by the middle of the 19th century, its efforts had been oriented to the production of relatively heavy-barreled rifles or revolvers. With the close of the Civil War, attempts were made to capture a portion of the foreign double-barrel shotgun market by developing a simple breechloading design using a drilled cast-steel barrel. Both Ethan Allen and Eli Whitney, Jr., made slight inroads into the import trade, but both were too expensive to seriously curtail the annual flood of Birmingham and Liège double-barreled guns. Even Charles Parker found it initially necessary to import unfinished Belgian damascus barrels to complete his early breechloaders economically. In 1878 Winchester paid silent testimony to the quality and low cost of the European product by importing several thousand English double barrels which were marked with the Winchester name and marketed in the New York area, a practice continued until 1884.

Although Parker was one of the first to devise a practical break-open mechanism, it was his employee Charles A. King who perfected the release mechanism in the 1870s and '80s that brought the Parker name to the forefront of American shotgun manufacturers. Likewise, both Colt and Remington owe more of their commercial success in the double-barrel shotgun trade to the early designs of A. E. Whitmore than to the improvements of their own staff designers. Lesser known are Alexander T. Brown, who transformed the early W. H. Baker designs into the popular L. C. Smith line, and entrepreneurs-inventors William M. Baker and Daniel M. Lefever, both of whose companies were eventually absorbed into the Ithaca Gun Co.

5O-O Parker Brothers "M1889" Inside Hammer Shotguns (color plate, above)

A hammerless model, this was available in 28", 30", or 32"-long barrels in 10, 12, or 16 ga. Each frame side is marked "Parker Bros.", and if the pistol grip incorporates a hard rubber end cap, it is marked "PARKER BROS." and "MERIDEN CONN." around its periphery. The center rib is marked "PARKER BROTHERS MAKERS, MERIDEN, CONN." followed by either "DAMASCUS STEEL" or "VULCAN STEEL." As with the 1882 model, the Deeley & Edge-type forestock is held by a patented spring catch marked "PATD MAR. 26, 1878". The barrel bottom is marked "PATD APR. 11, 1875" while the frame inside is marked "PAT'D JAN. 18.-AUG. 15 1887/MAY 7-OCT. 8 1889". Serial nos. are marked on most major parts and on the triggerguard strap. Automatic ejectors were added in 1902. Like all Parker shotguns, the hammerless versions came in a number of grades. **(A)**

L.C. Smith & Co./Hunter Arms Co. Inside Hammer Shotguns (color plate, below)

In 1883 Alexander T. Brown of L.C. Smith patented a new side swinging top lever release that was incorporated almost immediately into the line. Although L.C. Smith sold out to Hunter Arms Co. in 1888, it continued the "L.C. SMITH" marking that appears on both frame sides throughout the 1800s. The damascus barrels were available in 10, 12, or 16 ga. in 28", 30", or 32" (as shown) lengths. Steel barrels rather than damascus were also available. Serial nos. appear on barrel underside. **(A)**

5O-1 Baker (Ithaca Gun Co.) Inside Hammer Shotgun

In 1893 the renamed Ithaca Gun Co. introduced a hammerless model.

Like its predecessor the damascus or "English twist" model, barrels were offered in 30" or 32" lengths but only in 10 or 12 ga. The frame sides are marked "ITHACA GUN CO." within a wreath. 77,000 made to 1904. **(A)**

50-2 Colt M1878 Outside Hammer Shotguns

In 1878 Colt introduced this arm. The damascus barrels are "blued" or "browned" and usually are marked on the center rib, "COLT'S PT. F.A. MFG. CO. HARTFORD CT. U.S.A." in italic script. Various barrel lengths were special order, but 28", 30", 32" are standard. Gauges are 12 and 10 only. The flat lockplates are marked, "COLT'S PT. F.A. MFG. CO." in either engraved italics (high grade models) or block letters forward of the hammers. 22,683 made to 1889. **(A)**

50-3 Colt M1883 Inside Hammer Shotguns

The "blued" or "browned" damascus barrels were available on special order in lengths from 18" to 34", but standard lengths are 28", 30", and 32". Gauges available included 8, 10, or 12. The rib is marked "COLT'S PT. F.A. MFG. CO. HARTFORD, CT. U.S.A." either in italics or engraved on the frame side, and "PATENTED (arced)/AUG. 22, SEPT. 19, 1882" on frame bottom. 7,366 produced to 1895. **(B)**

50-4 N. R. Davis & Sons Outside Hammer Shotguns

These shotguns were probably not commercially available until c. 1885. The outside hammer version was offered only in 12 ga. with 30" or 32" damascus barrels. Flat lockplates are marked "N.R. DAVIS & SONS" forward of the hammers. The rib top is marked "laminated". **(A)**

50-5 D. M. Lefever Co./Lefever Arms Co. Inside Hammer Shotguns

Daniel M. Lefever and partner Francis S. Dangerfield were issued a patent in 1872 for a strong locking action for breechloaders. In 1878 the firm introduced a hammerless model, and in 1884 this arm was produced at Syracuse, N.Y. by the reorganized Lafever Arms Co. Various gauges and barrel lengths were offered, marked "LAFEVER ARMS CO/ SYRACUSE, N.Y. U.S.A." on side plates. Total production until 1906, when purchased by Ithaca, not known. **(B)**

50-6 Parker Brothers "M1868" Outside Hammer Shotguns

The earliest production of the firm (established in 1868) is marked by the "lifter" release forward of the triggerguard. The "blued" damascus barrels are standrd in 10 or 12 ga. in 30" lengths; however 8 ga., 16 ga., or 20 ga. were special orders as were non-standard barrel lengths. The flat lockplates are marked "PARKER BROS" in block letters or script forward of the hammers. In 1874 there were 11 grades available; by 1880, 16, though the differences are often minimal. **(A)**

50-7 Parker Brothers "M1882" Outside Hammer Shotguns

This year the firm incorporated Charles A. King's side swinging top release to replace the old "lifter" release below the frame. These arms were available in a number of grades with either 30" or 32" barrels in 10 or 12 ga. Barrels were damascus, "blued." Flat locks are marked "PARKER BROS." forward of the hammers. **(A)**